Hands-On Microservices with Rust

Build, test, and deploy scalable and reactive microservices with Rust 2018

Denis Kolodin

BIRMINGHAM - MUMBAI

Hands-On Microservices with Rust

Commissioning Editor: Richa Tripathi
Acquisition Editor: Shririam Shekhar
Content Development Editor: Manjusha Mantri
Technical Editor: Mayank Dubey
Copy Editor: Safis Editing
Language Support Editors: Mary McGowan and Safis Editing
Project Coordinator: Prajakta Naik
Proofreader: Safis Editing
Indexer: Priyanka Dhadke
Graphics: Jisha chirayil
Production Coordinator: Tom Scaria

First published: January 2019

Production reference: 1310119

Published by Packt Publishing Ltd.
Livery Place
35 Livery Street
Birmingham
B3 2PB, UK.

ISBN 978-1-78934-275-8

www.packtpub.com

`mapt.io`

Mapt is an online digital library that gives you full access to over 5,000 books and videos, as well as industry leading tools to help you plan your personal development and advance your career. For more information, please visit our website.

Why subscribe?

- Spend less time learning and more time coding with practical eBooks and Videos from over 4,000 industry professionals

- Improve your learning with Skill Plans built especially for you

- Get a free eBook or video every month

- Mapt is fully searchable

- Copy and paste, print, and bookmark content

Packt.com

Did you know that Packt offers eBook versions of every book published, with PDF and ePub files available? You can upgrade to the eBook version at `www.packt.com` and as a print book customer, you are entitled to a discount on the eBook copy. Get in touch with us at `customercare@packtpub.com` for more details.

At `www.packt.com`, you can also read a collection of free technical articles, sign up for a range of free newsletters, and receive exclusive discounts and offers on Packt books and eBooks.

Contributors

About the author

Denis Kolodin has been developing high-loaded network applications for more than 12 years. He has mastered and used different kinds of programming languages, including C, Java, and Python, for developing a variety of apps, from high-frequency trading robots to video broadcasting servers. Nowadays, he enjoys creating peer-to-peer networking applications and is inspired by distributed systems such as cryptocurrencies.

He has been using Rust since version 1.0 and is delighted with the features it provides, specifically WebAssembly support. He's the author of *Yew Framework*, which collected more than 6,000 stars on GitHub. He writes with Rust continuously as part of his job and believes that Rust will be used for everything in the future, including backend, frontend, operating systems, embedded software, games, and smart contracts.

About the reviewer

Daniel Durante is an avid coffee drinker/roaster, motorcyclist, archer, welder, and carpenter whenever he isn't programming. From the age of 12, he has been involved with web and embedded programming with PHP, Node.js, Golang, Rust, and C.

He has worked on text-based browser games that have reached over 1,000,000 active players, created bin-packing software for CNC machines, embedded programming with cortex-m and PIC circuits, high-frequency trading applications, and helped contribute to one of the oldest ORMs of Node.js (SequelizeJS).

He has also reviewed other books – *PostgresSQL Developer's Guide, PostgreSQL 9.6 High Performance, Rust Programming By Example*, and *Rust High Performance* – for Packt.

> *I would like to thank my parents, my brother, my mentors, and my friends who've all put up with my insanity of sitting in front of a computer day in and day out. I would not be here today if it wasn't for their patience, guidance, and love.*

Gaurav Aroraa has completed his M.Phil in computer science. He is an MVP, a lifetime member of the **Computer Society of India** (**CSI**), an advisory member of IndiaMentor, and is certified as a scrum trainer/coach, XEN for ITIL-F, and APMG for PRINCE-F and PRINCE-P. Gaurav is an open source developer, and the founder of Ovatic Systems Private Limited. Recently, he was awarded the title "Icon of the year – excellence in mentoring technology startups" for the year 2018-19 by Radio City, A Jagran Initiative, for his extraordinary work during his 20-year career in the industry in the field of technology mentoring. You can tweet Gaurav on his twitter handle: @g_arora.

Packt is searching for authors like you

If you're interested in becoming an author for Packt, please visit `authors.packtpub.com` and apply today. We have worked with thousands of developers and tech professionals, just like you, to help them share their insight with the global tech community. You can make a general application, apply for a specific hot topic that we are recruiting an author for, or submit your own idea.

Table of Contents

Preface

This book will introduce you to the development of microservices with Rust. I started using Rust not that long ago, back in 2015. It had only been a couple of months since the release of version 1.0 and, at that time, I didn't think that this tool would usher in a silent revolution that would disrupt the traditions associated with system programming, which, at that time, was tedious and in no way fashionable.

Maybe I'm exaggerating a little, but I have witnessed how companies stopped using the customary tools and began rewriting parts of their products or a number of services in Rust, and they were so happy with the outcome that they continue to do so time and again. Today, Rust is an important part of blockchain initiatives, the flagship for WebAssembly, and is an awesome tool for developing fast and reliable microservices that utilize all available server resources. Consequently, Rust has transformed itself from a hobby tool for curious developers into a strong foundation for modern products.

In this book, we will learn how to create microservices using Rust. We begin with a short introduction to microservices, and discuss why Rust is a good tool for writing them. Then, we will create our first microservice using the `hyper` crate, and learn how to configure microservices and log activities. After that, we will explore how to support different formats of requests and responses using the `serde` crate.

Who this book is for

This book is designed for two categories of reader—experienced Rust developers who are new to microservices, and advanced microservice developers who are new to Rust. I've tried to cover the ecosystem of useful tools and crates available for Rust developers today. This book describes the creation of microservices, from high-level frameworks to constructing low-level asynchronous combinators that produce responses with minimal resource blocking time. This book aims to allow you to find the solution to a specific task.

To be able to understand the topics covered in this book, you need a solid background in the Rust programming language (you should be able to write and compile applications using `cargo`, understand lifetimes and borrowing concepts, know how traits work, and understand how to use reference counters, mutexes, threads, and channels). If you are unfamiliar with Rust, take the time to understand these concepts before reading this book.

You also have to know how to write a minimal backend working on an HTTP protocol. You have to understand what REST is, and how to use it for applications. However, you don't have to understand how HTTP/2 works because we will use crates that provide abstractions agnostic to specific transport.

What this book covers

Chapter 1, *Introduction to Microservices*, introduces you to microservices and how they can be created with Rust. In this chapter, we also discuss the benefits of using Rust for creating microservices.

Chapter 2, *Developing a Microservice with Hyper Crate*, describes how to create microservices with the hyper crate, thereby allowing us to create a compact asynchronous web server with precise control over incoming requests (method, path, query parameters, and so on).

Chapter 3, *Logging and Configuring Microservices*, includes information about configuring a microservice using command-line arguments, environment variables, and configuration files. You will also see how to add logging to your projects, since this is the most important feature for the maintenance of microservices in production.

Chapter 4, *Data Serialization and Deserialization with Serde Crate*, explains how, in addition to customary HTTP requests, your microservice has to support formal requests and responses in a specific format, such as JSON, and CBOR, which is important for API implementation and in terms of organizing the mutual interaction of microservices.

Chapter 5, *Understanding Asynchronous Operations with Futures Crate*, delves into the deeper asynchronous concepts of Rust and how to use asynchronous primitives for writing combinators to process a request and prepare a response for a client. Without a clear understanding of these concepts, you cannot write effective microservices to utilize all available resources of a server, and to avoid the blocking of threads that execute asynchronous activities and require special treatment with execution runtime.

Chapter 6, *Reactive Microservices – Increasing Capacity and Performance*, introduces you to a reactive microservice that won't respond immediately to incoming requests, and that takes time to process a request and response when it's done. You will become familiar with remote procedure calls in Rust and how to use the language so that microservices can call one another.

Chapter 7, *Reliable Integration with Databases*, shows you how to interact with databases using Rust. You will get to know crates that provide interaction with databases, including MySQL, PostgreSQL, Redis, MongoDB, and DynamoDB.

Chapter 8, *Interaction to Database with Object-Relational Mapping*, explains how, in order to interact with SQL databases effectively and map database records to native Rust structs, you can use **object-relational mapping (ORM)**. This chapter demonstrates how to use diesel crates which require nightly compiler version and whose capabilities are used for generating bindings with tables.

Chapter 9, *Simple REST Definition and Request Routing with Frameworks*, explains how, in certain cases, you don't need to write stringent asynchronous code, and that it is sufficient to use frameworks that simplify microservice writing. In this chapter, you will become acquainted with four such frameworks—rouille, nickel, rocket, and gotham.

Chapter 10, *Background Tasks and Thread Pools in Microservices*, discusses multithreading in microservices and how to use pools of threads to perform tasks on a background, given that not every task can be performed asynchronously and requires a high CPU load.

Chapter 11, *Involving Concurrency with Actors and Actix Crate*, introduces you to the Actix framework, which uses the actor's model to provide you with abstractions that are easily compatible with Rust. This includes the balance of performance, the readability of the code, and task separation.

Chapter 12, *Scalable Microservices Architecture*, delves into an explanation of how to design loose-coupling microservices that don't need to know about sibling microservices, and that use message queues and brokers to interact with one another. We will write an example of how to interact with other microservices using RabbitMQ.

Chapter 13, *Testing and Debugging Rust Microservices*, explains how testing and debugging is a key component in terms of preparing for the release of microservices. You will learn how to test microservices from unit tests to cover a full application with integration tests. Afterward, we will then discuss how to debug an application using debuggers and logging capabilities. Also, we will create an example that uses distributed tracing based on the OpenTrace API – a modern tool for tracking the activities of complex applications.

Chapter 14, *Optimization of Microservices*, describes how to optimize a microservice and extract the maximum performance possible.

Chapter 15, *Packing Servers to Containers*, explains how, when a microservice is ready for release, there should be a focus on packing microservices to containers, because at least some microservices require additional data and environments to work, or even just to gain the advantage of fast delivery containers over bare binaries.

Chapter 16, *DevOps of Rust Microservices - Continuous Integration and Delivery*, continues with the theme of learning how to build microservices and explains how to use continuous integration to automate building and delivery processes for your product.

Chapter 17, *Bounded Microservices with AWS Lambda*, introduces you to serverless architecture, an alternative approach to writing services. You will become acquainted with AWS Lambda and you can use Rust to write fast functions that work as a part of serverless applications. Also, we will use the Serverless Framework to build and deploy the example application to the AWS infrastructure in a fully automated manner.

To get the most out of this book

You will require at least version 1.31 of Rust. Install it using the rustup tool: https://rustup.rs/. To compile examples from some chapters, you will need to install a nightly version of the compiler. You will also need to install Docker with Docker Compose to run containers with databases and message brokers to simplify the testing of example microservices from this book.

Download the example code files

You can download the example code files for this book from your account at www.packt.com. If you purchased this book elsewhere, you can visit www.packt.com/support and register to have the files emailed directly to you.

You can download the code files by following these steps:

1. Log in or register at www.packt.com.
2. Select the **SUPPORT** tab.
3. Click on **Code Downloads & Errata**.
4. Enter the name of the book in the **Search** box and follow the onscreen instructions.

Once the file is downloaded, please make sure that you unzip or extract the folder using the latest version of:

- WinRAR/7-Zip for Windows
- Zipeg/iZip/UnRarX for Mac
- 7-Zip/PeaZip for Linux

The code bundle for the book is also hosted on GitHub at https://github.com/PacktPublishing/Hands-On-Microservices-with-Rust. In case there's an update to the code, it will be updated on the existing GitHub repository.

We also have other code bundles from our rich catalog of books and videos available at https://github.com/PacktPublishing/. Check them out!

Download the color images

We also provide a PDF file that has color images of the screenshots/diagrams used in this book. You can download it here: https://www.packtpub.com/sites/default/files/downloads/9781789342758_ColorImages.pdf.

Conventions used

There are a number of text conventions used throughout this book.

CodeInText: Indicates code words in text, database table names, folder names, filenames, file extensions, pathnames, dummy URLs, user input, and Twitter handles. Here is an example: "Mount the downloaded WebStorm-10*.dmg disk image file as another disk in your system."

A block of code is set as follows:

```
let conn = Connection::connect("postgres://postgres@localhost:5432",
TlsMode::None).unwrap();
```

When we wish to draw your attention to a particular part of a code block, the relevant lines or items are set in bold:

```
#[derive(Deserialize, Debug)]
struct User {
    name: String,
    email: String,
}
```

Any command-line input or output is written as follows:

```
cargo run -- add user-1 user-1@example.com
cargo run -- add user-2 user-2@example.com
cargo run -- add user-3 user-3@example.com
```

Bold: Indicates a new term, an important word, or words that you see on screen. For example, words in menus or dialog boxes appear in the text like this. Here is an example: "Select **System info** from the **Administration** panel."

Warnings or important notes appear like this.

 Tips and tricks appear like this.

Get in touch

Feedback from our readers is always welcome.

General feedback: If you have questions about any aspect of this book, mention the book title in the subject of your message and email us at customercare@packtpub.com.

Errata: Although we have taken every care to ensure the accuracy of our content, mistakes do happen. If you have found a mistake in this book, we would be grateful if you would report this to us. Please visit www.packt.com/submit-errata, selecting your book, clicking on the Errata Submission Form link, and entering the details.

Piracy: If you come across any illegal copies of our works in any form on the internet, we would be grateful if you would provide us with the location address or website name. Please contact us at copyright@packt.com with a link to the material.

If you are interested in becoming an author: If there is a topic that you have expertise in, and you are interested in either writing or contributing to a book, please visit authors.packtpub.com.

Reviews

Please leave a review. Once you have read and used this book, why not leave a review on the site that you purchased it from? Potential readers can then see and use your unbiased opinion to make purchase decisions, we at Packt can understand what you think about our products, and our authors can see your feedback on their book. Thank you!

For more information about Packt, please visit packt.com.

Introduction to Microservices

1

This chapter will introduce you to the basics of microservices, including what a microservice is and how to break a monolithic server down into microservices. It will be useful if you are not familiar with the concept of microservices or if you have never implemented them using the Rust programming language.

The following topics will be covered in this chapter:

- What are microservices?
- How to transform a traditional server architecture into microservices
- The importance of Rust in microservices development

Technical requirements

This chapter hasn't got any special technical requirements, but now is a good time to install or update your Rust compiler. You can get this from Rust's official website: `https://www.rust-lang.org/`. I recommend that you use the `rustup` tool, which you can download from `https://rustup.rs/`.

If you have previously installed the compiler, you need to update it to the latest version using the following command:

```
rustup update
```

You can get the examples for this book from the GitHub page: `https://github.com/PacktPublishing/Hands-On-Microservices-with-Rust-2018/`.

What are microservices?

Modern users interact with microservices every day; not directly, but by using web applications. Microservices are a flexible software development technique that help to implement applications as a collection of independent services with weak relations.

In this section, we'll learn about why microservices are a good thing and why we need them. Microservices follow the REST architecture, which provides rules about using consistent HTTP methods. We will also look at how microservices can be deployed to the user, which is one of their main advantages.

Why we need microservices

Microservices are a modern software development approach that refers to the splitting of software into a suite of small services that are easier to develop, debug, deploy, and maintain. Microservices are tiny, independent servers that act as single business functions. For example, if you have an e-commerce suite that works as a monolith, you could split it into small servers that have limited responsibility and carry out the same tasks. One microservice could handle user authorization, the other could handle the users' shopping carts, and the remaining services could handle features such as search functionality, social-media integration, or recommendations.

Microservices can either interact with a database or be connected to other microservices. To interact with a database, microservices can use different protocols. These might include HTTP or REST, Thrift, ZMQ, AMQP for the messaging communication style, WebSockets for streaming data, and even the old-fashioned **Simple Object Access Protocol** (**SOAP**) to integrate them with the existing infrastructure. We will use HTTP and REST in this book, because this is the most flexible way to provide and interact with the web API. We'll explain this choice later.

Microservices have the following advantages over monolithic servers:

- You can use different programming languages
- The code base of a single server is smaller
- They have an independent DevOps process to build and deploy activities
- They can be scaled depending on their implementation
- If one microservice fails, the rest will continue to work
- They work well within containers
- Increased isolation between elements leads to better security
- They are suitable for projects involving the Internet of Things

- They are in line with the DevOps philosophy
- They can be outsourced
- They can be orchestrated after development
- They are reusable

There are, however, a few drawbacks of microservices. These include the following:

- Too many microservices overload the development process
- You have to design interaction protocols
- They can be expensive for small teams

A microservices architecture is a modern approach that can help you achieve the goal of having loosely coupling elements. This is where the servers are independent from one another, helping you to release and scale your application faster than a monolithic approach, in which you put all your eggs in one basket.

How to deploy a microservice

Since a microservice is a small but complete web server, you have to deploy it as a complete server. But since it has a narrow scope of features, it's also simpler to configure. Containers can help you pack your binaries into an image of the operating system with the necessary dependencies to simplify deployment.

This differs from the case with monoliths, in which you have a system administrator who installs and configures the server. Microservices need a new role to carry out this function—DevOps. DevOps is not just a job role, but a whole software engineering culture in which developers become system administrators and vice versa. DevOps engineers are responsible for packing and delivering the software to the end user or market. Unlike system administrators, DevOps engineers work with clouds and clusters and often don't touch any hardware except their own laptop.

DevOps uses a lot of automation and carries the application through various stages of the delivery process: building, testing, packaging, releasing, or deployment, and the monitoring of the working system. This helps to reduce the time it takes both to market a particular software and to release new versions of it. It's impossible to use a lot of automation for monolithic servers, because they are too complex and fragile. Even if you want to pack a monolith to a container, you have to deliver it as a large bundle and run the risk that any part of the application could fail. In this section, we'll have a brief look at containers and continuous integration. We will go into detail about these topics in Chapter 15, *Packing Servers to Containers*, and Chapter 16, *DevOps of Rust Microservices – Continuous Integration and Delivery*.

Docker

When we refer to containers, we almost always mean Docker containers (`https://www.docker.com/`). Docker is the most popular software tool for running programs in containers, which are isolated environments.

Containerization is a kind of virtualization where the scope of the application's resources is limited. This means the application works at its maximum performance level. This is different from full virtualization, where you have to run the full operating system with the corresponding overhead and run your application inside that isolated operating system.

Docker has become popular for a variety of reasons. One of these reasons is that it has a registry—the place where you can upload and download images of containers with applications. The public registry is Docker Hub (`https://hub.docker.com/explore/`), but you can have a private registry for a private or permissioned software.

Continuous Integration

Continuous Integration (**CI**) is the practice of keeping a master copy of the software and using tests and merging processes to expand the features of the application. The process of CI is integrated with the **Source Code Management** (**SCM**) process. When the source code is updated (for example, in Git), the CI tool checks it and starts the tests. If all tests pass, developers can merge the changes to the master branch.

CI doesn't guarantee that the application will work, because tests can be wrong, but it removes the need to run tests from developers on an automated system. This gives you the great benefit of being able to test all your upcoming changes together to detect conflicts between changes. Another advantage is that the CI system can pack your solution in a container, so the only thing that you have to do is deliver the container to a production cloud. The deployment of containers is also simple to automate.

How to split a traditional server into multiple microservices

Around 10 years ago, developers used to use the Apache web server with a scripting programming language to create web applications, rendering the views on the server-side. This meant that there was no need to split applications into pieces and it was simpler to keep the code together. With the emergence of **Single-Page Applications** (**SPAs**), we only needed server-side rendering for special cases and applications were divided into two parts: frontend and backend. Another tendency was that servers changed processing method from synchronous (where every client interaction lives in a separate thread) to asynchronous (where one thread processes many clients simultaneously using non-blocking, input-output operations). This trend promotes the better performance of single server units, meaning they can serve thousands of clients. This means that we don't need special hardware, proprietary software, or a special toolchain or compiler to write a tiny server with great performance.

The invasion of microservices happened when scripting programming languages become popular. By this, we are not only referring to languages for server-side scripting, but general-purpose high-level programming languages such as Python or Ruby. The adoption of JavaScript for backend needs, which had previously always been asynchronous, was particularly influential.

If writing your own server wasn't hard enough, you could create a separate server for special cases and use them directly from the frontend application. This would not require rendering procedures on the server. This section has provided a short description of the evolution from monolithic servers to microservices. We are now going to examine how to break a monolithic server into small pieces.

Reasons to avoid monoliths

If you already have a single server that includes all backend features, you have a monolithic service, even if you start two or more instances of this service. A monolithic service has a few disadvantages—it is impossible to scale vertically, it is impossible to update and deploy one feature without interrupting all the running instances, and if the server fails, it affects all features. Let's discuss these disadvantages a little further. This might help you to convince your manager to break your service down into microservices.

Impossible to scale vertically

There are two common approaches to scaling an application:

- **Horizontally**: Where you start a new instance of application
- **Vertically**: Where you improve an independent application layer that has a bottleneck

The simplest way to scale a backend is to start another instance of the server. This will solve the issue, but in many cases it is a waste of hardware resources. For example, imagine you have a bottleneck in an application that collects or logs statistics. This might only use 15% of your CPU, because logging might include multiple IO operations but no intensive CPU operations. However, to scale this auxiliary function, you will have to pay for the whole instance.

Impossible to update and deploy only one feature

If your backend works as a monolith, you can't update only a small part of it. Every time you add or change a feature, you have to stop, update, and start the service again, which causes interruptions.

When you have a microservice and you have find a bug, you can stop and update only this microservice without affecting the others. As I mentioned before, it can also be useful to split a product into separate development teams.

The failure of one server affects all features

Another reason to avoid monoliths is that every server crash also crashes all of the features, which causes the application to stop working completely, even though not every feature is needed for it to work. If your application can't load new user interface themes, the error is not critical, as long as you don't work in the fashion or design industry, and your application should still be able to provide the vital functions to users. If you split your monolith into independent microservices, you will reduce the impact of crashes.

Breaking a monolithic service into pieces

Let's look an example of an e-commerce monolith server that provides the following features:

- **User registration**
- **Product catalog**
- **Shopping cart**
- **Payment integration**
- **E-mail notifications**
- **Statistics collecting**

Old-fashioned servers developed years ago would include all of these features together. Even if you split it into separate application modules, they would still work on the same server. You can see an example structure of a monolithic service here:

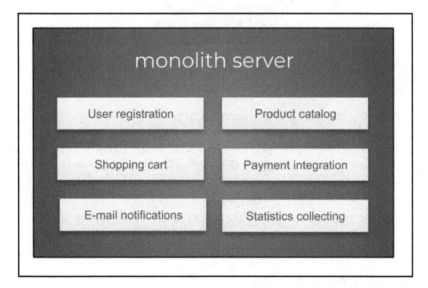

In reality, the real server contains more modules than this, but we have separated them into logical groups based on the tasks they perform. This is a good starting point to breaking your monolith into multiple, loosely coupled microservices. In this example, we can break it further into the pieces represented in the following diagram:

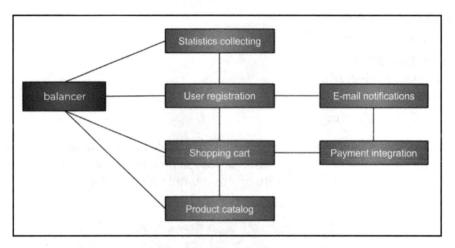

As you can see, we use a **balancer** to route requests to microservices. You can actually connect to microservices directly from the frontend application.

Shown in the preceding diagram is the potential communication that occurs between services. For simple cases, you can use direct connections. If the interaction is more complex, you can use message queues. However, you should avoid using a shared state such as a central database and interacting through records, because this can cause a bottleneck for the whole application. We will discuss how to scale microservices in Chapter 12, *Scalable Microservices Architecture*. For now, we will explore REST API, which will be partially implemented in a few examples throughout this book. We will also discuss why Rust is a great choice for implementing microservices.

Definition of a REST API

Let's define the APIs that we will use in our microservice infrastructure using the REST methodology. In this example, our microservices will have minimal APIs for demonstration purposes; real microservices might not be quite so "micro". Let's explore the REST specifications of the microservices of our application. We will start by looking at a microservice for user registration and go through every part of the application.

User registration microservice

The first service is responsible for the registration of users. It has to contain methods to add, update, or delete users. We can cover all needs with the standard REST approach. We will use a combination of methods and paths to provide this user registration functionality:

- POST request to /user/ creates a new user and returns its id
- GET request to /user/id returns information related to a user with id
- PUT request to /user/id applies changes to a user with id
- DELETE request to /user/id removes a user with id

This service can use the **E-mail notifications** microservice and call its methods to notify the user about registration.

E-mail notifications microservice

The **E-mail notifications** microservice can be extremely simple and contains only a single method:

- The POST request to /send_email/ sends an email to any address

This server can also count the sent emails to prevent spam or check that the email exists in the user's database by requesting it from the **User registration** microservice. This is done to prevent malicious use.

Product catalog microservice

The **Product catalog** microservice tracks the available products and needs only weak relations with other microservices, except for the **Shopping cart**. This microservice can contain the following methods:

- POST request to /product/ creates a new product and returns its id
- GET request to /product/id returns information about the product with id
- PUT request to /product/id updates information about the product with id
- DELETE request to /product/id marks the product with id as deleted
- GET request to /products/ returns a list of all products (can be paginated by extra parameters)

Shopping cart microservice

The **Shopping cart** microservice is closely integrated with the **User registration** and **Product catalog** microservices. It holds pending purchases and prepares invoices. It contains the following methods:

- POST request to /user/uid/cart/, which puts a product in the cart and returns the id of item in the user's cart with the uid
- GET request to /user/uid/cart/id, which returns information about the item with id
- PUT request to /user/uid/cart/id, which updates information about the item with id (alters the quantity of items)
- GET request to /user/uid/cart/, which returns a list of all the items in the cart

As you can see, we don't add an extra "s" to the /cart/ URL and we use the same path for creating items and to get a list, because the first handler reacts to the POST method, the second processes requests with the GET method, and so on. We also use the user's ID in the path. We can implement the nested REST functions in two ways:

- Use session information to get the user's id. In this case, the paths contain a single object, such as /cart/id . We can keep the user's id in session cookies, but this is not reliable.
- We can add the id of a user to a path explicitly.

Payment Integration microservice

In our example, this microservice will be a third-party service, which contains the following methods:

- POST request to /invoices creates a new invoice and returns its id
- POST request to /invoices/id/pay pays for the invoice

Statistics collecting microservice

This service collects usage statistics and logs a user's actions to later improve the application. This service exports API calls to collect the data and contains some internal APIs to read the data:

- POST request to /log logs a user's actions (the id of a user is set in the body of the request)

- `GET` request to `/log?from=?&to=?` works only from the internal network and returns the collected data for the period specified

This microservice doesn't conform clearly to the REST principles. It's useful for microservices that provide a full set of methods to add, modify, and remove the data, but for other services, it is excessively restrictive. You don't have follow a clear REST structure for all of your services, but it may be useful for some tools that expect it.

Transformation to microservices

If you already have a working application, you might transform it into a set of microservices, but you have to keep the application running at the highest rate and prevent any interruptions.

To do this, you can create microservices step by step, starting from the least important task. In our example, it's better to start from email activities and logging. This practice helps you to create a DevOps process from scratch and join it with the maintenance process of your app.

Reusing existing microservices

If your application is a monolith server, you don't need to turn all modules into microservices, because you can use existing third-party services and shrink the bulk of the code that needs rewriting. These services can help with many things, including storage, payments, logging, and transactional notifications that tell you whether an event has been delivered or not.

I recommend that you create and maintain services that determine your competitive advantage yourself and then use third-party services for other tasks. This can significantly shrink your expenses and the time to market.

In any case, remember the product that you are delivering and don't waste time on unnecessary units of your application. The microservices approach helps you to achieve this simply, unlike the tiresome coding of monoliths, which requires you to deal with numerous secondary tasks. Hopefully, you are now fully aware of the reasons why microservices can be useful. In the next section, we will look at why Rust is a promising tool for creating microservices.

Why Rust is a great tool for creating microservices

If you have chosen to read this book, you probably already know that Rust is an up-to-date, powerful, and reliable language. However, choosing it to implement microservices is not an obvious decision, because Rust is a system programming language that is often assigned to low-level software such as drivers or OS kernels. This is because you tend to have to write a lot of glue code or get into detailed algorithms with low-level concepts, such as pointers in system programming languages. This is not the case with Rust. As a Rust programmer, you've surely already seen how it can be used to create high-level abstractions with flexible language capabilities. In this section, we'll discuss the strengths of Rust: its strict and explicit nature, its high performance, and its great package system.

Explicit versus implicit

Up until recently, there hasn't been a well-established approach to using Rust for writing asynchronous network applications. Previously, developers tended to use two styles: either explicit control structures to handle asynchronous operations or implicit context switching. The explicit nature of Rust meant that the first approach outgrew the second. Implicit context switching is used in concurrent programming languages such as Go, but this model does not suit Rust for a variety of reasons. First of all, it has design limitations and it's hard or even impossible to share implicit contexts between threads. This is because the standard Rust library uses thread-local data for some functions and the program can't change the thread environment safely. Another reason is that an approach with context switching has overheads and therefore doesn't follow the zero-cost abstractions philosophy because you would have a background runtime. Some modern libraries such as `actix` provide a high-level approach similar to automatic context switching, but actually use explicit control structures for handling asynchronous operations.

Network programming in Rust has evolved over time. When Rust was released, developers could only use the standard library. This method was particularly verbose and not suitable for writing high-performance servers. This was because the standard library didn't contain any good asynchronous abstractions. Also, event `hyper`, a good crate for creating HTTP servers and clients, processed requests in separate threads and could therefore only have a certain number of simultaneous connections.

The `mio` crate was introduced to provide a clear asynchronous approach to make high-performance servers. It contained functions to interact with asynchronous features of the operating system, such as epoll or kqueue, but it was still verbose, which made it hard to write modular applications.

The next abstraction layer over `mio` was a `futures` and `tokio` pair of crates. The `futures` crate contained abstractions for implementing delayed operations (like the defers concept in Twisted, if you're familiar with Python). It also contained types for assembling stream processors, which are reactive and work like a finite state machine.

Using the `futures` crate was a powerful way to implement high-performance and high-accuracy network software. However, it was a middleware crate, which made it hard to solve everyday tasks. It was a good base for rewriting crates such as `hyper`, because these can use explicit asynchronous abstractions with full control.

The highest level of abstraction today are crates that use `futures`, `tokio`, and `hyper` crates, such as `rocket` or `actix-web`. Now, `rocket` includes high-level elements to construct a web server with the minimal amount of lines. `actix-web` works as a set of actors when your software is broken down into small entities that interact with one another. There are many other useful crates, but we will start with hyper as a basis for developing web servers from scratch. Using this crate, we will be between low-level crates, such as futures, and high-level crates, such as `rocket`. This will allow us to understand both in detail.

hyper *rocket, actix-web*
future, tokio
mio (epoll)

Minimal amount of runtime errors

There are many languages suitable for creating microservices, but not every language has a reliable design to keep you from making mistakes. Most interpreted dynamic languages let you write flexible code that decides on the fly which field of the object to get and which function to call. You can often even override the rules of function calling by adding meta-information to objects. This is vital in meta-programming or in cases where your data drives the behavior of the runtime.

The dynamic approach, however, has significant drawbacks for the software, which requires reliability rather than flexibility. This is because any inaccuracy in the code causes the application to crash. The first time you try to use Rust, you may feel that it lacks flexibility. This is not true, however; the difference is in the approach you use to achieve flexibility. With Rust, all your rules must be strict. If you create enough abstractions to cover all of the cases your application might face, you will get the flexibility you want.

Rust rookies who come from the JavaScript or the Python world might notice that they have to declare every case of serialization/deserialization of data, whereas with dynamic languages, you can simply unpack any input data to the free-form object and explore the content later. You actually have to check all cases of inconsistency during runtime and try and work out what consequences could be caused if you change one field and remove another. With Rust, the compiler checks everything, including the type, the existence, and the corresponding format. The most important thing here is the type, because you can't compile a program that uses incompatible types. With other languages, this sometimes leads to strange compilation errors such as a case where you have two types for the same crate but the types are incompatible because they were declared in different versions of the same crate. Only Rust protects you from shooting yourself in the foot in this way. In fact, different versions can have different rules of serialization/deserialization for a type, even if both declarations have the same data layout.

Great performance

Rust is a system programming language. This means your code is compiled into native binary instructions for the processor and runs without unwanted overhead, unlike interpreters such as JavaScript or Python.

Rust also doesn't use a garbage collector and you can control all allocations of memory and the size of buffers to prevent overflow.

Another reason why Rust is so fast for microservices is that it has zero-cost abstractions, which means that most abstractions in the language weigh nothing. They turn into effective code during compilation without any runtime overhead. For network programming, this means that your code will be effective after compilation, that is, once you have added meaningful constructions in the source code.

Minimal dependencies burden

Rust programs are compiled into a single binary without unwanted dependencies. It needs libc or another dynamic library if you want to use OpenSSL or similar irreplaceable dependencies, but all Rust crates are compiled statically into your code.

You may think that the compiled binaries are quite large to be used as microservices. The word microservice, however, refers to the narrow logic scope, rather than the size. Even so, statically linked programs remain tiny for modern computers.

What benefits does this give you? You will avoid having to worry about dependencies. Each Rust microservice uses its own set of dependencies compiled into a single binary. You can even keep microservices with obsolete features and dependencies besides new microservices. In addition, Rust, in contrast with the Go programming language, has strict rules for dependencies. This means that the project resists breaking, even if someone forces an update of the repository with the dependency you need.

How does Rust compare to Java? Java has microframeworks for building microservices, but you have to carry all dependencies with them. You can put these in a fat **Java ARchive (JAR)**, which is a kind of compiled code distribution in Java, but you still need **Java Virtual Machine (JVM)**. Don't forget, too, that Java will load every dependency with a class loader. Also, Java bytecode is interpreted and it takes quite a while for the **Just-In-Time (JIT)** compilation to finish to accelerate the code. With Rust, bootstrapping dependencies don't take a long time because they are attached to the code during compilation and your code will work with the highest speed from the start since it was already compiled into native code.

Summary

In this chapter, we have mastered the basics of microservices. Simply put, a microservice is a compact web server that handles specific tasks. For example, microservices can be responsible for user authentication or for email notifications. They make running units reusable. This means you don't need to recompile or restart units if they don't require any updates. This approach is simpler and more reliable in deployment and maintenance.

We have also discussed how to split a monolithic web server that contains all of its business logic in a single unit into smaller pieces and join them together through communication, in line with the ideology of loose coupling. To split a monolithic server, you should separate it into domains that are classified by what tasks the servers carry out.

In the last section of this chapter, we've looked at why Rust is a good choice for developing microservices. We touched on dependencies management, the performance of Rust, its explicit nature, and its toolchain. It's now time to dive deep into coding and write a minimal microservice with Rust.

In the next chapter we will start to writing microservices with Rust using `hyper` crate that provides all necessary features to write compact asynchronous HTTP server.

Further reading

You have learned about the basics of microservices in this chapter, which will serve as a point for you to start writing microservices on Rust throughout this book. If you want to learn more about topics discussed in this chapter, please consult the following list:

- *Microservices - a definition of this new architectural term*, 2014, Martin Fowler, available at `https://martinfowler.com/articles/microservices.html`. This article introduces the concept of microservices.
- `mio`, available at `https://github.com/carllerche/mio`. This is a crate that is widely used by other crates for asynchronous operations in Rust. We won't use it directly, but it is useful to know how it works.
- *Network Programming with Rust, 2018,* Abhishek Chanda, available at `https://www.packtpub.com/application-development/network-programming-rust`. This book explains more about network addresses, protocols and sockets, and how to use them all with Rust.

Developing a Microservice with the Hyper Crate

2

This chapter will provide a short introduction to creating microservices using Rust the and `hyper` crate. We will look at the basics of the HTTP protocol and the principles of routing. We'll also describe a minimal REST service written completely with Rust, using a simple method.

In this chapter, we'll cover the following topics:

- Using `hyper`
- Handling HTTP requests
- Using regular expressions for routing
- Getting parameters from the environment

Technical requirements

Because we're starting to write code in this chapter, you'll need to have certain software in order to compile and run examples:

- I recommend you use the `rustup` tool, which will keep your Rust instance up to date. If you don't have this tool, you can get it from `https://rustup.rs/`. When it's installed, run the `rustup update` command to update the current installation.
- The Rust compiler, at least version 1.31.
- The `hyper` crate, which we'll use to compile the code, requires the OpenSSL (`https://www.openssl.org/`) library. The most popular operating systems already include the OpenSSL package and you can follow the manual of your package manager to install it.

You can get the examples shown in this chapter from GitHub at `https://github.com/PacktPublishing/Hands-On-Microservices-with-Rust/tree/master/Chapter02`.

Binding a Tiny Server

In this section, we'll create a Tiny Server from scratch. We'll start with the necessary dependencies, declare a main function, and then try to build and run it.

Adding necessary dependencies

First, we need to create a new folder where we'll add the necessary dependencies to create our first microservice. Use `cargo` to make a new project called `hyper-microservice`:

```
> cargo new hyper-microservice
```

Open the created folder and add dependencies to your `Cargo.toml` file:

```
[dependencies]
hyper = "0.12"
```

The single dependency is the `hyper` crate. The latest release of this crate is asynchronous and lies on top of the `futures` crate. It also uses the `tokio` crate for runtime, which includes the scheduler, reactor, and asynchronous sockets. Some of the necessary types of the `tokio` crate are re-exported in the `hyper::rt` module. The main purpose of `hyper` is to operate with the HTTP protocol, which means that the crate can support other runtimes in the future.

The main function of the server

Let's start with the main function and add the necessary dependencies one by one, looking in detail at why we need each one. A minimal HTTP server needs the following:

- An address to bind to
- A `server` instance to handle incoming requests
- A default handler for any request
- A reactor (runtime) where the `server` instance will operate

Address of the server

The first thing we need is an address. A socket address consists of an IP address and a port number. We'll use IPv4 in this book because it's widely supported. In Chapter 6, *Reactive Microservices – Increasing Capacity and Performance*, where we'll discuss scaling and the intercommunication of microservices, I'll show a few examples using IPv6.

The standard Rust library contains an IpAddr type to represent the IP address. We'll use the SocketAddr struct, which contains both the IpAddr and the u16 for the port number. We can construct the SocketAddr from a tuple of the ([u8; 4], u16) type. Add the following code to our main function:

```
let addr = ([127, 0, 0, 1], 8080).into();
```

We used an implementation of the impl<I: Into<IpAddr>> From<(I, u16)> for SocketAddr trait here, which, in turn, uses impl From<[u8; 4]> for IpAddr. This lets us use the .into() method call to construct a socket address from the tuple. Similarly, we can create new SocketAddr instances with a constructor. In production applications, we will parse the socket addresses from external strings (command-line parameters or environment variables), and if no variants are set, we'll create SocketAddr from a tuple with default values.

Server instances

Now we can create a server instance and bind to this address:

```
let builder = Server::bind(&addr);
```

The preceding line creates a hyper::server::Server instance with a bind constructor that actually returns Builder, not a Server instance. The Server struct implements the Future trait. It has similar role to Result, but describes a value that isn't available immediately. You'll learn more about Future and other traits of the futures crate in Chapter 5, *Understanding Asynchronous Operations with the Futures Crate*.

Setting the requests handler

The `Builder` struct provides methods to tweak the parameters of the `server` created. For example, hyper's `server` supports both `HTTP1` and `HTTP2`. You can use a `builder` value to choose either one protocol or both. In the following example, we're using `builder` to attach a service for handling incoming HTTP requests using the `serve` method:

```
let server = builder.serve(|| {
    service_fn_ok(|_| {
        Response::new(Body::from("Almost microservice..."))
    })
});
```

Here, we're using the builder instance to attach a function that generates a `Service` instance. This function implements the `hyper::service::NewService` trait. The generated item then has to implement the `hyper::service::Service` trait. A service in a `hyper` crate is a function that takes a request and gives a response back. We haven't implemented this trait in this example; instead, we'll use the `service_fn_ok` function, which turns a function with suitable types into a service handler.

There are two corresponding structs: `hyper::Request` and `hyper::Response`. In the preceding code, we ignored a request argument and constructed the same response for every request. The response contains a body of static text.

Adding the server instance to a runtime

Since we now have a handler, we can start the server. The runtime expects a `Future` instance with the `Future<Item = (), Error = ()>` type, but the `Server` struct implements a `Future` with the `hyper::Error` error type. We can use this error to inform the user about issues, but in our example we'll just drop any error. As you might remember, the drop function expects a single argument of any type and returns a `unit` empty type. The `Future` trait uses the `map_err` method. It changes the error type using a function, which expects the original error type and returns a new one. Drop an error from the `server` using the following:

```
let server = server.map_err(drop);
```

We now have everything we need and can start the `server` with the specific runtime. Use the `hyper::rt::run` function to start the `server`:

```
hyper::rt::run(server);
```

Don't compile it yet, because we haven't imported types. Add it to the head of a source file:

```
use hyper::{Body, Response, Server};
use hyper::rt::Future;
use hyper::service::service_fn_ok;
```

We need to import the different `hyper` types that we are using: `Server`, `Response`, and `Body`. In the final line, we're using the `service_fn_ok` function. The `Future` import needs special attention; it's the re-exported trait of the `futures` crate and it's used everywhere in the `hyper` crate. In the next chapter, we'll examine this trait in detail.

Building and running

You can now compile the code and start the server with the following command:

```
cargo run
```

Use your browser to connect to the server. Enter `http://localhost:8080/` in the browser's address bar and the browser will connect to your server and show you a page with the text you entered in the previous code:

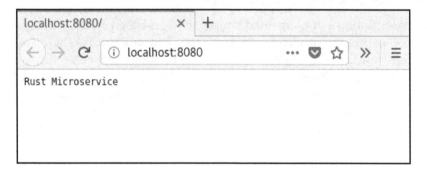

Rebuilding on changes

When you're working on developing web servers, it's useful to have instant access to compiled and running applications. It's tiresome to have to restart `cargo run` manually whenever you change the code. I recommend that you install and use the `cargo-watch` subcommand on `cargo`. This will monitor the changes made to the files of your project and restart the other commands you have chosen.

To install `cargo-watch`, perform the following steps:

1. Type the following command in the console:

```
cargo install cargo-watch
```

2. Use the `run` command with `watch`:

```
cargo watch -x "run"
```

You can add extra arguments to the `run` command between quotes or add extra arguments after the `--` characters.

Handling incoming requests

We've created a server, but it isn't very useful until it can respond to real requests. In this section, we'll add handlers to the requests and use the principles of REST.

Adding a service function

In the previous section, we implemented simple services based on `service_fn_ok` functions, which expect the service function not to throw any errors. There are also `service_fn` functions, which can be used to create handlers that can return an error. These are more suitable for asynchronous `Future` results. As we saw previously, the `Future` trait has two associated types: one for a successful result and one for an error.
The `service_fn` function expects the result to be converted into future with the `IntoFuture` trait. You can read more about the `futures` crate and its types in the next chapter.

Let's change the previous service function into one that returns the `Future` instance:

```
let server = builder.serve(|| service_fn(microservice_handler));
```

Then add this unimplemented service function:

```
fn microservice_handler(req: Request<Body>)
    -> impl Future<Item=Response<Body>, Error=Error>
{
    unimplemented!();
}
```

Similar to the previous one, this function expects a `Request`, but it doesn't return a simple `Response` instance. Instead, it returns a future result. Since `Future` is a trait (which doesn't have a size), we can't return an unsized entity from the function and we have to wrap it in a `Box`. However, in this case, we used a brand new approach, which is the `impl` trait. This allows us to return an implementation of the trait by value, rather than by reference. Our `future` can be resolved to a `hyper::Response<Body>` item or a `hyper::Error` error type. You should import the necessary types if you've started a project from scratch and aren't using the code examples included with this book:

```
use futures::{future, Future};
use hyper::{Body, Error, Method, Request, Response, Server, StatusCode};
use hyper::service::service_fn;
```

We also imported the `Future` trait from the `futures` crate. Make sure you're either using `edition = "2018"` in the `Cargo.toml` file, or importing the crates in `main.rs`:

```
extern crate futures;
extern crate hyper;
```

We started by importing the types to the code, but we still have to import the crates in the `Cargo.toml` file. Add these crates in the dependency list of your `Cargo.toml`:

```
[dependencies]
futures = "0.1"
hyper = "0.12"
```

Everything is now ready to implement a service handler.

> I prefer to order dependencies from generic to more specific. Alternatively, you can use alphabetical order.

Implementing a service function

Our service function will support two kinds of requests:

- `GET` requests to the `/` path with an index page response
- Other requests with a `NOT_FOUND` response

To detect the corresponding method and path, we can use the methods of the `Request` object. See the following code:

```
fn microservice_handler(req: Request<Body>)
    -> impl Future<Item=Response<Body>, Error=Error>
{
    match (req.method(), req.uri().path()) {
        (&Method::GET, "/") => {
            future::ok(Response::new(INDEX.into()))
        },
        _ => {
            let response = Response::builder()
                .status(StatusCode::NOT_FOUND)
                .body(Body::empty())
                .unwrap();
            future::ok(response)
        },
    }
}
```

I used a `match` expression to detect the corresponding method returned from the `req.method()` function, and also the path of the URI of the `Request` returned by the `req.uri().path()` method's chain call.

The `method()` function returns a reference to the `Method` instance. `Method` is an enumeration that contains all supported HTTP methods. Instead of other popular languages, which return strings for methods, Rust uses a strict set of methods from a finite enumeration. This helps to detect typos during compilation.

The `Future` instances created with the `future::ok` function are also returned. This function immediately resolves the future to a successful result with an item of the corresponding type. This is useful for static values; we don't need to wait to create them.

The future object is a long operation that won't return a result immediately. The runtime will poll the future until it returns the result. It's useful to perform asynchronous requests on a database. We'll do this in Chapter 7, *Reliable Integration with Databases*.

We can also return streams instead of a whole result. The `futures` crate contains a `Stream` trait for those cases. We'll look at this further in Chapter 5, *Understanding Asynchronous Operations with the Futures Crate*.

In our match expression, we used `Method::GET` and the `"/"` path to detect requests of the index page. In this case, we'll return a `Response` that constructs a `new` function and an HTML string as an argument.

In case no pages were found that match the `_` pattern, we'll return a response with the `NOT_FOUND` status code from the `StateCode` enumeration. This contains all of the status codes of the HTTP protocol.

We use the `body` method to construct the response, and we used an empty `Body` as an argument for that function. To check that we haven't used it before, we use `unwrap` to unpack the `Response` from the `Result`.

Index pages

The last thing we need is an index page. It's considered good form to return some information about a microservice when requested, but you may hide it for security reasons.

Our index page is a simple string with HTML content inside:

```
const INDEX: &'static str = r#"
 <!doctype html>
 <html>
     <head>
         <title>Rust Microservice</title>
     </head>
     <body>
         <h3>Rust Microservice</h3>
     </body>
 </html>
 "#;
```

This is a constant value that can't be modified. Pay attention to the start of the string, `r#"`, if you haven't used it before. This is a kind of multiline string in Rust that has to end with `"#`.

Now you can compile the code and view the pages with a browser. I opened Developer Tools to show the status codes of the requests:

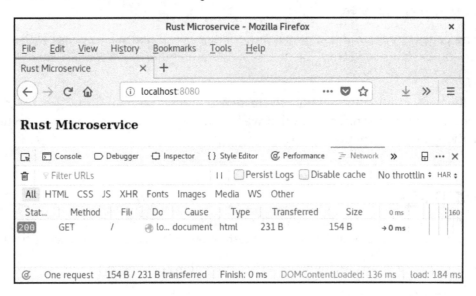

If you try to get a nonexistent resource, you'll get a `404` status code, which we set with the `StatusCode::NOT_FOUND` constant:

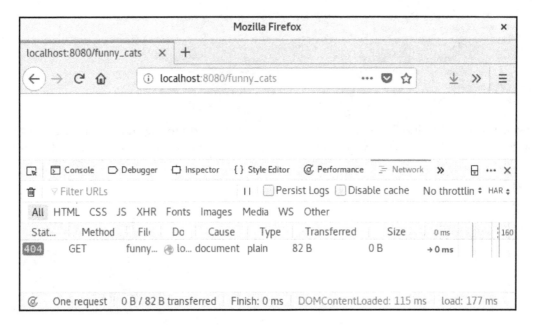

Implementing the REST principles

If everyone were to create rules of interaction with microservices from scratch, we'd have an excess of private standards of intercommunication. REST isn't a strict set of rules, but it's an architectural style intended to make interacting with microservices simple. It provides a suggested set of HTTP methods to create, read, update, and delete data; and perform actions. We'll add methods to our service and fit them to REST principles.

Adding a shared state

You may have already heard that shared data is a bad thing and a potential cause of bottlenecks, if it has to be changed from separate threads. However, shared data can be useful if we want to share the address of a channel or if we don't need frequent access to it. In this section, we need a user database. In the following example, I'll show you how to add a shared state to our generator function. This approach can be used for a variety of reasons, such as keeping a connection to a database.

A user database will obviously hold data about users. Let's add some types to handle this:

```
type UserId = u64;
struct UserData;
```

UserId represents the user's unique identifier. UserData represents the stored data, but we use an empty struct for serialization and parsing streams in this example.

Our database will be as follows:

```
type UserDb = Arc<Mutex<Slab<UserData>>>;
```

Arc is an atomic reference counter that provides multiple references to a single instance of data (in our case, this is the Mutex over the slab of data). Atomic entities can be safely used with multiple threads. It uses native atomic operations to prohibit the cloning of the reference. This is because two or more threads can corrupt the reference counter and can cause segmentation faults, leading to data loss or a memory leak if the counter was greater than the references in the code.

Mutex is a mutual-exclusion wrapper that controls access to mutable data. Mutex is an atomic flag that checks that only one thread has access to the data and other threads have to wait until the thread that has locked the mutex releases it.

You have take into account that if you have a locked `Mutex` in one thread and that thread panics, the `Mutex` instance become poisoned, and if you try to lock it from another thread, you'll get an error.

You may be wondering why we reviewed these types if the asynchronous server can work in a single thread. There are two reasons. First, you may need to run the server in multiple threads for scaling. Second, all types that provide interaction facilities, such as Sender objects (from a standard library, a `futures` crate, or anywhere else) or database connections, are often wrapped with these types to make them compatible with a multithreading environment. It can be useful to know what's going on under the hood.

You might be familiar with standard library types, but `Slab` may seem a little different. This type can be thought of as a silver bullet in web-server development. Most pools use this appliance. Slab is an allocator that can store and remove any value identified by an ordered number. It can also reuse the slots of removed items. It's similar to the `Vec` type, which won't resize if you remove the element, but will reuse free space automatically. For servers, it's useful to keep connections or requests, such as in the JSON-RPC protocol implementation.

In this case, we use `Slab` to allocate new IDs for users and to keep the data with the user. We use `Arc` with the `Mutex` pair to protect our database of data race, because different responses can be processed in different threads, which can both try to access the database. In fact, Rust won't let you compile the code without these wrappers.

We have to add an extra dependency, because the `Slab` type is available in the external `slab` crate. Add this using `Cargo.toml`:

```
[dependencies]
slab = "0.4"
futures = "0.1"
hyper = "0.12"
```

Import these necessary types in the `main.rs` file:

```
use std::fmt;
use std::sync::{Arc, Mutex};
use slab::Slab;
use futures::{future, Future};
use hyper::{Body, Error, Method, Request, Response, Server, StatusCode};
use hyper::service::service_fn;
```

Let's write a handler and a `main` function in the following section.

Accessing a shared state from a service function

To get access to a shared state, you need to provide a reference to the shared data. This is simple, because we've already wrapped our state with `Arc`, which provides us with a `clone()` function to duplicate the reference to the shared object.

Since our service function needs extra parameters, we have to rewrite the definition and call our `microservice_handler` function. Now it has an extra argument, which is the reference to the shared state:

```
fn microservice_handler(req: Request<Body>, user_db: &UserDb)
    -> impl Future<Item=Response<Body>, Error=Error>
```

We also have to send this expected reference to the `main` function:

```
fn main() {
    let addr = ([127, 0, 0, 1], 8080).into();
    let builder = Server::bind(&addr);
    let user_db = Arc::new(Mutex::new(Slab::new()));
    let server = builder.serve(move || {
        let user_db = user_db.clone();
        service_fn(move |req| microservice_handler(req, &user_db))
    });
    let server = server.map_err(drop);
    hyper::rt::run(server);
}
```

As you can see, we created a `Slab` and wrapped it with `Mutex` and `Arc`. After that, we moved the object, called `user_db`, into the `serve` function call of the `server` builder that's using the `move` keyword. When the reference moves into the closure, we can send it to `microservice_handler`. This is a handler function called by a closure sent to the `service_fn` call. We have to clone the reference to move it to a nested closure, because that closure can be called multiple times. We shouldn't move the object completely, however, because a closure sent to the `serve` function can be called multiple times and so the runtime might need the object again later.

In other words, both closures can be called multiple times. The closure of `service_fn` will be called in the same thread as the runtime, and we can use a reference for the value inside it.

Parsing paths in a microservice

A common task in web development is to use functions that work with persistent storage. These functions are often called **create, read, update, and delete** (**CRUD**) functions. They are the most common operations with data.

We can implement a CRUD set for our service, but first we have to identify the entity that we want to work with. Imagine that we need three types of entities: users, articles, and comments. In this case, I recommend that you separate the microservices, because the users microservice is responsible for identity, the articles microservice is responsible for the content, and the comments microservice handles content. However, you would get more benefits if you could reuse these entities for more than one context.

Before we implement all the handlers, we need a helper function that creates empty responses with the corresponding HTTP status codes:

```
fn response_with_code(status_code: StatusCode) -> Response<Body> {
    Response::builder()
        .status(status_code)
        .body(Body::empty())
        .unwrap()
}
```

This function carries out a few simple actions – it expects a status code, creates a new response builder, sets that status, and adds an empty body.

We can now add a new request handler that checks three path variants:

- The index page (path /)
- Actions with user data (prefix /user/)
- Other paths

We can use the `match` expression to fulfill all of these cases. Add the following code to the `microservices_handler` function:

```
let response = {
    match (req.method(), req.uri().path()) {
        (&Method::GET, "/") => {
            Response::new(INDEX.into())
        },
        (method, path) if path.starts_with(USER_PATH) => {
            unimplemented!();
        },
        _ => {
            response_with_code(StatusCode::NOT_FOUND)
```

```
        },
    }
};
future::ok(response)
```

As you can see, we used an `if` expression in the second branch to detect that the path starts with the `/user/` prefix. This prefix is actually stored in the `USER_PATH` constant:

```
const USER_PATH: &str = "/user/";
```

Unlike the previous example, in this case we'll use our brand new `response_with_code` function to return a `NOT_FOUND` HTTP response. We also assign a response to the `response` variable and use it to create a `Future` instance with the `future::ok` function.

Implementing REST methods

Our microservices can already distinguish between different paths. All that's left is to implement request handling for the users' data. All incoming requests have to contain the `/user/` prefix in their paths.

Extracting the user's identifier

To modify a specific user, we need their identifier. REST specifies that you need to get the IDs from a path, because REST maps data entities to URLs.

We can extract a user's identifier using the tail of the path, which we already have. This is why we use the `starts_with` method of the string, instead of checking for strong equality with `USER_PATH` to the path tails.

We previously declared the `UserId` type, which equals the `u64` unsigned number. Add this code to the second branch of the previously-declared `match` expression with the `(method, path)` pattern to extract the user's identifier from the path:

```
let user_id = path.trim_left_matches(USER_PATH)
        .parse::<UserId>()
        .ok()
        .map(|x| x as usize);
```

The `str::trim_left_matches` method removes the part of the string if it matches a provided string from the argument. After that, we use the `str::parse` method, which tries to convert a string (the remaining tail) to a type that implements the `FromStr` trait of the standard library. `UserId` already implements this, because it's equal to the `u64` type, which can be parsed from the string.

The parse method returns `Result`. We convert this to an `Option` instance with `Result::ok` functions. We won't try to handle errors with the IDs. The `None` value represents either the absence of a value or a wrong value.

We can also use a map of the returned `Option` instance to convert a value to the `usize` type. This is because `Slab` uses `usize` for IDs, but the real size of the `usize` type depends on the platform architecture, which can be different. It can be `u32` or `u64` depending on the largest memory address that you can use.

Why can't we use `usize` for `UserId` since it implements the `FromStr` trait? This is because a client expects the same behavior as an HTTP server, which doesn't depend on the architecture platform. It's bad practice to use unpredictable size parameters in HTTP requests.

Sometimes, it can be difficult to choose a type to identify the data. We use `map` to convert the `u64` value to `usize`. This doesn't work, however, for architectures where `usize` equals `u32`, because `UserId` can be larger than the memory limit. It's safe in cases where the microservices are tiny, but this is an important point to bear in mind for microservices that you'll use in production. Often, this problem will be simple to solve, because you can use the ID type of a database.

Getting access to the shared data

In this user handler, we need access to a database with users. Because the database is a `Slab` instance that's wrapped with a `Mutex` instance, we have to lock the mutex to have exclusive access to a slab. There's a `Mutex::lock` function that returns `Result<MutexGuard, PoisonError<MutexGuard>>`. `MutexGuard` is a scoped lock, which means it leaves the code block or scope in, and it implements the `Deref` and `DerefMut` traits to provide transparent access to data under the guard object.

It's a good practice to report all errors in the handler. You can log errors and return a 500 (Internal Error) HTTP code to the client. To keep it simple, we'll use an `unwrap` method and expect the mutex to lock correctly:

```
let mut users = user_db.lock().unwrap();
```

Here, we locked the `Mutex` for the duration of generating the request. In this case, where we're creating whole responses immediately, this is normal. In cases where the result is delayed or when we work with a stream, we shouldn't lock the mutex all time. This will create a bottleneck for all requests because the `server` can't process requests in parallel if all of them depend on a single shared object. For cases where you don't have results immediately, you can clone the reference to the mutex and lock it for the short time you need access to the data.

REST methods

We want to cover all basic CRUD operations. Using the principles of REST, there are suitable HTTP methods that fit these operations—POST, GET, PUT, and DELETE. We can use the `match` expression to detect the corresponding HTTP method:

```
match (method, user_id) {
    // Put other branches here
    _ => {
        response_with_code(StatusCode::METHOD_NOT_ALLOWED)
    },
}
```

Here, we used a tuple with two values—a method and a user identifier, which is represented by the `Option<UserId>` type. There is a default branch that returns the METHOD_NOT_ALLOWED message (the 405 HTTP status code) if a client requests an unsupported method.

Let's discuss every branch of match expression for every operation.

POST – Creating data

When the `server` has just started, it doesn't contain any data. To support data creation, we use the POST method without the user's ID. Add the following branch to the `match (method, user_id)` expression:

```
(&Method::POST, None) => {
    let id = users.insert(UserData);
    Response::new(id.to_string().into())
}
```

This code adds a `UserData` instance to the user database and sends the associated ID of the user in a response with the OK status (an HTTP status code of 200). This code was set by the `Response::new` function by default.

UserData is an empty struct in this case. In real applications, however, it would have to contain real data. We use an empty struct to avoid serialization, but you can read more about serialization and deserialization based on the serde crate in Chapter 4, *Data Serialization and Deserialization with the Serde Crate.*

What if the client sets the ID with a POST request? You can interpret this case in two ways—ignore it or try to use the provided ID. In our example, we'll inform the client that the request was wrong. Add the following branch to handle this case:

```
(&Method::POST, Some(_)) => {
    response_with_code(StatusCode::BAD_REQUEST)
}
```

This code returns a response with the BAD_REQUEST status code (a 400 HTTP status code).

GET – Reading data

When data is created, we need to be able to read it. For this case, we can use the HTTP GET method. Add the following branch to the code:

```
(&Method::GET, Some(id)) => {
    if let Some(data) = users.get(id) {
        Response::new(data.to_string().into())
    } else {
        response_with_code(StatusCode::NOT_FOUND)
    }
}
```

This code uses the user database to try to find the user by the ID that's provided in the path. If the user is found, we'll convert its data to a String and into a Body to send with a Response.

If the user isn't found, the handler branch will respond with the NOT_FOUND status code (the classic 404 error).

To make the UserData convertible to a String, we have to implement the ToString trait for that type. However, it's typically more useful to implement the Display trait, because ToString will be derived automatically for every type that implements the Display trait. Add this code somewhere in the main.rs source file:

```
impl fmt::Display for UserData {
    fn fmt(&self, f: &mut fmt::Formatter) -> fmt::Result {
        f.write_str("{}")
    }
}
```

In this implementation, we return a string with an empty JSON object "{}". Real microservices have to use the `serde` trait for such conversions.

PUT – Updating data

Once the data is saved, we might want to provide the ability to modify it. This is a task for the PUT method. Use this method to handle changes to the data:

```
(&Method::PUT, Some(id)) => {
    if let Some(user) = users.get_mut(id) {
        *user = UserData;
        response_with_code(StatusCode::OK)
    } else {
        response_with_code(StatusCode::NOT_FOUND)
    }
},
```

This code tries to find a `user` instance in the user database with the `get_mut` method. This returns a mutable reference wrapped with either a `Some` option, or a `None` option if the corresponding value isn't found. We can use a dereference operator, *, to replace the data in the storage.

If the user's data was found and replaced, the branch returns an OK status code. If there's no user with the requested ID, the branch returns NOT_FOUND.

DELETE – Deleting data

When we don't need data anymore, we can delete it. This is the purpose of the DELETE method. Use it in the branch as follows:

```
(&Method::DELETE, Some(id)) => {
    if users.contains(id) {
        users.remove(id);
        response_with_code(StatusCode::OK)
    } else {
        response_with_code(StatusCode::NOT_FOUND)
    }
},
```

This code checks whether the `Slab` contains the data and removes it with the `remove` method. We don't use the `remove` method right away because this expects the data to exist in the storage beforehand, and therefore panics if the data is absent.

 Often, web services don't actually remove data and instead just mark it as deleted. This is a reasonable thing to do because it allows you to explore the data later and improve the efficiency of the service or the company. However, this is a risky practice. Users should be able to remove their data completely, because sensitive data can represent a threat. New laws, such as the GDPR law (`https://en.wikipedia.org/wiki/General_Data_ Protection_Regulation`), protect the user's right to own their data and stipulate certain requirements for data protection. Violation of such laws may result in a fine. It's important to remember this when you work with sensitive data.

Routing advanced requests

In the preceding example, we used pattern matching to detect the destination of a request. This isn't a flexible technique, because the path often contains extra characters that have to be taken into account. The `/user/1/` path, for example, contains the trailing slash, `/`, which can't be parsed with a user ID in the previous version of our microservice. There's a flexible tool to fix this issue: regular expressions.

Defining paths with regular expressions

A regular expression is a sequence of characters that express a pattern to be searched for in a string. Regular expressions provide you with the ability to create tiny parsers that split a text into parts using a formal declaration. Rust has a crate called `regex`, a popular abbreviation of *regular expression collocation*. You can learn more about this crate here: `https://crates.io/crates/regex`.

Adding the necessary dependencies

To use regular expressions in our `server`, we need two crates: `regex` and `lazy_static`. The first provides a `Regex` type to create and match regular expressions with strings. The second helps to store `Regex` instances in a static context. We can assign constant values to static variables, because they're created when a program loads to memory. To use complex expressions, we have to add an initialization code and use it to execute expressions, assigning the result to a static variable. The `lazy_static` crate contains a `lazy_static!` macro to do this job for us automatically. This macro creates a static variable, executes an expression, and assigns the evaluated value to that variable. We can also create a regular expression object for every request in a local context using a local variable, rather than a static one. However, this takes up runtime overhead, so it's better to create it in advance and reuse it.

Add both dependencies to the `Cargo.toml` file:

```
[dependencies]
slab = "0.4"
futures = "0.1"
hyper = "0.12"
lazy_static = "1.0"
regex = "1.0"
```

Add two imports, in addition to the imports in the `main.rs` source file from the previous example:

```
use lazy_static::lazy_static;
use regex::Regex;
```

We'll use the `lazy_static` macro and the `Regex` type to construct a regular expression.

Writing regular expressions

Regular expressions contain a special language, used to write a pattern to extract data from a string. We need three patterns for our example:

- A path for the index page
- A path for user management
- A path for the list of users (a new feature for our example server)

There's a `Regex::new` function that creates regular expressions. Remove the previous `USER_PATH` constant and add three new regular expression constants in a lazy static block:

```
lazy_static! {
    static ref INDEX_PATH: Regex =
Regex::new("^/(index\\.html?)?$").unwrap();
    static ref USER_PATH: Regex =
Regex::new("^/user/((?P<user_id>\\d+?)/?)?$").unwrap();
    static ref USERS_PATH: Regex = Regex::new("^/users/?$").unwrap();
}
```

As you can see, regular expressions look complex. To understand them better, let's analyze them.

Path for index page

The `INDEX_PATH` expression matches the following paths:

- `/`
- `/index.htm`
- `/index.html`

The expression that fits these paths is `"^/(index\\.html?)?$"`.

The `^` symbol means there must be a string beginning, while the `$` symbol means there must be a string ending. When we place these symbols on either side, we prevent all prefixes and suffixes in the path and expect exact matching.

The `( )` brackets implies there must be a group. An expression in a group is treated as an indivisible unit.

The `?` symbol means that the previous character is optional. We place it after the `l` character to allow the file in the path to have both `.htm` and `.html` extensions. As you'll see later, we don't have an index file to read. We use it as an alias of the root path handler. The question mark is also used after a whole group with a file name to fit the empty root path, `/`.

The dot symbol (`.`) fits any character, but we need a real dot symbol. To treat a dot as a symbol, we have to add a backslash (`\`) before it. A single backslash, however, will be interpreted as a beginning-of-escape expression, so we have to use pair of backslashes (`\\`) to make the backslash a plain symbol.

All other characters are treated as is, including the `/` symbol.

Path for user management

The USER_PATH expression can fit the following paths:

- /user/
- /user/<id>, where <id> means group of digits
- /user/<id>/, the same as the previous one, but with a trailing backslash

These cases can be handled with the "^/user/((?P<user_id>\\d+?)/?)?$" regular expression. This expression is a bit complex. It includes two groups (one is nested) and some other strange characters. Let's have a closer look.

?P<name> is a grouping attribute that sets the name of the capturing group. Every group in brackets can be accessed by the regex::Captures object. Named groups can be accessed by names.

\\d is a special expression that matches any digit. To specify that we have one or more digits, we should add the + symbol, which tells us how many repetitions it may have. The * symbol can also be added, which tells us that there are zero or more repetitions, but we haven't used this in our regular expression.

There are two groups. The first is nested with the name user_id. It must include digits only to be parsed to the UserId type. The second is an enclosing group that contains the optional trailing slash. This whole group is optional, meaning that the expression can include a /user/ path without any identifier.

Path for the users list

The USERS_PATH is a new pattern, which we didn't have in the previous example. We'll use it to return a full list of users on the server. This pattern fits only two variants of the path:

- /users/ (with a trailing slash)
- /users (without a trailing slash)

The regular expression to handle these cases is quite simple: "^/users/?$". We've already seen all the symbols in this pattern. It expects a string to begin with the ^ symbol and the slash symbol. After that, it expects users with an optional slash at the tail /?. Finally, it expects the end of a string with the $ symbol.

Matching expressions

We have to reorganize the code of `microservice_handler` because we can't use regular expressions in a `match` expression. We have to extract the method with the path at the start, because we need it for most responses:

```
let response = {
    let method = req.method();
    let path = req.uri().path();
    let mut users = user_db.lock().unwrap();

    // Put regular expressions here
};
futures::ok()
```

The first thing we'll check is the index page requests. Add the following code:

```
if INDEX_PATH.is_match(path) {
    if method == &Method::GET {
        Response::new(INDEX.into())
    } else {
        response_with_code(StatusCode::METHOD_NOT_ALLOWED)
    }
```

This uses the `INDEX_PATH` regular expression to check whether the request's path matches the index page request using the `Regex::is_match` method, which returns a `bool` value. Here, we're checking the method of a request, so only `GET` is allowed.

We'll then continue the `if` clause with an alternative condition for the user list request:

```
} else if USERS_PATH.is_match(path) {
    if method == &Method::GET {
        let list = users.iter()
            .map(|(id, _)| id.to_string())
            .collect::<Vec<String>>()
            .join(",");
        Response::new(list.into())
    } else {
        response_with_code(StatusCode::METHOD_NOT_ALLOWED)
    }
```

This code uses the `USERS_PATH` pattern to check whether the client requested the list of users. This is a new path route. After this, we iterate over all the users in the database and join their IDs in a single string.

The following code is used to handle REST requests:

```
} else if let Some(cap) = USER_PATH.captures(path) {
    let user_id = cap.name("user_id").and_then(|m| {
        m.as_str()
            .parse::<UserId>()
            .ok()
            .map(|x| x as usize)
    });
    // Put match expression with (method, user_id) tuple
```

This code uses the USER_PATH and the Regex::captures method. It returns a Captures object with the values of all captured groups. If the pattern doesn't match the method, it returns a None value. If the pattern does match, we get an object stored in the cap variable. The Captures struct has the name method to get a captured value by name. We use the user_id as the name of the group. This group can be optional and the name method returns an Option. We use the and_then method of the Option to replace it with the parsed UserId. Finally, the user_id variable takes the Option<UserId> value, in the same way as the previous version of our microservice. To avoid repetition, I skipped the block where the request is the same as the (method, user_id) tuple – just copy this part from the example in the previous section of this chapter.

The last part is a default handler that returns a response with a NOT_FOUND status code:

```
} else {
    response_with_code(StatusCode::NOT_FOUND)
}
```

The service is now complete, so it can be compiled and run. In Chapter 13, *Testing and Debugging Rust Microservices*, you'll find out how to debug microservices. For now, however, you can use the curl command to send some POST requests and check the result in the browser. Type the following command in the shell to add three users and remove the second user with the ID of 1:

```
$ curl -X POST http://localhost:8080/user/
0
$ curl -X POST http://localhost:8080/user/
1
$ curl -X POST http://localhost:8080/user/
2
$ curl -X DELETE http://localhost:8080/user/1
$ curl http://localhost:8080/users
0,2
```

If you fetch the list of users in the browser, it should display the following:

As you can see, we used the /users request without a trailing slash with curl, and /users/ with the trailing slash in the browser. This result means that regular expressions and request routing both work.

Summary

In this chapter, we created a microservice using a hyper crate. We started with a minimal example that only responds with the *Rust Microservice* message. Then, we created a microservice that has two distinct paths – the first being the index page request and the second, the NOT_FOUND response.

Once we learned the basics, we then started to use the match expression to make the microservice REST-compliant. We also added the ability to handle users' data with four basic operations—create, read, update, and delete.

To expand the routing capabilities in the last example of the chapter, we implemented routing based on regular expressions. Regular expressions are compact patterns that check and extract data from a text.

In this chapter, we encountered various crates—hyper, futures, slab, regex, and lazy_static. We'll discuss these in detail in the next chapter.

Since we have learned to create minimal HTTP microservice in the next chapter we will learn how to make it configurable and how to attach logging to it, because microservices work at remote servers and we need a capability to configure it without recompilation and be able to see all issues that happened with a microservices in logs.

3
Logging and Configuring Microservice

Microservices work in the real world, which is dynamic. To be useful, they have to be configurable, so that you can change an address or port to bind the server's socket. Often, you will need to set tokens, secrets, and the addresses of other microservices. Even if you have configured them correctly, your microservices may fail. In this case, you need to be able to use the server's logs.

In this chapter, we'll learn the following skills:

- How to use logging with the `log` crate
- How to read command-line parameters with the `clap` crate
- How to read environment variables with the `dotenv` crate
- How to declare and use configuration files

Technical requirements

This chapter explains how to add logging to a service and parse command-line parameters or the environment variables required to configure a microservice. You don't need any special software except the Rust compiler, version 1.31 or above. Install it using the rustup tool.

You can find the code for the examples of this chapter on GitHub: `https://github.com/PacktPublishing/Hands-On-Microservices-with-Rust-2018/tree/master/Chapter3`.

Adding logging to a microservice

We can't use or debug a microservice if it doesn't record the actions that it carries out. In this section, we will start to use logging with our microservices to understand what is going on inside them. We will create a microservice that generates random values and attach a logger to a microservice to record the actions it carries out. Afterward, we will configure logging using environment variables.

Random-value-generating microservices

To discuss these more advanced topics, we need a microservices architecture that has a more useful purpose than generating *hello* messages. We will create a microservice application for generating random values. This is simple enough to implement and will provide us with sufficient opportunities to use logging and configuration.

However, we won't start completely from scratch; let's take the example from the previous chapter and add a dependency to it:

```
[dependencies]
hyper = "0.12"
rand = "0.5"
```

A `rand` crate provides the utilities necessary to generate random values in Rust. Import the necessary types in the `main.rs` file:

```
use hyper::{Body, Response, Server};
use hyper::rt::Future;
use hyper::service::service_fn_ok;
```

Add two lines to the `service_fn_ok` function to handle incoming requests:

```
fn main() {
    let addr = ([127, 0, 0, 1], 8080).into();
    let builder = Server::bind(&addr);
    let server = builder.serve(|| {
        service_fn_ok(|_| {
            let random_byte = rand::random::<u8>();
            Response::new(Body::from(random_byte.to_string()))
        })
    });
    let server = server.map_err(drop);
    hyper::rt::run(server);
}
```

To learn more about the preceding code, please refer to the previous chapter, where we explored the `hyper` crate.

As you can see, we have added two lines in the closure provided to the `service_fn_ok` function. The first line generates a random byte with the `random` function of the `rand` crate. We set the generated type in the type parameter of the `rand::random::<u8>()` call. Now, `u8` is an unsigned byte integer.

In the second line, we simply convert the generated byte to a string and return it as a `Body` of the `Response`. Try to run the code to test it:

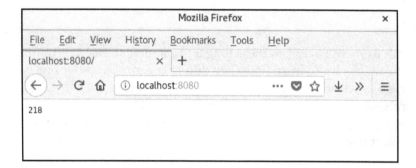

From the preceding screenshot, you can see that the service returned the generated random value successfully.

The log crate

Logging is the process of recording the activities of a program. Logs can be a textual flow in a specified format, which prints to a console or writes to a file. Rust has a great logging ecosystem based on the `log` crate. It is worth noting that the `log` crate contains macros without a real logger implementation. This gives you an opportunity to use different loggers depending on what you need them for. In this section, we will start to use the log crate in our microservices to learn how logging levels work and how to set the desired level of logs you want to see.

Loggers

The actual logger implementations that are contained in some crates are as follows:

- `env_logger`
- `simple_logger`
- `simplelog`
- `pretty_env_logger`
- `stderrlog`
- `flexi_logger`
- `log4rs`
- `fern`

It can be difficult to choose between these logger implementations. I recommend that you explore them on `crates.io` to learn how they differ. The most popular one is `env_logger`, which is the one that we are going to use. `env_logger` reads the `RUST_LOG` environment variable to configure logging and prints logs to `stderr`. There is also the `pretty_env_logger` crate, which is built on top of `env_logger` and prints logs with a compact and colorful format. Both use the same environment variable for configuration.

 `stderr` is one of three standard streams—`stdin`, where your program reads the input data with the console; `stdout`, where the program sends the output data; and `stderr`, which has the special purpose of showing errors or other information about working with the application. Loggers often use `stderr` to avoid affecting the output data. For example, let's say that you have a tool that decodes an input stream. You want the tool to send the decoded data only to the output stream. How will the program inform you about any issues it is experiencing? In this case, we can use the `stderr` stream, which works as an output stream, but doesn't pollute `stdout`? There is `stderr` stream that works as output stream, but doesn't pollute `stdout`.

Add the logger to the dependencies list of your `Cargo.toml` file:

```
[dependencies]
log = "0.4"
pretty_env_logger = "0.2"
hyper = "0.12"
rand = "0.5"
```

Then add these types to your `main.rs` file:

```
use hyper::{Body, Response, Server};
use hyper::rt::Future;
use hyper::service::service_fn_ok;
use log::{debug, info, trace};
```

Log levels

As we discussed earlier, with the `log` crate, we need to import the following logging macros. We can use the following:

- `trace!`
- `debug!`
- `info!`
- `warn!`
- `error!`

These are ordered by the importance of the information they print, with `trace!` being the least important and `error!` being the most important:

- `trace!`: Used to print verbose information about any pivotal activity. It allows web servers to trace any incoming chunk of data.
- `debug!`: Used for less verbose messages, such as the incoming server requests. It is useful for debugging.
- `info!`: Used for important information such as the runtime or server configuration. It is rarely used in library crates.
- `warn!`: Informs the user about non-critical errors, such as if the client has used broken cookies or if the necessary microservice is temporarily unavailable and cached data is used for responses instead.
- `error!`: Provides an alert about critical errors. This is used when the database connection is broken.

We imported the necessary macro directly from the `log` crate.

Logging messages

Logging is not useful without the contextual data of the code. Every logging macro expects a text message that can contain positional parameters. For example, take a look at the println! macro:

```
debug!("Trying to bind server to address: {}", addr);
```

The preceding code will work for types that implement the Display trait. As in the println! macro, you can add types that implement the Debug trait with the {:?} formatter. It's useful to derive the Debug trait for all types in your code with #[derive(Debug)] and set the #![deny(missing_debug_implementations)] attribute for the whole crate.

Custom level of messages

Levels have an important role in the logging process. They are used for filtering the records by their priority. If you set the info level for the logger, it will skip all the debug and trace records. Obviously, you need more verbose logging for debugging purposes and less verbose logging to use the server in production.

Internally, every macro of the log crate uses the log! macro, which has an argument to set the level:

```
log!(Level::Error, "Error information: {}", error);
```

It takes an instance of the Level enumeration that has the following variants—Trace, Debug, Info, Warn, and Error.

Checking logging is enabled

Sometimes, logging may require a lot of resources. In this case, you can use the log_enabled! macro to check that a certain logging level has been enabled:

```
if log_enabled!(Debug) {
    let data = get_data_which_requires_resources();
    debug!("expensive data: {}", data);
}
```

Own target

Every log record has a target. A typical logging record looks as follows:

```
RUST_LOG=debug cargo run                                              ×

File  Edit  View  Search  Terminal  Help
INFO   random_service_with_logging > Rand Microservice - v0.1.0
DEBUG  random_service_with_logging > Trying to bind server to address: 127.0.0.1:8080
INFO   random_service_with_logging > Used address: 127.0.0.1:8080
DEBUG  random_service_with_logging > Run!
DEBUG  hyper::proto::h1::io        > read 747 bytes
DEBUG  hyper::proto::h1::io        > parsed 9 headers
DEBUG  hyper::proto::h1::conn      > incoming body is empty
DEBUG  random_service_with_logging > Generated value is: 106
DEBUG  hyper::proto::h1::io        > flushed 78 bytes
DEBUG  hyper::proto::h1::io        > read 747 bytes
DEBUG  hyper::proto::h1::io        > parsed 9 headers
DEBUG  hyper::proto::h1::conn      > incoming body is empty
DEBUG  random_service_with_logging > Generated value is: 142
DEBUG  hyper::proto::h1::io        > flushed 78 bytes
```

The log record consists of the logging level, the time (not shown in this output), the target, and the message. You can think about the target as a namespace. If no target is specified, the `log` crate uses the `module_path!` macro to set one. We can use the target to detect the module where an error or warning has happened or use it for filtering records by name. We will see how to set filtering by environment variable in the following section.

Using logging

We can now add logging to our microservice. In the following example, we will print information about the socket address, the incoming request, and a generated random value:

```
fn main() {
    logger::init();
    info!("Rand Microservice - v0.1.0");
    trace!("Starting...");
    let addr = ([127, 0, 0, 1], 8080).into();
    debug!("Trying to bind server to address: {}", addr);
    let builder = Server::bind(&addr);
    trace!("Creating service handler...");
    let server = builder.serve(|| {
        service_fn_ok(|req| {
            trace!("Incoming request is: {:?}", req);
            let random_byte = rand::random::<u8>();
            debug!("Generated value is: {}", random_byte);
```

```
                Response::new(Body::from(random_byte.to_string()))
        })
    });
    info!("Used address: {}", server.local_addr());
    let server = server.map_err(drop);
    debug!("Run!");
    hyper::rt::run(server);
}
```

Using logging is quite simple. We can use macros to print the address of the socket and information about the request and response.

Configuring a logger with variables

There are some environment variables that you can use to configure a logger. Let's take a look at each variable.

RUST_LOG

Compile this example. To run it with an activated logger, you have to set the RUST_LOG environment variable. The env_logger crate reads it and configures the logger using filters from this variable. A logger instance must be configured with a corresponding logging level.

 You can set the RUST_LOG variable globally. If you use the Bash shell, you can set it in your .bashrc file.

You can set RUST_LOG temporarily before the cargo run command:

```
RUST_LOG=trace cargo run
```

However, this will also print a lot of cargo tool and compiler records, because the Rust compiler also uses the log crate for logging. You can exclude all records except for those of your program using filtering by name. You only need to use part of the target name, as follows:

```
RUST_LOG=random_service=trace,warn cargo run
```

This value of the RUST_LOG variable filters all records by the *warn* level and uses the *trace* level for targets starting with the random_service prefix.

RUST_LOG_STYLE

The RUST_LOG_STYLE variable sets the style of printed records. It has three variants:

- **auto**: Tries to use the style characters
- **always**: Always uses the style characters
- **never**: Turns off the style characters

See the following example:

```
RUST_LOG_STYLE=auto cargo run
```

I recommend that you use the never value if you redirect the stderr output a file or if you want to use grep or awk to extract values with special patterns.

Changing the RUST_LOG variable to your own

If you release your own product, you may need to change the name of the RUST_LOG and the RUST_LOG_STYLE variable to your own. New releases of the env_logger contain the init_from_env special function to fix this. This expects one argument—an instance of the Env object. Take a look at the following code:

```
let env = env_logger::Env::new()
    .filter("OWN_LOG_VAR")
    .write_style("OWN_LOG_STYLE_VAR");
env_logger::init_from_env(env);
```

It creates an Env instance and sets the OWN_LOG_VAR variable to configure logging and the OWN_LOG_STYLE_VAR variable to control the style of the logs. When the env object is created, we will use it as an argument for the init_from_env function call of the env_logger crate.

Reading environment variables

In the previous example, we used a value of the RUST_LOG environment variable to set filtering parameters for logging. We can use other environment variables to set parameters for our server as well. In the following example, we will use the ADDRESS environment variable to set the address of the socket we want to bind.

Standard library

There are enough functions in the `std::env` standard module to work with environment variables. It contains the `var` function to read external values. This function returns a `Result` with a `String` value of the variable if it exists, or a `VarError` error if it doesn't exist. Add the import of the `env` module to your `main.rs` file:

```
use std::env;
```

We need to replace the following line:

```
let addr = ([127, 0, 0, 1], 8080).into();
```

Replace it with the following:

```
let addr = env::var("ADDRESS")
    .unwrap_or_else(|_| "127.0.0.1:8080".into())
    .parse()
    .expect("can't parse ADDRESS variable");
```

This new code reads the `ADDRESS` value. If this value doesn't exist, we won't let the code throw a panic. Instead, we will replace it with the default value, `"127.0.0.1:8080"`, using the `unwrap_or_else` method call. As the `var` function returns a `String`, we also have to convert `&'static str` into a `String` instance with the `into` method call.

If we can't parse an address, we will throw a panic in the `except` method call.

Your server will now use the `addr` variable, which takes a value from the `ADDRESS` environment variable or from the default value.

Environment variables are a simple way of configuring your application. They are also widely supported with hosting or cloud platforms and Docker containers.

Remember that all sensitive data is visible to the system administrator of the host. In Linux, the system administrator can read this data simply by using the `cat /proc/`pidof random-service-with-env`/environ` | tr '\0' '\n'` command. This means that it's not a good idea to set the secret key of your bitcoin wallet to the environment variable.

Using the .env file

Setting many environment variables is time-consuming. We can simplify this using configuration files, which we will explore further at the end of this chapter. However, configuration files can't be used in cases where the crates or dependencies use environment variables.

To make this process simple, we can use the dotenv crate. This is used to set environment variables from a file. This practice appeared as part of *The Twelve-Factor App* methodology (https://12factor.net/).

The Twelve-Factor App approach is a methodology for building **Software as a Service (SaaS)** applications to fulfill the following three objectives:

- Configurations in declarative formats
- Maximum portability with operating systems and clouds
- Continuous deployment and scaling

This methodology encourages you to use environment variables to configure the application. The *Twelve-Factor App* approach doesn't require disk space for configuration and it is extremely portable, meaning that all operating systems support the environment variables.

Using the dotenv crate

The dotenv crate allows you to set environment variables in a file called .env and join them with variables set in the traditional way. You don't need to read this file manually. All you need to do is add the dependency and call the initialization method of the crate.

Add this crate to the list of dependencies :

```
dotenv = "0.13"
```

Add the following imports to the main.rs file of the previous example to use the dotenv crate:

```
use dotenv::dotenv;
use std::env;
```

Initialize it with the dotenv function, which will try to find the .env file. It will return a Result with a path to this file. Call the ok method of the Result to ignore it if the file hasn't been found.

Adding variables to the .env file

The .env file contains pairs of names and values of environment variables. For our service, we will set the RUST_LOG, RUST_BACKTRACE, and ADDRESS variables:

```
RUST_LOG=debug
RUST_BACKTRACE=1
ADDRESS=0.0.0.0:1234
```

As you can see, we set all the targets of the logger to the debug level, because cargo doesn't use dotenv and therefore skips these settings.

The RUST_BACKTRACE variable sets the flag to print a backtrace of the application in the case of panic.

Store this file in the working directory from which you will run the application. You can have multiple files and use them for different configurations. This file format is also compatible with Docker and can be used to set variables to the container.

 I recommend that you add the .env file to your .gitignore to prevent leaking of sensitive or local data. This means that every user or developer who works with your project has their own environment and needs their own version of the .env file.

Parsing command-line arguments

Environment variables are useful for using with containers. If you use your application from a console or you want to avoid a conflict of names with other variables, you can use command-line parameters. This is a more conventional way for developers to set parameters to the program.

You can also get command-line arguments with the env module. This contains the args function, which returns an Args object. This object is not an array or vector, but it's iterable and you can use the for loop processes all command-line arguments:

```
for arg in env::args() {
    // Interpret the arg here
}
```

This variant may come in handy in simple cases. For parsing arguments with complex rules, however, you have to use a command-line argument parser. A good implementation of this is contained in the clap crate.

Using the clap crate

To use the `clap` crate for parsing arguments, you have to build a parser and use it for arguments. To build a parser, you start by creating an instance of the `App` type. To use it, add all the necessary imports.

Adding dependencies

Add a dependency to `Cargo.toml`:

```
clap = "2.32"
```

This crate provides useful macros for adding meta information about the program. These are as follows:

- `crate_name!`: Returns the name of the crate
- `crate_version!`: Returns the version of the crate
- `crate_authors!`: Returns the list of authors
- `crate_description!`: Provides the description of the crate

All information for these macros is taken from the `Cargo.toml` file.

Import the necessary types. We need two types, which are `App` and `Arg`, and the macros mentioned previously:

```
use clap::{crate_authors, crate_description, crate_name, crate_version,
Arg, App};
```

Building a parser

The process of building a parser is quite simple. You will create an `App` instance and feed this type with the `Arg` instances. The `App` also has methods that can be used to set information about the application. Add the following code to the `main` function of our server:

```
let matches = App::new(crate_name!())
        .version(crate_version!())
        .author(crate_authors!())
        .about(crate_description!())
        .arg(Arg::with_name("address")
            .short("a")
            .long("address")
```

```
            .value_name("ADDRESS")
            .help("Sets an address")
            .takes_value(true))
    .arg(Arg::with_name("config")
            .short("c")
            .long("config")
            .value_name("FILE")
            .help("Sets a custom config file")
            .takes_value(true))
    .get_matches();
```

First, we create an `App` instance with a `new` method that expects the name of the crate. We provide this using the `crate_name!` macro. After that, we use the `version`, `author`, and `about` methods to set this data using the corresponding macros. We can chain these method calls, because every method consumes and returns the updated `App` object. When we set meta-information about the application, we have to declare the supported arguments with the `arg` method.

To add an argument, we have to create an `Arg` instance with the `with_name` method, provide the name, and set extra parameters using chaining-of-methods calls. We can set a short form of the argument with the `short` method and the long form with the `long` method. You can set the name of the value for the generated documentation using the `value_name` method. You can provide a description of an argument using the `help` method. The `takes_value` method is used to indicate that this argument requires a value. There is also a `required` method to indicate that an option is required, but we didn't use that here. All options are optional in our server.

We added the `--address` argument using these methods to set the address of the socket that we will use to bind the server. It also supports the short form `a` of the argument. We will read this value later.

The server will support the `--config` argument to set a configuration file. We have added this argument to the builder, but we will use it in the next section of this chapter.

After we create the builder, we call the `get_matches` method. This reads arguments with `std::env::args_os` and returns an `ArgMatches` instance, which we can use to get the values of the command-line parameters. We assign it to the `matches` local variable.

We should add the `get_matches` method before any logging call because it also prints help messages. We should avoid printing logs with the help description.

Reading arguments

To read arguments, `ArgMatches` contains a `value_of` method, where you add the name of a parameter. In this case, it is convenient to use constants to avoid typos. Extract the `--address` argument, and if this does not exist, then check the `ADDRESS` environment variable. This means that the command-line argument is a higher priority than the environment variable and you can override the parameters from the `.env` file with command-line parameters:

```
let addr = matches.value_of("address")
    .map(|s| s.to_owned())
    .or(env::var("ADDRESS").ok())
    .unwrap_or_else(|| "127.0.0.1:8080".into())
    .parse()
    .expect("can't parse ADDRESS variable");
```

In this code, we have converted all of the provided string references with the `&str` type to solid `String` objects. This is useful if you want to use the object later in the code or if you need to move it elsewhere.

Usage

When you use the `clap` crate in your application, you can use command-line parameters to tweak it. The `clap` crate adds a `--help` argument, which the user can use to print information about all the arguments. This description was generated automatically by the crate, as can be seen in the following example:

```
$ ./target/debug/random-service-with-args --help
random-service-with-env 0.1.0
Your Name
Rust Microservice

USAGE:
    random-service-with-env [OPTIONS]

FLAGS:
    -h, --help       Prints help information
    -V, --version    Prints version information

OPTIONS:
    -a, --address <ADDRESS>    Sets an address
    -c, --config <FILE>        Sets a custom config file
```

Our application successfully printed the usage info: it provided us with all flags, options, and usage variants. If you need to add your own help description, you can use the `help` method of the `App` instance to set any string as a help message.

If you use the `cargo run` command, you can also set command-line parameters after the `--` parameter. This means that it stops reading the `run` command and passes all remaining arguments to the running application:

```
$ cargo run -- --help
```

You can now start the server and set an address using the `--address` parameter with value:

```
$ cargo run -- --address 0.0.0.0:2345
```

The server has started and prints to the console:

```
     Finished dev [unoptimized + debuginfo] target(s) in 0.10s
  Running `target/debug/random-service-with-args --address '0.0.0.0:2345'`
  INFO 2018-07-26T04:23:52Z: random_service_with_env: Rand Microservice -
v0.1.0
DEBUG 2018-07-26T04:23:52Z: random_service_with_env: Trying to bind server
to address: 0.0.0.0:2345
  INFO 2018-07-26T04:23:52Z: random_service_with_env: Used address:
0.0.0.0:2345
DEBUG 2018-07-26T04:23:52Z: random_service_with_env: Run!
DEBUG 2018-07-26T04:23:52Z: tokio_reactor::background: starting background
reactor
```

How to add subcommands

Some popular applications, such as `cargo` and `docker`, use subcommands to provide multiple commands inside a single binary. We can also support subcommands with the `clap` crate. A microservice might have two commands: one to run the server and one to generate a secret for the HTTP cookies. Take a look at the following code:

```
let matches = App::new("Server with keys")
    .setting(AppSettings::SubcommandRequiredElseHelp)
    .subcommand(SubCommand::with_name("run")
        .about("run the server")
        .arg(Arg::with_name("address")
            .short("a")
            .long("address")
            .takes_value(true)
            .help("address of the server"))
```

```
.subcommand(SubCommand::with_name("key")
    .about("generates a secret key for cookies")))
.get_matches();
```

Here, we have used two methods. The `setting` method tweaks the builder and you can set it with variants of the `AppSettings` enumeration.

The `SubcommandRequiredElseHelp` method requires us to use subcommands or prints help message if no subcommands are provided. To add a subcommand, we use the `subcommand` method with the `SubCommand` instance that we created with the `with_name` method. A subcommand instance also has methods to set meta information about a subcommand, like we did with the `App` instance. Subcommands can also take arguments.

In the preceding example above, we added two subcommands—`run`, to run the server, and `key`, to generate secrets. You can use these when you start the application:

```
$ cargo run -- run --address 0.0.0.0:2345
```

We have two `run` arguments because the cargo has a command with the same name.

Reading the configuration from file

Environment variables and command-line arguments are useful to add temporary change parameters for a single run. They are a more convenient way to configure servers to use configuration files. This approach doesn't conform to The *Twelve-Factor App* methodology, but it's useful in cases when you need to set long parameters.

There are many formats that can be used for configuration files. The popular ones include TOML, YAML, and JSON. We will use TOML, because it is widely used with the Rust programming language.

Adding the TOML config

The TOML file format is implemented in the `toml` crate. It previously used the now-obsolete `rustc-serialize` crate, but the last few versions have used the `serde` crate for serialization and deserialization. We will use both the `toml` and the `serde` crates.

Adding dependencies

We actually need not only the serde crate but also the serde_derive crate. Both crates help with the serialization struct in various serialization formats. Add all three crates to the dependencies list in Cargo.toml:

```
serde = "1.0"
serde_derive = "1.0"
toml = "0.4"
```

The full list of imports in the main.rs file contains the following:

```
use clap::{crate_authors, crate_description, crate_name, crate_version,
Arg, App};
use dotenv::dotenv;
use hyper::{Body, Response, Server};
use hyper::rt::Future;
use hyper::service::service_fn_ok;
use log::{debug, info, trace, warn};
use serde_derive::Deserialize;
use std::env;
use std::io::{self, Read};
use std::fs::File;
use std::net::SocketAddr;
```

As you can see, we haven't imported the serde crate here. We won't use it directly in the code because it's necessary to use the serde_derive crate instead. We have imported all macros from the serde_derive crate, because the serde crate contains the Serialize and Deserialize traits and serde_derive helps us to derive these for our structs.

Microservices often need to serialize and deserialize data when interacting with the client. We will cover this topic in the next chapter.

Declaring a struct for configuration

We have now imported all the necessary dependencies and can declare our configuration file structure. Add the Config struct to your code:

```
#[derive(Deserialize)]
struct Config {
    address: SocketAddr,
}
```

This struct contains only one field with the address. You can add more, but remember that all fields have to implement the `Deserialize` trait. The `serde` crate already has implementations for standard library types. For our types, we have to derive the implementation of `Deserialize` with the macro of the `serde_derive` crate.

Everything is ready for us to read the configuration from the file.

Reading the configuration file

Our server will expect to find a configuration file in the current working folder with the name `microservice.toml`. To read a configuration and convert it to the `Config` struct, we need to find and read this file if it exists. Add the following code to the `main` function of the server:

```
let config = File::open("microservice.toml")
    .and_then(|mut file| {
        let mut buffer = String::new();
        file.read_to_string(&mut buffer)?;
        Ok(buffer)
    })
    .and_then(|buffer| {
        toml::from_str::<Config>(&buffer)
            .map_err(|err| io::Error::new(io::ErrorKind::Other, err))
    })
    .map_err(|err| {
        warn!("Can't read config file: {}", err);
    })
    .ok();
```

The preceding code is a chain of method calls that start with the `File` instance. We use the `open` method to open the file and provide the name `microservice.toml`. The call returns a `Result`, which we will process in the chain. At the end of the processing, we will convert it to an option using the `ok` method and ignore any errors that occur during the parsing of the config file. This is because our service also supports environment variables and command-line parameters and has defaults for unset parameters.

When the file is ready, we will try to convert it into a `String`. We created an empty string, called a buffer, and used the `read_to_string` method of the `File` instance to move all of the data into the buffer. This is a synchronous operation. It's suitable for reading a configuration but you shouldn't use it for reading files to send to the client, because it will lock the runtime of the server until the file is read.

After we have read the `buffer` variable, we will try to parse it as a TOML file into the `Config` struct. The `toml` crate has a `from_str` method in the root namespace of the crate. It expects a type parameter to deserialize and an input string. We use the `Config` struct for the output type and our `buffer` for the input. But there is a problem: the `File` uses `io::Error` for errors, but `from_str` uses `toml::de:Error` for the error type. We can convert the second type to `io::Error` to make it compatible with the chain of calls.

The penultimate part of the chain is the `map_err` method call. We use this to write any errors with the configuration file to logs. As you can see, we used the `Warn` level. Issues with the configuration file are not critical, but it is important to be aware of them because they can affect the configuration. This makes the `microservices.toml` file optional.

Joining all values by a priority

Our server has four sources of address settings:

- The configuration file
- The environment variable
- The command-line parameter
- The default value

We have to join these in this order. It's simple to implement this using a set of options and using the `or` method to set a value if the option doesn't contain anything. Use the following code to get address values from all of the sources:

```
let addr = matches.value_of("address")
    .map(|s| s.to_owned())
    .or(env::var("ADDRESS").ok())
    .and_then(|addr| addr.parse().ok())
    .or(config.map(|config| config.address))
    .or_else(|| Some(([127, 0, 0, 1], 8080).into()))
    .unwrap();
```

At first, this code takes a value from the `--address` command-line parameter. If it doesn't contain any value, the code tries to get a value from the `ADDRESS` environment variable. After that, we try to parse a textual value to the socket address. If all these steps fail, we can try to get a value from the `Config` instance that we read from `microservice.toml`. We will use the default address value if the value wasn't set by a user. In the previous address-parsing code, we also parsed the default value from a string. In this code, we use a tuple to construct the `SocketAddr` instance. Since we are guaranteed to get a value, we `unwrap` the option to extract it.

Creating and using the configuration file

We can now create a configuration file and run the server. Create the `microservice.toml` file in the root folder of the project and add the following line to it:

```
address = "0.0.0.0:9876"
```

Compile and start the service and you will see it has bound to that address:

Summary

In this chapter, we added logging to the server and learned how to activate the `logger` and set filters to it. After that, we transformed our unflexible server to a configurable microservice that can read settings from different sources—the configuration file, the environment variable, and the command-line parameters. We became familiar with *The Twelve-Factor App* methodology and used the `dotenv` crate, which helped us to read environment variables from a file. We also used the `clap` crate to add a command-line parser. Finally, we touched on the `serde` crate, which introduced us to the world of serialization.

In the next chapter we will learn how to use `serde` crate for needs of a microservices: to deserialize request and serialize responses to a certain format like JSON, CBOR, BSON, MessagePack, etc.

4
Data Serialization and Deserialization with the Serde Crate

Microservices can either interact with clients or each other. To implement interaction, you have to choose a protocol and a format to send messages from one communication participant to another. There are many formats and RPC frameworks that simplify the interaction process. In this chapter, we'll discover features of the serde crate, which helps you to make structs serializable and deserializable and compatible with different formats, such as JSON, CBOR, MessagePack, and BSON.

The following topics will be covered in this chapter:

- How to serialize and deserialize data
- How to make custom types types serializable
- Which serialization formats to choose and which to avoid

Technical requirements

In this chapter, we'll explore some of the features that are available in the serde crates family. This family includes the inseparable pair – the serde and serde_derive crates. It also includes crates such as serde_json, serde_yaml, and toml that provide you support for special formats, such as JSON, YAML, and TOML. All of these crates are pure Rust and don't require any external dependencies.

You can get the source code of the examples in this chapter from GitHub at: `https://github.com/PacktPublishing/Hands-On-Microservices-with-Rust-2018/tree/master/Chapter04`.

Data formats for interaction with microservices

Microservices can interact with different participants, such as clients, other microservices, and third-party APIs. Typically, interactions are performed by the network using serialized data messages in a certain format. In this section, we'll learn how to choose a format for these interactions. We'll also explore the basic features of a `serde` crate – how to make our structs serializable and use a specific format.

The serde crate

When I started to use Rust in my projects, I used to use the popular `rustc_serialize` crate. This wasn't bad, but I found that it wasn't flexible enough. For example, I couldn't use generic data types in my own structs. The `serde` crate was created to eliminate the shortcomings of the `rustc_serialize` crate. `serde` has been the main crate for serialization and deserialization in Rust since the `serde` crate reached the 1.0 release branch.

We used this crate in the previous chapter to deserialize a configuration file. We're now going to use it to transform request and response data to text or binary data.

To explore serialization, we'll use a microservice that generates random numbers. We'll rewrite a very simple version without logging, reading arguments, environment variables, or configuration files. It will use the HTTP body to specify a range of random values and a random distribution to generate a number from.

Our service will handle requests for the `/random` path only. It will expect both a request and a response in JSON format. As mentioned, the `serde` crate provides serialization capabilities to the code. We also need the `serde_derive` crate to derive the serialization method automatically. The `serde` crate contains only core types and traits to make the serialization process universal and reusable, but specific formats are implemented in other crates. We'll use `serde_json`, which provides a `serializer` in JSON format.

Copy the code of the minimal random-number-generating service and add these dependencies to `Cargo.toml`:

```
[dependencies]
futures = "0.1"
hyper = "0.12"
rand = "0.5"
serde = "1.0"
```

```
serde_derive = "1.0"
serde_json = "1.0"
```

Import these crates into the `main.rs` source file:

```
extern crate futures;
extern crate hyper;
extern crate rand;
#[macro_use]
extern crate serde_derive;
extern crate serde_json;
```

As you can see, we imported a macro from the `serde_derive` and `serde_json` crates to use a JSON `serializer`. We don't import the `serde` crate, because we won't use it directly, but it's necessary to use the macro. We can now look at the different parts of the code. At first, we'll examine the request and response types. After that, we'll implement a handler to use it.

Serializing responses

The service returns random numbers represented as the `f64` type. We want to return it packed to a JSON object, because we may need to add more fields to the object. It's simple to use objects in JavaScript. Declare the `RngResponse` struct and add the `#[derive(Serailize)]` attribute. This makes this struct serializable, as follows:

```
#[derive(Serialize)]
struct RngResponse {
    value: f64,
}
```

To make this struct deserializable, we should derive the `Deserialize` trait. Deserialization may be useful it you want to use the same type for requests and responses. It's also important to derive both `Serialize` and `Deserialize` if you want to use the same type in a server and a client.

The serialized object will be represented as a string, as follows:

```
{ "value": 0.123456 }
```

Deserializing requests

The service will support complex requests in which you can specify a distribution and parameters. Let's add this enumeration to the source file:

```
#[derive(Deserialize)]
enum RngRequest {
    Uniform {
        range: Range<i32>,
    },
    Normal {
        mean: f64,
        std_dev: f64,
    },
    Bernoulli {
        p: f64,
    },
}
```

You may want to know what the serialized value looks like. `serde_derive` provides extra attributes, which you can use to tweak the serialization format. The current `deserializer` expects a `RngRequest` instance, as follows:

```
RngRequest::Uniform {
        range: 1..10,
}
```

This will be represented as the string:

```
{ "Uniform": { "range": { "start": 1, "end": 10 } } }
```

If you create your own protocol from scratch, there won't be any problems with the layout, because you can easily make it conform to any restrictions specified by serializers that are automatically generated by the `serde` crate. If you have to use an existing protocol, however, you can try to add extra attributes to a declaration. If this doesn't help, you can implement the `Serialize` or `Deserialize` traits manually. For example, let's say we want to use the following request format:

```
{ "distribution": "uniform", "parameters": { "start": 1, "end": 10 } } }
```

Add the `serde` attributes to the `RngRequest` declaration, which transform the `deserializer` to support the preceding format. The code will look as follows:

```
#[derive(Deserialize)]
#[serde(tag = "distribution", content = "parameters", rename_all =
"lowercase")]
enum RngRequest {
```

```
Uniform {
    #[serde(flatten)]
    range: Range<i32>,
},
Normal {
    mean: f64,
    std_dev: f64,
},
Bernoulli {
    p: f64,
},
}
```

Now, the enumeration uses the aforementioned request format. There are a lot of attributes in the `serde_derive` crate and it's important to explore them in more detail.

Tweaking serialization

`serde_derive` supports a lot of attributes that help you to avoid manual implementations of the `serializer` or `deserializer` for the struct. In this section, we take a look at useful attributes in detail. We'll learn how to change the letter case of variants, how to remove a level of nesting, and how to use specific names for a tag and for a content of an enumeration.

Changing the case of names

`serde_derive` maps names of fields in the code to fields of data. For example, the `title` field of a struct will expect the `title` field of a data object. If the protocol uses other names for fields, you have to take this into account to avoid warnings. For example, a struct in a protocol might contain the `stdDev` field, but if you use the name of this field in Rust, you get the following warning:

```
warning: variable `stdDev` should have a snake case name such as `std_dev`
```

You can fix this adding the `#![allow(non_snake_case)]` attribute, but this makes the code unsightly. A better solution is to use the `#[serde(rename="stdDev")]` attribute and use the other naming convention for serialization and deserialization only.

There are two variants of renaming attributes:

- Changing the naming convention for all variants
- Changing the name of a field

To change all variants of an enumeration, add the `#[serde(rename_all="...")]`
attribute with one of the following values: `"lowercase"`, `"PascalCase"`, `"camelCase"`,
`"snake_case"`, `"SCREAMING_SNAKE_CASE"`, or `"kebab-case"`. To be more
representative, naming values are written according to the rules of their own convention.

To change the name of a field, use the `#[serde(rename="...")]` attribute with the name
of the field used in the serialization process. You can see an example of the usage of this
attribute in `Chapter 17`, *Bounded Microservices with AWS Lambda*.

Another reason to use renaming is when the names of fields are keywords in Rust. For
example, a struct can't contain a field with the popular name `type`, because it's a keyword.
You can rename it to `typ` in the struct and add `#[serde(rename="type")]` to it.

Removing a nesting

The `serializer` derived automatically uses the same nesting structure as your type. If you
need to reduce the levels of nesting, you can set the `#[serde(flatten)]` attribute to use
fields without enclosing objects. In the previous example, we used the `Range` type from the
standard library to set a range in which to generate a random value, but we also want to see
the implementation details in the serialized data. To do this, we need the `start` and `end`
fields of the `Range`. We added this attribute to the field to cut out the `{ "range": ... }`
level of the structure.

For enumeration, `serde_derive` uses a tag as the name of the object. For example, the
following JSON-RPC contains two variants:

```
#[derive(Serialize, Deserialize)]
enum RpcRequest {
    Request { id: u32, method: String, params: Vec<Value> },
    Notification { id: u32, method: String, params: Vec<Value> },
}
```

The `params` field contains an array of any JSON values represented by
the `serde_json::Value` type, we'll explore this type later in this chapter. If you serialize
an instance of this struct, it will include the name of a variant. Consider the following, for
example:

```
{ "Request": { "id": 1, "method": "get_user", "params": [123] } }
```

This request isn't compatible with the JSON-RPC specification (`https://www.jsonrpc.org/
specification#request_object`). We can drop the enclosing object with
the `#[serde(untagged)]` attribute and the struct becomes as follows:

```
{ "id": 1, "method": "get_user", "params": [123] }
```

After this change, this serialized data can be sent as JSON-RPC. However, if you still want to keep the variant value in a serialized data form, you have to use another approach, which is described in the next section.

Using specific names for a tag and content

In our example, we want to have two fields in a serialized data form: distribution and parameters. In the first field, we want to hold a variant of enumeration, but renamed so that it's in lowercase. In the second field, we'll keep the parameters of the specific variant.

To achieve this, you can write your own Serializer and Deserializer, an approach that we'll explore later in this chapter. For this case, however, we can use the #[serde(tag = "...")] and #[serde(context = "...")] attributes. context can only be used in a pair with tag.

We have added this to our RngRequest:

```
#[serde(tag = "distribution", content = "parameters", rename_all =
"lowercase")]
```

This attribute specifies the distribution key of the serialized object to hold a variant of the enumeration. The variants of the enumeration move to the parameters field of the serialized object. The last attribute, rename_all, changes the case of the name of a variant. Without renaming, we would be forced to use title case for distributions, such as "Uniform" instead of the tidier "uniform".

Sometimes, a serialized value has to include an object with a dynamic structure. Formats such as JSON support free data structures. I don't like unspecified structures, but we may need them to create services that are compatible with existent services.

Any Value

If you want to keep a certain part of your data deserialized but you don't know the structure of the data and you want to explore it later in runtime, you can use the generic serde_json::Value, which represents a value of any type. For example, the serde_json crate includes a Value object and a method to deserialize types from an instance of Value. This may be useful in difficult deserialization cases in which you need to reorder the representation before it's completely deserialized.

To use a generic `Value`, add it to your struct. Consider the following, for example:

```
#[derive(Deserialize)]
struct Response {
    id: u32,
    result: serde_json::Value,
}
```

Here, we used a generic value of the `serde_json` crate. When you need to deserialize it to a `User` struct, for example, you can use the `serde_json::from_value` function:

```
let u: User = serde_json::from_value(&response)?;
```

In this section, we learned about deserialization processes. It's now time to add a handler to our server to process requests. This handler will deserialize the data, generate a random value, and return the data back in its serialized form to the client.

 If I write a proxy service, should I deserialize and serialize requests to send them unchanged to another service? This depends on the purpose of the service. Serialization and deserialization take up a substantial amount of CPU resources. If the service is used to balance requests, you don't need the inner data of the request. This is especially the case if you only use HTTP headers to choose the destination of the request. However, you might want to use the processing benefits of deserialized data – for example, you can patch some values of the data before sending it to other microservices.

Using hyper

We added the `RngRequest` and `Response` types and implemented the `Serialize` and `Deserialize` traits. Now we can use them with `serde_json` in a handler. In this section, we'll explore how get the full body of a request, deserialize it into an instance of a specific type, and serialize a response.

Reading a body from a stream

In fact, the body of a request in a `hyper` crate is a stream. You can't get access to the full body immediately, but you can read incoming chunks, write them to a vector, and use the resulting data set as a single object.

We don't have access to the whole body because it may be a huge block of data that we can't keep in the memory. Our service could be used, for example, to upload multiple terabytes of data files or for video streaming.

Since we're using an asynchronous approach, we can't block the current thread while we read the stream to the end. This is because it would block the thread and cause the program to stop working, because the same thread is used for polling streams.

 The serde crate doesn't support the deserialization of a continuous flow of data, but you can create and use a Deserializer instance directly to handle infinite streams.

To read data from a stream, you have to take a Stream instance and put it into a Future object, which will collect the data from that stream. We'll explore this topic in the next chapter in more detail. Let's implement a Future that collects data from a Stream instance. Add the following code to a branch of the /random path in the match expression of the handler:

```
(&Method::POST, "/random") => {           Stream trait (aka Iterator)
    let body = req.into_body().concat2() Future (aka Result)
        .map(|chunks| {                   Deserializer
            let res = serde_json::from_slice::<RngRequest>(chunks.as_ref()) Result <T, Err>
                .map(handle_request) T = Rng Request -> Rng Response
                .and_then(|resp| serde_json::to_string(&resp));
            match res {  String
                Ok(body) => {              Rng Response -> Result < String, Error>
                    Response::new(body.into())
                },
                Err(err) => {       serde_json:: Error
                    Response::builder()
                        .status(StatusCode::UNPROCESSABLE_ENTITY)
                        .body(err.to_string().into())
                        .unwrap()           ↑
                },
            }                        std:: Convert ::Into
        }
    });                             hyper:: Body
    Box::new(body)                    impl < String> for Body
}
```

(&Method::POST, annotations: Request / Body above `req.into_body()`)

The `Request` instance has the `into_body` method, which returns the body of the request. We used the `Body` type to represent a body for our handler. The `Body` type is a stream of chunks that implement the `Stream` trait. It has the `concat2` method, which concatenates all chunks to a single object. This is possible because the `Chunk` type implements the `Extend` trait and can be extended with the other `Chunk`. The `concat2` method transforms the `Stream` to `Future`.

> If you aren't familiar with the `futures` crate, you can learn more about it in the next chapter. For now, you can think of a `Future` object as a `Result` that will be completed later. You can think of a `Stream` as an `Iterator` that doesn't have a reference to any item and has to poll for the next item from a data stream.

After we take the whole body of a request, we can use deserialize. `serde_derive` derives a generic `deserializer`, so we have to use a crate to get a specific serialization format. In this case, we'll use the JSON format, so we'll use the `serde_json` crate. This includes a `from_slice` function, which creates a `Deserializer` for our type and uses it to read an instance from a buffer.

The `from_slice` method returns a `Result<T, serde_json::Error>` and we'll map this result to our own `handle_request` function, which reads the request and generates a response. We'll discuss this function later in this section.

When the result is ready, we use the `serde_json::to_string` function to convert the response to a JSON string. We use `and_then`, because `to_string` returns a Result and we have to handle errors if there are any.

We now have a `Result`, which contains a serialized response or `serde_json::Error` if anything goes wrong. We'll use the `match` expression to return a successful `Response` if the response is created and serialized to a `String` successfully or a response with the `UNPROCESSABLE_ENTITY` status and a body with an error message.

In our case, we created a `Future` object, which doesn't have any results. We have to add that future to a reactor to execute it.

When discussing the preceding code, we mentioned the `handle_request` function. Let's take a closer look at the implementation of this function:

```
fn handle_request(request: RngRequest) -> RngResponse {
    let mut rng = rand::thread_rng();
    let value = {
        match request {
            RngRequest::Uniform { range } => {
```

```
            rng.sample(Uniform::from(range)) as f64
        },
        RngRequest::Normal { mean, std_dev } => {
            rng.sample(Normal::new(mean, std_dev)) as f64
        },
        RngRequest::Bernoulli { p } => {
            rng.sample(Bernoulli::new(p)) as i8 as f64
        },
    }
  };
  RngResponse { value }
}
```

The function takes a `RngRequest` value. The first line of the implementation uses a `rand::thread_rng` function to create a random-number-generator instance. We'll use the `sample` method to generate a random value.

Our request supports three kinds of distributions: `Uniform`, `Normal`, and `Bernoulli`. We used destructuring patterns to get the parameters of a request to create a distribution instance. After this, we used a deserialized request for sampling and converted the result into the `f64` type to pack it into the `RngResponse` value.

Custom types

When your microservice uses custom data structures, it needs a custom serialization format. You can add your own serialization by implementing the `Serialize` and `Deserialize` traits, or by adding special attributes to your struct or field of struct. We'll explore both approaches here.

Custom serialization

We'll extend our random-number-generating service with two features – generating random colors and shuffling an array of bytes. For the first feature, we need to add the `Color` struct to hold the color components. Create a new file, `color.rs`, and add the following code to it:

```
#[derive(Clone, PartialEq, Eq)]
pub struct Color {
    pub red: u8,
    pub green: u8,
    pub blue: u8,
}
```

Add two constant colors that we'll use later:

```
pub const WHITE: Color = Color { red: 0xFF, green: 0xFF, blue: 0xFF };
pub const BLACK: Color = Color { red: 0x00, green: 0x00, blue: 0x00 };
```

The struct also implements `PartialEq` and `Eq` to compare a value with these constants.

We'll use a textual representation of color that's compatible with CSS. We'll support RGB colors in hex format and two textual colors: `black` and `white`. To convert a color to a string, implement the `Display` trait for `Color`:

```
impl fmt::Display for Color {
    fn fmt(&self, f: &mut fmt::Formatter) -> fmt::Result {
        match self {
            &WHITE => f.write_str("white"),
            &BLACK => f.write_str("black"),
            color => {
                write!(f, "#{:02X}{:02X}{:02X}", color.red, color.green,
color.blue)
            },
        }
    }
}
```

This implementation writes three color components to a string with the `'#'` prefix. Every color component byte is written in hex format with the `'0'` prefix for nonsignificant digits and with a width of two characters.   *0 FA*

We can now use this formatter to implement the `Serialize` trait for the `Color` struct:

```
impl Serialize for Color {
    fn serialize<S>(&self, serializer: S) -> Result<S::Ok, S::Error>
    where
        S: Serializer,
    {
        serializer.serialize_str(&self.to_string())
    }
}
```

This `Serialize` implementation calls the `serialize_str` method of the `Serializer` to store a hex representation of a color to a string. Before implementing a custom deserialization, add all necessary imports to the `color.rs` file:

```
use std::fmt;
use std::str::FromStr;
use std::num::ParseIntError;
use serde::{de::{self, Visitor}, Deserialize, Deserializer, Serialize,
```

```
Serializer};
```

Custom deserialization

Our `Color` type has to be convertible from a string. We can do this by implementing the `FromStr` trait, which makes it possible to call the `parse` method of `str` to parse the struct from a string:

```
impl FromStr for Color {
    type Err = ColorError;

    fn from_str(s: &str) -> Result<Self, Self::Err> {
        match s {
            "white" => Ok(WHITE.to_owned()),
            "black" => Ok(BLACK.to_owned()),
            s if s.starts_with("#") && s.len() == 7 => {
                let red = u8::from_str_radix(&s[1..3], 16)?;
                let green = u8::from_str_radix(&s[3..5], 16)?;
                let blue = u8::from_str_radix(&s[5..7], 16)?;
                Ok(Color { red, green, blue })
            },
            other => {
                Err(ColorError::InvalidValue { value: other.to_owned() })
            },
        }
    }
}
```

In this implementation, we use a match expression with four branches to check the cases. We indicate that the expression should have a textual value of either "white" or "black", or that it can start with a #, and that it should contain exactly seven characters. Otherwise, an error should be returned to indicate that an unsupported format has been provided.

To implement the `Deserialization` trait, we need to add the `ColorVisitor` struct, which implements the `Visitor` trait of the `serde` crate. The `Visitor` trait is used to extract a value of a specific type from different input values. For example, we can use the `u32` and `str` input types to deserialize decimal values. The `ColorVisitor` in the following example tries to parse the incoming strings to a color. It has the following implementation:

```
struct ColorVisitor;

impl<'de> Visitor<'de> for ColorVisitor {
    type Value = Color;
```

```
    fn expecting(&self, formatter: &mut fmt::Formatter) -> fmt::Result {
        formatter.write_str("a color value expected")
    }

    fn visit_str<E>(self, value: &str) -> Result<Self::Value, E> where E:
de::Error { bstr
        value.parse::<Color>().map_err(|err|
de::Error::custom(err.to_string()))
    }

    fn visit_string<E>(self, value: String) -> Result<Self::Value, E> where
E: de::Error {
        self.visit_str(value.as_ref())
    }
}
}
```

As you can see, we use the `parse` method of `str`, which works with types that implement the `FromStr` trait to convert a string to a `Color` instance. We implemented two methods to extract values from different types of strings – the first for `String` instances and the second for `str` references. We can now add the `Color` type as a field in the other deserializable struct. Let's take a closer look at the `ColorError` type before we look closer at working with binary data.

Custom error types with the failure crate

The preceding parsing needs its own error type to cover both errors—incorrect parsing of numbers, and invalid variants. Let's declare the `ColorError` type in this section.

Error handling in Rust is particularly easy. There's a `Result` type that wraps successful and unsuccessful outcomes in a single entity. `Result` interprets any type as an error type and you can transform one result to another using the `try!` macro or the ? operator. Joining different error types, however, is much more complicated. There's the `std::error::Error` trait, which provides a generic interface for all errors, but it's a little clumsy. To create errors in a more user-friendly way, you can use the `failure` crate.

This crate helps with error handling and contains extensive `failure::Error` types, which are compatible with other errors that implement the `std::Error::Error` trait. You can convert any error type that implements this trait to a generic `failure::Error`. This crate also includes macros that can be used to derive your own error type and the `failure::Fail` trait to implement extra features, such as `Backtrace`, which provides extra information about the primary cause of an error at runtime. *std :: Error :: Error*

failure :: Error ✓

Fail

Declare this type in the `color.rs` file:

```
#[derive(Debug, Fail)]
pub enum ColorError {
    #[fail(display = "parse color's component error: {}", _0)]
    InvalidComponent(#[cause] ParseIntError),
    #[fail(display = "invalid value: {}", value)]
    InvalidValue {
        value: String,
    },
}
```

The `ColorError` enumeration has two variants: `InvalidComponent` for parsing issues and `InvalidValue` if the wrong value is provided. To implement the necessary error traits for this type, we derive the `Fail` trait with the `#[derive(Debug, Fail)]` attribute. The `Debug` trait implementation is also necessary for `Fail` deriving.

To create error messages, we added the `fail` attribute with a `display` parameter that expects a message with parameters to interpolate into a format string. For fields, you can use names, such as `value`, and numbers with the underscore prefix to indicate their field position. To insert the first field, for example, use the name `_0`. To mark a field as a nested error, use the `#[cause]` attribute.

Deriving the `Fail` trait won't implement `From` for types that we used as variants of the `ColorError` enum. You should do this yourself:

```
impl From<ParseIntError> for ColorError {
    fn from(err: ParseIntError) -> Self {
        ColorError::InvalidComponent(err)
    }
}
```

The `ColorError` type is now ready to use with the `?` operator, and we can add random color generation to our microservice, together with the shuffling of a binary array.

Binary data

Before improving the microservice, add all the necessary dependencies to `Cargo.toml`:

```
failure = "0.1"
futures = "0.1"
hyper = "0.12"
rand = "0.5"
serde = "1.0"
serde_derive = "1.0"
```

```
serde_json = "1.0"
base64 = "0.9"
base64-serde = "0.3"
```

We're using a lot of dependencies that work well with each other, thanks to Rust and crates. As you might have noticed, we have added the `base64` crate and the `base64-serde` crate. The first is a binary-to-text converter and the second is necessary to work with a converter in the serialization processes of `serde`. Import all of these to `main.rs`:

```
#[macro_use]
extern crate failure;
extern crate futures;
extern crate hyper;
extern crate rand;
extern crate serde;
#[macro_use]
extern crate serde_derive;
extern crate serde_json;
extern crate base64;
#[macro_use]
extern crate base64_serde;

mod color;

use std::ops::Range;
use std::cmp::{max, min};
use futures::{future, Future, Stream};
use hyper::{Body, Error, Method, Request, Response, Server, StatusCode};
use hyper::service::service_fn;
use rand::Rng;
use rand::distributions::{Bernoulli, Normal, Uniform};
use base64::STANDARD;
use color::Color;
```

We also added the `color` module and used `color:Color` from that module. We also imported macros from the `failure` and `base64_serde` crates.

Add two extra variants to the `RngRequest` enumeration for color generation and array shuffling:

```
#[derive(Deserialize)]
#[serde(tag = "distribution", content = "parameters", rename_all =
"lowercase")]
enum RngRequest {
    Uniform {
        #[serde(flatten)]
        range: Range<i32>,
```

```
    },
    Normal {
        mean: f64,
        std_dev: f64,
    },
    Bernoulli {
        p: f64,
    },
    Shuffle {
        #[serde(with = "Base64Standard")]
        data: Vec<u8>,
    },
    Color {
        from: Color,
        to: Color,
    },
}
```

The `Shuffle` variant has field data of the `Vec<u8>` type. Since JSON doesn't support binary data, we have to convert it to text. We added the `#[serde(with = "Base64Standard")]` attribute, which requires us to use the `Base64Standard` type for deserialization. You can customize fields with your own serialization and deserialization functions; now, we have to declare `Base64Standard`:

```
base64_serde_type!(Base64Standard, STANDARD);
```

We have to declare this since `base64_serde` doesn't contain predefined deserializers. This is because Base64 needs extra parameters that can't have universal values.

The `Color` variant contains two fields, which can be used to specify a range in which the color will be generated.

Add some new variants of a response to the `RngResponse` enumeration:

```
#[derive(Serialize)]
#[serde(rename_all = "lowercase")]
enum RngResponse {
    Value(f64),
    #[serde(with = "Base64Standard")]
    Bytes(Vec<u8>),
    Color(Color),
}
```

We now have to improve the `handle_request` function with additional variants:

```
fn handle_request(request: RngRequest) -> RngResponse {
    let mut rng = rand::thread_rng();
```

```
match request {
    RngRequest::Uniform { range } => {
        let value = rng.sample(Uniform::from(range)) as f64;
        RngResponse::Value(value)
    },
    RngRequest::Normal { mean, std_dev } => {
        let value = rng.sample(Normal::new(mean, std_dev)) as f64;
        RngResponse::Value(value)
    },
    RngRequest::Bernoulli { p } => {
        let value = rng.sample(Bernoulli::new(p)) as i8 as f64;
        RngResponse::Value(value)
    },
    RngRequest::Shuffle { mut data } => {
        rng.shuffle(&mut data);
        RngResponse::Bytes(data)
    },
    RngRequest::Color { from, to } => {
        let red = rng.sample(color_range(from.red, to.red));
        let green = rng.sample(color_range(from.green, to.green));
        let blue = rng.sample(color_range(from.blue, to.blue));
        RngResponse::Color(Color { red, green, blue})
    },
}
}
```

We refactored the code a bit here and there are two extra branches. The first branch, for the `RngRequest::Shuffle` variant, uses the `shuffle` method of the `Rng` trait to shuffle incoming binary data and return it as converted to Base64 text.

The second variant, `RngRequest::Color`, uses the `color_range` function that we'll declare. This branch generates three colors in a range and returns a generated color. Let's explore the `color_range` function:

```
fn color_range(from: u8, to: u8) -> Uniform<u8> {
    let (from, to) = (min(from, to), max(from, to));
    Uniform::new_inclusive(from, to)
}
```

This function creates a new `Uniform` distribution with an inclusive range using `from` and `to` values. We're now ready to compile and test our microservice.

Compiling, running, and testing

Compile this example and run it with the `cargo run` command. Use `curl` to send requests to the service. In the first request, we'll generate a random number with a uniform distribution:

```
$ curl --header "Content-Type: application/json" --request POST \
    --data '{"distribution": "uniform", "parameters": {"start": -100,
"end": 100}}' \
    http://localhost:8080/random
```

We sent a `POST` request to the `localhost:8080/random` URL with a JSON body. This will return `{"value":-55.0}`.

The next command requests a shuffle of the `"1234567890"` binary string converted to Base64:

```
$ curl --header "Content-Type: application/json" --request POST \
    --data '{"distribution": "shuffle", "parameters": { "data":
"MTIzNDU2Nzg5MA==" } }' \
    http://localhost:8080/random
```

The expected response will be `{"bytes":"MDk3NjgxNDMyNQ=="}`, which equals the string `"0976814325"`. You'll get another value for this request.

The next request will take a random color:

```
$ curl --header "Content-Type: application/json" --request POST \
    --data '{"distribution": "color", "parameters": { "from": "black",
"to": "#EC670F" } }' \
    http://localhost:8080/random
```

Here, we used both representations of a color value: a string value of `"black"` and a hex value of `"#EC670F"`. The response will be something similar to `{"color":"#194A09"}`.

The last example shows what happens if we try to send a request with an unsupported value:

```
$ curl --header "Content-Type: application/json" --request POST \
    --data '{"distribution": "gamma", "parameters": { "shape": 2.0,
"scale": 5.0 } }' \
    http://localhost:8080/random
```

Since the service doesn't support `"gamma"` distribution, it will return an error reading `"unknown variant `gamma`, expected one of `uniform`, `normal`, `bernoulli`, `shuffle`, `color` at line 1 column 24"`.

Microservices with multiple formats

Sometimes microservices have to be flexible and support multiple formats. For example, some modern clients use JSON, but some need XML or another format. In this section, we'll improve our microservices by adding the **Concise Binary Object Representation (CBOR)** serialization format.

 CBOR is a binary data serialization format based on JSON. It's more compact, supports binary strings, works faster, and is defined as a standard. You can read more about this at `https://tools.ietf.org/html/rfc7049`.

Different formats

We need two extra crates: `queryst` for parsing parameters from the query string, and the `serde_cbor` crate to support the CBOR serialization format. Add these to your `Cargo.toml`:

```
queryst = "2.0"
serde_cbor = "0.8"
```

Also, import them in `main.rs`:

```
extern crate queryst;
extern crate serde_cbor;
```

Instead of using `serde_json::to_string` directly in the handler, we'll move it to a separate function that serializes data depending on the expected format:

```
fn serialize(format: &str, resp: &RngResponse) -> Result<Vec<u8>, Error> {
    match format {
        "json" => {
            Ok(serde_json::to_vec(resp)?)
        },
        "cbor" => {
            Ok(serde_cbor::to_vec(resp)?)
        },
        _ => {
            Err(format_err!("unsupported format {}", format))
        },
    }
}
```

P9

failure::Error

In this code, we used a match expression to detect a format. Significantly, we changed the `String` result to a binary type, `Vec<u8>`. We also used `failure::Error` as an error type, because both `serde_json` and `serde_cbor` have their own error types and we can convert them to a generic error using the `?` operator.

If the provided format is unknown, we can construct an `Error` with the `format_err!` macro of the `failure` crate. This macro works like the `println!` function, but it creates a generic error based on a string value.

We also changed the `Error` type in import section. Previously, it was the `hyper::Error` type from the `hyper` crate, but we'll now use the `failure::Error` type instead and use a crate name prefix for errors.

Parsing a query

The HTTP URI can contain a query string with parameters that we can use to tune a request. The `Request` type has a method, `uri`, which returns a query string if it's available. We added the `queryst` crate, which parses a query string to `serde_json::Value`. We'll use this value to extract the `"format"` parameters from the query string. If the format isn't provided, we'll use `"json"` as a default value. Add the format-extracting block to the branch that handles requests to the `/random` path and use the `serialize` function that we previously declared:

```
(&Method::POST, "/random") => {
    let format = {                 uri    query string
        let uri = req.uri().query().unwrap_or("");
        let query = queryst::parse(uri).unwrap_or(Value::Null);  -> Value
        query["format"].as_str().unwrap_or("json").to_string()
    };
    let body = req.into_body().concat2()
        .map(move |chunks| {
            let res = serde_json::from_slice::<RngRequest>(chunks.as_ref())
                .map(handle_request)
                .map_err(Error::from)
                .and_then(move |resp| serialize(&format, &resp));
            match res {
                Ok(body) => {
                    Response::new(body.into())
                },
                Err(err) => {
                    Response::builder()
                        .status(StatusCode::UNPROCESSABLE_ENTITY)
                        .body(err.to_string().into())
                        .unwrap()
```

```
            },
        }
    });
    Box::new(body)
},
```

This code extracts a format value from a query string, processes a request, and returns a serialized value using a chosen format.

Checking different formats

Compile the code, run it, and use `curl` to check the result. First, let's check the traditional JSON format:

```
$ curl --header "Content-Type: application/json" --request POST \
        --data '{"distribution": "uniform", "parameters": {"start": -100,
"end": 100}}' \
        "http://localhost:8080/random?format=json"
```

This will return a JSON response that we've seen before: `{"value":-19.0}`. The next request will return a CBOR value:

```
$ curl --header "Content-Type: application/json" --request POST \
        --data '{"distribution": "uniform", "parameters": {"start": -100,
"end": 100}}' \
        "http://localhost:8080/random?format=cbor"
```

This command won't print a response to the console, because it's in binary format. You'll see the following warning message:

```
Warning: Binary output can mess up your terminal. Use "--output -" to tell
Warning: curl to output it to your terminal anyway, or consider "--output
Warning: <FILE>" to save to a file.
```

Let's try to request a response in XML format:

```
$ curl --header "Content-Type: application/json" --request POST \
  --data '{"distribution": "uniform", "parameters": {"start": -100, "end":
100}}' \
  "http://localhost:8080/random?format=xml"
```

This has worked correctly; it printed `unsupported format xml` to indicate that it doesn't support XML format. Let's now move on to discussing transcoding `serde` values and looking at why XML isn't a format that's widely supported by `serde`.

Transcoding

Sometimes, you'll be faced with situations in which you need to convert one format to another. In this instance, you can use the `serde_transcode` crate, which converts one format to another using a standard `serde` serialization process. The crate has a `transcode` function that expects a `serializer` and a `deserializer` as arguments. You can use it as follows:

```
let mut deserializer = serde_json::Deserializer::from_reader(reader);
let mut serializer = serde_cbor::Serializer::pretty(writer);
serde_transcode::transcode(&mut deserializer, &mut serializer).unwrap();
```

This code converts incoming JSON data into CBOR data. You can read more about this crate at: `https://crates.io/crates/serde-transcode`.

XML support

`serde` doesn't provide very good support for XML. The main reason for this is the complexity of the format. It has so many rules and exceptions that you can't describe the expected format in a simple form. However, there are also some implementations that aren't compatible with `serde`. The following links explain streaming, reading, and writing XML data: `https://crates.io/crates/xml-rs` and `https://crates.io/crates/quick-xml`.

Another format that isn't compatible with the `serde` infrastructure is Protocol Buffers (`https://developers.google.com/protocol-buffers/`). Developers often choose this format for performance reasons and to use one scheme of data for different applications. To use this format in Rust code, try to use the `protobuf` crate: `https://crates.io/crates/protobuf`.

In my opinion, it's better to use a format that's compatible with the `serde` crate in Rust for the following reasons:

- It's simpler to use in a code.
- Structs don't need a scheme, because they're strict.
- You can use a separated crate with a determined protocol.

The only situation in which you shouldn't follow the `serde` approach is if you have to support a format that isn't compatible with `serde`, but has been used in existing services or clients.

Summary

In this chapter, we discussed serialization and deserialization processes using the `serde` crate. We looked at how `serde` supports multiple formats and can automatically derive `Serialize` and `Deserialize` implementations for structs or enumerations. We implemented a service that generates random numbers from incoming parameters serialized in JSON format.

After that, you learned how to implement these traits yourself and add extra features to shuffle an array or to generate a random color. Finally, we discussed how to support multiple formats in one handler.

In the next chapter, you'll learn how to use full potential of asynchronous code, and write microservices with Rust that can handle thousands of clients simultaneously.

5
Understanding Asynchronous Operations with Futures Crate

Rust is a modern language and has many approaches and crates that we can use to implement microservices. We can split these into two categories—synchronous frameworks and asynchronous frameworks. If you want to write synchronous microservices, you can implement a handler as a sequence of expressions and methods calls. But writing asynchronous code is hard in Rust, because it doesn't use a garbage collector and you have to take into account the lifetimes of all objects, including callbacks. This is not a simple task, because you can't stop the execution at any line of the code. Instead, you have to write code that won't block the execution for a long period of time. This challenge can be elegantly solved with the `futures` crate.

In this chapter, you will learn about how the `futures` crate works. We will study two basic types—`Future` and `Stream`. We will also explore the **Multi-Producer Single-Consumer** (**MPSC**) module, which is an alternative to a similar module of the `std` crate, but supports asynchronous access to channels. At the end of the chapter, we will create a microservice that uses `Future` and `Stream` traits to process incoming data and return a processed result to a client.

The `futures` crate contains asynchronous primitives only. We will also use the `tokio` crate, which provides asynchronous input and output capabilities to read and write image files for our microservice.

We will cover the following topics in this chapter:

- Basic asynchronous types
- Creating an image service

Technical requirements

This chapter requires Rust installation. We will develop microservices using the `futures` and `tokio` crates.

You can find the source code of the projects of this chapters on GitHub: `https://github.com/PacktPublishing/Hands-On-Microservices-with-Rust/tree/master/Chapter04`.

Basic asynchronous types

Microservices can be implemented in two different ways—synchronously and asynchronously. The approach refers to when the next task has to wait for the completion of the current task. To run tasks in parallel using code, we have to run a pool of threads and run tasks in the threads of the pool. The asynchronous approach is when you use non-blocking operations and a single thread performs multiple tasks. If an operation can't be completed, it returns a flag that means the task has not yet completed and we have to try to run it again later.

In the past, Rust developers used synchronous operations only, which meant that if we wanted to read data from a socket, we would have to block an executing thread. Modern operating systems have two approaches to avoid blocking—non-blocking input/output functions, and a scalable I/O event notification system, such as **epoll**.

Asynchronous activity refers to the ability to use the resources of the working for multiple concurrent activities. In contrast to synchronous handlers, asynchronous handlers use non-blocking operations. If resources are not available to finish the handler, it will be suspended until the next attempt to get access to resources. There is a well-established approach that involves a reactor and promises. A reactor allows a developer to run multiple activities in the same thread, while a promise represents a delayed result that will be available later. A reactor keeps a set of promises and continues to poll until it is completed and the result is returned.

Since the standard Rust library doesn't contain useful modules to write asynchronous applications and to work with reactors and promises, you need a third-party crate. An example of this type of crate is the `futures` crate, which we have used indirectly by using the `hyper` crate. It's now time to explore this crate in detail. In this section, we will discuss the different types of the `futures` crate that are available, how to use channels to pass messages between tasks, and how to use reactors, which are needed to run tasks.

Basic types of future crate

The `futures` crate was created to provide Rust developers zero-cost abstractions for asynchronous programming. The crate fits the borrowing system of Rust and helps to create types that poll resources and return results when they are available.

For everyday use, you need only a few types of the `futures` crate. The three basic types are `Future`, `Stream`, and `Sink`. Let's explore all of these types in detail.

[handwritten: poll() → Async::Ready, Pending]

Using the Future trait

[handwritten: Future aka Result { Item / Error]

`Future` is a trait that returns a result in the future and represents an operation that can't be completed immediately. Like the `Result` enumeration, `Future` has two outcome variants that are represented by the associated types `Item` and `Error`. The trait has a `poll` method, which is what retrieves the result. This method will be called by a reactor until it returns `Error` or an `Async::Ready` value. `Async` is an enumeration that has both `Ready` and `Pending` variants, which are used to represent a result of an asynchronous operation. `Ready` means the value is ready to use, while `Pending` means the value is not yet available and will be ready later.

As you can see, `Future` is used for a similar purpose to `Result`. Unlike `Result`, however, `Future` is a trait, which means the implementation is not specified and many types can implement it. A useful feature is the `FutureExt` trait which can be implemented for all the `Future` instances. This has multiple methods to process the result in a delayed manner. For example, if we want to convert an obtained value to another type, the trait has a `map` method for this purpose. Take a look at the following:

```
let fut = future::ok(10u64);
let mapped_fut = fut.map(|x| x as f64);
```

[handwritten: FutureExt → map, FutureResult impl]

In this example, we created a `FutureResult` struct from a constant. This type implements the `Future` trait and represents a value that is immediately ready. Afterward, we called the `map` method from `FutureExt` for `FutureResult`, which expects a closure and returns.

You have to use a reactor to get the result for types that implement the `Future` trait. We will discuss reactors later in this section. Remember that you can't get the result immediately and use it in the next expression; instead, you have to create chains of futures or streams to get the appropriate result. Keep reading! We will now look into the `Stream` trait.

[handwritten: Future → { chain of future / stream]

Recall ← Iterature

Using the Stream trait

Stream aka Iterator { poll → Item / Error

`Stream` is a trait that represents a sequence of deferred items. It works in a similar way to the `Iterator` trait, but it uses the poll method to get the next `Item` or to return `Error` in the case of failure. The stream can either be incoming data from a socket or data that can be read from a file. `Stream` can be converted to `Future` and vice versa if the `Future` instance returns a `Stream`.

StreamEx { filter split

To use streams effectively, you should learn the methods of the `StreamExt` trait. This lets you make a chain to process every item of the stream or even join multiple streams into one. For example, you can filter some elements from `Stream` using the `filter` method with a predicate:

```
let stream = stream::iter_ok::<_, ()>(vec![-1, 0, 1, 2, 3]);
let filtered_stream = stream.filter(|x| x > 0);
```

The `iter_ok` method creates a `Stream` from the `Iterator`. It is useful if you want to provide your own values from a `Vec` instance.

Future → Stream

A useful feature is the conversion of a `Future` instance that contains a `Stream` as a result to just a `Stream`. For example, when you try to connect by TCP using the `TcpStream::connect` method of the `tokio` crate, it will return `ConnectFuture`, which implements the `Future` trait and returns a `TcpStream` instance.

TcpStream :: Connect → ConnectFuture

Using Sink to send data back

`Future` and `Stream` objects supply data from a source, but if you want to send a piece of data to the source, you have to use `Sink` objects. `Sink` is a trait that is similar to `Stream`, but works in the opposite direction. It contains two associated types—`SinkItem` and `SinkError`. The first determines the type of item that can be sent using a specific sink. The second represents an error if the sending process goes wrong. To interact with a `Sink`, you should use the methods of the `SinkExt` trait, which contains send methods to send an item to a recipient. The `send` method returns a `Send` struct that implements the `Future` trait, which means you can't send an item immediately. The call of the `send` methods returns a future that has to be executed with a reactor. If you are not concerned about the result of the sending process, you can use the `spawn` method to send the future in a separate task.

SinkExt { send → Send Future / spawn

Sink (source) { Sink Item / Sink Error

channel (tx, rx) Sender ← jwin

Future Stream (dest) ?poll → StreamExt { split → { Split Sink / Split Stream

The Sink object comes with Stream and you have to call the split method of StreamExt to get an instance of Sink attached to a stream. This call returns a tuple with both SplitSink and SplitStream objects. These are necessary to let you read an input and write an output concurrently. Later, both of these can be reunited using the reunite method of any of these objects. If you are writing a complex interaction, you have to use a Sink trait many times. It's hard to do this using split every time, but there are two alternative approaches that you can use. The first is to implement all interactions in a separate implementation of the Stream trait and work with a Stream and a Sink using the poll method. The second approach is to split a sink and join it with a Receiver object of a channel. You can then use a Sender of this channel to send an item without splitting the stream every time. We will implement an example of this kind of interaction in the next section, in which we will discuss channels.

Sink : Stream : StreanExt } split → Sink
(Split Sink
Split Stream)
reunite
join

The channel module

Concurrent activities often need to interact with each other. It's likely that you are already familiar with the mpsc module of the standard library, which uses blocking operations to send in channels, but this is not suitable for a sophisticated reactor that blocks completely if any operation blocks the working thread. Fortunately, however, there is the channel module in the futures crate which is capable of carrying out cross-task communication. The channel module contains two modules—mpsc and oneshot. Let's look at both.

Channels for sending multiple messages

As a rule, channels are a one-way interaction primitive. A channel has a sender to send messages and a receiver to extract messages. Internally, a channel works as an array or list that is protected from data races (when two or more threads try to write the same memory cell) using an atomic flag or lock-free data types. Channels implement one of the queue access patterns we will discuss in the following sections.

Single-Producer Single-Consumer

This approach means that only one producer can send messages and only one consumer can read them. In Rust, this means we have a single Sender and a single Receiver, neither of which can be cloned. The standard library has an internal implementation of a **Single-Produce Single-Consumer (SPSC)** queue, but this type is not available for users. If you need this type of queue, try the bounded-spsc-queue crate.

Multi-Producer Single-Consumer

This is the most popular queue type in Rust. Both the standard library and the `futures` crate provide this kind of channel. It's popular because channels are often used to provide access to a resource that lives in a single thread for other multiple threads. For this type of queue, the `Sender` can be cloned, but the `Receiver` can't.

Multi-Producer Multi-Consumer

This type of queue allows us to use a `Sender` and a `Receiver` with any amount of threads. Both the `Sender` and the `Receiver` can be cloned and used in multiple threads. If multiple threads read messages from `Receiver`, you can't predict which thread will get a specific message. You can find this functionality in the `crossbeam-channel` crate.

Example of usage

To send a message from one thread to another, you are likely to use the `mpsc` module of the standard library. The `mpsc` module of the `futures` crate works in a similar way, but the `Sender` returns the `Sink` instance when you call the `send` method to send an item to the message stream. The `Receiver` implements the `Stream` trait, which means you have to use a reactor to poll the stream for new messages:

```
fn multiple() {
    let (tx_sink, rx_stream) = mpsc::channel::<u8>(8);
    let receiver = rx_stream.fold(0, |acc, value| {
        future::ok(acc + value)
    }).map(|x| {
        println!("Calculated: {}", x);
    });
    let send_1 = tx_sink.clone().send(1);
    let send_2 = tx_sink.clone().send(2);
    let send_3 = tx_sink.clone().send(3);
    let execute_all = future::join_all(vec![
        to_box(receiver),
        to_box(send_1),
        to_box(send_2),
        to_box(send_3),
    ]).map(drop);
    drop(tx_sink);
    tokio::run(execute_all);
}
```

In this example, we created a channel that delivers messages of the u8 type. We used the fold method of the Receiver to add all the values and print the result when the channel is closed. We used the Sender to send values to the Receiver. At the end, we combined all the futures to a single future with the future::join_all method and passed the resultant future to an executor of the tokio crate. The join_all function expects a Vec of specific types that implements the Future trait. We added the to_box function which converts a type into a Future with the IntoFuture trait, drops the result and an error, and boxes it:

```
fn to_box<T>(fut :T) -> Box<dyn Future<Item=(), Error=()> + Send>
where
    T: IntoFuture,
    T::Future: Send + 'static,
    T::Item: 'static,
    T::Error: 'static,
{
    let fut = fut.into_future().map(drop).map_err(drop);
    Box::new(fut)
}
```

Sender . send → Receiver
↳ Sink
↳ Stream
(poll)
↓
Reactor

To close the Sender, all we need to do is drop it. If we don't drop the Sender, the channel remains open and tokio::run will never finish.

One-shot

The oneshot module implements a channel of a single message. It also has its own Sender and Receiver types, but these work in a different way. The Sender has a send method that completes oneshot and consumes an instance completely. Sender doesn't need to implement the Sink trait, because we can't send multiple items. It has a preallocated cell for an item that will be put into the cell immediately and we don't have any queue.

The Receiver implements the Future trait, which means you have to use a reactor to get an item from it:

Sender . send → Receiver
↳ Future
↓
Reactor

```
fn single() {
    let (tx_sender, rx_future) = oneshot::channel::<u8>();
    let receiver = rx_future.map(|x| {
        println!("Received: {}", x);
    });
    let sender = tx_sender.send(8);
    let execute_all = future::join_all(vec![
        to_box(receiver),
        to_box(sender),
    ]).map(drop);
```

```
        tokio::run(execute_all);
}
```

In this example, we created a `Sender` and a `Receiver` for a `oneshot` channel. The sender is an object that will be consumed with the `send` method call. The `Receiver` implements the `Future` trait and we can use the `map` method to get access to a value.

Previously, we mentioned that we can send messages to `Sink` from multiple sources. Let's implement this example using channels.

Using channels to use Sink in multiple places

As mentioned previously, you can use a channel to send data with `Sink` from different places and at any time. Look at the following example:

```
fn alt_udp_echo() -> Result<(), Error> {
    let from = "0.0.0.0:12345".parse()?;
    let socket = UdpSocket::bind(&from)?;
    let framed = UdpFramed::new(socket, LinesCodec::new());  Stream
    let (sink, stream) = framed.split();
    let (tx, rx) = mpsc::channel(16);
    let rx = rx.map_err(|_| other("can't take a message"))
        .fold(sink, |sink, frame| {
            sink.send(frame)
        });
    let process = stream.and_then(move |args| {
        tx.clone()
            .send(args)
            .map(drop)
            .map_err(other)
    }).collect();
    let execute_all = future::join_all(vec![
        to_box(rx),
        to_box(process),
    ]).map(drop);
    Ok(tokio::run(execute_all))
}
```

This example creates a `UdpSocket` instance that represents a UDP socket and binds it to the `0.0.0.0:12345` address. After that, we wrap a socket with the `UdpFramed` type, which implements a `Stream` of data that is generated with the provided codec. We will use `LinesCodec` from the `tokio::codec` module. This reads an input and uses a line delimiter to split the data into pieces that represent lines of text.

We will split the framed stream and create a channel to send the UDP datagrams from different places. We will get familiar with the channel module in the next section and learn how tasks can interact with each other asynchronously using the Sender and Receiver objects.

The channel method returns the Sender and Receiver objects. We use the Receiver to forward all incoming messages to a Sink of the UDP connection and we read all data from the stream and send it back with the channel. This echo server can be implemented more effectively without channels, but we have used them here for demonstrative purposes. To send a message, we used a Sender of the created channel. The advantage of this approach is that you can clone and use a sender instance everywhere to send messages to a channel at any time.

Sometimes, Future and Stream differ with regard to their Item or Error type parameters. To counteract this, we add an other method that wraps any error instance with the io::Error type. We use this function to convert one error type to another:

```
fn other<E>(err: E) -> io::Error
where
    E: Into<Box<std::error::Error + Send + Sync>>,
{
    io::Error::new(io::ErrorKind::Other, err)
}
```

You can compile this echo server and check how it works using the netcat utility. You should install this if your operating system doesn't contain it already. Type the nc command with the --verbose (short form: -v), --udp (short form: -u), and --no-dns (short form: -n) arguments and enter any text. As an example, we have typed "Text Message":

```
$ nc -vnu 0.0.0.0 12345
Ncat: Version 7.60 ( https://nmap.org/ncat )
Ncat: Connected to 0.0.0.0:12345.
Text Message
Text Message
^C
```

As you can see, the server has sent us back the provided string. All these examples used an executor to run the tasks concurrently. Before we start to implement a server, let's learn how executors work.

Executors

Since asynchronous tasks can be executed in a single thread, we need a way to execute all tasks, even if some tasks generate new tasks during execution. There are two approaches to run all tasks:

- Run futures and collect streams directly with blocking
- Use an executor to run futures and streams

Let's explore them both in the following sections.

Running futures and streams with blocking

The first approach is to use the `block_on` or `block_on_stream` functions of the `executor` module. Both functions block the current thread to wait for the result. It is a naive approach that is not very flexible, but it is great in the following circumstances:

- If you have only one task
- If none of your tasks read or write streams
- If you want to complete the task from a separate thread that can be blocked

You should remember that you must not call this function in asynchronous code, because the call will block the executor and your program will stop working.

Using an executor

The second approach is to execute all tasks with an `Executor` instance. This allows you to run multiple tasks in a single thread, even if some tasks can't be completed immediately. To use an `Executor`, you have to create and run it, but it will block the current thread and you should add all the necessary tasks to be executed at the start.

For example, if you want to open a socket and process the stream of every incoming connection, you have to create a main `Future` that will read the `Stream` of incoming connections and spawn a handler for processing the `Stream` of the data of the connection using the `tokio::spawn` method. After you have created it, you have to `spawn` the whole processing future with the executor. Take a look at the following example:

```
fn send_spawn() {
    let (tx_sink, rx_stream) = mpsc::channel::<u8>(8);
    let receiver = rx_stream.fold(0, |acc, value| {
        println!("Received: {}", value);
        future::ok(acc + value)
```

```
    }).map(drop);
    let spawner = stream::iter_ok::<_, ()>(1u8..11u8).map(move |x| {
        let fut = tx_sink.clone().send(x).map(drop).map_err(drop);
        tokio::spawn(fut);
    }).collect();
    let execute_all = future::join_all(vec![
        to_box(spawner),
        to_box(receiver),
    ]).map(drop);
    tokio::run(execute_all);
}
```

In this example, we have created a channel. We have also created a stream from a sequence of integers using the stream::iter_ok method. We send all items of the stream to the channel, which reads all the incoming values and prints them to a console. We have already dealt with a similar example. In the current version, we use the tokio::spawn function to spawn a task in an executor of the current thread.

As you can see, to use the futures crate, you have to build chains of handlers. The resultant code is hard to maintain and improve. To simplify asynchronous code, the Rust compiler has started to support the async/await syntax.

The async/await syntax

Some programming languages, such as JavaScript and C#, have async and await operators which help to write asynchronous code that looks like synchronous code. The nightly version of the Rust compiler supports a new syntax and adds async and await (actually, this is a macro) keywords to the language to simplify the writing of asynchronous applications. The new code might look as follows:

```
async fn http_get(addr: &str) -> Result<String, std::io::Error> {
    let mut conn = await!(NetwrokStream::connect(addr))?;
    let _ = await!(conn.write_all(b"GET / HTTP/1.0\r\n\r\n"))?;
    let mut buf = vec![0;1024];
    let len = await!(conn.read(&mut buf))?;
    let res = String::from_utf8_lossy(&buf[..len]).to_string();
    Ok(res)
}
```

This is not stable yet and may be changed before release. async is a new keyword that converts a standard function to asynchronous. await! is a macro that is built in in unstable Rust versions. It suspends the execution of a function and waits for the result from a Future instance provided to await! as argument. This macro uses the generators feature to interrupt execution until the Future under await! has been completed.

In the remaining part of this chapter, we are going to look at a proxy that uses streams to process incoming and outgoing data.

Creating an image service

In this section, we will create a microservice that allows clients to upload images and then download them. At first, we implement a handler to upload images and save them to a filesystem asynchronously using the tokio crate. After that, we will implement a downloading handler that allows the user to download original images from files that were uploaded before.

Uploading images

Let's start implementing a microservice to store and serve images with an uploading files feature. To get incoming files, we have to read an incoming Stream of a Request. The Stream might be huge, so we shouldn't hold the whole file in memory. We will read the incoming data in chunks and write them immediately to a file. Let's create the main function of our microservice:

```
fn main() {
    let files = Path::new("./files");
    fs::create_dir(files).ok();
    let addr = ([127, 0, 0, 1], 8080).into();
    let builder = Server::bind(&addr);
    let server = builder.serve(move || {
        service_fn(move |req| microservice_handler(req, &files))
    });
    let server = server.map_err(drop);
    hyper::rt::run(server);
}
```

This looks like the other examples that we've created but here we set a std::path::Path to a directory that will keep all incoming files. We will create the directory with the path we set before using the create_dir function of the std::fs module. If the creation of the directory fails, we will ignore it, but for production code it's better to stop creating a server and return an Error or print the necessary information. This is suitable for demonstrative purposes, but it's not reliable, because locally stored files can be lost in the server and your service will be corrupted. In real microservices, you may prefer to use a third-party service, such as AWS S3, to store and deliver files to clients.

After we create a directory to store files, we will start a `Server` with a `microservice_handler` that we will define later. Pay attention to when we pass a reference to a `Path`. Providing a path as a parameter is useful if you want to set another folder using command-line arguments.

We can now define the `microservice_handler` function that will handle four cases:

- Returning an index page on the / path
- Storing a file to the /upload path
- Returning the uploaded file with the /download path
- Returning 404 errors for other requests

The function has the following definition:

```
fn microservice_handler(req: Request<Body>, files: &Path)
    -> Box<Future<Item=Response<Body>, Error=std::io::Error> + Send>
```

This is a similar handler definition to that we used in Chapter 2, *Developing a Microservice with Hyper Crate,* and Chapter 3, *Logging and Configuring Your Microservices,* but we use `std::io::Error` instead of `hyper::Error`. This is because we are not only working with requests and responses, but we are also using a filesystem that can cause errors of other types. We also expect an argument of the `Path` type to determine a directory in which we will store files.

Lets add a `match` expression to match the parameters of an incoming request. We will consider only two branches here—the first is when a client sends a GET request to the root path, and the second is for all other requests. We will add other branches later:

```
match (req.method(), req.uri().path().to_owned().as_ref()) {
    (&Method::GET, "/") => {
        Box::new(future::ok(Response::new(INDEX.into())))
    },
    _ => {
        response_with_code(StatusCode::NOT_FOUND)
    },
}
```

We used similar pattern matching in Chapter 2, *Developing a Microservice with Hyper Crate.* Previously, we had a `match` expression to check the method and the path of incoming requests. This time, we need a copy of `Uri::path`, because we will need to use a path copy in regular expressions of other branches later.

The `response_with_code` function returns a `Future` instance now, instead of `Request`:

```
fn response_with_code(status_code: StatusCode)
    -> Box<Future<Item=Response<Body>, Error=Error> + Send>
{
    let resp = Response::builder()
        .status(status_code)
        .body(Body::empty())
        .unwrap();
    Box::new(future::ok(resp))
}
```

Let's add the remaining branches to the `match` expression. Let's add one to handle the uploading of files:

```
(&Method::POST, "/upload") => {
    let name: String =
thread_rng().sample_iter(&Alphanumeric).take(20).collect();
    let mut filepath = files.to_path_buf();
    filepath.push(&name);
    let create_file = File::create(filepath);
    let write = create_file.and_then(|file| {
        req.into_body()
            .map_err(other)
            .fold(file, |file, chunk| {
            tokio::io::write_all(file, chunk)
                .map(|(file, _)| file)
        })
    });
    let body = write.map(|_| {
        Response::new(name.into())
    });
    Box::new(body)
}
```

This request-handling branch expects the `POST` method and the `"/upload"` path. We don't check the user credentials and we allow everyone to upload a file, but in a real microservice, you should filter incoming traffic to avoid spam or malicious use.

In the first line of the branch, we generate a random name for the incoming file. We can provide the client with an opportunity to set the name of the file, but this is a dangerous practice. If you don't check the paths of incoming requests, a client can request a file from any folder in the server. We take an instance of random number generator that implements the Rng trait with `thread_rng` function call of the `rand` crate. Afterward, we use the generator to get an `Iterator` of samples by the `sample_iter` method call of the Rng trait and provide an `Alphanumeric` distribution to it that generates random characters and digits. We take 20 items from the iterator and collect them in a `String`. Then, we convert the `files` variable to `PathBuf` using the `to_path_buf` method and add the generated filename to the path.

In the next line, we create a `File` with the generated name. Here lies the most important difference of asynchronous applications—we use the `tokio::fs::File` type instead of the `std::fs::File` type, so we return a `Future` instance instead of a file reference. The future will be completed when the file is created. After that, we use the created file to write some data to this file asynchronously. The `tokio::fs::File` type wraps `std::fs::File`, but implements the `AsyncRead` and `AsyncWrite` traits. At any time, you can call the `into_std` method to unwrap the standard `File` type. Before we do this, however, we will write an incoming stream to the created file. Let's take a closer look at the `tokio` crate and some important issues to do with the asynchronous reading and writing of files.

The tokio crate

The `tokio` crate provides the functionality to work with the network connections of files in an asynchronous manner. It includes wrappers for the TCP and UDP sockets—`TcpStream` and `UdpSocket`. It also includes types to access a filesystem through the `Future` and `Stream` traits. There is no cross-platform approach to work with files asynchronously, because operating systems have their own implementations of non-blocking APIs. Some operating systems, however, don't have good asynchronous APIs at all. To provide cross-platform asynchronous access to filesystems, `tokio` uses the `tokio_threadpool` crate, which has a `blocking` method that runs a task in a separate thread. This helps to implement asynchronous interaction for types that can block the thread using input/output operations. It isn't the most effective way to interact with a filesystem, but it does allow us to convert synchronous APIs to asynchronous. The `tokio` crate also contains an `Executor` trait and a `Timer` module. We've considered executors before. The `timer` module contains the `Timeout` and `Interval` types to create a `Future` and a `Stream` that generate values whenever a specified time period has elapsed.

Asynchronous input/output of files

We now have to create a chain to read all incoming chunks and write them to the created file. As you might remember, `File::create` returns a `Future` that returns a `File` instance. We won't take the result immediately, because I/O operations take some time and can cause the current running thread to be blocked. We have to use the `Future::and_then` method to move the result (when it is ready) to other `Future` instance that will send all chunks to the file. To do that, we will use a `Body` instance that we get with the `into_body` method call of the `Request` that is stored in the `req` variable. The `Body` implements a `Stream` of the `Chunk` instances, but it can produce a `hyper::Error`. Since `File::create` can produce an `io::Error`, we have to convert the `hyper::Error` to an `io::Error` using the `other` function call as follows:

```
fn other<E>(err: E) -> Error
where
    E: Into<Box<std::error::Error + Send + Sync>>,
{
    Error::new(ErrorKind::Other, err)
}
```

The preceding function creates an `io::Error` with `ErrorKind::Other` based on any `Error` provided with the single argument. We use the `other` function with the `map_err` of the `StreamExt` to convert failures of the stream to `io::Error`. When the `Stream` of the `Body` is compatible with the type of error, we can create a `Future` that will move incoming binary data to the file. To do that, we can use a `fold` method of a `StreamExt` trait. If you are familiar with functional programming, you might know how this works already. The `fold` function takes two arguments—an initial value, which will be reused in every iteration, and a function, which carries out some processing with the initial value. Processing functions have to return a `Future` instance on every call, with one condition—the `Future` has to return the same type as the type of the initial value.

We will provide a `File` instance as an initial value and we will call `tokio::io::write_all` to write an incoming chunk of the request's body to a file. The `write_all` function expects an output stream and a binary slice. It returns a `Future`, which returns a tuple with an output stream and a provided slice on success. We have to use the `map` method of the returned `Future` to drop the slice and keep the file. The resultant chain will `fold` the whole `Stream` to a `Future`, which will return a filled `File` instance when all chunks are written to the file. We store this `Future` to write a variable and use the map method of `FutureExt` to drop the file instance (the real file with the written data will remain on the drive), and return a `Response` with the name of the stored file.

We have now successfully implemented file uploading. We should now discuss how to upload files using HTML forms and add a downloading feature to our service.

Multipart form requests

So far in this chapter, we have used requests with binary bodies. This is suitable for microservices, but if you want to send files with an HTML form, you should use a request with a `multipart/form-data` type of content. This allows a client to include multiple files in a single request, but it also needs a parser to split files from the body of a request. The `hyper` crate doesn't include a parser for multipart requests, and you can use other crates such as the `multipart` crate to parse requests instead. This, however, doesn't work asynchronously, so you should use the `multipart-async` crate with the latest versions of the `hyper` crate. You can also implement multipart requests yourself. To implement this, you can create a struct that implements the `Stream` trait and parses incoming chunks of data. Multipart requests have the `multipart/form-data` content type with a boundary value such as `boundary=53164434ae464234f`. Its body contains a separator and the embedded files:

```
---------------------------53164434ae464234f
Content-Disposition: form-data; name="first_file"; filename="file1.txt"
Content-Type: text/plain
Contents of the file1.txt
---------------------------53164434ae464234f
Content-Disposition: form-data; name="second_file"; filename="file2.txt"
Content-Type: text/plain
Contents of the file2.txt
---------------------------53164434ae464234f
```

Your stream has to implement `Stream<Item=FileEntry>`, which reads a request and extracts files using the provided boundary.

Downloading images

Let's implement a branch to download images. The handler can download files using the `/download/filename` path. To extract the name of the file, we use a regular expression:

```
lazy_static! {
    static ref DOWNLOAD_FILE: Regex =
Regex::new("^/download/(?P<filename>\\w{20})?$").unwrap();
}
```

We will use `startwith` to detect the `/download` part of the path. Take a look at the implementation:

```
(&Method::GET, path) if path.starts_with("/download") => {
    if let Some(cap) = DOWNLOAD_FILE.captures(path) {
        let filename = cap.name("filename").unwrap().as_str();
        let mut filepath = files.to_path_buf();
        filepath.push(filename);
        let open_file = File::open(filepath);
        let body = open_file.map(|file| {
            let chunks = FileChunkStream::new(file);
            Response::new(Body::wrap_stream(chunks))
        });
        Box::new(body)
    } else {
        response_with_code(StatusCode::NOT_FOUND)
    }
}
```

In this example, we expect a GET method and check that the paths match with the DOWNLOAD_FILE regular expression. We use the name `"filename"` to extract a string with the name of the file. Since we have the filepath variable with a path to a folder, we convert the `Path` value to the `PathBuf` type using the `to_path_buf` method of the `Path` instance and push a filename to it. After that, we use the file type of the `tokio` crate to open a file, which has asynchronous reading and writing capabilities to work with the file's content. The `open` method of the file returns an `OpenFuture` instance that resolves to a `File` instance when it is successful.

We wrap a file with `FileChunkStream`, imported from the `hyper_staticfile` crate. This stream reads a `File` and returns chunks of bytes. The body has a `wrap_stream` method and we can send the whole stream as a response. When the stream is forwarded to a client, the opened `File` will be closed when the stream is dropped.

The last thing we should do is return a `Body` instance.

sendfile for sending files

Forwarding files from one file to another is not effective, because this approach copies every chunk of data to the memory before sending it. Popular servers such as **NGINX** use the `sendfile` system call to send files from one file descriptor to another. This helps to save a lot of resources, because `sendfile` allows for zero copy, which means that we can write the buffer directly to the necessary device. To use `sendfile` with `tokio`, you have to implement a wrapper for it, but I don't think it's a good idea to serve static files with a microservice. You may prefer to use NGINX for this task or use object storage such as **AWS S3**, which can provide static files to a client.

Testing the service

The image service is now ready for testing. Compile it, download any image from the internet, and use `curl` to upload it to our service:

```
$ curl https://www.rust-lang.org/logos/rust-logo-128x128.png | curl -X POST
--data-binary @- localhost:8080/upload
```

```
I4tcxkp9SnAjkbJwzy0m
```

This request downloads the Rust logo and uploads it to our microservice. It will return the name of the uploaded image with a response. Put it after the `/download/` path and try to download it with your browser:

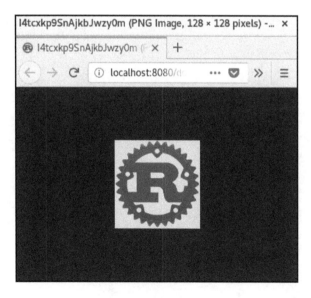

Summary

In this chapter, we have examined the `futures` and `tokio` crates. The `futures` crate contains types to work with delayed results and streams. We have compared the `Future` and `Result` types and the `Stream` and `Iterator` types. After that, we implemented a microservice that stores images and sends them back to the client.

We will improve microservice of this chapter using threads and background tasks in `Chapter 10`, *Background Tasks and Thread Pools in Microservices*. But in the next chapter, we will take a look at reactive microservices and using remote procedure calls as an alternative way to implement of microservices.

6
Reactive Microservices - Increasing Capacity and Performance

If you adhere to a microservices architecture for your application, you'll get the benefits of loose coupling, meaning that every microservice is standalone enough to be developed and maintained by separate teams. This is a kind of asynchronous approach to business tasks, but it's not the only benefit; there are others. You can increase your capacity and performance by only scaling the microservices that take a huge load. To achieve this, your microservice has to be reactive, and it has to be self-sustaining, interacting with other microservices via message passing.

In this chapter, you will learn what a reactive microservice is, and how to use message passing to ensure the connectivity of microservices. Also, we will discuss whether reactive microservices can be asynchronous.

In this chapter, we will cover the following topics:

- What is a reactive microservice?
- JSON-RPC
- gRPC

Technical requirements

This chapter will cover using **remote procedure calls** (**RPCs**) in Rust. You'll need a working Rust compiler, because we will create two examples with the `jsonrpc-http-server` and `grpc` crates.

If you want to test TLS connections, you'll need OpenSSL version 0.9, because the `grpc` crate doesn't support version 1.0 or higher yet. Most modern operating systems have switched to 1.0 already, but you can build the examples to a Docker image that supports version 0.9, or wait till the `grpc` crate is updated to the latest OpenSSL version. We will build test examples without TLS.

You can find the sources of the examples from this chapter in the GitHub repository at, `https://github.com/PacktPublishing/Hands-On-Microservices-with-Rust/tree/master/Chapter06`.

What is a reactive microservice?

A microservices architecture implies the presence of multiple parts in an application. In the past, most applications were monoliths, with all of the parts contained in a single code base. The microservices approach gives us the opportunity to split a code base between multiple teams and developers, to have an individual life cycle for every microservice, and for parts to interact with a common protocol.

Does this mean that your application will be free from all of the flaws of a monolithic application? No. You can write microservices that are so closely related to each other that you can't even properly update them.

How is this possible? Imagine that you have a microservice that has to wait for the response of another microservice to send a response to a client. The other microservice, in turn, also has to wait for another microservice, and so on. If you closely link the microservices of an application, you will find the same drawbacks that you have with monoliths.

You have to write microservices as independent applications that can be reused for multiple projects, not only yours. How can you achieve that? Develop a reactive microservice. Let's look at what that is.

Loose coupling

Loose coupling is a software design approach that implies every part of an application should know little information about the other parts. In traditional applications, if you write a GUI component, such as a button, it has to be possible to use it everywhere, for any application. As another example, if you develop a library to work with sound hardware, this also means you can use it with every application; the library is not limited to use in one kind of application. In microservices, however, loose coupling means that a microservice doesn't know anything about other microservices, or how many there are.

If you develop an application, you should write parts of it—microservices—as standalone applications. For example, a notification service that sends push notifications to mobile platforms won't know about CRM, accounting, or even the users. Is it possible to do this? Yes! You can write a microservice that uses a common protocol and interacts with other services via message passing. This is called a **message-driven application**.

Message-driven applications

Traditional microservices have an API that immediately returns a result and every participant of a working application has to know about the other parts. This approach keeps the relations of microservices close. Such an application is hard to maintain, update, and scale.

It is much more convenient if your application interacts via messages that are handled by other microservices. This approach is called **message-driven**, when you use messages as a unit of interaction. Messages help you to reduce the coupling of microservices, because you can process a message for multiple services simultaneously or add an extra processing message for a particular message type.

To have totally uncoupled microservices, you should use a message queue or a message broker service. We will learn this approach in detail in Chapter 12, Scalable Microservices Architecture, in which we talk about scalable architecture.

Asynchronous

Since reactive microservices use message passing, you have to process message asynchronously. This doesn't mean you have to use asynchronous crates such as tokio or futures. But it means no one message can block the service; every message is processed in a short period of time and if the service has to perform a long task it should do it as a background task and inform the thread issued that task about the result by sending a message with that result. To achieve this behavior, you can use multiple threads without asynchronous code. But what about using asynchronous code for reactive microservices?

Should a reactive microservice be asynchronous?

Very often, confusion is caused by asynchronous applications being called **reactive**, because their event loops wait for external events and don't waste server resources while they're waiting. Reactive microservices don't waste resources to keep incoming connection to return a result, because when a client connects to a reactive microservices for a short time, put the task and disconnects. After a client waits for asynchronous response from a microservice. Reactive microservices don't need to be asynchronous, but they can be.

When you choose message passing for interaction, you have to take into account that microservices have to be asynchronous and can handle multiple messages simultaneously. Traditional synchronous code can't process as many messages as asynchronous code does, because synchronous code has to wait for I/O resources, but asynchronous code reacts to I/O events and utilizes as many resources as possible.

More simply, if your microservices have to process hundreds of thousands of messages, you should use asynchronous code. If your microservices do not have a heavy load, it's enough to use a modest synchronous algorithm.

Reactive microservices with futures and streams

If you have decided to implement a reactive microservice using asynchronous code, you can consider using a future crate as a basis. This crate provides you with types to construct reactive chains to process all messages asynchronously. But remember, it can be hard to write all `Future` instances manually. There is an upcoming feature in the Rust compiler that provides `async/await` operators, which simplifies the `Future` trait implementation by writing traditional functions with the `Result` return type. This feature is unstable and we won't consider it in this book.

If you don't want to write low-level code, I recommend you use the `actix` crate. This is a really good framework that lets you write asynchronous code like synchronous code.

If you need the lowest level of control, you can use the `mio` crate that's used as a base by the `futures` crate. It provides you with full control of I/O events, and you can squeeze the maximum speed from the resources of your server.

async/await

lapin-futures — futures   actix   msg queue   event handler
lapin-async   mio   └─> thread pool
AMQP   msg

Message brokers

Message brokers let you send all messages to a central point that routes and delivers messages to the necessary microservices. In some cases, this can be a bottleneck, because the full load will fall on a single application—the message broker. But in most cases, it's a great approach that helps you to decouple microservices and update any microservices imperceptibly.

To use message brokers, it's sufficient to support the AMQP protocol. All popular message brokers are compatible with that protocol. The `lapin-futures` crate provides types and methods to use the AMQP protocol through the API of the `futures` crate. If you want to use the low-level control of the `mio` crate, there is the `lapin-async` crate.

Remote procedure calls

If you want to connect microservices to each other directly, you can use RPCs to allow the functions of a service to be called remotely by another service. There are a lot of RPC frameworks with different formats and speed potential. Let's look at some popular protocols.

JSON-RPC

The JSON-RPC protocol uses messages serialized to JSON format. It uses a special format for requests and responses, described here: `https://www.JSON-RPC.org/specification`. The protocol can use different transports, such as, HTTP, Unix sockets, or even stdio. Later in this chapter, you will find an example of the usage of this protocol.

gRPC

The gRPC protocol was created by Google and uses the Protocol Buffer serialization format for messages. Also, the protocol lies on benefits of the `HTTP/2` transport and allows you to achieve excellent performance. You can find more about the protocol here: `https://grpc.io/docs/`. There is also an example of using this protocol later in this chapter.

Thrift

Apache Thrift is a binary communication protocol developed by Facebook. Despite the fact the protocol is binary, there are a lot of supported languages, such as C++, Go, and Java. Supported transports are file, memory, and socket.

Other RPC frameworks

There are other RPC protocols, such as Cap'n Proto, XML-RPC, and even vintage SOAP. Some have implementations for Rust, but I recommend considering choosing between JSON-RPC, gRPC, and Thrift, because they are the most commonly used for microservices.

RPC and REST

You may ask if it is possible to implement reactive microservices with a REST API or a traditional web API. Of course—yes! You can do it one of two ways:

- There are gateways that translate REST requests to JSON-RPC or other protocols. For example, gRPC has one ready to use: `https://github.com/grpc-ecosystem/grpc-gateway`. You can even write your own gateway—it's not so hard for simple or specific cases.
- You can use a Web API to send messages from one server to another. A microservice doesn't have to have a single API path, but you can add a special handler for messages in JSON or other formats. For transport, you can use not only HTTP, but also the WebSocket protocol.

Reactive manifesto

If you look at the reactive architecture as a standardized approach, you won't find a guide or rules for how to turn your microservice reactive, but there is The Reactive Manifesto, which you can find here: `https://www.reactivemanifesto.org/`. It contains a list of principles you can use to be inspired by ideas for the improvement of your application.

Now we can create an example of a reactive microservice for the JSON-RPC procotol.

Understanding JSON-RPC

There are some crates that provide functionality to support the JSON-RPC protocol. Mostly, crates support only the server or the client side, not both. Some crates don't support asynchronous computations either.

How JSON-RPC works

The JSON-RPC protocol uses JSON messages in the following format for a request:

```
{"jsonrpc": "2.0", "method": "substring", "params": [2, 6, \"string\"],
"id": 1}
```

The preceding JSON message calls the substring remote method of a server that can return a result like this:

```
{"jsonrpc": "2.0", "result": "ring", "id": 1}
```

It's worth nothing that a client determines the identifier of the request and has to track those values. Servers are ID-agnostic and they use a connection to track requests.

There are two versions of the protocol—1.0 and 2.0. They are similar, but in the second version there is a separation of the client and the server. Also, it is transport independent, because the first version uses connection events to determine behavior. There are improvements for errors and parameters as well. You should use version 2.0 for new projects.

To support JSON-RPC, your server has to respond to these kind of JSON requests. The protocol is really simple to implement, but we will use the jsonrpc-http-server crate, which uses HTTP transport and provides types to bootstrap a server.

Creating a microservice

In this section, we will create an example of a microservice that supports the JSON-RPC protocol and has two methods. The microservice will support working as a part of a ring of microservices. We will send a message to one microservice, which will send a message to the next microservice in the ring, and that microservice will send the message further.

We will create a ring example, because if it is implemented incorrectly your microservice will be blocked, because they can't process requests in parallel like reactive services have to do.

Dependencies

First, we need to import the necessary dependencies:

```
failure = "0.1"
JSON-RPC = { git = "https://github.com/apoelstra/rust-JSON-RPC" }
jsonrpc-http-server = { git = "https://github.com/paritytech/JSON-RPC" }
log = "0.4"
env_logger = "0.6"
serde = "1.0"
serde_derive = "1.0"
```

Most likely, you are familiar with most crates except `jsonrpc` and `json-rpc-server`. The first is a JSON-RPC client that's based on the `hyper` crate. The second also uses the `hyper` crate and provides server functionality of JSON-RPC.

Let's import the necessary types and talk a little about them:

```
use failure::Error;
use JSON-RPC::client::Client;
use JSON-RPC::error::Error as ClientError;
use JSON-RPC_http_server::ServerBuilder;
use JSON-RPC_http_server::JSON-RPC_core::{IoHandler, Error as ServerError,
Value};
use log::{debug, error, trace};
use serde::Deserialize;
use std::env;
use std::fmt;
use std::net::SocketAddr;
use std::sync::Mutex;
use std::sync::mpsc::{channel, Sender};
use std::thread;
```

The JSON-RPC crate has the `Client` type that we will use to call the remote methods of other services. We also imported `Error` from that crate as `ClientError` to avoid a name conflict with `Error` from the failure crate.

For the server side, we will use `ServerBuilder` from the `jsonrpc-http-server` crate. Also, we need `Error` to be renamed to `ServerError` from that crate. To implement function handlers, we need to import `IoHandler`, which can be used to attach functions as RPC methods. Also, we need a `Value` (actually, this type is reimported from the `serde_json` crate), which is used as a result type for RPC methods.

To avoid mistakes in method names, because we will use them twice for the server implementation and then in a client, we declare names as string constants:

```
const START_ROLL_CALL: &str = "start_roll_call";
const MARK_ITSELF: &str = "mark_itself";
```

The first method will start sending messages from one microservice to the next. The second method is used to stop this roll-calling process.

Client

To interact with other microservice instances and to call their remote methods, we will create a separate struct, because it's more convenient than using the JSON-RPC `Cilent` directly. But in any case, we use this type internally in our struct:

```
struct Remote {
    client: Client,
}
```

We will use the `Remote` struct to make calls to remote services. To create the struct, we will use the following constructor:

```
impl Remote {
    fn new(addr: SocketAddr) -> Self {
        let url = format!("http://{}", addr);
        let client = Client::new(url, None, None);
        Self {
            client
        }
    }
}
```

The `Client` struct expects the `String` URL as a parameter, but we will use `SocketAddr` to create a URL.

Also, we need a generic function that will use the `Client` instance to call remote methods. Add the `call_method` method to the implementation of the `Remote` struct:

```
fn call_method<T>(&self, meth: &str, args: &[Value]) -> Result<T,
ClientError>
where
    T: for<'de> Deserialize<'de>,
{
    let request = self.client.build_request(meth, args);
    self.client.send_request(&request).and_then(|res|
res.into_result::<T>())
}
```

The calling of the JSON-RPC method using the JSON-RPC crate is simple. Use the `build_request` method of the `Client` instance to create a `Request` and send it using the `send_request` method of the same `Client`. There is a method called `do_rpc` that does this in a single call. We will use a more verbose approach to show that you can predefine requests and use them to speed up the preparation for calling. Also, it's more pleasant to use business-oriented struct methods instead of a raw `Client`. We isolate an implementation using a wrapper that hides the details of RPC calls. What if you decide to change to another protocol, such as gRPC?

Add special methods to the `Remote` struct implementation to make calls using the `call_method` method. First, we need the `start_roll_call` function:

```
fn start_roll_call(&self) -> Result<bool, ClientError> {
    self.call_method(START_ROLL_CALL, &[])
}
```

It won't pass any parameters with a call, but it expects the `bool` type of the result. We used a constant for the remote method's name.

Add the `mark_itself` method to the `Remote` struct:

```
fn mark_itself(&self) -> Result<bool, ClientError> {
    self.call_method("mark_itself", &[])
}
```

It doesn't send any parameters either and returns the `bool` value.

Now we can add a worker to separate outgoing method calls from incoming calls.

Worker

Since we have two methods, we will add a struct to perform remote calls of these methods from a worker thread. Add the `Action` enumeration to the code:

```
enum Action {
    StartRollCall,
    MarkItself,
}
```

It has two variants: `StartRollCall` to perform the remote `start_roll_call` method call, and the `MarkItself` variant to call the remote `mark_itself` method.

Now we can add a function to spawn a worker in a separate thread. If we will perform outgoing calls immediately in incoming method handlers, we can block the execution, because we have a ring of microservices and blocking one microservice will block the whole ring's interaction.

 No blocking is an important property of a reactive microservice. The microservices have to process all calls in parallel or asynchronously, but never block execution for a long time. They should work like actors in the actors model we have discussed.

Look at the `spawn_worker` function:

```
fn spawn_worker() -> Result<Sender<Action>, Error> {
    let (tx, rx) = channel();
    let next: SocketAddr = env::var("NEXT")?.parse()?;
    thread::spawn(move || {
        let remote = Remote::new(next);
        let mut in_roll_call = false;
        for action in rx.iter() {
            match action {
                Action::StartRollCall => {
                    if !in_roll_call {
                        if remote.start_roll_call().is_ok() {
                            debug!("ON");
                            in_roll_call = true;
                        }
                    } else {
                        if remote.mark_itself().is_ok() {
                            debug!("OFF");
                            in_roll_call = false;
                        }
                    }
                }
                Action::MarkItself => {
```

```
                        if in_roll_call {
                            if remote.mark_itself().is_ok() {
                                debug!("OFF");
                                in_roll_call = false;
                            }
                        } else {
                            debug!("SKIP");
                        }
                    }
                }
            }
        });
        Ok(tx)
    }
```

This function creates a channel and spawns a new thread with a routine that processes all received messages from a channel. We create the Remote instance with the address extracted from the NEXT environment variable.

There is a flag that shows that the start_roll_call method has been called. We set it to true when the StartRollCall message is received and the start_roll_call method of the remote server is called. If the flag is already set to true and the routine received the StartRollCall message, the thread will call the mark_itself remote method. In other words, we will call the start_roll_call methods of all running service instances. When all services set the flag to true, we will call the mark_itself methods of all services.

Let's start a server and run a ring of services.

Server

The main function activates a logger and spawns a worker. Then, we extract the ADDRESS environment variable to use this address value to bind a socket of a server. Loot at the following code:

```
fn main() -> Result<(), Error> {
    env_logger::init();
    let tx = spawn_worker()?;
    let addr: SocketAddr = env::var("ADDRESS")?.parse()?;
    let mut io = IoHandler::default();
    let sender = Mutex::new(tx.clone());
    io.add_method(START_ROLL_CALL, move |_| {
        trace!("START_ROLL_CALL");
        let tx = sender
            .lock()
```

```
            .map_err(to_internal)?;
        tx.send(Action::StartRollCall)
            .map_err(to_internal)
            .map(|_| Value::Bool(true))
    });
    let sender = Mutex::new(tx.clone());
    io.add_method(MARK_ITSELF, move |_| {
        trace!("MARK_ITSELF");
        let tx = sender
            .lock()
            .map_err(to_internal)?;
        tx.send(Action::MarkItself)
            .map_err(to_internal)
            .map(|_| Value::Bool(true))
    });
    let server = ServerBuilder::new(io).start_http(&addr)?;
    Ok(server.wait())
}
```

To implement JSON-RPC methods, we use the `IoHandler` struct. It has the `add_method` method, which expects the name of the method and needs a closure with an implementation of this method.

We added two methods, `start_roll_call` and `mark_itself`, using constants as names for these methods. The implementation of these methods is simple: we only prepare the corresponding `Action` messages and send them to the worker's thread.

The JSON-RPC method implementation has to return the `Result<Value, ServerError>` value. To convert any other errors to `ServerError` we use the following function:

```
fn to_internal<E: fmt::Display>(err: E) -> ServerError {
    error!("Error: {}", err);
    ServerError::internal_error()
}
```

The function only prints the current error message and creates an error with the `InternalError` code using the `internal_error` method of the `ServerError` type.

At the end of main function, we create a new `ServerBuilder` instance with the created `IoHandler` and start the HTTP server to listen for JSON-RPC requests with the `start_http` server.

Now we can start a ring of services to test it.

Compiling and running

Compile this example with the `cargo build` subcommand, and let's start three instances of the service using the following commands (run every command in a separate terminal window to see the logs):

```
RUST_LOG=JSON-RPC_ring=trace ADDRESS=127.0.0.1:4444 NEXT=127.0.0.1:5555
target/debug/JSON-RPC-ring
RUST_LOG=JSON-RPC_ring=trace ADDRESS=127.0.0.1:5555 NEXT=127.0.0.1:6666
target/debug/JSON-RPC-ring
RUST_LOG=JSON-RPC_ring=trace ADDRESS=127.0.0.1:6666 NEXT=127.0.0.1:4444
target/debug/JSON-RPC-ring
```

When the three services are started, prepare and send a JSON-RPC call request with `curl` from another terminal window:

```
curl -H "Content-Type: application/json" --data-binary '{"JSON-
RPC":"2.0","id":"curl","method":"start_roll_call","params":[]}'
http://127.0.0.1:4444
```

With this command, we start the interaction of all services, and they will call each other in a ring. You will see the logs of every service. The first prints something like this:

```
[2019-01-14T10:45:29Z TRACE JSON-RPC_ring] START_ROLL_CALL
[2019-01-14T10:45:29Z DEBUG JSON-RPC_ring] ON
[2019-01-14T10:45:29Z TRACE JSON-RPC_ring] START_ROLL_CALL
[2019-01-14T10:45:29Z DEBUG JSON-RPC_ring] OFF
[2019-01-14T10:45:29Z TRACE JSON-RPC_ring] MARK_ITSELF
[2019-01-14T10:45:29Z DEBUG JSON-RPC_ring] SKIP
```

The second will print something like this:

```
[2019-01-14T10:45:29Z TRACE JSON-RPC_ring] START_ROLL_CALL
[2019-01-14T10:45:29Z DEBUG JSON-RPC_ring] ON
[2019-01-14T10:45:29Z TRACE JSON-RPC_ring] MARK_ITSELF
[2019-01-14T10:45:29Z DEBUG JSON-RPC_ring] OFF
```

And the third will output the following logs:

```
[2019-01-14T10:45:29Z TRACE JSON-RPC_ring] START_ROLL_CALL
[2019-01-14T10:45:29Z DEBUG JSON-RPC_ring] ON
[2019-01-14T10:45:29Z TRACE JSON-RPC_ring] MARK_ITSELF
[2019-01-14T10:45:29Z DEBUG JSON-RPC_ring] OFF
```

All services works as independent participants of the process, react to incoming messages, and send messages to other services when there is something to send.

Learning about gRPC

In this section, we will rewrite the JSON-RPC ring example to gRPC. This protocol differs from JSON-RPC because it requires a protocol declaration—a predefined interaction schema. This restriction is good for large projects, because you can't make a mistake in a message's layout, but with Rust, JSON-RPC is also reliable because you have to declare all structs exactly and you will get an error if you take an incorrect JSON message. With gRPC, you don't have to care about it at all.

How gRPC works

The benefit of gRPC in comparison with JSON-RPC is speed. gRPC can work faster, because it uses a fast serialization format—Protocol Buffers. Both gRPC and Protocol Buffers were originally developed by Google and are proven in high-performance cases.

gRPC uses `HTTP/2` for transport. It's a really fast and good transport protocol. First, it's binary: all requests and responses are squeezed into a compact portion of bytes and compressed. It's multiplexed: you can send a lot of requests simultaneously, but `HTTP/1` demands respect for the order of requests.

gRPC needs a scheme and uses Protocol Buffers as the **Interface Definition Language** (**IDL**). Before you start writing an implementation of a service, you have to write the `proto` file that contains a declaration of all types and services. After that, you need to compile the declaration to sources (in the Rust programming language in our case) and use them to write the implementation.

The `protobuf` crate and the common gRPC crates use that crate as a basis. Actually, there are not many crates; just two: the `grpcio` crate, which is a wrapper over the original gRPC core library, and the `grpc` crate, which is the pure Rust implementation of the protocol.

Now we can rewrite the previous example from JSON-RPC protocol to gRPC. At first, we have to add all the necessary dependencies and write a declaration of our service.

Creating a microservice

The gRPC example is very complex, because we have to declare an interaction protocol. We also have to add the `build.rs` file to generate Rust sources from a protocol description.

Since it's hard to make a gRPC call from curl, we will also add a client that helps us to test services. You can also use other tools that are available for debugging gRPC applications.

Dependencies

Create a new binary crate and open `Cargo.toml` in an editor. We will explore every section of this file, because building a gRPC example is more complex than services that use flexible interaction protocols such as JSON-RPC. We'll use Edition 2018, as we do for most examples in this book:

```
[package]
name = "grpc-ring"
version = "0.1.0"
authors = ["your email"]
edition = "2018"
```

In dependencies, we need a basic set of crates—`failure`, `log`, and `env_logger`. Also, we add the `protobuf` crate. We won't use it directly, but it's used by generated Rust sources that we will get from a protocol description later in this section. The most important crate from the current example is grpc. We will use a version from GitHub, because the crate is in active development:

```
[dependencies]
env_logger = "0.6"
failure = "0.1"
grpc = { git = "https://github.com/stepancheg/grpc-rust" }
log = "0.4"
protobuf = "2.2"
```

Actually, the GitHub repository of the `grpc` crate is a workspace and also contains the `protoc-rust-grpc` crate, which we will use to generate a protocol declaration in Rust using the `build.rs` file. Add this dependency to the `[build-dependencies]` section of `Cargo.toml`:

```
[build-dependencies]
protoc-rust-grpc = { git = "https://github.com/stepancheg/grpc-rust" }
```

The example crate we create will produce two binary files—server and client. As I said, we need a client, because it's simpler than preparing calls manually, and use curl to call gRPC methods.

The first binary is a server built from the `src/server.rs` file:

```
[[bin]]
name = "grpc-ring"
path = "src/server.rs"
test = false
```

The second binary uses the `src/client.rs` file to build a client:

```
[[bin]]
name = "grpc-ring-client"
path = "src/client.rs"
test = false
```

We also have `src/lib.rs` for common parts, but we have to describe a protocol and create the `build.rs` file.

Protocol

gRPC uses a special language for protocol declarations. There are two versions of the language—`proto2` and `proto3`. We will use the second as it's more modern. Create a `ring.proto` file and add the following declaration:

```
syntax = "proto3";

option java_multiple_files = true;
option java_package = "rust.microservices.ring";
option java_outer_classname = "RingProto";
option objc_class_prefix = "RING";

package ringproto;

message Empty { }

service Ring {
  rpc StartRollCall (Empty) returns (Empty);
  rpc MarkItself (Empty) returns (Empty);
}
```

As you can see, we specified the syntax as `proto3`. Options give you the ability to set the properties for the generation of source files for different languages if you will interact with a service from other applications or other microservices. We don't need to set these options for our example, but you might have this part in a file if you take it from another developer.

The protocol declaration contains a package name set with the `package` specifier and a package name that we set to `ringproto`.

Also, we added the `Empty` message with no fields. We will use this type as the input and output parameter for all methods, but it's better to use different types for real microservices. Firstly, you can't have methods without input and output parameters. The second reason is future service improvements. If you want to add extra fields to the protocol later, you can do it. Moreover, the protocol can easily cope with different versions of the protocol; often you can use both new and old microservices, because Protocol Buffers work fine with extra fields, and you can extend the protocol later when you need it.

The service declaration is contained in the `service` section. You can have multiple services' declarations in a protocol declaration file and use only the necessary declared services in an implementation. But we need only one service declaration for our ring example. Add the `Ring` service and include two RPC methods with the `rpc` specifier. We added the `StartRollCall` method and `MakeItself`. The same as we did in the previous example. Both take the `Empty` value as an input argument and return `Empty` as well.

The name of a service is important, because it will be used as a prefix for multiple types in generated Rust sources. You can create sources using the `protoc` tool, but it's more convenient to create a build script that will generate sources with protocol types during compilation.

Generating interfaces

Rust build scripts let you implement a function that will do some additional preparation for project compilation. In our case, we have the `ring.proto` file with a protocol definition and we want to convert it to Rust sources using the `protoc-rust-grpc` crate.

Create the `build.rs` file in the project and add the following content:

```
extern crate protoc_rust_grpc;

fn main() {
    protoc_rust_grpc::run(protoc_rust_grpc::Args {
        out_dir: "src",
        includes: &[],
        input: &["ring.proto"],
        rust_protobuf: true,
        ..Default::default()
    }).expect("protoc-rust-grpc");
}
```

Build scripts use the `main` function as an entry point, in which you can implement any activities you want. We used the run function of the `protoc-rust-grpc` crate with `Args`—we set the output directory in the `out_dir` field, set the `ring.proto` file as input declaration with the `input` field, activate the `rust_protobuf` Boolean flag to generate sources for the `rust-protobuf` crate (you don't need it if you are already using the `protobuf` crate and generating types with it), then set the `includes` field to an empty array.

Then, when you run `cargo build`, it will produce two modules in the `src` folder: `ring.rs` and `ring_grpc.rs`. I don't put its sources here, because generated files are large, but we will use it to create a wrapper for a gRPC client, as we did in the previous example.

Shared client

Open the `lib.rs` source file and add two generated modules:

```
mod ring;
mod ring_grpc;
```

Import some types we need to create a wrapper for a gRPC client:

```
use crate::ring::Empty;
use crate::ring_grpc::{Ring, RingClient};
use grpc::{ClientConf, ClientStubExt, Error as GrpcError, RequestOptions};
use std::net::SocketAddr;
```

As you can see, the generated modules contain types we declared in the `ring.proto` file. The `ring` module contains the `Empty` struct, and the `ring_grpc` module contains the `Ring` trait, which represents an interface of a remote service. Also, `protoc_rust_grpc` in the build script generated the `RingClient` type. This type is a client that can be used to call remote methods. We wrap it with our own struct, because `RingClient` generates `Future` instances and we will use the `Remote` wrapper to perform them and get the result.

We also use types from the `grpc` crate. The `Error` type is imported as `GrpcError`; `RequestOptions`, which is necessary to prepare method call requests; `ClientConf`, which is used to add extra configuration parameters for the `HTTP/2` connection (we will use the default values); and `ClientStubExt`, which provides connection methods for clients.

Add the `Remote` struct holding the `RingClient` instance inside:

```
pub struct Remote {
    client: RingClient,
}
```

We use this struct for both client and server. Add a new method to construct new instances of `Remote` from the provided `SocketAddr`:

```
impl Remote {
    pub fn new(addr: SocketAddr) -> Result<Self, GrpcError> {
        let host = addr.ip().to_string();
        let port = addr.port();
        let conf = ClientConf::default();
        let client = RingClient::new_plain(&host, port, conf)?;
        Ok(Self {
            client
        })
    }
}
```

Since generated clients expect separate host and port values, we extract them from the `SocketAddr` value. Also, we create the default `ClientConf` configuration and use all these values to create the `RingClient` instance to put it to the new `Remote` instance.

We create the `Remote` struct to have simple methods to call remote methods. Add the `start_roll_call` method to the `Remote` implementation to call the `StartRollCall` gRPC method:

```
pub fn start_roll_call(&self) -> Result<Empty, GrpcError> {
    self.client.start_roll_call(RequestOptions::new(), Empty::new())
        .wait()
        .map(|(_, value, _)| value)
}
```

`RingClient` already has this method, but it expects parameters that we want to hide, and returns a `Future` instance that we want to perform immediately using the wait method call. The `Future` returns a tuple with three items, but we need only one value, because other values contain metadata that we don't need.

Implement the `mark_itself` method in a similar way to call the `MarkItself` gRPC method:

```
pub fn mark_itself(&self) -> Result<Empty, GrpcError> {
    self.client.mark_itself(RequestOptions::new(), Empty::new())
        .wait()
        .map(|(_, value, _)| value)
}
```

Now we can implement a client and a server, because both need the `Remote` struct to perform RPC calls.

Client

Add the `src/client.rs` file and import a few types:

```
use failure::Error;
use grpc_ring::Remote;
use std::env;
```

We need a generic `Error` from the `failure` crate, because it's a universal type for most error handling cases, and import the `Remote` struct we created before.

The client is an extremely simple tool. It calls the `StartRollCall` remote gRPC method of a service with the address provided in the `NEXT` environment variable:

```
fn main() -> Result<(), Error> {
    let next = env::var("NEXT")?.parse()?;
    let remote = Remote::new(next)?;
    remote.start_roll_call()?;
    Ok(())
}
```

Create the `Remote` instance with the parsed `SocketAddr` value and perform a call. This is it. The server is very complex. Let's implement it.

Server implementation

Add the `src/server.rs` source file and add generated modules to it:

```
mod ring;
mod ring_grpc;
```

We need these modules because we will implement the `Ring` trait for our RPC handler. Look at the types we will use:

```
use crate::ring::Empty;
use crate::ring_grpc::{Ring, RingServer};
use failure::Error;
use grpc::{Error as GrpcError, ServerBuilder, SingleResponse,
RequestOptions};
use grpc_ring::Remote;
use log::{debug, trace};
use std::env;
use std::net::SocketAddr;
use std::sync::Mutex;
use std::sync::mpsc::{channel, Receiver, Sender};
```

The types you are not familiar with yet are `ServerBuilder`, which is used to create a server instance and fill it with service implementations, and `SingleResponse` is the result of handler calls. The other types you already know.

Service implementation

We need our own type that will implement the `Ring` trait to implement RPC interface of a service. But we also have to keep a `Sender` for a worker to send actions to it. Add the `RingImpl` struct with a `Sender` of `Action` wrapped with `Mutex`, because the `Ring` trait requires the `Sync` trait implementation as well:

```
struct RingImpl {
    sender: Mutex<Sender<Action>>,
}
```

We will construct an instance from the `Sender` instance:

```
impl RingImpl {
    fn new(sender: Sender<Action>) -> Self {
        Self {
            sender: Mutex::new(sender),
        }
    }
}
```

For every incoming method call, we need to send `Action` to a worker and we can add a method to the `RingImpl` implementation to reuse it in all handlers:

```
fn send_action(&self, action: Action) -> SingleResponse<Empty> {
    let tx = try_or_response!(self.sender.lock());
    try_or_response!(tx.send(action));
    let result = Empty::new();
    SingleResponse::completed(result)
}
```

The `send_action` function takes the `Action` value and locks a `Mutex` to use a `Sender`. At the end, it creates an `Empty` value and returns it as a `SingleResponse` instance. If you have noticed, we used the `try_or_response!` macro that we defined, because `SingleResponse` is a `Future` instance and we have to return this type in any success or failure cases.

This macro works like the `try!` macro of the standard library. It uses match to extract a value or return a result if there is an error value:

```
macro_rules! try_or_response {
    ($x:expr) => {{
        match $x {
            Ok(value) => {
                value
            }
            Err(err) => {
                let error = GrpcError::Panic(err.to_string());
                return SingleResponse::err(error);
            }
        }
    }};
}
```

The preceding macro creates the `SingleResponse` instance with the `Panic` variant of `GrpcError`, but uses a description of an error from the existing error value.

Handlers

Now we can implement gRPC methods of the `Ring` service we declared in the `ring.proto` file before. We have the `Ring` trait with the same names of the methods. Every method expects the `Empty` value and has to return this type, because we defined this in the declaration. Also, every method has to return the `SingleResponse` type as a result. We already defined the `send_action` method that sends the `Action` value to a worker and returns the `SingleResponse` response with the `Empty` value. Let's use the `send_action` method for both methods we have to implement:

```
impl Ring for RingImpl {
    fn start_roll_call(&self, _: RequestOptions, _: Empty) ->
SingleResponse<Empty> {
        trace!("START_ROLL_CALL");
        self.send_action(Action::StartRollCall)
    }

    fn mark_itself(&self, _: RequestOptions, _: Empty) ->
SingleResponse<Empty> {
        trace!("MARK_ITSELF");
        self.send_action(Action::MarkItself)
    }
}
```

We have a pretty simple implementation of gRPC methods handlers, but you can also add more sensible implementations and produce `SingleResponse` from a Future asynchronously.

The main function

Everything is ready for the implementation of the `main` function:

```
fn main() -> Result<(), Error> {
    env_logger::init();
    let (tx, rx) = channel();
    let addr: SocketAddr = env::var("ADDRESS")?.parse()?;
    let mut server = ServerBuilder::new_plain();
    server.http.set_addr(addr)?;
    let ring = RingImpl::new(tx);
    server.add_service(RingServer::new_service_def(ring));
    server.http.set_cpu_pool_threads(4);
    let _server = server.build()?;

    worker_loop(rx)
}
```

[handwritten: event handler part to get action]

[handwritten: Main thread to call peer in ring loop]

We initialized a logger and created a channel that we will use to send actions from `RingImpl` to a worker. We extracted `SocketAddr` from the `ADDRESS` environment variable and used this value to bind a server to the provided address.

We created a `ServerBuilder` instance with the `new_plain` method. It creates a server without TLS, since gRPC supports secure connections and we have to provide a type parameter for `ServerBuilder` that implements the `TldAcceptor` trait. But with `new_plain` we use the `TlasAcceptor` stub from the `tls_api_stub` crate. The `ServerBuilder` struct contains the `http` field of the `httpbis::ServerBuilder` type. We can use this file to set the address to which to bind the server's socket.

After, we create the `RingImpl` instance and use the `add_service` method of `ServiceBuilder` to attach a service implementation, but we have to provide the generic `grpc::rt::ServerServiceDefinition` definition of the service and we use `new_service_def` of the `RingServer` type to create it for the `RingImpl` instance.

At the end, we set the quantity of threads in the pool that will be used to handle incoming requests and call the `build` method of `ServiceBuilder` to start a server. But wait—if you leave the `build` call method, the main thread will be terminated and you will have to add a loop or other routine to keep the main thread alive.

Luckily, we need a worker and we can use the main thread to run it. If you only need to run the gRPC server, you can use a loop with the `thread::park` method call, which will block the thread till it is unblocked by the unpark method call. This approach is used internally by asynchronous runtimes.

We will use the `worker_loop` function call, but we have not implemented this function yet.

Worker

We already implemented the worker in the JSON-RPC example. In the gRPC version, we use have same code, but expect a `Receiver` value and don't spawn a new thread:

```
fn worker_loop(receiver: Receiver<Action>) -> Result<(), Error> {
    let next = env::var("NEXT")?.parse()?;
    let remote = Remote::new(next)?;
    let mut in_roll_call = false;
    for action in receiver.iter() {
        match action { /* Action variants here */ }
    }
    Ok(())
}
```

Let's compile and run this example.

Compiling and running

Build both the server and the client with the `cargo build` subcommand.

If you want to specify binary, use the --bin parameter with the name of a binary.

Also, you can use `cargo watch` tool for building.

If you use the `cargo watch` tool, then the `build.rs` script will generate files with gRPC types and `watch` will continuously restart the build. To prevent this, you can set the `--ignore` argument to the command with a pattern of files' names to ignore. For our example, we have to run the `cargo watch --ignore 'src/ring*'` command.

When both binaries are built, run three instances in separate terminals:

```
RUST_LOG=grpc_ring=trace ADDRESS=127.0.0.1:4444 NEXT=127.0.0.1:5555
target/debug/grpc-ring
RUST_LOG=grpc_ring=trace ADDRESS=127.0.0.1:5555 NEXT=127.0.0.1:6666
target/debug/grpc-ring
RUST_LOG=grpc_ring=trace ADDRESS=127.0.0.1:6666 NEXT=127.0.0.1:4444
target/debug/grpc-ring
```

When all of the services start, use a client to send a request to the first service:

```
NEXT=127.0.0.1:4444 target/debug/grpc-ring-client
```

This command will call a remote method, `start_roll_call`, and you will see similar server logs to what you saw in the preceding JSON-RPC example.

Summary

This chapter covered good practices for creating reactive microservices architecture. We started our learning from basic concepts: what a reactive approach is, how to implement it, and how remote procedure calls helps to implement message-driven architecture. Also, we discussed existing RPC frameworks and crates that you can use simply with Rust.

To demonstrate how reactive applications work, we created two examples of microservices that use RPC methods to interact with each other. We created an application that uses a ring of running microservices that send requests to each other in a loop till every instance is informed about an event.

We also created an example that uses the JSON-RPC protocol for instance interaction and used the `jsonrpc-http-server` crate for the server side and the JSON-RPC crate for the client side.

After that, we created an example that uses the gRPC protocol for microservice interaction, and we used the `grpc` crate, which covers both the client and server sides.

In the next chater we will start to integrate microservices with database and explore available crates to interact with the follwoing databases: PostgreSQL, MySQL, Redis, MongoDB, DynamoDB.

7
Reliable Integration with Databases

Persistent microservices have to store and load data. If you want to keep this data organized and reliable, you should use a database. Rust has third-party crates that support popular databases, and in this chapter, you'll learn about how to use different databases with Rust, including the following:

- PostgreSQL
- MySQL
- Redis
- MongoDB
- DynamoDB

We will create utilities that will allow you to insert or remove data to and from the database, and to query the data held in the database.

Technical requirements

In this chapter, you'll need database instances to run our examples. The most effective way to run and work with a database for testing purposes is to use Docker. You can install databases locally, but seeing as we'll also need Docker for the remaining chapters, it's best to install and use it from this chapter.

We will use the following official images from Docker Hub:

- `postgres:11`
- `mysql:8`
- `redis:5`
- `mongo:4`
- `amazon/dynamodb-local:latest`

You can get to know more about these images on the Docker Hub repository pages: `https://hub.docker.com/`.

We will also use the `DynamoDB` database, which is provided as part of Amazon Web Services: `https://aws.amazon.com/dynamodb/`.

If you want to interact with databases to check whether our examples work successfully, you'll also have to install the corresponding clients for each database.

You can find all of the examples for this chapter in the `Chapter07` folder on GitHub: `https://github.com/PacktPublishing/Hands-On-Microservices-with-Rust-2018/`.

PostgreSQL

PostgreSQL is a reliable and mature database. In this section, we will explore how to start an instance of this database in a container, and how to connect to it from Rust using third-party crates. We will look at simple interactions with this database, and at the use of connection pools to get extra performance. We will start an instance of the database with Docker and create a tool to add records to a table and to query the list of added records before printing them to a console.

Setting up a test database

To create our database, you can use Docker, which automatically pulls all the necessary layers of the images containing the preinstalled PostgreSQL database. It's important to note that PostgreSQL has official images on Docker Hub, and you should opt to use these instead of unofficial ones, because the latter have a greater risk of malicious updates.

We need to start a container with a PostgreSQL database instance. You can do this using the following command:

```
                       volume
docker run -it --rm --name test-pg -p 5432:5432 postgres
          interact                              image
```

What does this command do? It starts a container from the `postgres` image (the latest version) and uses port `5432` on the localhost to forward it to the inner port, `5432`, of the container (that is, the port exposed by the image). We also set a name with the `--name` argument. We give the container the name `test-pg`. You can use this name later to stop the container. The `--rm` flag will remove the anonymous volumes associated with the container when it's stopped. So that we can interact with the database from a Terminal, we've added `-it` flags.

The database instance will start and print something like the following to the Terminal:

```
creating subdirectories ... ok
selecting default max_connections ... 100
selecting default shared_buffers ... 128MB
selecting dynamic shared memory implementation ... posix
creating configuration files ... ok
running bootstrap script ... ok
performing post-bootstrap initialization ... ok
syncing data to disk ... ok
........
```

The database is now ready for use. You can check it with the `psql` client, if you have it locally. The default parameters of the image are as follows:

```
psql --host localhost --port 5432 --username postgres
```

If you don't need the database anymore, you can use the following command to shut it down:

```
docker stop test-pg
```

But don't shut it down yet—let's connect to it with Rust.

Simple interaction with a database

The easiest way to interact with a database is to create a single connection directly to the database. Simple interaction is a straightforward database connection that doesn't use connection pools or other abstractions to maximize performance.

To connect to a PostgreSQL database, we can use two crates: `postgres` or `r2d2_postgres`. The first is a generic connection driver. The second, `r2d2_postgres`, is a crate for the `r2d2` connection pools crate. We will start by using the `postgres` crate directly, without a pool from the `r2d2` crate, and work on a simple utility to create a table, before adding commands to manipulate the data in that table.

Adding dependencies

Let's create a new project with all the necessary dependencies. We will create a binary utility for managing users in a database. Create a new binary crate:

```
cargo new --bin users
```

Next, add the dependencies:

```
cargo add clap postgres
```

But wait! Cargo doesn't contain an `add` command. I've installed `cargo-edit` tool for managing dependencies. You can do this with the following command:

```
cargo install cargo-edit
```

The preceding command installs the `cargo-edit` tool. If you don't install it, your local `cargo` won't have an `add` command. Install the `cargo-edit` tool and add the `postgres` dependency. You can also add dependencies manually by editing the `Cargo.toml` file, but as we are going to create more complex projects, the `cargo-edit` tool can be used to save us time.

> The Cargo tool can be found here: `https://github.com/killercup/cargo-edit`. This tool contains three useful commands to manage dependencies: `add` to add a dependency, `rm` to remove an unnecessary dependency, and `upgrade` to upgrade versions of dependencies to their latest versions. Furthermore, with the awesome Edition 2018 of Rust, you don't need to use an `extern crate ...` declaration. You can simply add or remove any crates and all of them will be available immediately in every module. But what about if you add a crate that you don't need, and end up forgetting about it? Since the Rust compiler allows unused crates, you can add the following crate-wide attribute, `#![deny(unused_extern_crates)]`, to your crate. This is necessary in case you accidentally add a crate that you won't use.

Also, add the `clap` crate. We need it for parsing arguments for our tool. Add the usages of all the necessary types, as follows:

```
extern crate clap;
extern crate postgres;

use clap::{
    crate_authors, crate_description, crate_name, crate_version,
    App, AppSettings, Arg, SubCommand,
};
use postgres::{Connection, Error, TlsMode};
```

All necessary dependencies have been installed, and our types have been imported, so we can create the first connection to a database.

Creating a connection

Before you can execute any query on a database, you have to establish a connection with the database you started in a container. Create a new `Connection` instance with the following command:

```
let conn = Connection::connect("postgres://postgres@localhost:5432",
TlsMode::None).unwrap();
```

The created `Connection` instance has `execute` and `query` methods. The first method is used to execute SQL statements; the second is used to query data with SQL. Since we want to manage users, let's add three functions that we'll use with our `Connection` instance: `create_table`, `create_user`, and `list_users`.

The first function, `create_table`, creates a table for users:

```
fn create_table(conn: &Connection) -> Result<(), Error> {
    conn.execute("CREATE TABLE users (
                id SERIAL PRIMARY KEY,
                name VARCHAR NOT NULL,
                email VARCHAR NOT NULL
            )", &[])
        .map(drop)
}
```

This function uses a `Connection` instance to execute a statement to create a `users` table. Since we don't need a result, we can simply `drop` it with the `map` command on `Result`. As you can see, we use an immutable reference to a connection, because `Connection` contains a reference to a shared struct, so we don't need to change this value to interact with a database.

 There are a lot of discussions about which approach to use: immutable references with runtime locks and Mutexes, or mutable references even if we need runtime locks. Some crates use the first approach, while others use the second. In my opinion, it's good to fit your approach to the environment in which it will be called. In some cases, it's more convenient to avoid mutable references, but in most cases, it's safer to require mutability for an interface object, such as `Connection` from the `postgres` crate. The developers of the crate also have a plan to move to mutable references. You can read more about it here: `https://github.com/sfackler/rust-postgres/issues/346`.

The next function is `create_user`:

```
fn create_user(conn: &Connection, name: &str, email: &str) -> Result<(),
Error> {
    conn.execute("INSERT INTO users (name, email) VALUES ($1, $2)",
                 &[&name, &email])
        .map(drop)
}
```

This function also uses the `execute` method of `Connection` to insert a value, but it also adds parameters to a call to fill the provided statement with values (the `create_table` function leaves these parameters empty). The result of the execution is dropped and we keep `Error` only. You may need the returning value if the request returns an identifier of an inserted record.

The last function, `list_users`, queries a database to get a list of users from the `users` table.

```
fn list_users(conn: &Connection) -> Result<Vec<(String, String)>, Error> {
    let res = conn.query("SELECT name, email FROM users", &[])?.into_iter()
        .map(|row| (row.get(0), row.get(1)))
        .collect();
    Ok(res)
}
```

This function, `list_users`, uses the `query` method of `Connection`. We use a simple `SELECT` SQL statement here, convert it into an iterator of rows, and extract pairs of names and email addresses of the users.

Wrapping with a tool

We've prepared all queries, so now we can join them in a binary tool with a command-line interface. In the following code, we will parse some parameters with the `clap` crate, and run functions to manage users with an established `Connection`.

Our tool will support three commands. Declare their names as constants:

```
const CMD_CREATE: &str = "create";
const CMD_ADD: &str = "add";
const CMD_LIST: &str = "list";
```

Now, we can create the `main` function using the `clap` crate to parse our command-line arguments:

```
fn main() -> Result<(), Error> {

    let matches = App::new(crate_name!())
        .version(crate_version!())
        .author(crate_authors!())
        .about(crate_description!())
        .setting(AppSettings::SubcommandRequired)
        .arg(
            Arg::with_name("database")
            .short("d")
            .long("db")
            .value_name("ADDR")
            .help("Sets an address of db connection")
            .takes_value(true),
            )
        .subcommand(SubCommand::with_name(CMD_CREATE).about("create users
table"))
        .subcommand(SubCommand::with_name(CMD_ADD).about("add user to the
table")
                        .arg(Arg::with_name("NAME")
                            .help("Sets the name of a user")
                            .required(true)
                            .index(1))
                        .arg(Arg::with_name("EMAIL")
                            .help("Sets the email of a user")
                            .required(true)
                            .index(2)))
        .subcommand(SubCommand::with_name(CMD_LIST).about("print list of
users"))
        .get_matches();
    // Add connection here
}
```

The `main` function returns `postgres::Error` in case of failure, because all operations we will do relate to our Postgres database connection. We create a `clap::App` instance here, and add a `--database` argument to let users change the address of the connection. We also added three subcommands, `create`, `add`, and `list`, along with extra arguments to the `add` command that requires the name and email address of a user so that we can insert this into a database.

To create a `Connection` instance, we use a database argument to extract a connection URL provided by a user with the `--db` command-line argument, and if it isn't provided, we will use the default URL value, `postgres://postgres@localhost:5432`:

```
let addr = matches.value_of("database")
    .unwrap_or("postgres://postgres@localhost:5432");
let conn = Connection::connect(addr, TlsMode::None)?;
```

We used a `Connection::connect` method with an address, and set the `TlsMode` parameter to `TlsMode::None`, because we don't use TLS in our demo. We created a `Connection` instance named `conn` to call our functions to interact with our database.

Finally, we can add branches for subcommands:

```
match matches.subcommand() {
    (CMD_CREATE, _) => {
        create_table(&conn)?;
    }
    (CMD_ADD, Some(matches)) => {
        let name = matches.value_of("NAME").unwrap();
        let email = matches.value_of("EMAIL").unwrap();
        create_user(&conn, name, email)?;
    }
    (CMD_LIST, _) => {
        let list = list_users(&conn)?;
        for (name, email) in list {
            println!("Name: {:20}    Email: {:20}", name, email);
        }
    }
    _ => {
        matches.usage(); // but unreachable
    }
}
Ok(())
```

The first branch matches the `crate` subcommand and creates a table by calling the `create_table` function.

The second branch is for the `add` subcommand. It extracts pairs of required arguments for the name and email of a user, and calls the `create_user` function to create a user record with the provided values. We use `unwrap` to extract it, because both arguments are required.

The penultimate branch handles the `list` command and takes a list of users with the `list_users` function call. After the value has been taken, it is used in a `for` loop to print all the records of the users to the console.

The last branch is unreachable because we set `AppSettings::SubcommandRequired` to `clap::App`, but we leave it in for consistency. It is especially useful if you want to provide a default behavior when a subcommand value hasn't been set.

Compiling and running

At the beginning of this chapter, we started an instance of the PostgreSQL database that we will use to check our tool. Compile the example we created with Cargo and print the available subcommands with the following command:

```
cargo run -- --help You will see the next output:
USAGE:
    users [OPTIONS] <SUBCOMMAND>
FLAGS:
    -h, --help       Prints help information
    -V, --version    Prints version information
OPTIONS:
    -d, --db <ADDR>    Sets an address of db connection
SUBCOMMANDS:
    add       add user to the table
    create    create users table
    help      Prints this message or the help of the given subcommand(s)
    list      print list of users
```

Cargo looks like a cute tool for managing the database of an application. Let's create a table with it, like so:

```
cargo run -- create
```

This command creates a `users` table. If you try to run it again, you will get an error:

```
Error: Error(Db(DbError { severity: "ERROR", parsed_severity: Some(Error),
code: SqlState("42P07"), message: "relation \"users\" already exists",
detail: None, hint: None, position: None, where_: None, schema: None,
table: None, column: None, datatype: None, constraint: None, file:
Some("heap.c"), line: Some(1084), routine: Some("heap_create_with_catalog")
}))
```

If you check your tables with the `psql` client, you will see the table that resides in our database:

```
postgres=# \dt
            List of relations
  Schema | Name  | Type  |  Owner
 --------+-------+-------+----------
  public | users | table | postgres
 (1 row)
```

To add a new user, call the `add` subcommand with the following parameters:

```
cargo run -- add user-1 user-1@example.com
cargo run -- add user-2 user-2@example.com
cargo run -- add user-3 user-3@example.com
```

We added three users, which you can see in the list if you enter the `list` subcommand:

```
cargo run -- list
Name: user-1    Email: user-1@example.com
Name: user-2    Email: user-2@example.com
Name: user-3    Email: user-3@example.com
```

In the following example, we will use a pool of database connections to add multiple users in parallel.

Connection pools

The tool we created uses a single connection to a database. It works fine for a small amount of queries. If you want to run multiple queries in parallel, you'll have to use connection pools. In this section, we improve the tool with the `import` command, which imports bulk user data from a CSV file. We will use a `Pool` type from the `r2d2` crate, add a command that will read users from a file, and execute statements to add users to a table in parallel.

Creating a pool

To create a connection pool, we will use the r2d2 crate that can hold multiple connections and provide one for us from the pool. This crate is generic, so you'll need a specific implementation for every database to connect to it. The r2d2 crate can connect to the following databases using adapter crates:

- PostgreSQL
- Redis
- MySQL
- SQLite
- Neo4j
- Diesel ORM
- CouchDB
- MongoDB
- ODBC

For our example, we need the r2d2-postgres adapter crate to connect to the PostgreSQL database. Add it to our dependencies with the r2d2 crate:

```
[dependencies]
clap = "2.32"
csv = "1.0"
failure = "0.1"
postgres = "0.15"
r2d2 = "0.8"
r2d2_postgres = "0.14"
rayon = "1.0"
serde = "1.0"
serde_derive = "1.0"
```

We also keep the postgres dependency, and add failure for error-handling and rayon to execute SQL statements in parallel. We also added a set of serde crates to deserialize User records from the CSV file, along with the csv crate to read that file.

You will be much more comfortable using Rust structs that represent data records in a database. Let's add a User type that represents a user record in a database with the following struct:

```
#[derive(Deserialize, Debug)]
struct User {
  name: String,
  email: String,
}
```

Since we have our special User type, we can improve the create_user and list_users functions to use this new type:

```
fn create_user(conn: &Connection, user: &User) -> Result<(), Error> {
    conn.execute("INSERT INTO users (name, email) VALUES ($1, $2)",
                &[&user.name, &user.email])
        .map(drop)
}

fn list_users(conn: &Connection) -> Result<Vec<User>, Error> {
    let res = conn.query("SELECT name, email FROM users", &[])?.into_iter()
        .map(|row| {
            User {
                name: row.get(0),
                email: row.get(1),
            }
        })
        .collect();
    Ok(res)
}
```

It hasn't changed dramatically: we still use the same Connection type, but we use the fields from the User struct to fill our create statements and extract values from our get list query. The create_table function has not changed.

Add a constant for the import command:

```
const CMD_IMPORT: &str = "import";
```

Then, add it as a SubCommand to App:

```
.subcommand(SubCommand::with_name(CMD_IMPORT).about("import users from csv"))
```

Almost all branches have changed and we should explore those changes. The add command creates a User instance to call the create_user function:

```
(CMD_ADD, Some(matches)) => {
    let name = matches.value_of("NAME").unwrap().to_owned();
    let email = matches.value_of("EMAIL").unwrap().to_owned();
    let user = User { name, email };
    create_user(&conn, &user)?;
}
```

The list subcommand returns a list of User struct instances. We have to take this change into account:

```
(CMD_LIST, _) => {
    let list = list_users(&conn)?;
    for user in list {
        println!("Name: {:20}    Email: {:20}", user.name, user.email);
    }
}
```

The import command is more complex, so let's discuss this in more detail in the following section.

Parallel imports with the rayon crate

Since we have a pool of connections, we can run multiple requests to a database in parallel. We will read users from a standard input stream in CSV format. Let's add a branch to the match expression we declared before, for the import subcommand, and open stdin with csv::Reader. After that, we will use the deserialize method of the reader, which returns an iterator of deserialized instances to our desired type. In our case, we deserialize the CSV data to a list of User structs and push them to a vector:

```
(CMD_IMPORT, _) => {
    let mut rdr = csv::Reader::from_reader(io::stdin());
    let mut users = Vec::new();
    for user in rdr.deserialize() {
        users.push(user?);
    }
    // Put parallel statements execution here
}
```

Rayon

To run requests in parallel, we'll use the `rayon` crate, which provides a parallel iterator with the `par_iter` method. The parallel iterator divides a list into separate tasks that run across a pool of threads:

```
users.par_iter()
    .map(|user| -> Result<(), failure::Error> {
        let conn = pool.get()?;
        create_user(&conn, &user)?;
        Ok(())
    })
    .for_each(drop);
```

The parallel iterator returns items much like a traditional iterator. We can get a connection from the pool using the `Pool::get` method, and call the `create_user` function with a reference to a connection. We also ignore results here, and if any request fails, it will be skipped silently, as in the demonstration, we cannot take care of values that have not been inserted. Since we use multiple connections, we can't use transactions to roll back changes if any statement does fail.

The `rayon` crate looks really impressive and simple to use. You may ask: *could you use this crate in microservices?* The answer is: *yes!* But remember that to collect data, you have to call the `for_each` method, which blocks the current thread until all tasks are completed. If you call it in reactor's context (which we discussed in `Chapter 5`, *Understanding Asynchronous Operations with Futures Crate*) in asynchronous `Future`, it will block the reactor for a while.

In the next section, we will rewrite this example for a MySQL database.

MySQL

MySQL is one of the most popular databases, so Rust naturally has crates to interact with it. There are two good crates that I recommend that you use: the `mysql` crate and its asynchronous version, the `mysql_async` crate.

In this section, we'll rewrite the previous example of managing users with support for a MySQL database. We'll also bootstrap a local instance of the database in a container, and create a command-line utility that connects to a database instance, sends queries to create table, and allows us to add and remove users. We will use the latest example for PostgreSQL, which uses the `r2d2` pool.

Database for tests

To bootstrap the database, we also will use a Docker image. You can install MySQL locally, but a container is a more flexible approach that doesn't clog the system, and you can easily start an empty database for testing purposes in seconds.

There is an official image, `mysql`, of the MySQL database that you can find here: `https://hub.docker.com/_/mysql`. You can load and run the container using these images with the following command:

```
docker run -it --rm --name test-mysql -e MYSQL_ROOT_PASSWORD=password -e
MYSQL_DATABASE=test -p 3306:3306 mysql
```

There are two necessary parameters that you can set with environment variables. First, the `MYSQL_ROOT_PASSWORD` environment variable sets a password for the root user. Second, the `MYSQL_DATABASE` environment variable sets the name of a default database that will be created on the first start of a container. We named our container `test-mysql` and forwarded the local port `3306` to port `3306` inside our container.

To make sure that our container has started, you can use the `mysql` client, if it's installed locally:

```
mysql -h 127.0.0.1 -P 3306 -u root -p test
```

The preceding command connects to `127.0.0.1` (to avoid using sockets) on port `3306`, with user as `root`. The `-p` argument asks for a password for the connection. We set a password for our testing container because the database images require it.

Our database is ready to use. You can also stop it with the following command:

```
docker stop test-mysql
```

Connecting with the r2d2 adapter

In the previous section, we used a connecting pool from the r2d2 crate with a PostgreSQL database. There is also a connection manager for MySQL in the r2d2-mysql crate that allows you to use a MySQL connection with the r2d2 crate. The r2d2-mysql crate is based on the mysql crate. Using the pool is also simple, just as we did for the PostgreSQL database, but here, we use the MysqlConnectionManager as a type parameter for r2d2::Pool. Let's modify all functions with queries to use a pool from our MySQL database.

Adding dependencies

First, we have to add dependencies to establish a connection to MySQL. We use all the same dependencies as in the previous example, but have replaced postgres with the mysql crate, and r2d2_postgres with the r2d2_mysql crate:

```
mysql = "14.1"
r2d2_mysql = "9.0"
```

We still need the csv, rayon, r2d2, and serde family crates.

You also have to declare other types to use them in the code, as follows:

```
use mysql::{Conn, Error, Opts, OptsBuilder};
use r2d2_mysql::MysqlConnectionManager;
```

Database interaction functions

Now, we can replace our `Connection` instance from the `postgres` crate with `Conn` from the `mysql` crate to provide our interaction functions. The first function, `create_table`, uses a mutable reference to a `Conn` instance:

```
fn create_table(conn: &mut Conn) -> Result<(), Error> {
    conn.query("CREATE TABLE users (
                    id INT(6) UNSIGNED AUTO_INCREMENT PRIMARY KEY,
                    name VARCHAR(50) NOT NULL,
                    email VARCHAR(50) NOT NULL
                )")
        .map(drop)
}
```

Also, we used the `query` method of the `Conn` connection object to send a query. This method doesn't expect parameters. We still ignore the successful result of a query and `drop` it with `map`.

The next function, `create_user`, has transformed into the following form:

```
fn create_user(conn: &mut Conn, user: &User) -> Result<(), Error> {
    conn.prep_exec("INSERT INTO users (name, email) VALUES (?, ?)",
                (&user.name, &user.email))
        .map(drop)
}
```

We use the `prep_exec` method of `Conn`, which expects a tuple of parameters that we have extracted from `User` struct fields. As you can see, we used the `?` char to specify where to insert the value.

The last function, `list_users`, collects users from a query. It's more complex than the version for PostgreSQL. We used the `query` method which returns a `QueryResult` type that implements the `Iterator` trait. We use this property to convert the result in to an iterator, and try to fold values to a vector in the `try_fold` method of the `Iterator` implementation:

```
fn list_users(conn: &mut Conn) -> Result<Vec<User>, Error> {
    conn.query("SELECT name, email FROM users")?
        .into_iter()
        .try_fold(Vec::new(), |mut vec, row| {
            let row = row?;
```

```
            let user = User {
                name: row.get_opt(0).unwrap()?,
                email: row.get_opt(1).unwrap()?,
            };
            vec.push(user);
            Ok(vec)
        })
    }
```

For the `try_fold` method call, we provide a closure that expects two arguments: the first is a vector that we pass with the `try_fold` call, while the second is a Row instance. We use `try_fold` to return Error if any row conversion to user fails.

We use the `get_opt` method of the Row object to get a value of a corresponding type, and use the ? operator to extract it from a result, or return Error with `try_fold`. In every iteration, we return a vector with a new, appended value.

Creating a connection pool

We will reuse the arguments parser from the previous example, but will rewrite the code that establish a connection, because we're using MySQL instead of PostgreSQL now. First, we replaced the database link with the `mysql` scheme. We will use the same parameters for the connection as those that we used to bootstrap the MySQL server instance.

We convert the address string to the Opts - options of a connections, the type of mysql crate that's used to set parameters for connections. But `MysqlConnectionManager` expects us to provide an `OptsBuilder` object. Look at the following code:

```
let addr = matches.value_of("database")
    .unwrap_or("mysql://root:password@localhost:3306/test");
let opts = Opts::from_url(addr)?;
let builder = OptsBuilder::from_opts(opts);
let manager = MysqlConnectionManager::new(builder);
let pool = r2d2::Pool::new(manager)?;
let mut conn = pool.get()?;
```

Now, we can create `MysqlConnectionManager` using `builder`, and we can create `r2d2::Pool` with a `manager` instance. We also get a mutable `conn` reference to a connection to provide it for subcommands.

The good news is that it's enough to start. We don't need to change anything in our branches, except the type of reference. Now, we have to pass a mutable reference to the connection:

```
(CMD_CRATE, _) => {
    create_table(&mut conn)?;
}
```

Try to start and check how the tool works. We will provide it a CSV file with content in the following format:

```
name,email
user01,user01@example.com
user02,user02@example.com
user03,user03@example.com
```

If you want to check whether the database has really changed, try importing user data from our CSV file:

```
cargo run -- import < users.csv
```

You can use the `mysql` client to print the `users` table:

```
mysql> SELECT * FROM users;
+----+--------+---------------------+
| id | name   | email               |
+----+--------+---------------------+
|  1 | user01 | user01@example.com  |
|  2 | user03 | user03@example.com  |
|  3 | user08 | user08@example.com  |
|  4 | user06 | user06@example.com  |
|  5 | user02 | user02@example.com  |
|  6 | user07 | user07@example.com  |
|  7 | user04 | user04@example.com  |
|  8 | user09 | user09@example.com  |
|  9 | user10 | user10@example.com  |
| 10 | user05 | user05@example.com  |
+----+--------+---------------------+
10 rows in set (0.00 sec)
```

It works! As you can see, users were added in an unpredictable order, because we used multiple connections and real concurrency. Now you have knowledge of how to use SQL databases. It's time to look at interacting with NoSQL databases through the `r2d2` crate.

Redis

When writing microservices, you may sometimes need a data store that can keep values by keys; for example, if you want to store session, you can store a protected identifier of the session and keep additional information about users in a persistent cache. It's not a problem if a session's data is lost; on the contrary, it is a best practice to clean sessions periodically in case a user's session identifier is stolen.

Redis is a popular in-memory data structure store for this use case. It can be used as a database, as a message broker, or as a cache. In the following section, we will run a Redis instance with Docker and create a command-line tool that helps manage a users' sessions in Redis.

Bootstrap database for tests

Redis has an official image, `redis`, on Docker Hub. To create and run a container, use the following command:

```
docker run -it --rm --name test-redis -p 6379:6379 redis
```

This command runs a container from the `redis` image with the name `test-redis`, and forwards local port `6379` to the internal port `6379` of the container.

An interesting fact about Redis is that it uses a very plain and simple interaction protocol. You can even use `telnet` to interact with Redis:

```
telnet 127.0.0.1 6379
Trying 127.0.0.1...
Connected to 127.0.0.1.
Escape character is '^]'.
SET session-1 "Rust"
+OK
GET session-1
$4
Rust
^]
```

The native client is more comfortable to use, but it expects the same commands as the raw protocol.

To shut down a container running Redis, use this command:

```
docker stop test-redis
```

Let's create a tool to manage sessions in Redis.

Creating a connection pool

We have started a Redis instance in a Docker container, so now, we can start creating a command-line tool to allow us to connect to that database instance and put some information into it. This utility will be different from the ones we created for PostgreSQL and MySQL, because Redis doesn't use the SQL language. We will use specific API methods that are available in Redis.

In this section, we will create a new binary crate and add functions that set or get data from Redis using r2d2::Pool. After this, we will call them in response to subcommands that a user specified as command-line arguments for the command.

Dependencies

Create a new binary crate and add all of the necessary dependencies to the Cargo.toml file of that crate:

```
[dependencies]
clap = "2.32"
failure = "0.1"
r2d2 = "0.8"
r2d2_redis = "0.8"
redis = "0.9"
```

We added the dependencies that we used in the previous examples of this chapter—clap, failure, and r2d2. Also, we need the redis and r2d2_redis crates, which contain a connection manager for Redis so that we can use it with Pool from the r2d2 crate.

Next, let's import the types we need to create a tool:

```
use clap::{
    crate_authors, crate_description, crate_name, crate_version,
    App, AppSettings, Arg, SubCommand,
};
use redis::{Commands, Connection, RedisError};
use r2d2_redis::RedisConnectionManager;
use std::collections::HashMap;
```

Note the usage of some types. We imported `Connection` as a main connection type, which we will use to connect to a Redis instance. We also imported `RedisConnectionManager` from the `r2d2_redis` crate. This type allows `Pool` to create new connections. The last thing you should note is the `Command` trait. This trait contains methods that reflect the Redis client API. The names of methods are the same (but in lowercase), as you can see in the Redis protocol. We tested it manually in a previous section. The `Command` trait, implemented by a `Connection` struct, allows you to call methods of the Redis API.

 Redis supports a lot of commands. You can find a full list at `https://redis.io/commands`. The `redis` crate provides most of them as methods of the `Command` trait.

Adding commands and interaction functions

The tool that we are creating for Redis will support three commands:

- `add` - adds a new session record
- `remove` - removes a session record by key (that is, by username)
- `list` - prints all session records

We need constants for the name of every subcommand to prevent mistakes in strings in the code:

```
const SESSIONS: &str = "sessions";
const CMD_ADD: &str = "add";
const CMD_REMOVE: &str = "remove";
const CMD_LIST: &str = "list";
```

This list also contains the `SESSION` constant as the name of the `HashMap` in Redis. Now, we can declare functions to manipulate session data.

Data manipulation functions

Our example needs three functions. The first function, add_session, adds an association between the token and user ID:

```
fn add_session(conn: &Connection, token: &str, uid: &str) -> Result<(),
RedisError> {
    conn.hset(SESSIONS, token, uid)
}
```

This function only calls the hset method of a Connection and sets the uid value by the token key in the SESSIONS map. It returns RedisError if something is wrong with a set operation.

The next function, remove_session, is also pretty simple and calls the hdel method of Connection:

```
fn remove_session(conn: &Connection, token: &str) -> Result<(), RedisError>
{
    conn.hdel(SESSIONS, token)
}
```

This function deletes a record with the token key from the SESSIONS map.

The last function, list_sessions, returns all token-uid pairs as a HashMap instance from the SESSION map. It uses the hgetall method of Connection, which calls the HGETALL method in Redis:

```
fn list_sessions(conn: &Connection) -> Result<HashMap<String, String>,
RedisError> {
    conn.hgetall(SESSIONS)
}
```

As you can see, all functions map to raw Redis commands, which looks pretty simple. But all functions do a good job in the background too, converting values to their corresponding Rust types.

Now, we can create an arguments parser for the session tool.

Parsing arguments

Since our command supports three subcommands, we have to add them to a `clap::App` instance:

```
let matches = App::new(crate_name!())
    .version(crate_version!())
    .author(crate_authors!())
    .about(crate_description!())
    .setting(AppSettings::SubcommandRequired)
    .arg(
        Arg::with_name("database")
        .short("d")
        .long("db")
        .value_name("ADDR")
        .help("Sets an address of db connection")
        .takes_value(true),
        )
    .subcommand(SubCommand::with_name(CMD_ADD).about("add a session")
                .arg(Arg::with_name("TOKEN")
                    .help("Sets the token of a user")
                    .required(true)
                    .index(1))
                .arg(Arg::with_name("UID")
                    .help("Sets the uid of a user")
                    .required(true)
                    .index(2)))
    .subcommand(SubCommand::with_name(CMD_REMOVE).about("remove a session")
                .arg(Arg::with_name("TOKEN")
                    .help("Sets the token of a user")
                    .required(true)
                    .index(1)))
    .subcommand(SubCommand::with_name(CMD_LIST).about("print list of
sessions")))
    .get_matches();
```

As in previous examples, this can also use the `--database` argument with a link to a Redis connection. It supports two subcommands. The `add` subcommand expects a session `TOKEN` and the `UID` of the user. The `remove` command expects a session `TOKEN` only to remove it from a map. The `list` command doesn't expect any parameters and prints a list of sessions.

Imagine the structure of data in this example as a cache for sessions that holds associations between `token` and `uid`. After authorization, we can send the token as a secure cookie and extract the user's `uid` for the provided token for every microservice to achieve loose coupling between microservices. We will explore this concept in detail later.

Now, we are ready to connect to Redis with `r2d2::Pool`.

Connecting to Redis

The `r2d2` connection to Redis looks similar to other databases:

```
let addr = matches.value_of("database")
    .unwrap_or("redis://127.0.0.1/");
let manager = RedisConnectionManager::new(addr)?;
let pool = r2d2::Pool::builder().build(manager)?;
let conn = pool.get()?;
```

We get the address from the `--database` argument, but if it isn't set, we will use the default value, `redis://127.0.0.1/`. After that, we will create a new `RedisConnectionManager` instance and pass it to the `Pool::new` method.

Executing subcommands

We use the structure of branches to match subcommands from our previous examples:

```
match matches.subcommand() {
    (CMD_ADD, Some(matches)) => {
        let token = matches.value_of("TOKEN").unwrap();
        let uid = matches.value_of("UID").unwrap();
        add_session(&conn, token, uid)?;
    }
    (CMD_REMOVE, Some(matches)) => {
        let token = matches.value_of("TOKEN").unwrap();
        remove_session(&conn, token)?;
    }
    (CMD_LIST, _) => {
        println!("LIST");
        let sessions = list_sessions(&conn)?;
        for (token, uid) in sessions {
            println!("Token: {:20}   Uid: {:20}", token, uid);
```

```
        }
    }
    _ => { matches.usage(); }
}
```

For the `add` subcommand, we extract the `TOKEN` and `UID` values from arguments and pass them to the `add_session` function with a reference to a `Connector`. For the `remove` subcommand, we extract only the `TOKEN` value and call the `remove_session` function with its corresponding parameters. For the `list` subcommand, we call the `list_session` function as is, because we don't need any extra parameters to get all values from a map. This returns a vector of pairs. The first item of the pair contains `token`, and the second contains `uid`. We print the values using a fixed width specifier of `{:20}`.

Testing our Redis example

Let's compile and test the tool. We will add three sessions of users:

```
cargo run -- add 7vQ2MhnRcyYeTptp a73bbfe3-df6a-4dea-93a8-cb4ea3998a53
cargo run -- add pTySt8FI7TIqId4N 0f3688be-0efc-4744-829c-be5d177e0e1c
cargo run -- add zJx3mBRpJ9WTkwGU f985a744-6648-4d0a-af5c-0b71aecdbcba
```

To print the list, run the `list` command:

```
cargo run -- list
```

With this, you will see all the sessions you have created:

```
LIST
Token: pTySt8FI7TIqId4N     Uid: 0f3688be-0efc-4744-829c-be5d177e0e1c
Token: zJx3mBRpJ9WTkwGU     Uid: f985a744-6648-4d0a-af5c-0b71aecdbcba
Token: 7vQ2MhnRcyYeTptp     Uid: a73bbfe3-df6a-4dea-93a8-cb4ea3998a53
```

We've learned how to use Redis. It's useful to store messages for caching something. Next in line is the last NoSQL database we'll look at: MongoDB.

MongoDB

MongoDB is a popular NoSQL database that has great features and good performance. It's really good for data that changes structure quickly, such as the following:

- Operational intelligence (logs and reports)
- Product data management (product catalog, hierarchies, and categories)
- Content management systems (posts, comments, and other records)

We will create an example that stores the activities of a user.

Bootstrapping a database for testing

We will use the official Docker image to bootstrap a MongoDB instance. You can do it simply with the following command:

```
docker run -it --rm --name test-mongo -p 27017:27017 mongo
```

This command runs a container with the name `test-mongo` from the `mongo` image, and forwards the local port `27017` to the same internal port of the container. The data that container produces will be removed after container shutdown.

If you have a `mongo` client, you can use it to connect to an instance of database inside the container:

```
mongo 127.0.0.1:27017/admin
```

When you need to shut down the container, use the `stop` subcommand of `docker` and specify the `name` of the container:

```
docker stop test-mongo
```

It can also be terminated with *Ctrl* + *C* if you attached the container to a Terminal with `-it` arguments, as I did previously.

Now, we can look how to connect to a database using `mongo` and the `r2d2-mongo` crate.

Connecting to a database using the r2d2 pool

By tradition, we will use a `Pool` from the `r2d2` crate, but in this example (as in the Redis example), we don't use multiple connections at once. Add all of the necessary dependencies to a new binary crate:

```
[dependencies]
bson = "0.13"
chrono = { version = "0.4", features = ["serde"] }
clap = "2.32"
failure = "0.1"
mongodb = "0.3"
r2d2 = "0.8"
r2d2-mongodb = "0.1"
serde = "1.0"
serde_derive = "1.0"
url = "1.7"
```

The list is not small. Besides the crates you already familiar with, we've added the `bson`, `chrono`, and `url` crates. The first crate we need to work with data in the database; the second, to use the `Utc` type; and the last to split URL strings into pieces.

Import all the necessary types, as follows:

```
use chrono::offset::Utc;
use clap::{
    crate_authors, crate_description, crate_name, crate_version,
    App, AppSettings, Arg, SubCommand,
};
use mongodb::Error;
use mongodb::db::{Database, ThreadedDatabase};
use r2d2::Pool;
use r2d2_mongodb::{ConnectionOptionsBuilder, MongodbConnectionManager};
use url::Url;
```

This user's logging tool will support two commands: `add` to add a record, and `list` to print a list of all records. Add the following necessary constants:

```
const CMD_ADD: &str = "add";
const CMD_LIST: &str = "list";
```

To set and get structured data, we need to declare an `Activity` struct that will be used to create a BSON document and to restore it from BSON data, because MongoDB uses this format for data interaction. The `Activity` struct has three fields, `user_id`, `activity`, and `datetime`:

```
#[derive(Deserialize, Debug)]
struct Activity {
    user_id: String,
    activity: String,
    datetime: String,
}
```

Interaction functions

Since we have a declared structure, we can add functions to work with databases. The first function we will add is `add_activity` which adds an activity record to a database:

```
fn add_activity(conn: &Database, activity: Activity) -> Result<(), Error> {
    let doc = doc! {
        "user_id": activity.user_id,
        "activity": activity.activity,
        "datetime": activity.datetime,
    };
    let coll = conn.collection("activities");
    coll.insert_one(doc, None).map(drop)
}
```

This function only converts the `Activity` struct into a BSON document, and does this by extracting fields from a struct and construct BSON document with the same fields. We can derive the `Serialize` trait for the structure and use automatic serialization, but I used the `doc!` macro for demonstration purposes to show you that you can add a free-form document that can be constructed on the fly.

To add `Activity`, we get a collection called `activities` from a `Database` instance by reference to the `collection()` method, and call the `insert_one` method of `Collection` to add a record.

The next method is `list_activities`. This method uses a `Database` instance to find all values in the *activities* collection. We use the `find()` method of `Collection` to get data, but make sure to set filter (the first argument) to `None`, and options (the second argument) to `None`, to get all of the values from a collection.

You can tweak these parameters for filtering, or to limit the quantity of records you retrieve:

```
fn list_activities(conn: &Database) -> Result<Vec<Activity>, Error> {
    conn.collection("activities").find(None, None)?
        .try_fold(Vec::new(), |mut vec, doc| {
            let doc = doc?;
            let activity: Activity =
bson::from_bson(bson::Bson::Document(doc))?;
            vec.push(activity);
            Ok(vec)
        })
}
```

To convert every record returned by the find query as a BSON document, we can use the bson::from_bson method, since we have derived the Deserialize trait for the Activity struct. The try_fold method lets us interrupt folding if conversion should fail. We push all successfully converted values to the vector that we provided as the first argument to the try_fold method call. Now, we can parse arguments so that we can prepare a pool to use for calling declared interaction functions.

Parsing arguments

Our tool expects two subcommands: add and list. Let's add them to a clap::App instance. Like all previous examples, we also added a --database argument to set the connection URL. Look at the following code:

```
let matches = App::new(crate_name!())
    .version(crate_version!())
    .author(crate_authors!())
    .about(crate_description!())
    .setting(AppSettings::SubcommandRequired)
    .arg(
        Arg::with_name("database")
        .short("d")
        .long("db")
        .value_name("ADDR")
        .help("Sets an address of db connection")
        .takes_value(true),
        )
        .subcommand(SubCommand::with_name(CMD_ADD).about("add user to the
table")
                .arg(Arg::with_name("USER_ID")
```

```
                              .help("Sets the id of a user")
                              .required(true)
                              .index(1))
                      .arg(Arg::with_name("ACTIVITY")
                              .help("Sets the activity of a user")
                              .required(true)
                              .index(2)))
          .subcommand(SubCommand::with_name(CMD_LIST).about("print activities
  list of users"))
          .get_matches();
```

The `add` subcommand expects two parameters: `USER_ID` and `ACTIVITY`. Both are represented as `String` type values in the `Activity` struct. We will require these arguments, but we'll get any provided values without any restrictions. The `list` subcommand has no extra arguments.

Creating a connections pool

To connect to a database, we extract the connection URL from the `--database` command-line argument. If it isn't set, we use the `mongodb://localhost:27017/admin` default value:

```
let addr = matches.value_of("database")
    .unwrap_or("mongodb://localhost:27017/admin");
let url = Url::parse(addr)?;
```

But we also parse it to the `Url` struct. This is necessary because MongoDB connections expect options sets to be collected by separate values:

```
let opts = ConnectionOptionsBuilder::new()
    .with_host(url.host_str().unwrap_or("localhost"))
    .with_port(url.port().unwrap_or(27017))
    .with_db(&url.path()[1..])
    .build();

let manager = MongodbConnectionManager::new(opts);

let pool = Pool::builder()
    .max_size(4)
    .build(manager)?;

let conn = pool.get()?;
```

In the preceding code, we create a new `ConnectionOptionsBuilder` instance and populate it with values from a parsed `Url` instance. We set `host`, `port`, and the `db` name. As you can see, we skip the first character of the path so that we can use it as the name of the database. Call the `build` method to build the `ConnectionOptions` struct. Now, we can create a `MongodbConnectionManager` instance and use it to create a `Pool` instance. But, in this example, we called the `builder` method, instead of `new`, to show you how you can set the number of connections in a `Pool` instance. We set this to 4. After that, we called the `build` method to create a `Pool` instance. As in previous examples, we call the `get` method of a `Pool` to get a `Database` connection object from a pool.

Implementing subcommands

The implementation of subcommands is simple. For the `add` subcommand, we extract two arguments, `USER_ID` and `ACTIVITY`, and use them to create an `Activity` struct instance. We also get the current time with the `Utc::now` method and save it to a `datetime` field of `Activity`. Finally, we call the `add_activity` method to add the `Activity` instance to the MongoDB database:

```
match matches.subcommand() {
    (CMD_ADD, Some(matches)) => {
        let user_id = matches.value_of("USER_ID").unwrap().to_owned();
        let activity = matches.value_of("ACTIVITY").unwrap().to_owned();
        let activity = Activity {
            user_id,
            activity,
            datetime: Utc::now().to_string(),
        };
        add_activity(&conn, activity)?;
    }
    (CMD_LIST, _) => {
        let list = list_activities(&conn)?;
        for item in list {
            println!("User: {:20}    Activity: {:20}    DateTime: {:20}",
                    item.user_id, item.activity, item.datetime);
        }
    }
    _ => { matches.usage(); }
}
```

The list subcommand calls the `list_activities` function, and then iterates over all records to print them to a Terminal. The logging tool is finished – we can test it now.

Testing

Compile and run the tool with the following command:

```
cargo run -- add 43fb507d-4cee-431a-a7eb-af31a1eeed02 "Logged In"
cargo run -- add 43fb507d-4cee-431a-a7eb-af31a1eeed02 "Added contact
information"
cargo run -- add 43fb507d-4cee-431a-a7eb-af31a1eeed02 "E-mail confirmed"
```

Print a list of added records with the following command:

```
cargo run -- list
```

This will print the following output:

```
User: 43fb507d-4cee-431a-a7eb-af31a1eeed02    DateTime: 2018-11-30
14:19:26.245957656 UTC    Activity: Logged In
User: 43fb507d-4cee-431a-a7eb-af31a1eeed02    DateTime: 2018-11-30
14:19:42.249548906 UTC   Activity: Added contact information
User: 43fb507d-4cee-431a-a7eb-af31a1eeed02    DateTime: 2018-11-30
14:19:59.035373758 UTC    Activity: E-mail confirmed
```

You can also check the result with the `mongo` client:

```
mongo admin
> db.activities.find()
{ "_id" : ObjectId("5c0146ee6531339934e7090c"), "user_id" :
"43fb507d-4cee-431a-a7eb-af31a1eeed02", "activity" : "Logged In",
"datetime" : "2018-11-30 14:19:26.245957656 UTC" }
{ "_id" : ObjectId("5c0146fe653133b8345ed772"), "user_id" :
"43fb507d-4cee-431a-a7eb-af31a1eeed02", "activity" : "Added contact
information", "datetime" : "2018-11-30 14:19:42.249548906 UTC" }
{ "_id" : ObjectId("5c01470f653133cf34391c1f"), "user_id" :
"43fb507d-4cee-431a-a7eb-af31a1eeed02", "activity" : "E-mail confirmed",
"datetime" : "2018-11-30 14:19:59.035373758 UTC" }
```

You did it! It works well! Now, you know how to use all popular databases with Rust. In the next chapter, we will improve on this knowledge with **object-relational mapping** (**ORM**), which helps to simplify database structure declaration, interaction, and migrations.

DynamoDB

We used local database instances in this chapter. The disadvantage of maintaining databases yourself is that you also have to take care of scalability yourself. There are a lot of services that provide popular databases that automatically scale to meet your needs. But not every database can grow without limits: traditional SQL databases often experience speed performance issues when tables become huge. For large datasets, you should choose to use key-value databases (such as NoSQL) that provide scalability by design. In this section, we will explore the usage of DynamoDB, which was created by Amazon, to provide an easily scalable database as a service.

To use AWS services, you need the AWS SDK, but there is no official SDK for Rust, so we will use the rusoto crate, which provides the AWS API in Rust. Let's start by porting the tool, which we created earlier in this chapter, to DynamoDB. First, we should create a table in the DynamoDB instance.

Bootstrapping a database for testing

Since AWS services are paid-for, it's better to bootstrap a local instance of the DynamoDB database for development or testing your application. There is an image of DynamoDB on Docker Hub. Run the instance with this command:

```
docker run -it --rm --name test-dynamodb -p 8000:8000 amazon/dynamodb-local
```

This command creates an instance of a database and forwards port 8000 of a container to a local port with the same number.

To work with this database instance, you need the AWS CLI tool. This can be installed using the instructions from https://docs.aws.amazon.com/cli/latest/userguide/cli-chap-install.html. On Linux, I use the following command:

```
pip install awscli --upgrade --user
```

This command doesn't need administration privileges to be installed. After I installed the tool, I created a user with programmatic access, as detailed here: https://console.aws.amazon.com/iam/home#/users$new?step=details. You can read more about creating a user account to access the AWS API here: https://docs.aws.amazon.com/IAM/latest/UserGuide/getting-started_create-admin-group.html.

When you have a user for programmatic access, you can configure the AWS CLI using the `configure` subcommand:

```
aws configure
AWS Access Key ID [None]: <your-access-key>
AWS Secret Access Key [None]: <your-secret-key>
Default region name [None]: us-east-1
Default output format [None]: json
```

The subcommand asks you for your user credentials, default region, and desired output format. Fill in those fields as appropriate.

Now, we can create a table using the AWS CLI tool. Enter the following command into the console:

```
aws dynamodb create-table --cli-input-json file://table.json --endpoint-url
http://localhost:8000 --region custom
```

This command creates a table from a declaration in JSON format from the `table.json` file in the local database, with an endpoint of `localhost:8000`. This is the address of the container we have started. Look at the contents of this table declaration file:

```json
{
    "TableName" : "Locations",
    "KeySchema": [
        {
            "AttributeName": "Uid",
            "KeyType": "HASH"
        },
        {
            "AttributeName": "TimeStamp",
            "KeyType": "RANGE"
        }
    ],
    "AttributeDefinitions": [
        {
            "AttributeName": "Uid",
            "AttributeType": "S"
        },
        {
            "AttributeName": "TimeStamp",
            "AttributeType": "S"
        }
    ],
    "ProvisionedThroughput": {
        "ReadCapacityUnits": 1,
        "WriteCapacityUnits": 1
```

```
      }
  }
```

This file contains a declaration of a table with two required attributes:

- `Uid` - This stores user identifiers. This attribute will be used as a partition key.
- `TimeStamp` - This stores a timestamp when location data is produced. This attribute will be used as a sorting key to order records.

You can check whether the database instance contains this new table with the following command:

```
aws dynamodb list-tables --endpoint-url http://localhost:8000 --region
custom
```

It prints the list of tables that the database instance contains, but our list is rather short, as we only have one table:

```
{
    "TableNames": [
        "Locations"
    ]
}
```

The database is prepared. Now, we will create a tool to add records to this table using Rust.

Connecting to DynamoDB

In this section, we will create a tool to add records to a table in our `DynamoDB` database, and also print all records from the table. First, we need to add all of the necessary crates.

Adding dependencies

To work with the AWS API, we will use the `rusoto` crate. Actually, it isn't a single crate, but a set of crates where every single crate covers some functionality of the AWS API. The basic crate is `rusoto_core`, which contains the `Region` struct that represents an address of the AWS API endpoint. `Region` is often necessary for other crates. Also, the `rusoto_core` crate re-exports the `rusoto_credential` crate, which contains types for loading and managing AWS credentials to access the API.

To interact with the `DynamoDB` database, we need to add the `rusoto_dynamodb` dependency. The full list looks like this:

```
chrono = "0.4"

clap = "2.32"

failure = "0.1"

rusoto_core = "0.36.0"

rusoto_dynamodb = "0.36.0"
```

We also added the `chrono` dependency to generate timestamps and convert them to ISO-8601 format strings. We use the `clap` crate to parse command-line arguments, and the `failure` crate to return a generic `Error` type from the `main` function.

We need the following types in our code:

```
use chrono::Utc;

use clap::{App, AppSettings, Arg, SubCommand,
    crate_authors, crate_description, crate_name, crate_version};

use failure::{Error, format_err};

use rusoto_core::Region;

use rusoto_dynamodb::{AttributeValue, DynamoDb, DynamoDbClient,
    QueryInput, UpdateItemInput};

use std::collections::HashMap;
```

It's worth paying attention to types that are imported from the `rusoto_core` and `rusoto_dynamodb` crates. We imported the `Region` struct, which is used to set the location of the AWS endpoint. The `DynamoDb` trait, `DynamoDbClient`, is used to get access to a database. `AttributeValue` is a type used to represent values stored in DynamoDB's tables. `QueryInput` is a struct to prepare `query` and `UpdateItemInput` is a struct to prepare an `update_item` request.

Let's add functions to interact with the `DynamoDB` database.

Interaction functions

In this section, we will create a tool that stores location records to a database and query location points for a specific user. To represent a location in the code, we declare the following `Location` struct:

```
#[derive(Debug)]
struct Location {
    user_id: String,
    timestamp: String,
    longitude: String,
    latitude: String,
}
```

This struct keeps `user_id`, which represents the partition key, and `timestamp`, which represents the sort key.

 DynamoDB is a key-value storage, where every record has a unique key. When you declare tables, you have to decide which attributes will be the key of a record. You can choose up to two keys. The first is required and represents a partition key that's used to distribute data across database partitions. The second key is optional and represents an attribute that's used to sort items in a table.

The `rusoto_dynamodb` crate contains an `AttributeValue` struct, which is used in queries and results to insert or extract data from tables. Since every record (that is, every item) of a table is a set of attribute names to attribute values, we will add the `from_map` method to convert the `HashMap` of attributes to our `Location` type:

```
impl Location {
    fn from_map(map: HashMap<String, AttributeValue>) -> Result<Location,
Error> {
        let user_id = map
            .get("Uid")
            .ok_or_else(|| format_err!("No Uid in record"))
            .and_then(attr_to_string)?;
        let timestamp = map
            .get("TimeStamp")
            .ok_or_else(|| format_err!("No TimeStamp in record"))
            .and_then(attr_to_string)?;
        let latitude = map
            .get("Latitude")
            .ok_or_else(|| format_err!("No Latitude in record"))
            .and_then(attr_to_string)?;
        let longitude = map
            .get("Longitude")
```

```
                .ok_or_else(|| format_err!("No Longitude in record"))
                .and_then(attr_to_string)?;
            let location = Location { user_id, timestamp, longitude, latitude
    };

            Ok(location)
        }
    }
```

We need four attributes: `Uid`, `TimeStamp`, `Longitude`, and `Latitude`. We extract every attribute from the map and convert it into a `Location` instance using the `attr_to_string` method:

```
fn attr_to_string(attr: &AttributeValue) -> Result<String, Error> {
    if let Some(value) = &attr.s {
        Ok(value.to_owned())
    } else {
        Err(format_err!("no string value"))
    }
}
```

The `AttributeValue` struct contains multiple fields for different types of values:

- `b` - A binary value represented by `Vec<u8>`
- `bool` - A boolean value with the `bool` type
- `bs` - A binary set, but represented as `Vec<Vec<u8>>`
- `l` - A list of attributes of a `Vec<AttributeValue>` type
- `m` - A map of attributes of a `HashMap<String, AttributeValue>` type
- `n` - A number stored as a `String` type to keep the exact value without any precision loss
- `ns` - A set of numbers as a `Vec<String>`
- `null` - Used to represent a null value and stored as `bool`, which means the value is null
- `s` - A string, of the `String` type
- `ss` - A set of strings, of the `Vec<String>` type

You might notice that there is no data type for timestamps. This is true, as `DynamoDB` uses strings for most types of data.

We use the `s` field to work with string values that we'll add with the `add_location` function:

```
fn add_location(conn: &DynamoDbClient, location: Location) -> Result<(),
Error> {
```

```rust
let mut key: HashMap<String, AttributeValue> = HashMap::new();
key.insert("Uid".into(), s_attr(location.user_id));
key.insert("TimeStamp".into(), s_attr(location.timestamp));
let expression = format!("SET Latitude = :y, Longitude = :x");
let mut values = HashMap::new();
values.insert(":y".into(), s_attr(location.latitude));
values.insert(":x".into(), s_attr(location.longitude));
let update = UpdateItemInput {
    table_name: "Locations".into(),
    key,
    update_expression: Some(expression),
    expression_attribute_values: Some(values),
    ..Default::default()
};
conn.update_item(update)
    .sync()
    .map(drop)
    .map_err(Error::from)
}
```

This function expects two parameters: a reference to a database client, and a `Location`
instance to store. We have to prepare data manually to get it as an attributes map for
storage, because `DynamoDbClient` takes values of the `AttributeValue` type only. The
attributes included in the key are inserted into the `HashMap`, with values extracted from
the `Location` instance and converted into `AttributeValue` using the `s_attr` function,
which has the following declaration:

```rust
fn s_attr(s: String) -> AttributeValue {
    AttributeValue {
        s: Some(s),
        ..Default::default()
    }
}
```

After we've filled the `key` map, we can set other attributes with expressions. To set
attributes to an item, we have to specify them in DynamoDB syntax, along the lines of `SET
Longitude = :x, Latitude = :y`. This expression means that we add two attributes
with the names `Longitude` and `Latitude`. In the preceding expression, we used the
placeholders of `:x` and `:y`, which will be replaced with real values that we pass in from
the `HashMap`.

More information about expressions can be found here: `https://docs.`
`aws.amazon.com/amazondynamodb/latest/developerguide/Expressions.`
`html`.

When all of the data prepared, we fill the `UpdateItemInput` struct and set `table_name` to `"Locations"`, because it requires this as an argument for the `update_item` method of `DynamoDbClient`.

The `update_item` method returns `RusotoFuture`, which implements the `Future` trait that we explored in Chapter 5, *Understanding Asynchronous Operations with Futures Crate*. You can use the `rusoto` crate in asynchronous applications. Since we don't use a reactor or asynchronous operations in this example, we will call the `sync` method of `RusotoFuture`, which blocks the current thread and waits for `Result`.

We have implemented a method to create new data items to the table and now we need a function to retrieve data from this table. The following `list_locations` function gets a list of `Location` for a specific user from the `Locations` table:

```rust
fn list_locations(conn: &DynamoDbClient, user_id: String) ->
Result<Vec<Location>, Error> {
    let expression = format!("Uid = :uid");
    let mut values = HashMap::new();
    values.insert(":uid".into(), s_attr(user_id));
    let query = QueryInput {
        table_name: "Locations".into(),
        key_condition_expression: Some(expression),
        expression_attribute_values: Some(values),
        ..Default::default()
    };
    let items = conn.query(query).sync()?
        .items
        .ok_or_else(|| format_err!("No Items"))?;
    let mut locations = Vec::new();
    for item in items {
        let location = Location::from_map(item)?;
        locations.push(location);
    }
    Ok(locations)
}
```

The `list_locations` function expects a reference to the `DynamoDbClient` instance and a string with if of user. If there are items in the table for the requested user, they are returned as a `Vec` of items, converted into the `Location` type.

In this function, we use the `query` method of `DynamoDbClient`, which expects a `QueryInput` struct as an argument. We fill it with the name of the table, the condition of the key expression, and values to fill that expression. We use a simple `Uid = :uid` expression that queries items with the corresponding value of the `Uid` partition key. We use a `:uid` placeholder and create a `HashMap` instance with a `:uid` key and a `user_id` value, which is converted into `AttributeValue` with the `s_attr` function call.

Now, we have two functions to insert and query data. We will use them to implement a command-line tool to interact with `DynamoDB`. Let's start with parsing arguments for our tool.

Parsing command-line arguments

AWS is divided by regions, where each has its own endpoint to connect to services. Our tool will support two arguments to set a region and endpoint:

```
.arg(
    Arg::with_name("region")
    .long("region")
    .value_name("REGION")
    .help("Sets a region")
    .takes_value(true),
    )
.arg(
    Arg::with_name("endpoint")
    .long("endpoint-url")
    .value_name("URL")
    .help("Sets an endpoint url")
    .takes_value(true),
    )
```

We add both to `App` instance. The tool will support two commands to add a new item and to print all items. The first subcommand is `add` and it expects three arguments: `USER_ID`, `LONGITUDE`, and `LATITUDE`:

```
.subcommand(SubCommand::with_name(CMD_ADD).about("add geo record to the
table")
            .arg(Arg::with_name("USER_ID")
                .help("Sets the id of a user")
                .required(true)
                .index(1))
            .arg(Arg::with_name("LATITUDE")
                .help("Sets a latitudelongitude of location")
                .required(true)
                .index(2))
```

```
            .arg(Arg::with_name("LONGITUDE")
                .help("Sets a longitude of location")
                .required(true)
                .index(3)))
```

The `list` subcommand requires `USER_ID` in arguments only:

```
.subcommand(SubCommand::with_name(CMD_LIST).about("print all records for
the user")
            .arg(Arg::with_name("USER_ID")
                .help("User if to filter records")
                .required(true)
                .index(1)))
```

Add all of the preceding code to the `main` function. We can use these arguments to create a `Region` instance that we can use for a connection with `DynamoDB`:

```
let region = matches.value_of("endpoint").map(|endpoint| {
    Region::Custom {
        name: "custom".into(),
        endpoint: endpoint.into(),
    }
}).ok_or_else(|| format_err!("Region not set"))
.or_else(|_| {
    matches.value_of("region")
        .unwrap_or("us-east-1")
        .parse()
})?;
```

The code works according to the following logic: if a user sets the `--endpoint-url` parameter, we create a `Region` with a custom name and provide an `endpoint` value. If `endpoint` is not set, we try to parse the `--region` parameter to the `Region` instance, or just use the `us-east-1` value by default.

 AWS takes the region value seriously, and if you create a table in one region, you can't access that table from another region. We used a custom name for the region, but for production tools, it's better to use the `~/.aws/config` file or provide the flexibility to customize these settings.

Now, we can use the `Region` value to create a `DynamoDbClient` instance:

```
let client = DynamoDbClient::new(region);
```

The `DynamoDbClient` struct is used for sending queries to our `DynamoDB` instance. We will use this instance in the implementation of our commands. Do you remember the `match` expression that parses command-line arguments? Add this implementation for the `add` subcommand first, which puts a new item in a table, as follows:

```
(CMD_ADD, Some(matches)) => {
    let user_id = matches.value_of("USER_ID").unwrap().to_owned();
    let timestamp = Utc::now().to_string();
    let latitude = matches.value_of("LATITUDE").unwrap().to_owned();
    let longitude = matches.value_of("LONGITUDE").unwrap().to_owned();
    let location = Location { user_id, timestamp, latitude, longitude };
    add_location(&client, location)?;
}
```

The implementation is simple—we extract all provided arguments, generate a timestamp using the `Utc::now` call, and convert it into a `String` type in the ISO-8601 format. Lastly, we fill the `Location` instance and call the `add_location` function that we declared before.

 Have you ever wondered why databases use the ISO-8601 format to represent dates, which look like YEAR-MONTH-DATE HOUR:MINUTE:SECOND? That's because dates stored in strings in this format are ordered chronologically if sorted alphabetically. It's very convenient: you can sort dates to get the earliest on top and the latest at the bottom.

We still need to implement the `list` subcommand:

```
(CMD_LIST, Some(matches)) => {
    let user_id = matches.value_of("USER_ID").unwrap().to_owned();
    let locations = list_locations(&client, user_id)?;
    for location in locations {
        println!("{:?}", location);
    }
}
```

This command extracts USER_ID arguments and calls the `list_locations` function with the provided `user_id` value. Finally, we iterate over all locations and print them to the Terminal.

The implementation is finished and we can try it now.

Testing

To test the tool, start the `DynamoDB` instance with Docker and create a table, like we did before in this chapter. Let's add four locations of two users:

```
cargo run -- --endpoint-url http://localhost:8000 add
651B4984-1252-4ECE-90E7-0C8B58541E7C 52.73169 41.44326
cargo run -- --endpoint-url http://localhost:8000 add
651B4984-1252-4ECE-90E7-0C8B58541E7C 52.73213 41.44443
cargo run -- --endpoint-url http://localhost:8000 add
651B4984-1252-4ECE-90E7-0C8B58541E7C 52.73124 41.44435
cargo run -- --endpoint-url http://localhost:8000 add 7E3E27D0-D002-43C4-
A0DF-415B2F5FF94D 35.652832 139.839478
```

We also set the `--endpoint-url` argument to target our client to a local `DynamoDB` instance. When all records have been added, we can use the `list` subcommand to print all of the values of the specified user:

```
cargo run -- --endpoint-url http://localhost:8000 list
651B4984-1252-4ECE-90E7-0C8B58541E7C
```

This command prints something like the following:

```
Location { user_id: "651B4984-1252-4ECE-90E7-0C8B58541E7C", timestamp:
"2019-01-04 19:58:26.278518362 UTC", latitude: "52.73169", longitude:
"41.44326" }
Location { user_id: "651B4984-1252-4ECE-90E7-0C8B58541E7C", timestamp:
"2019-01-04 19:58:42.559125438 UTC", latitude: "52.73213", longitude:
"41.44443" }
Location { user_id: "651B4984-1252-4ECE-90E7-0C8B58541E7C", timestamp:
"2019-01-04 19:58:55.730794942 UTC", latitude: "52.73124", longitude:
"41.44435" }
```

As you can see, we retrieved all of the values in a sorted order, because we use the `TimeStamp` attribute as a sorting key of the table. Now, you know enough to create microservices that uses databases, but if you use the SQL database, you can add an extra abstraction layer and work with records of a database as native Rust structs, without writing glue code. In the next chapter, we will examine this approach with object-relational mappings.

Summary

In this chapter, we've covered a lot to do with databases. We started by creating a plain connection to PostgreSQL. After that, we added a pool of connections with the `r2d2` crate and used the `rayon` crate to execute SQL statements in parallel. We created a tool to manage our `users` database, and reimplemented it for our MySQL database.

We have also mastered some ways of interacting with NoSQL databases, in particular, Redis and MongoDB.

The last database we explored was DynamoDB, which is part of Amazon Web Services and can be scaled very easily.

For all examples, we run database instances in containers, because it's the simplest way to test interactions with databases. We haven't use database connections in microservices yet, because it requires a separate thread to avoid blocking. We will learn how to use background tasks with asynchronous code later, in `Chapter 10`, *Background Tasks and Thread Pools in Microservices*.

In the next chapter, we will explore a different approach to using databases—object-relational mapping with the `diesel` crate.

8
Interaction to Database with Object-Relational Mapping

In this chapter, we will continue to interact with databases, but this time we will explore **object-relational mapping** (**ORM**) using the `diesel` crate. This crate helps with generating Rust types that represent tables and records in SQL databases. ORM allows you to use native data structs in code and maps records and database tables to them. It's useful because the compiler takes care of matching types of data columns in a database and structs in source code.

After reading this chapter you will be familiar with the following:

- Using the `diesel` crate with `r2d2` pools
- Generating and applying migrations
- Accessing data with ORM types

Technical requirements

In this chapter, we will use the SQLite embedded database. You don't need to install and run databases, but you need development packages from the PostgreSQL, MySQL, and SQLite databases. Install them on your system.

You can find examples of this chapter on GitHub: `https://github.com/PacktPublishing/Hands-On-Microservices-with-Rust/tree/master/Chapter08`.

The diesel crate

In the previous chapter, we learned about interacting with different databases. But the approach we discussed has potential difficulties—you have to check the raw requests you add to your application. It's better if the Rust compiler controls the structure of the data and generates all the necessary requests for the declared structs. This formal and strict approach is possible with the diesel crate.

Rust has an awesome feature that creates macros and generates code. It allowed the creators of the diesel crate to create a domain-specific language to query data from a database. To start using this crate, we need to add it to a new project.

Adding the necessary dependencies

Create a new crate and add the following dependencies:

```
[dependencies]
clap = "2.32"
diesel = { version = "^1.1.0", features = ["sqlite", "r2d2"] }
failure = "0.1"
r2d2 = "0.8"
serde = "1.0"
serde_derive = "1.0"
uuid = { version = "0.5", features = ["serde", "v4"] }
```

We have added the clap, r2d2, and serde crates along with the serde_derive crate. We also need the uuid crate for generating user IDs. We also added the diesel crate with the following features:

- sqlite: To adapt the crate to use the SQLite database
- r2d2: To use a pool instead of a plain connection

The next thing you need is the diesel_cli tool.

diesel_cli

diesel_cli is needed to create migrations and apply them. To install the tool, use cargo with the following parameters:

```
cargo install diesel_cli
```

However you need development packages for PostgreSQL, MySQL, and SQLite to build this tool. If you don't have or can't install them, you can pass special parameters to `cargo install`. For example, if you want to use `diesel_cli` with the example in this chapter, it's enough to install the tool with the `sqlite` feature only:

```
cargo install diesel_cli --no-default-features --features "sqlite"
```

When you have installed the `diesel-cli` tool, run it to prepare the application using the `setup` command to use the `diesel` crate:

```
diesel setup
```

Now, we have to prepare all the necessary migrations for our example.

Creating migrations

This command creates a `migrations` folder, where you can store migrations using the following command:

```
diesel migration generate <name>
```

This command creates a migration called `<name>` and stores it in the `migrations` folder. For example, if you set the name of the created migration to `create_tables`, you will see in the following structure in the `migrations` folder:

```
migrations/
└── 2018-11-22-192300_create_tables/
    ├── up.sql
    └── down.sql
```

For every migration, the `generate` command creates a folder and a pair of files:

- `up.sql`: Statements for applying migrations
- `down.sql`: Statements for reverting migrations

All migrations are handwritten. Add all the necessary statements for the migrations yourself. For our example, we need the following statements in the `up.sql` file:

```
CREATE TABLE users (
    id TEXT PRIMARY KEY NOT NULL,
    name TEXT NOT NULL,
    email TEXT NOT NULL
);
```

The opposite statement is in the down.sql file:

```
DROP TABLE users;
```

Applying the up.sql script creates the users database with the same struct we used in the previous chapter. The revert script drops the users table.

Now, we can create the database and apply all the migrations with this command:

```
DATABASE_URL=test.db diesel migration run
```

We set DATABASE_URL to test.db to create a SQLite database in the current folder. The run command runs all the migrations in order. You can have multiple migrations and move from one structure level to another, both forward and backward.

 Be careful! You can have multiple migrations, but you can't have competing migrations from different projects to the same database. The problem of automatic migrations is that you can't do it from multiple services, or you can't even start a microservice if it will try to migrate the database after another microservice has already migrated it.

We have created migrations, and now we have to declare the data structure in Rust sources.

Declaring the data structure

Our tool will have two modules with a data structure. The first is the src/schema.rs module, which contains a table! macro call that declares the fields of every table. In our case, this module contains the following declaration:

```
table! {
    users (id) {
        id -> Text,
        name -> Text,
        email -> Text,
    }
}
```

This file was automatically generated by the diesel setup command. When you run a setup, it creates a diesel.toml configuration file with the following contents:

```
# For documentation on how to configure this file,
# see diesel.rs/guides/configuring-diesel-cli
[print_schema]
file = "src/schema.rs"
```

As you can see, the config has a schema module reference. A `schema.rs` file is also generated, and will be updated on every compilation. The `table!` macro creates the required declaration of DSL for the tables used.

Models

Schema declaration defines a table structure only. To map tables to Rust types, you have to add a module with models that will be used to convert records from the `users` table to native Rust types. Let's create one and call it `models.rs`. It will contain the following code:

```
use serde_derive::Serialize;
use super::schema::users;

#[derive(Debug, Serialize, Queryable)]
pub struct User {
    pub id: String,
    pub name: String,
    pub email: String,
}

#[derive(Insertable)]
#[table_name = "users"]
pub struct NewUser<'a> {
    pub id: &'a str,
    pub name: &'a str,
    pub email: &'a str,
}
```

We declared two models here: `User` to represent a user in a database and `NewUser` for creating a new record of a user. We derive the necessary traits for the `User` struct. The `Queryable` trait is implemented to allow you get this type from a database using queries.

There is the `Insertable` trait, which is derived from the `NewUser` struct. This trait allows a struct to be inserted as a new row in a table. This derivation requires an annotation with the name of the table. We can set it to the `users` table with the `#[table_name = "users"]` annotation.

The database structure has been prepared, and we can start to use the database from an application.

Connecting to a database

In our tool, we will implement two subcommands—add to add a new user, and list to retrieve all available users from the database. Import all the necessary dependencies and add the modules with schema and models:

```
extern crate clap;
#[macro_use]
extern crate diesel;
extern crate failure;
extern crate serde_derive;

use clap::{
    crate_authors, crate_description, crate_name, crate_version,
    App, AppSettings, Arg, SubCommand,
};
use diesel::prelude::*;
use diesel::r2d2::ConnectionManager;
use failure::Error;

pub mod models;
pub mod schema;
```

Since we are using the r2d2 crate, we also have to import ConnectionManager to use diesel's abstraction over the traditional database connection.

Modules declared with the pub modifier make them available in documentation. It's useful for modules that are generated by the diesel crate so that you can explore the functions provided by a generated DSL.

Parsing arguments

Similar to the examples in the previous chapter, we have a parser for arguments. It has the following declaration:

```
let matches = App::new(crate_name!())
    .version(crate_version!())
    .author(crate_authors!())
    .about(crate_description!())
    .setting(AppSettings::SubcommandRequired)
    .arg(
        Arg::with_name("database")
        .short("d")
        .long("db")
```

```
                .value_name("FILE")
                .help("Sets a file name of a database")
                .takes_value(true),
            )
        .subcommand(SubCommand::with_name(CMD_ADD).about("add user to the
    table")
                        .arg(Arg::with_name("NAME")
                            .help("Sets the name of a user")
                            .required(true)
                            .index(1))
                        .arg(Arg::with_name("EMAIL")
                            .help("Sets the email of a user")
                            .required(true)
                            .index(2)))
        .subcommand(SubCommand::with_name(CMD_LIST).about("prints a list with
    users"))
        .get_matches();
```

We can get `--database` arguments with a path to a database file. The `add` subcommand requires two arguments—NAME with the name of a user, and EMAIL with their email. The `list` subcommand doesn't require extra arguments and will print a list of users.

Creating a connection

To create a connection, we extract the path to a database. Since we are using the SQLite database, in contrast to the previous examples, we don't expect a URL, but instead a path to a database file. That's why we use the `test.db` filename instead of a URL:

```
let path = matches.value_of("database")
    .unwrap_or("test.db");
let manager = ConnectionManager::<SqliteConnection>::new(path);
let pool = r2d2::Pool::new(manager)?;
```

`r2d2::Pool` requires a `ConnectionManager` instance to establish connections with a database, and we can provide `SqliteConnection` as an associated type to use the SQLite database. We provide a path to a database extracted from command-line arguments. Now let's look at how to use a generated DSL to interact with a database.

Implementing subcommands using a DSL

The `diesel` crate generates a DSL for us to construct typed queries in a simple way. All instructions are generated as a submodule of schema and are available for every generated table mapping with a module path such as the following:

```
use self::schema::users::dsl::*;
```

Let's implement two commands using generated typed relations.

Adding a user subcommand implementation

The first subcommand of our users management tool is `add`. This command extracts the `NAME` and `EMAIL` of the user from the arguments and generates a new user identifier using the `uuid` crate. We will use this type across all our microservices. Look at the following code:

```
(CMD_ADD, Some(matches)) => {
    let conn = pool.get()?;
    let name = matches.value_of("NAME").unwrap();
    let email = matches.value_of("EMAIL").unwrap();
    let uuid = format!("{}", uuid::Uuid::new_v4());
    let new_user = models::NewUser {
        id: &uuid,
        name: &name,
        email: &email,
    };
    diesel::insert_into(schema::users::table)
        .values(&new_user)
        .execute(&conn)?;
}
```

After we have extracted all the parameters, we create a `NewUser` instance from the `models` module. It requires references to values, and we don't need to pass ownership to values and reuse them in multiple requests.

The last line uses the `insert_into` function, which generates an `INSERT INTO` statement for the provided tables, but instead of textual names of tables, such as `"users"`, we use the `table` type from the users `module` of schema. It helps you to see all the mistypes at compile time. We set the value for this request with the `values` function call. As a value, we use a reference to the `NewUser` instance because this map is already mapped to the ***users*** table in the struct declaration. To execute a statement, we call the `execute` function of the `InsertStatement` instance which is generated by the `values` method call.

The `execute` method expects a reference to a connection that we have already extracted from a pool.

Listing users subcommand implementation

In the previous example of data insertion, we didn't use the generated `users` type, and used the `table` nested type only. To list users in the implementation of the `list` subcommand, we will use types from the `dsl` submodule.

If you build some documentation and look into the `users::schema::users::dsl` module, you will see the following items:

```
pub use super::columns::id;
pub use super::columns::name;
pub use super::columns::email;
pub use super::table as users;
```

All types are quite complex, and you can see all the features in the documentation. Since the `users` table type implements the `AsQuery` trait, we can use the `load` method of the `RunQueryDsl` trait for the `users` type. We set the associated type to `model::Users` to extract this type from the table. We also don't need any manual extractions like we did in the previous chapter. The `load` method expects a `Connection` that we get from a `Pool` instance:

```
(CMD_LIST, _) => {
    use self::schema::users::dsl::*;
    let conn = pool.get()?;
    let mut items = users
        .load::<models::User>(&conn)?;
    for user in items {
        println!("{:?}", user);
    }
}
```

Now, we can simply iterate over the users collections. That's pretty simple.

If you want to construct more complex requests, you can use other DSL functions that are generated by the `diesel` crate during building. For example, you can filter users by domain name and limit the quantity of users in a list with the following DSL expression:

```
let mut items = users
    .filter(email.like("%@example.com"))
    .limit(10)
    .load::<models::User>(&conn)?;
```

We have filtered all users by the `example.com` domain using the `filter` method with a parameter created by the `like` method call of the `email` column.

Testing

Let's test our tool. Compile and run it with the following commands:

```
cargo run -- add user1 user1@example.com
cargo run -- add user2 user2@example.com
cargo run -- add userx userx@xample.com
```

If you add filtering and call the `list` subcommand, you will see the following output:

```
cargo run -- list
User { id: "a9ec3bae-c8c6-4580-97e1-db8f988f10f8", name: "user1", email:
"user1@example.com" }
User { id: "7f710d18-aea5-46f9-913c-b60d4e4529c9", name: "user2", email:
"user2@example.com" }
```

We got a perfect example of mapping pure Rust types to relational database types.

Complex database structure

We have covered one example with a single table. In this section, we will create an example with a complex table structure to cover holistic database interaction. We will develop a separate crate for database interaction that covers the functionality of a complex chat application—chat with users, channels, and roles. Also, we will test the functionality we have implemented and show you how to test the database interaction layer of the Rust application.

Business logic of the example application

In this section, we will learn how to transform data relations into ORM models. We will implement a database interaction crate for a chat application. Imagine, we need to express these data relations in Rust:

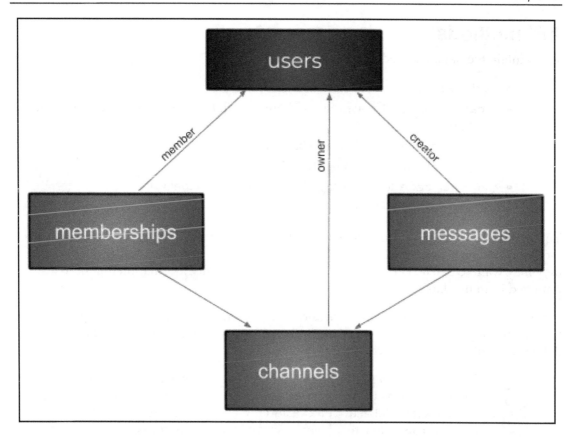

We have four tables. The first table contains users. It's the main table and is used by all the other tables. Every user can create a channel and become the owner of a channel. The second table contains channels, and every channel has the owner represented by a record in the users table.

In our chat application, every user can join a channel and post messages to it. To maintain this relation, we will add a memberships table that contains records with two references—a user who is a member of a channel and a channel record that contains a user as a member.

Also, users can post messages to channels. We will keep all messages in a separate messages table. Every message has two relations: the channel that contains the message and the user who posted the message.

API methods

To maintain the data, we need to provide the following methods:

- `register_user`: Adds a new user to the `users` table
- `create_channel`: Creates a new channel with the provided user as the owner of the channel
- `publish_channel`: Makes the channel public
- `add_member`: Adds a member to a channel
- `add_message`: Adds a message from a user to a channel
- `delete_message`: Deletes a message

You may have noticed that we don't have methods to delete a channel, but we have a method to delete a message. That's because users can post a message accidentally, which they may want to delete. Perhaps the user posts some private information that they want removed from the database.

We don't allow the deletion of channels and users, because they are an important part of the business logic. If user deletes a channel, then all the messages from other users will be deleted as well. It's not a behavior other users want.

> If you need a deleting feature, you can add a boolean column to every table that means the record was deleted. Don't delete the physical record, but mark it as deleted. You can add it yourself to this example. In real cases you also have to take into account the laws in the country that the user lives in, because they can require the physical deletion of records.

Now, we can express these relations in Rust with ORM using the `diesel` crate.

Database structure and migrations

Let's start by creating the database structure. We need four tables:

- `users`: Contains users' accounts
- `channels`: Contains channels created by users
- `memberships`: Users belonging to a channel
- `messages`: Messages of users in channels

To add these tables, we will add four migrations to a new project:

```
cargo new --lib chat
cd chat
diesel setup
diesel migration generate create_users
diesel migration generate create_channels
diesel migration generate create_memberships
diesel migration generate create_messages
```

The preceding commands created these migrations:

```
00000000000000_diesel_initial_setup
2019-01-06-192329_create_users
2019-01-06-192333_create_channels
2019-01-06-192338_create_memberships
2019-01-06-192344_create_messages
```

As you may remember, every migration folder contains two files: up.sql and down.sql. Now, we can add SQL statements to execute the necessary migration operations.

Diesel initial setup

The first migration is diesel_initial_setup. It was created by the diesel CLI tool automatically and contains a function to set a trigger to update the updated_at column of a table. We will use this feature for the channel table. Like every migration, it consists of two files.

up.sql

This SQL file contains two statements. The first is the diesel_manage_updated_at function, whichcreates a trigger for a table to call the diesel_set_updated_at function for each row update:

```
CREATE OR REPLACE FUNCTION diesel_manage_updated_at(_tbl regclass) RETURNS
VOID AS $$
BEGIN
    EXECUTE format('CREATE TRIGGER set_updated_at BEFORE UPDATE ON %s
                    FOR EACH ROW EXECUTE PROCEDURE
diesel_set_updated_at()', _tbl);
END;
$$ LANGUAGE plpgsql;
```

This function only executes the CREATE TRIGGER statement for a table you provided with the _tbl argument.

The second function is `diesel_set_updated_at`, which updates the `updated_at` column with the current timestamp if the processed row has changed:

```
CREATE OR REPLACE FUNCTION diesel_set_updated_at() RETURNS trigger AS $$
BEGIN
    IF (
        NEW IS DISTINCT FROM OLD AND
        NEW.updated_at IS NOT DISTINCT FROM OLD.updated_at
    ) THEN
        NEW.updated_at := current_timestamp;
    END IF;
    RETURN NEW;
END;
$$ LANGUAGE plpgsql;
```

To make this function work, you have to add the `updated_at` column to your table and a field with the same name to your model. We will do this for the `channel` table later in this section.

down.sql

The down script removes both functions, if they exist:

```
DROP FUNCTION IF EXISTS diesel_manage_updated_at(_tbl regclass);
DROP FUNCTION IF EXISTS diesel_set_updated_at();
```

This was a default migration created by the `diesel` tool. As you can see, it contains a functionality you can drop or replace with your own. Now, we can add the `users` table to the next migration.

Users table

The second migration is `create_users`. It creates a `users` table that is required to keep all the users' accounts in a database. To create this table, we create a separate migration that contains two scripts—one to create the `users` table and one to drop it.

up.sql

Add the following statement to the `up.sql` script:

```
CREATE TABLE users (
  id SERIAL PRIMARY KEY,
  email TEXT NOT NULL UNIQUE
);
```

As you can see, the table has two columns. `id` represents the unique ID of the user, and we will use this identifier in other tables later. The `email` column contains the unique e-mail of the user. For real applications, the `users` table also has to contain a hashed password, and two columns to store when the user was created and updated.

down.sql

The down script drops the `users` table:

```
DROP TABLE users;
```

Now, we can use the users' IDs to create channels.

Channels table

The third migration is `create_channels`. It creates a `channels` table that contains all of the channels that have been created by users. Channels can be private or public, and each has a title. Let's look at a script that creates a table of channels in a database.

up.sql

The up script contains a statement that creates the `channels` table. Columns includes the channel `id` and `user_id`, which refers to the user in the `users` table. The channel also has a `title` column and an `is_public` column that contains a flag that represents the visibility of the channel. If `is_public` equals `TRUE`, it means the channel is public. Look at the following statement:

```
CREATE TABLE channels (
    id SERIAL PRIMARY KEY,
    user_id INTEGER NOT NULL REFERENCES users,
    title TEXT NOT NULL,
    is_public BOOL NOT NULL,
    created_at TIMESTAMP NOT NULL DEFAULT CURRENT_TIMESTAMP,
    updated_at TIMESTAMP NOT NULL DEFAULT CURRENT_TIMESTAMP
);

SELECT diesel_manage_updated_at('channels');
```

The table also has two columns—`create_at`, which takes the current timestamp when the row is created, and `updated_at`, which contains the timestamp of the latest update of the row. By default, the `updated_at` column takes the current timestamp as the default value on creation.

As we mentioned before, diesel creates a `diesel_manage_updated_at` function that sets a trigger to a table, which updates the `updated_at` column of rows automatically when the row is updated. Since we have the `updated_at` column in the table declaration, we can call this function in the `SELECT` statement.

down.sql

The down script drops the `channels` table:

```
DROP TABLE channels;
```

In the `up.sql` script, we created a trigger with a `diesel_manage_updated_at` call, but we don't need to drop it manually, because it is automatically removed with the table.

Memberships table

The fourth migration is `create_memberships`. It creates a `memberships` table that is necessary to manage the participants of the channel who can read messages and write new ones. This table depends on both the `users` and `channels` tables.

up.sql

The `up` script is simple and contains a statement that creates the memberships table with three fields—the `id` of a membership, the `id` of a channel in the `channel_id` column whose member is a user with the `user_id` column:

```
CREATE TABLE memberships (
  id SERIAL PRIMARY KEY,
  channel_id INTEGER NOT NULL REFERENCES channels,
  user_id INTEGER NOT NULL REFERENCES users
);
```

down.sql

The down script drops the table:

```
DROP TABLE memberships;
```

We now need to add a table that stores messages that users have posted to the channels.

Messages table

The fifth migration is `create_messages`. It creates a `messages` table that contains every message that has been written by the users.

up.sql

Look at the following up script:

```
CREATE TABLE messages (
    id SERIAL PRIMARY KEY,
    timestamp TIMESTAMP NOT NULL,
    channel_id INTEGER NOT NULL REFERENCES channels,
    user_id INTEGER NOT NULL REFERENCES users,
    text TEXT NOT NULL
);
```

It creates a table that contains a message that is associated with a channel and a user by ID. Also, it contains a timestamp showing when the messages were added, as well as the text of each message.

down.sql

The down script drops the table:

```
DROP TABLE messages;
```

We have finished all the migrations, and now we can look at the schema that was generated by the `diesel` tool.

Schema

`diesel` creates a schema file that contains macro calls that generate a DSL language to use in the sources of your crate. A schema of tables that have relations to each other need extra declarations. Let's explore a generated schema in the `src/schema.rs` file to see how it differs from the simple schema we created earlier in this chapter.

The first table is `users`. It has the same columns we declared in the SQL file:

```
table! {
    users (id) {
        id -> Int4,
        email -> Text,
    }
```

```
}
```

The `table!` macro will be expanded during compilation to some type and trait implementations that you can see with the following command:

```
cargo rustc -- -Z unstable-options --pretty=expanded
```

This command prints all expanded macros to a Terminal.

The diesel tool has also generated a DSL declaration for the `channels` table:

```
table! {
    channels (id) {
        id -> Int4,
        user_id -> Int4,
        title -> Text,
        is_public -> Bool,
        created_at -> Timestamp,
        updated_at -> Timestamp,
    }
}
```

For the `memberships` table, we have this declaration:

```
table! {
    memberships (id) {
        id -> Int4,
        channel_id -> Int4,
        user_id -> Int4,
    }
}
```

And for the `messages` table, we have this declaration:

```
table! {
    messages (id) {
        id -> Int4,
        timestamp -> Timestamp,
        channel_id -> Int4,
        user_id -> Int4,
        text -> Text,
    }
}
```

But you might have noticed that the table declarations don't contain any information about relations. Relations created by the `joinable!` macro expect a table name and a parent table with the ID column name:

```
joinable!(channels -> users (user_id));
joinable!(memberships -> channels (channel_id));
joinable!(memberships -> users (user_id));
joinable!(messages -> channels (channel_id));
joinable!(messages -> users (user_id));
```

All relations are listed with the `joinable!` macro, but the schema also contains a `allow_tables_to_appear_in_same_query!` macro call that represents which tables can be used in JOIN queries:

```
allow_tables_to_appear_in_same_query!(
    channels,
    memberships,
    messages,
    users,
);
```

Since we have a complete schema declaration with all relations, we can declare models with the same relations as native Rust structs.

Models

Now, we can use the generated schema to create all the necessary models that represent database records to native Rust structs. First, we have to import the `NaiveDateTime` type, because we have the timestamp column. Also, we have to import all tables: `users`, `channels`, `memberships`, and `messages`:

```
use chrono::NaiveDateTime;
use crate::schema::{users, channels, memberships, messages};
```

We will use the `i32` type as the identifier of records, but it's better to use an alias to make its intent more clear:

```
pub type Id = i32;
```

Let's add a model to represent a record in the `users` table.

User

To represent a user stored in the `users` table, we will add a `User` struct with the following declaration:

```
#[derive(Debug, Identifiable, Queryable, Serialize, Deserialize)]
#[table_name = "users"]
```

```
pub struct User {
    pub id: Id,
    pub email: String,
}
```

As you can see, we use the `Id` type for the ID column that has the `SERIAL` SQL type. For the email field, we use the String type, which maps to the `TEXT` column type in PostgreSQL.

There is also the `table_name` attribute to bind this struct with a table. We also derive some traits for this model—`Debug` for printing the model's value to a terminal, and the `Serialize` and `Deserialize` traits to make this model convertible to any serialization format. Theser are basic traits that I recommend to implement for database models, especially if you want to use the same types in a REST API.

The `Queryable` trait represents the result of SQL expressions that can be converted in a struct that implements the trait. This lets us convert tuples to the `User` struct in our database interaction API later.

The `Identifiable` trait means the struct that implements this trait represents a single record in a table. This trait has an associated `Id` type that is set to the corresponding type in the SQL table. This trait also contains an `id` method that returns the identifier of a record in a table.

Channel

The next model is `Channel`, which represents a record in the `channels` table:

```
#[derive(Debug, Identifiable, Queryable, Associations, Serialize,
Deserialize)]
#[belongs_to(User)]
#[table_name = "channels"]
pub struct Channel {
    pub id: Id,
    pub user_id: Id,
    pub title: String,
    pub is_public: bool,
    pub created_at: NaiveDateTime,
    pub updated_at: NaiveDateTime,
}
```

This model binds to a table using the `table_name` attribute and contains all the fields that map to the corresponding columns of the table. To represent the `TIMESTAMP` SQL type, we use `NaiveDateTime` from the `chrono` crate.

The model has a `user_id` field that maps to a record in the `users` table. To indicate whether a `User` model belongs to the `users` table, we added the `belongs_to` attribute to this model. The model also has to implement the `Associations` trait. If the model does that, you can use the `belonging_to` method of a model to get records belonging to other records with a parental relation.

Membership

To represent records in the memberships model, we added the `Membership` model:

```
#[derive(Debug, Identifiable, Queryable, Associations, Serialize,
Deserialize)]
#[belongs_to(Channel)]
#[belongs_to(User)]
#[table_name = "memberships"]
pub struct Membership {
    pub id: Id,
    pub channel_id: Id,
    pub user_id: Id,
}
```

This model has set relations with the `Channel` and `User` models. For example, if you want to get all the memberships of a user, you can use the `belonging_to` method:

```
let memberships = Membership::belonging_to(&user)
    .load::<Membership>(&conn);
```

Message

The last model we need is `Message`, which relates to the records in the `messages` table:

```
#[derive(Debug, Identifiable, Queryable, Associations, Serialize,
Deserialize)]
#[belongs_to(Channel)]
#[belongs_to(User)]
#[table_name = "messages"]
pub struct Message {
    pub id: Id,
    pub timestamp: NaiveDateTime,
    pub channel_id: Id,
    pub user_id: Id,
    pub text: String,
}
```

This model also uses derived traits which we discussed in the first example. Now, we can implement our database interaction crate using the generated schema and the declared models.

Database interaction API crate

Let's add an implementation of the database interaction API to the `lib.rs` source file. We need to import the `diesel` crate and declare the module:

```
#[macro_use]
extern crate diesel;

mod models;
mod schema;
```

You can see that we have added two modules: `models` and `schema`. In the implementation, we need the following types:

```
use diesel::{Connection, ExpressionMethods, OptionalExtension,
PgConnection, QueryDsl, RunQueryDsl, insert_into};
use chrono::Utc;
use failure::{Error, format_err};
use self::models::{Channel, Id, Membership, Message, User};
use self::schema::{channels, memberships, messages, users};
use std::env;
```

The imports include all models and all tables. We also imported the `Connection` trait to the `establish` connection, the `ExpressionMethods` trait to use the `eq` method of DSL to set the equality of columns to values, the `OptionalExtension` trait to use the `optional` method to try to get a record that cannot be in a table, the `QueryDsl` trait that has the `filter` method, and `RunQueryDsl` to use the `get_result` method that tries to convert a record to the Rust type. The `insert_into` method lets us insert new records into a table. Now, we have everything we need to declare the `Api` struct.

Api

We will declare a struct with a connection instance inside and add methods over this connection:

```
pub struct Api {
    conn: PgConnection,
}
```

The `Api` struct can be created with the `connect` method, which uses the `DATABASE_URL` environment variable to bootstrap a connection to PostgreSQL:

```
impl Api {
    pub fn connect() -> Result<Self, Error> {
        let database_url = env::var("DATABASE_URL")
            .unwrap_or("postgres://postgres@localhost:5432".to_string());
        let conn = PgConnection::establish(&database_url)?;
        Ok(Self { conn })
    }
}
```

We use a direct connection here without an `r2d2` pool, but you can also make the `Api` struct compatible with concurrent access. Let's add first the API method for registering new users.

Register user

To register a new user with an email address, add the following method:

```
pub fn register_user(&self, email: &str) -> Result<User, Error> {
    insert_into(users::table)
        .values((
                users::email.eq(email),
                ))
        .returning((
                users::id,
                users::email
                ))
        .get_result(&self.conn)
        .map_err(Error::from)
}
```

The `register_user` function expects a string with the email of a user, adds a record to a database, and returns a `User` instance, which represents a record in the `users` table.

We use the `insert_into` method with a table type from the users scope, which is automatically created by the `table!` macro in the `schema` module. This method returns an `IncompleteInsertStatement` instance that provides a `values` method to set values with an `INSERT` statement. We set the `email` column equal to the `email` variable. The `values` method call returns an `InsertStatement` type instance that has the `returning` method to set columns that will be returned with this statement. We set the returning values to the `id` and `email` columns of the `users` table. The `returning` method takes ownership of a statement and returns a new `InsertStatement` instance with the returning values.

At the end, we call the `get_result` method of the `InsertStatement` struct to execute the statement and convert the result to the `User` model. Because we have a different error type of `Result`, we have to convert the `diesel::result::Error` type returned by the `get_result`, method call to the `failure::Error` type.

Create channel

The next method is `create_channel`, which creates a new channel for a user. Take a look at the implementation:

```
pub fn create_channel(&self, user_id: Id, title: &str, is_public: bool)
    -> Result<Channel, Error>
{
    self.conn.transaction::<_, _, _>(|| {
        let channel: Channel = insert_into(channels::table)
            .values((
                    channels::user_id.eq(user_id),
                    channels::title.eq(title),
                    channels::is_public.eq(is_public),
                    ))
            .returning((
                    channels::id,
                    channels::user_id,
                    channels::title,
                    channels::is_public,
                    channels::created_at,
                    channels::updated_at,
                    ))
            .get_result(&self.conn)
            .map_err(Error::from)?;
        self.add_member(channel.id, user_id)?;
```

```
            Ok(channel)
    })
}
```

The function expects `user_id`, the `title` of a channel, and the `is_public` flag, which means the channel is public.

Since we have to add the user who created the channel as the first member of a created channel, we will join two statements to a single transaction. To create a transaction with `diesel`, you can use the `transaction` method of the `Connection` instance. This method expects three type parameters—successful value type, error value type, and a type of a closure provided as a single argument with a function call. We skip all types, because the compiler can detect them.

In the transaction implementation we create a `Channel` model instance that represents a new record in a database. After that, we use the `add_member` method of our `Api` struct. As you can see, neither the transaction and connection instances need a mutable reference, and we can combine multiple methods to get an immutable reference to a `Connection` instance. You will see the implementation of the `add_member` method later, but now we will add a method to update a channel's record in a table.

Publish channel

We will add a method that sets the `is_public` flag of a channel record to `true`. Look at the following implementation:

```
pub fn publish_channel(&self, channel_id: Id) -> Result<(), Error> {
    let channel = channels::table
        .filter(channels::id.eq(channel_id))
        .select((
                channels::id,
                channels::user_id,
                channels::title,
                channels::is_public,
                channels::created_at,
                channels::updated_at,
                ))
        .first::<Channel>(&self.conn)
        .optional()
        .map_err(Error::from)?;
    if let Some(channel) = channel {
        diesel::update(&channel)
            .set(channels::is_public.eq(true))
            .execute(&self.conn)?;
```

```
            Ok(())
        } else {
            Err(format_err!("channel not found"))
        }
    }
```

The function expects `channel_id`, and we use the `table` value to create a statement. We use the `filter` method of the `QueryDsl` trait to get a single record with the provided ID, and the `select` method of the same trait to extract values from the table needed for conversion to the `Channel` model instance. Then, we call the `first` method that returns the first record found with the executed statement. If no record is found, it will return an error, but since `Result` types are returned, we can drop the error part of this by converting it in `Option` with the `optional` method call. It lets us decide later what to do if a record hasn't been found later.

If a record is found, we use the `update` method with a reference to a `Channel` model. This call returns an `UpdateStatement` value, which has a `set` method that we use to set the `is_public` column to `true`. At the end, we `execute` this statement for a connection instance. This call also updates the `updated_at` column of the record automatically since we registered a trigger for the `channels` table. Now, we can implement the `add_member` function.

Add member

The `add_member` function requires a channel ID and a user ID to add a membership record to the `memberships` table:

```
pub fn add_member(&self, channel_id: Id, user_id: Id)
    -> Result<Membership, Error>
{
    insert_into(memberships::table)
        .values((
                memberships::channel_id.eq(channel_id),
                memberships::user_id.eq(user_id),
                ))
        .returning((
                memberships::id,
                memberships::channel_id,
                memberships::user_id,
                ))
        .get_result(&self.conn)
        .map_err(Error::from)
}
```

The implementation is simple and it uses the `insert_into` function call to prepare the `INSERT` statement to insert a new `Membership` value in the table. We also need a function to add new messages to a channel.

Add message

The `add_message` method adds a message related to a channel and a user to the `messages` table:

```
pub fn add_message(&self, channel_id: Id, user_id: Id, text: &str)
    -> Result<Message, Error>
{
    let timestamp = Utc::now().naive_utc();
    insert_into(messages::table)
        .values((
                messages::timestamp.eq(timestamp),
                messages::channel_id.eq(channel_id),
                messages::user_id.eq(user_id),
                messages::text.eq(text),
                ))
        .returning((
                messages::id,
                messages::timestamp,
                messages::channel_id,
                messages::user_id,
                messages::text,
                ))
        .get_result(&self.conn)
        .map_err(Error::from)
}
```

The implementation also uses the `insert_into` function, but we also created the timestamp manually. You can avoid setting this field manually and set a default value to the current timestamp in the `timestamp` column.

Delete message

If you posted a message and decided to remove it, we need a method to delete messages from `messages` table. Look at `delete_message` method implementation:

```
pub fn delete_message(&self, message_id: Id) -> Result<(), Error> {
    diesel::delete(messages::table)
        .filter(messages::id.eq(message_id))
        .execute(&self.conn)?;
```

```
        Ok(())
    }
```

This function uses the `delete` method, which returns a `DeleteStatement` instance, which has a `filter` method as well. We set a filter with the `id` column equal to the provided `message_id` and execute the generated `DELETE` SQL statement.

Testing the crate

That's all, and now we have a crate that can be used to interact with a database. Since it's not binary, we need to guarantee that the code works correctly. It's a good practice to cover your code with tests, and we will do that now.

Add the following code to the `lib.rs` file:

```rust
#[cfg(test)]
mod tests {
    use super::Api;

    #[test]
    fn create_users() {
        let api = Api::connect().unwrap();
        let user_1 = api.register_user("user_1@example.com").unwrap();
        let user_2 = api.register_user("user_2@example.com").unwrap();
        let channel = api.create_channel(user_1.id, "My Channel",
false).unwrap();
        api.publish_channel(channel.id).unwrap();
        api.add_member(channel.id, user_2.id).unwrap();
        let message = api.add_message(channel.id, user_1.id,
"Welcome!").unwrap();
        api.add_message(channel.id, user_2.id, "Hi!").unwrap();
        api.delete_message(message.id).unwrap();
    }
}
```

We added a `test` module and a `create_users` testing function. This function tests all the API methods we implemented. It creates an `Api` instance with a connect method call and uses that instance to register two users with the following emails—"`user_1@example.com`" and "`user_2@example.com`". After that, it creates a channel for the first user, publishes it, and add the second user as a member. At the end, it adds two messages and deletes the first one. Let's run this test, but you have to run a PostgreSQL database instance with Docker. You can read how to do this in the previous chapter.

Apply all the migrations and run the test:

```
DATABASE_URL=postgres://postgres@localhost:5432 diesel migration run &&
cargo test
```

When the testing is over, you will get a message with from the `psql` client:

```
postgres=# select * from messages;
 id | timestamp | channel_id | user_id | text
----+--------------------------+------------+---------+------
 2 | 2019-01-08 18:30:48.465001 | 1 | 2 | Hi!
(1 row)
```

As you can see, the test added two records and removed the first. In `Chapter 13`, *Testing and Debugging Rust Microservices*, we will discuss testing microservices in detail.

Summary

In this chapter, we have learned how to use object-relational mapping to store and load pure Rust types to databases. First, we created migrations with the `diesel-cli` tool that comes with the `diesel` crate. After that, we added models to map columns to Rust types and created a minimal connection using the `r2d2` crate with a `diesel` crate abstraction.

We also touched on DSL constructs. however the `diesel` crate provides a lot of features, and if you want to construct more complex queries, you can refer to the documentation.

In the next chapter, we will learn about some frameworks that simplify writing microservices and let you implement your ideas faster.

Simple REST Definition and Request Routing with Frameworks
9

In this chapter, we'll have a look at alternative frameworks for creating microservices. In the previous chapters, we used a `hyper` crate to handle HTTP interaction, but it required us to write asynchronous code. If you don't need low-level control, if a microservice you've created won't work with a high load, or if you need to write one simply and quickly, you can try using the following crates to create microservices:

- rouille
- nickel
- rocket
- gotham

In this chapter, we will create four microservices that use database interaction concepts from previous chapters.

Technical requirements

This chapter introduces you to new crates—`rouille`, `nickel`, `rocket`, and `gotham`. You don't need to install special software instead of `cargo` and the Rust compiler, but you need a nightly version, because the Rocket framework requires it.

To make the examples complex, we will use SQL Database and an SMTP server. But you don't need to install this software locally. It's sufficient to start containers with PostgreSQL and Postfix servers using Docker.

You can get the sources for this chapter from the relevant project on GitHub: `https://github.com/PacktPublishing/Hands-On-Microservices-with-Rust/tree/master/Chapter09`.

Rouille

The `rouille` crate helps you to create a microservice with a simple routing declaration using the `route!` macro. This framework provides a synchronous API and every request is processed by a thread from a pool.

Creating a microservice

Let's write a microservice for user registration using the Rouille framework. It allows users to create an account and authorize the use of other microservices. We can start by creating a server instance.

Bootstrapping a server

The Rouille framework is very simple to use. It contains `start_server` functions that expect a function to handle every incoming request. Let's create a `main` function that uses a `diesel` crate with an `r2d2` pool feature and calls a function to handle requests:

```
fn main() {
    env_logger::init();
    let manager = ConnectionManager::<SqliteConnection>::new("test.db");
    let pool = Pool::builder().build(manager).expect("Failed to create
pool.");
    rouille::start_server("127.0.0.1:8001", move |request| {
        match handler(&request, &pool) {
            Ok(response) => { response },
            Err(err) => {
                Response::text(err.to_string())
                    .with_status_code(500)
            }
        }
    })
}
```

We created a `ConnectionManager` for a local `test.db` SQLite database and a `Pool` instance with this manager. We discussed this in previous chapters. We are interested in the line with the `rouille::start_server` function call. This function takes two arguments: a listening address and a closure for handling requests. We moved `pool` to the closure and called `handler` functions, which we declared underneath it to generate a response for a request with `Pool` as an argument.

Since `handler` functions have to return a `Response` instance, we have to return a response with a 500 status code if a `handler` function returns an error. Looks pretty simple, doesn't it? Let's look at a `handler` function declaration.

Handling requests

The Rouille framework contains a `router!` macro that helps you declare a handler for every path and HTTP method. If we add a `handler` function that is called from a closure we used in the `start_server` function call, the `router!` macro expects a request instance as the first argument and the desired number of request handlers. Let's analyze the four handler functions in order.

Root handler

The following is a simple handler that expects a GET method and returns a text response:

```
(GET) (/) => {
    Response::text("Users Microservice")
},
```

Sign-up handler

To handle sign-up requests, we need a POST method handler for the /signup path. We can declare it in the following way:

```
(POST) (/signup) => {
    let data = post_input!(request, {      ← form
        email: String,
        password: String,
    })?;
    let user_email = data.email.trim().to_lowercase();
    let user_password = pbkdf2_simple(&data.password, 12345)?;
    {
        use self::schema::users::dsl::*;
        let conn = pool.get()?;
        let user_exists: bool =
```

```
select(exists(users.filter(email.eq(user_email.clone()))))
            .get_result(&conn)?;
        if !user_exists {
            let uuid = format!("{}", uuid::Uuid::new_v4());
            let new_user = models::NewUser {
                id: &uuid,
                email: &user_email,
                password: &user_password,
            };
    diesel::insert_into(schema::users::table).values(&new_user).execute(&conn)?
;
            Response::json(&())
        } else {
            Response::text(format!("user {} exists", data.email))
                .with_status_code(400)
        }
    }
}
```

This handler is more complex and also demonstrates how to parse the parameters of a request. We need to parse an HTML form with two parameters—email and password. To do this, we used the post_input! macro, which expects a request instance and a form declaration with types. The form structure declaration looks like a simple struct declaration without a name, but with fields. We added two necessary fields and the post_input! macro parsed a request to fill an object with the corresponding fields.

Since parsed parameters only fit types, we also had to add extra processing to it. The email field is a String type, and we used the trim method to remove unnecessary spacing and the to_lowercase method to convert it to lowercase. We used the password field without any changes and passed it as a parameter to the pbkdf2_simple method of the rust-crypto crate.

 PBKDF2 is an algorithm that adds computational cost to an encrypted value to prevent brute-force attacks. If your microservice is attacked and your password is stolen, it won't be easy for attackers to find a password value to access the service with someone else's account. If you use hashes, then the attacker will be able to find the matching password quickly.

After we prepared parameters, we used them with object-relational mapping methods. First, to check whether the user with the provided email exists, we use a DSL generated by the `diesel` crate and, if the user doesn't exist, we generate a unique ID for the user using the `uuid` crate. The handler fills the `NewUser` instance with corresponding values and inserts it into a database. Upon success, it returns an empty JSON response. If the user already exists, the handler returns a response with a 400 status code (Bad Response) with a message to the effect that the user with the provided email already exists. Let's look at how to sign in with a stored user value.

Sign-in handler

The following code represents a handler for the /signin request path and parses a query with the data from the HTML form using post_input!:

```
(POST) (/signin) => {
    let data = post_input!(request, {
        email: String,
        password: String,
    })?;
    let user_email = data.email;
    let user_password = data.password;
    {
        use self::schema::users::dsl::*;
        let conn = pool.get()?;
        let user = users.filter(email.eq(user_email))
            .first::<models::User>(&conn)?;
        let valid = pbkdf2_check(&user_password, &user.password)
            .map_err(|err| format_err!("pass check error: {}", err))?;
        if valid {
            let user_id = UserId {
                id: user.id,
            };
            Response::json(&user_id)
                .with_status_code(200)
        } else {
            Response::text("access denied")
                .with_status_code(403)
        }
    }
}
```

When the data has been extracted, we get a connection from a pool and use types generated by the `diesel` crate to send a query to the database. The code gets the first record from the users table with the provided email value. After that, we use the `pbkdf2_check` function to check that the password matches the stored one. If the user is valid, we return a JSON value with the user's ID. In the next chapters, we won't provide this service directly but will use it from another microservice. If the password doesn't match, we will return a response with a `403` status code.

Default handler

For cases where there is no path or method pair matched for the request, we can add a default handler. Our microservice returns a `404` error for all unknown requests. Add this to the `router!` macro call:

```
_ => {
    Response::empty_404()
}
```

Compiling and running

Prepare the database and run the server using the following commands:

```
DATABASE_URL=test.db diesel migration run
cargo run
```

When the server is started, try to send sign-in and sign-up requests:

```
curl -d "email=user@example.com&password=password" -X POST
http://localhost:8001/signup
curl -d "email=user@example.com&password=password" -X POST
http://localhost:8001/signin
```

The second request will return a response with a user identifier in JSON format that looks like this:

```
{"id":"08a023d6-be15-46c1-a6d6-56f0e2a04aae"}
```

Now we can try to implement another service with the `nickel` crate.

Nickel

Another framework that helps us create a microservice very simply is `nickel`. In terms of the design of its handlers, it's very similar to `hyper`, but it's synchronous.

Creating a microservice

Let's create a service that sends emails to any address. This microservice will also build the email's body content from a template. To start with, we have to add the necessary dependencies to start a server instance.

Bootstrapping a server

To write a mailer microservice, we need two dependencies: the `nickel` crate and the `lettre` crate. The first is a framework inspired by the Express framework for Node.js. The second implements the SMTP protocol and lets us interact with a mail server such as Postfix. Add these dependencies to `Cargo.toml`:

```
failure = "0.1"
lettre = { git = "https://github.com/lettre/lettre" }
lettre_email = { git = "https://github.com/lettre/lettre" }
nickel = "0.10"
```

For the `lettre` crate, we're using version 0.9.0 from GitHub, because it's not available on crates.io at the time of writing. We need to import some types from these crates:

```
use lettre::{ClientSecurity, SendableEmail, EmailAddress, Envelope,
SmtpClient, SmtpTransport, Transport};
use lettre::smtp::authentication::IntoCredentials;
use nickel::{Nickel, HttpRouter, FormBody, Request, Response,
MiddlewareResult};
use nickel::status::StatusCode;
use nickel::template_cache::{ReloadPolicy, TemplateCache};
```

Types from the `std` and `failure` crates are not presented in the preceding code. Now we can declare the `Data` struct that represents the shared state of the server:

```
struct Data {
    sender: Mutex<Sender<SendableEmail>>,
    cache: TemplateCache,
}
```

This struct contains two fields—a `Sender` to send messages to the mailer worker that we will implement later, and `TemplateCache`, which lets us load and render templates from a local directory. We will use it directly for the body of emails only, because this microservice won't render HTML responses.

The following code spawns a mail sender worker, creates an instance of the `Data` struct, creates a `Nickel` server, and binds it to the `127.0.0.1:8002` socket address:

```
fn main() {
    let tx = spawn_sender();

    let data = Data {
        sender: Mutex::new(tx),
        cache: TemplateCache::with_policy(ReloadPolicy::Always),
    };

    let mut server = Nickel::with_data(data);
    server.get("/", middleware!("Mailer Microservice"));
    server.post("/send", send);
    server.listen("127.0.0.1:8002").unwrap();
}
```

In the `cache` field of the `Data` struct, we set a `TemplateCache` instance that needs `ReloadPolicy` as an argument. The `ReloadPolicy` parameter controls how often templates will be reloaded. We use the `Always` variant, which means templates will be reloaded on every rendering. It lets an administrator update templates without interrupting the service.

To start the server, we need to create a `Nickel` instance, which we initialize with the `Data` instance using the `with_data` method. Since `Data` will be shared across threads, we have to wrap `Sender` with `Mutex`. `TemplateCache` already implements `Sync` and `Send` and can be shared safely.

We add two methods to the `Nickel` server instance using the `get` and `post` methods. We add two handlers. The first is for the root path, `/`, which uses the `middleware!` macro from the `nickel` crate to attach a handler that returns a text response. The second handles requests with the `/send` path and calls the `send` function, which is implemented beneath that. The last method call, `listen`, binds the server's socket to an address. Now we can move forward and implement a handler.

Handling requests

Handlers of the Nickel framework take two parameters: a mutable reference to a `Request` struct and an owned `Response` instance that we can fill with data. Handlers have to return `MiddlewareResult`. Every input and output type has a type parameter of a shared data type.

The `nickel` crate contains the `try_with!` macro. It needs to unwrap the `Result` type, but returns an HTTP error if the result equals `Err`. I created the `send_impl` method to use the usual `?` operator; `failure::Error` is the error type. I've found this to be more common than using a special macro such as `try_with!`:

```
fn send<'mw>(req: &mut Request<Data>, res: Response<'mw, Data>) ->
MiddlewareResult<'mw, Data> {
    try_with!(res, send_impl(req).map_err(|_| StatusCode::BadRequest));
    res.send("true")
}
```

We mapped the result to BadRequest. If the method returns `Ok`, we will send a JSON `true` value as a response. We don't need to use serialization for this simplest type of JSON value.

The following code is the `send_impl` function implementation. Let's take it apart piece by piece:

```
fn send_impl(req: &mut Request<Data>) -> Result<(), Error> {
    let (to, code) = {
        let params = req.form_body().map_err(|_| format_err!(""))?;
        let to = params.get("to").ok_or(format_err!("to field not
set"))?.to_owned();
        let code = params.get("code").ok_or(format_err!("code field not
set"))?.to_owned();
        (to, code)
    };
    let data = req.server_data();
    let to = EmailAddress::new(to.to_owned())?;
    let envelope = Envelope::new(None, vec![to])?;
    let mut params: HashMap<&str, &str> = HashMap::new();
    params.insert("code", &code);
    let mut body: Vec<u8> = Vec::new();
    data.cache.render("templates/confirm.tpl", &mut body, &params)?;
    let email = SendableEmail::new(envelope, "Confirm email".to_string(),
Vec::new());
    let sender = data.sender.lock().unwrap().clone();
    sender.send(email).map_err(|_| format_err!("can't send email"))?;
    Ok(())
}
```

The `Request` instance has the `from_body` method, which returns query parameters as a `Params` struct instance. The `get` method of `Params` returns a parameter called `Option`. If any of the parameters are not provided, we return an `Err` value, because the method requires all parameters to be set.

To get access to a shared server's data, there is the `server_data` method of `Request`, which returns a `Data` instance, because we set this type as a type parameter of a `Request` and provided an instance of `Data` to the server.

When we have got all the parameters, we can extract a `Sender` instance (used to send tasks to a worker) compose an email using a template from the cache, and send it to a worker. We create an `EmailAddress` instance from the `to` parameter of the query. Then, we fill `HashMap` with parameters for a template that contains the `code` parameter with a confirmation code value.

The parameters have been prepared and we use the `cache` field of the `Data` instance to get access to `TemplateCache`. The `render` method of the cache loads a template and fills it with the provided parameters. The `render` method expects a buffer to fill the rendered content. After we get it, we create a `SendableEmail` instance, we clone a `Sender`, and use the cloned instance to send an email to a worker. Let's look at how an email worker is implemented.

Worker for sending emails

We use a separate thread that receives `SendableEmail` values and send them using the SMTP protocol. The following code creates an instance of `SmtpClient` and uses the `credentials` method to set the credentials for a connection:

```
fn spawn_sender() -> Sender<SendableEmail> {
    let (tx, rx) = channel();
    let smtp = SmtpClient::new("localhost:2525", ClientSecurity::None)
        .expect("can't start smtp client");
    let credentials = ("admin@example.com", "password").into_credentials();
    let client = smtp.credentials(credentials);
    thread::spawn(move || {
        let mut mailer = SmtpTransport::new(client);
        for email in rx.iter() {
            let result = mailer.send(email);
            if let Err(err) = result {
                println!("Can't send mail: {}", err);
            }
        }
        mailer.close();
```

```
        });
        tx
    }
```

`StmpClient` has moved to the new thread's context. It's wrapped with `SmtpTransport` and is used to send every received `SendableEmail` instance.

The worker implements a non-transactional email sender. If you want a guarantee of email delivery, you need to implement more diverse interaction with a mail server, or you can even embed an email server, or use a third-party service. I recommend you use as many external services as possible; they will cost you, but you will save much more on maintenance. We implemented the mailer service for demonstration purposes only to show how to integrate multiple services together later.

Compiling and running

Before we start our microservice, we need a working SMTP server. Let's create one with Docker. The following command creates a container with a Postfix server instance:

```
docker run -it --rm --name test-smtp -p 2525:25  \
        -e SMTP_SERVER=smtp.example.com \
        -e SMTP_USERNAME=admin@example.com \
        -e SMTP_PASSWORD=password \
        -e SERVER_HOSTNAME=smtp.example.com \
        juanluisbaptiste/postfix
```

The server exposes port *25* and we remap it to local port *2525*. The command sets all the necessary parameters using environment variables and now the mailer microservice is ready to compile and run. Do so using the `cargo run` command, and when it starts, check it using the following command:

```
curl -d "to=email@example.com&code=passcode" -X POST
http://localhost:8002/send
```

When you call this command, the microservice will build and send an email to the Postfix server. Actually, the email won't be delivered, because our mail server works as a relay only and many mail services will reject emails from this kind of mail server. If you want to receive emails, you need to configure the service accordingly.

Rocket

The next framework we will explore is Rocket. It's a simple-to-use framework that uses the nightly compiler's features to provide a tool that converts a set of Rust functions into a complete web service. The Rocket framework is different than the frameworks we've discussed before. It implements application configurations with environment variables and logging. The imperfection of this approach is that tuning and replacing parts is a little complex, but the positive side of this approach is that you spend next to no time coding the logging and configuration capabilities of your microservice.

Creating a microservice

Let's create a microservice that implements the commenting features of our application. It will take new comments and store them in a database. Also, a client can request any and all comments from the microservice. To start with, we need to bootstrap a new server with the Rocket framework.

Bootstrapping a server

To start a server instance, we have to prepare a database interaction. But it doesn't work directly as it did with the `diesel` crate. To connect a database, we have to add the crates we need and activate the necessary features of the `rocket_contrib` crate:

```
rocket = "0.4.0-rc.1"
rocket_contrib = { version = "0.4.0-rc.1", features =
["diesel_sqlite_pool"] }
serde = "1.0"
serde_json = "1.0"
serde_derive = "1.0"
diesel = { version = "1.3", features = ["sqlite", "r2d2"] }
diesel_migrations = "1.3"
log = "0.4"
```

We used the `diesel_sqlite_pool` feature of the `rocket_contrib` crate and `sqlite` with r2d2 from the `diesel` crate. The following lines of code import macros from all of the crates we need, add the `comment` module that we will create later, and import all necessary types:

```
#![feature(proc_macro_hygiene, decl_macro)]

#[macro_use]
extern crate rocket;
```

```
#[macro_use]
extern crate diesel;
#[macro_use]
extern crate diesel_migrations;
#[macro_use]
extern crate log;
#[macro_use]
extern crate serde_derive;
#[macro_use]
extern crate rocket_contrib;

mod comment;

use rocket::fairing::AdHoc;
use rocket::request::Form;
use rocket_contrib::json::Json;
use diesel::SqliteConnection;
use comment::{Comment, NewComment};
```

You will also see that we used two features from the nightly release:
`proc_macro_hygiene` and `decl_macro`. Without these features, you can't declare handlers.

> The nightly Rust compiler contains a lot of cool but unstable features. Unstable doesn't mean you can't use them in production applications; it means the features may be changed or even removed. Their being unstable means that it's risky to use these, because you may need to rewrite your code later. The Rocket framework requires you to use some unstable features. You can find the complete list of unstable features in the Unstable Book: `https://doc.rust-lang.org/stable/unstable-book/`.

Now we can connect to SQLite Database in the code. To do so, we create a wrapper for `SqliteConnection` and the user database attribute to assign a database connection is set in the `global.database.sqlite_database` parameters:

```
#[database("sqlite_database")]
pub struct Db(SqliteConnection);
```

Another feature we used is migration embedding, which includes all of the SQL scripts from the `migrations` folder in a program:

```
embed_migrations!();
```

Now we can create and launch a server instance. We create a `Rocket` instance with the `ignite` method call, but before we launch it, we add two middleware called fairings in the Rocket framework. The first is created for the `Db` database wrapper and provides a database pool in requests. The second is the `AdHoc` fairing, which tries to run migrations for a database. Look at the following code:

```
fn main() {
    rocket::ignite()
        .attach(Db::fairing())
        .attach(AdHoc::on_attach("Database Migrations", |rocket| {
            let conn = Db::get_one(&rocket).expect("no database
connection");
            match embedded_migrations::run(&*conn) {
                Ok(_) => Ok(rocket),
                Err(err) => {
                    error!("Failed to run database migrations: {:?}", err);
                    Err(rocket)
                },
            }
        }))
        .mount("/", routes![list, add_new])
        .launch();
}
```

After that, we call the `mount` method to add routes to the root path. Routes are created by the `routes!` macro, where we include all of the routes defined later in this section. When the `Rocket` instance is built, we run it with the `launch` method call.

Handling requests

Our microservice contains two handlers. The first handles the request for the `/list` path and returns all comments from a database:

```
#[get("/list")]
fn list(conn: Db) -> Json<Vec<Comment>> {
    Json(Comment::all(&conn))
}
```

As you can see, a handler in the Rocket framework is a function that takes parameters that **rocket** automatically binds and expects a function to return a result. Our `list` function returns a list of comments in JSON format. We use the `Comment` model declared in the `comment` module to extract all comments using a connection from a pool provided as an argument of function.

To declare a method and a path, we add the `get` attribute to a function declaration with the path we need. The get attribute allows you to call a handler with the GET method. Also, there is the `post` attribute, which we use for adding the comment handler:

```
#[post("/new_comment", data = "<comment_form>")]
fn add_new(comment_form: Form<NewComment>, conn: Db) {
    let comment = comment_form.into_inner();
    Comment::insert(comment, &conn);
}
```

The preceding function expects two parameters: Form, which can be parsed to the NewComment object, and the Db instance. The Form wrapper holds the inner value of the provided type. To extract it, we call the into_inner method, which returns the NewComment struct in our case. If form doesn't provide a request, the method won't even be called. We set the data bind in the post attribute to set an argument that stores the provided data. At the end, we use the insert method of the Comment type to insert the NewComment struct into the database using the provided Connection.

That's all! The microservice has been declared. It's pretty simple, isn't it? But the final thing we need is a schema declaration. Let's add that.

Database schema and models

Comments will be stored in a comments table that has three fields: the id of a comment, the uid of a user, and the text of a comment:

```
mod schema {
    table! {
        comments {
            id -> Nullable<Integer>,
            uid -> Text,
            text -> Text,
        }
    }
}
```

The Comment struct has the following declaration:

```
#[table_name="comments"]
#[derive(Serialize, Queryable, Insertable, Debug, Clone)]
pub struct Comment {
    pub id: Option<i32>,
    pub uid: String,
    pub text: String,
}
```

We repeated the same field in the `Comment` struct and added the `NewComment` struct without `id`:

```
#[derive(FromForm)]
pub struct NewComment {
    pub uid: String,
    pub text: String,
}
```

And now for something new—we derive the `FormForm` type for the `NewComment` struct. It helps Rocket convert a query into a `Form` instance. The next `Comment` struct implementation adds two methods:

```
impl Comment {
    pub fn all(conn: &SqliteConnection) -> Vec<Comment> {
all_comments.order(comments::id.desc()).load::<Comment>(conn).unwrap()
    }

    pub fn insert(comment: NewComment, conn: &SqliteConnection) -> bool {
        let t = Comment { id: None, uid: comment.uid, text: comment.text };
diesel::insert_into(comments::table).values(&t).execute(conn).is_ok()
    }
}
```

We use the generated method with the `diesel` crate to interact with a database using a `Connection` instance. If you want to know more about the `diesel` crate, you can read more in `Chapter 8`, *Interaction to Database with Object-Relational Mapping*.

Compiling and running

To run a microservice created with `Rocket`, you need to create a `Rocket.toml` configuration file. This allows you to configure a microservice before starting. Look at the following `Rocket.toml` contents:

```
[global]
template_dir = "static"
address = "127.0.0.1"
port = 8003

[global.databases.sqlite_database]
url = "test.db"
```

In this configuration, we declared global parameters such as: the `template_dir` directory with templates (if we use it), `address` and `port`, and a `url` for a database connection.

You can override any parameter using environment variables. For example, if we need to set the `port` parameter to 80, we can run a microservice with a command:

```
ROCKET_PORT=3721 cargo run
```

The Rocket framework also supports three different types of environment: `development`, `staging`, and `production`. It allows you to have three configurations in one. Add an extra section in addition to the `global` section and run a microservice with the corresponding mode:

```
ROCKET_ENV=staging cargo run
```

To test a microservice, it's sufficient to start it with a simple cargo run without extra parameters. When the service starts, we can add a comment with the following command and print a list of all comments:

```
curl -d 'uid=user_id&text="this is a comment"' -X POST
http://localhost:8003/new_comment
curl http://localhost:8003/list
```

This command prints all comments in JSON format. As you can see, we don't convert any structs directly to JSON. Rocket does this automatically.

Gotham

We have learned how to use three frameworks that simplify writing microservices: Rouille, Nickel, and Rocket. But all of these frameworks are synchronous. If you want to write an asynchronous microservice, you have three paths to choose from: using the `hyper` crate directly, as we did in Chapter 2, *Developing a Microservice with Hyper Crate*; using the `gotham` crate, which uses `hyper` and `tokio` internally; or using the `actix-web` framework. In this section, we will learn how to use the `gotham` crate with the asynchronous `tokio-postgres` crate to work with PostgreSQL asynchronously. We will learn about the `actix-web` crate later, in Chapter 11, *Involving Concurrency with Actors and Actix Crate*.

As an example of using the `gotham` crate, we will create a microservice that takes the User-Agent header from a request and stores it in a PostgreSQL database. We will create a completely asynchronous application and also learn about the `tokio-postgres` crate.

Creating a microservice

Create a new binary crate and add the following dependencies:

```
failure = "0.1"
futures = "0.1"
gotham = "0.3"
gotham_derive = "0.3"
hyper = "0.12"
mime = "0.3"
tokio = "0.1"
tokio-postgres = { git = "https://github.com/sfackler/rust-postgres" }
```

As you can see, we added the gotham and gotham_derive crates. The first is a framework and the second helps us derive an implementation of the StateData trait for the shared state with the connection we need. The gotham_derive crate can also be used to derive the NewMiddleware trait for middleware, but we don't need special middleware for our example.

We also added the tokio-postgres crate to dependencies. It contains an implementation of an asynchronous database connector for PostgreSQL.

Types of framework

We need a lot of types for the microservice. Let's talk a little about every type we import here:

```
use failure::{Error, format_err};
use futures::{Future, Stream, future};
use gotham::handler::HandlerFuture;
use gotham::middleware::state::StateMiddleware;
use gotham::pipeline::single::single_pipeline;
use gotham::pipeline::single_middleware;
use gotham::router::Router;
use gotham::router::builder::{DefineSingleRoute, DrawRoutes, build_router};
use gotham::state::{FromState, State};
use gotham_derive::StateData;
use hyper::Response;
use hyper::header::{HeaderMap, USER_AGENT};
use std::sync::{Arc, Mutex};
use tokio::runtime::Runtime;
use tokio_postgres::{Client, NoTls};
```

Most likely, you are familiar with types from `failure` and `futures` crates, because we used them a lot in the first part of the book. The most interesting are types of the `gotham` crate. There are modules that cover different parts of the framework; the `handler` module contains `HandlerFuture`, which is an alias to the `Future` trait with predefined types:

```
type HandlerFuture = dyn Future<
    Item = (State, Response<Body>),
    Error = (State, HandlerError)
    > + Send;
```

We will use this `Future` alias in our asynchronous handlers. Also, this module contains the `IntoHandlerFuture` trait, which is implemented for a tuple that can be converted into a response.

The `middleware` module contains `StateMiddleware`, which we will use to attach a state to our microservice.

The `pipeline` module contains two functions we will use: `single_middleware` and `single_pipeline`. The first creates a `Pipeline` with a single provided middleware inside. The second function is necessary to create a pipeline chain from a single pipeline instance.

The `router` module includes types we need to construct a routing table for our microservice. The `Router` struct is a type that contains routes and we have to instantiate and provide it for a server. We will do this with the `build_router` function call.

For the `DrawRoutes` trait, we need to have methods of `Router` to add paths. It adds `get`, `get_or_head`, `put`, `post`, and other methods to register paths with corresponding HTTP methods. Calling those methods returns the `SingleRouteBuilder` instance and we need to use the `DefineSingleRoute` trait for the `to` method, which allows us to map a registered path to a `Handler`.

The `state` module provides us with the capability to use generic `State` and convert it to a type we need by calling the `borrow_from` method of the `FromState` trait that implemented the types that implement the `StateData` trait.

Generic `State` in `gotham` is a very flexible concept and provides the capability to get references to different parts of the environment. You can get a reference to your own state type or to the request data.

We need some types from the hyper crate, because the crate is used in the gotham implementation and in some types of hyper. We imported the Response type to create responses for a client and the HeaderMap to get access to request headers, because we need to get a value for the USER_AGENT header.

Since we are developing an asynchronous application, we have to use the same reactor to execute all tasks in the same runtime. To do this, we will use a manually created Runtime from the tokio crate.

To connect to a database, we need to import the Client type from the tokio-postgres crate and NoTls to configure a connection.

Now we have imported all we need to write the main function of the application.

The main function

In the main function implementation, we create a Runtime instance, which we will use for database queries and to process HTTP requests. Look at the following code:

```
pub fn main() -> Result<(), Error> {
    let mut runtime = Runtime::new()?;

    let handshake =
tokio_postgres::connect("postgres://postgres@localhost:5432", NoTls);
    let (mut client, connection) = runtime.block_on(handshake)?;
    runtime.spawn(connection.map_err(drop));

    // ...
}
```

We create a Runtime instance. After that, we can create a new database connection by calling the connect function of the tokio-postgres crate. It returns a Future that we have to execute immediately. To run a Future, we will use the same Runtime we have already created. Runtime has the block_on method, which we have already discussed in Chapter 5, *Understanding Asynchronous Operations with Futures Crate*. We call it with a Connect future and take a pair of results: Client and Connection instances.

Client is a type that provides a method to create statements. We will store this instance in ConnState, which we will declare later in this section.

The Connection type is a task that performs actual interaction with a database. We have to spawn this task within Runtime. If you forget to do this, your database queries will be blocked and will never be sent to a database server.

Now we can use the `Client` instance to execute SQL statements. The first statement we need creates a table to log `User-Agent header` values. The `Client` struct has the `batch_execute` method, which executes multiple statements from a string. We've used only one statement, but this call is useful if you want to create more than one table:

```
let execute = client.batch_execute(
    "CREATE TABLE IF NOT EXISTS agents (
        agent TEXT NOT NULL,
        timestamp TIMESTAMPTZ NOT NULL DEFAULT NOW()
    );");
runtime.block_on(execute)?;
```

`batch_execute` returns a `Future` instance and we have to execute it immediately to initialize the database before inserting a record into it. We use the `block_on` method of a `Runtime` instance to execute the statement.

Before we finish implementing the main function, let's look at the `ConnState` struct implementation:

```
#[derive(Clone, StateData)]
struct ConnState {
    client: Arc<Mutex<Client>>,
}
```

The struct is very simple and contains the atomic reference counter, `Arc`, to a database `Client` wrapped with a `Mutex`. We need only one method to simplify instance creation:

```
impl ConnState {
    fn new(client: Client) -> Self {
        Self {
            client: Arc::new(Mutex::new(client)),
        }
    }
}
```

But you can also add a method to get the inner value of this state. It's useful if you want to declare a state type in a separate module. We will use the `client` field directly.

Also, you might notice that `ConnState` derives `Clone` and `StateData` traits. The struct has to be cloneable, because a state is cloned by Gotham for every request. `StateData` allows us to attach an instance of this struct to `StateMiddleware`.

Now we can finish the `main` function implementation:

```
let state = ConnState::new(client);
let router = router(state);

let addr = "127.0.0.1:7878";
println!("Listening for requests at http://{}", addr);
gotham::start_on_executor(addr, router, runtime.executor());
runtime
    .shutdown_on_idle()
    .wait()
    .map_err(|()| format_err!("can't wait for the runtime"))
```

We created the `ConnState` state with a `Client` value. We stored the result to the `state` variable and used it for the `router` function call, which we will declare later.

After that, we can start a Gotham server by calling the `start_on_executor` function. It expects three arguments: the *address* that we set to the `"127.0.0.1:7878"` value, the *router* value that we created with the `router` function call, and the `TaskExecutor` instance that we extracted from our `Runtime`.

Actually, the `start_on_executor` function call the spawns a task to the asynchronous reactor and we have to start our `Runtime` instance. We can do this with the `shutdown_on_idle` method call. It returns the `Shutdown` future that we run in the current thread using the `wait` method call. The `main` function ends when all tasks are complete.

Let's look at the `router` function implementation that creates the `Router` instance for our application:

```
fn router(state: ConnState) -> Router {
    let middleware = StateMiddleware::new(state);
    let pipeline = single_middleware(middleware);
    let (chain, pipelines) = single_pipeline(pipeline);
    build_router(chain, pipelines, |route| {
        route.get("/").to(register_user_agent);
    })
}
```

In the function implementation, we create a `StateMiddleware` instance and provide `ConnState` to it. We add a middleware to a pipeline with the `single_middleware` call and create a chain by calling the `single_pipeline` function call. It returns a pair of a chain and a set of pipelines.

We pass these values to the `build_router` function, which returns the `Router` instance, but we can tune the resulting `Router` by calling methods of `RouterBuilder` in a closure that we pass as a third argument to the `build_router` function.

We called the get method of `RouterBuilder` to set a handler implemented in the `register_user_agent` function to the root path, `/`. The Gotham framework supports scopes of routes that help you group handlers by a path prefix, like this:

```
route.scope("/checkout", |route| {
    route.get("/view").to(checkout::view);
    route.post("/item").to(checkout::item::create);
    route.get("/item").to(checkout::item::read);
    route.put("/item").to(checkout::item::update);
    route.patch("/item").to(checkout::item::update);
    route.delete("/item").to(checkout::item::delete);
}
```

We now only have to implement a handler.

Handler implementation

Every handler in Gotham has to return the `HandlerFuture` implementation of a tuple that can be converted to `HandlerFuture`. Also, a handler has to accept a `State` parameter:

```
fn register_user_agent(state: State) -> Box<HandlerFuture> {
    // Implementation
}
```

If you remember, we need to extract the `User-Agent` header from a request. We can do this using a `State` value, because we can borrow `HeaderMap` from a `State` with the `borrow_from` method call. It returns a map that we can use to get the `User-Agent` HTTP `header` by using the `USER_AGENT` key imported from the `hyper` crate:

```
let user_agent = HeaderMap::borrow_from(&state)
    .get(USER_AGENT)
    .map(|value| value.to_str().unwrap().to_string())
    .unwrap_or_else(|| "<undefined>".into());
```

`HeaderMap` returns `HeaderValue` as a value of `header` and we have to get the string value using the `to_str` method and convert it to an owned string with the `to_string` method. If the `header` was not provided, we use the `"<undefined>"` value.

Now we can borrow the `ConnState` value from `State` and add a new record to the database:

```
let conn = ConnState::borrow_from(&state);
let client_1 = conn.client.clone();
let client_2 = conn.client.clone();

let res = future::ok(())
    .and_then(move |_| {
        let mut client = client_1.lock().unwrap();
        client.prepare("INSERT INTO agents (agent) VALUES ($1)
                        RETURNING agent")
    })
    .and_then(move |statement| {
        let mut client = client_2.lock().unwrap();
        client.query(&statement, &[&user_agent]).collect().map(|rows| {
            rows[0].get::<_, String>(0)
        })
    })
    .then(|res| {
        let mut builder = Response::builder();
        let body = {
            match res {
                Ok(value) => {
                    let value = format!("User-Agent: {}", value);
                    builder.status(StatusCode::OK);
                    value.into()
                }
                Err(err) => {
                    builder.status(StatusCode::INTERNAL_SERVER_ERROR);
                    err.to_string().into()
                }
            }
        };
        let response = builder.body(body).unwrap();
        Ok((state, response))
    });
Box::new(res)
```

We need two references to a `Client`, because we have to resolve two futures: one is to prepare a query, the second to execute that query. To prepare a query, we will use the `prepare` method, which expects a string with a SQL statement. The method call returns a `Future` instance that returns a `Statement` instance, but we can't create that `Future` directly in the function's body, because we have to lock `Mutex` to get access to the `Client` and it will be blocked after the `Future` statement is resolved.

To use `Client` twice, we need two references to the `Client` and use them in separate closures in a chain of futures. We start creating a futures chain with the `future::ok` method call, which returns a successful `Future`. We use the `and_then` method to add the first step: statement preparation. We lock the `Mutex` to get a mutable reference to a `Client`. Then, we call the `prepare` method to create a `Future` that returns a `Statement`.

Beyond that, we can add the next step to the futures chain to fill a `Statement` with values. We lock the second `Mutex` clone to the call query method of a `Client`. The method expects a statement as a first parameter and a reference to an array with references to values. Since we know that the statement we're using inserts a new record and returns exactly one row, we extract a `String` value from the first position of the first row.

At the end of the chain, we then use the method to convert a `Result` of the query execution into a `Response`. We create a new `Builder` for a `Response`. If the query returns a successful result, we return it to a client. If the query fails, we print an error with the `500` status code. The closure returns a tuple with a pair: the `State` and `Response` instances. Gotham uses this result to return the response to the client.

The implementation is finished and now we can check it with a database instance.

Running and testing

To run this example, we need a PostgreSQL database instance. The simplest way to run it is to start a Docker container. We already did that in Chapter 7, *Reliable Integration with Databases*, where we studied how to use Rust with databases. You can start a new container with a PostgreSQL database instance using the following command:

```
docker run -it --rm --name test-pg -p 5432:5432 postgres
```

When the container is started, run the example server we wrote in this section with the `cargo run` command. It prints after compilation and the server is ready to accept requests:

```
Listening for requests at http://127.0.0.1:7878
```

Now you can use the link provided to log visits from your browser. If it is configured successfully, you will see the response in the browser:

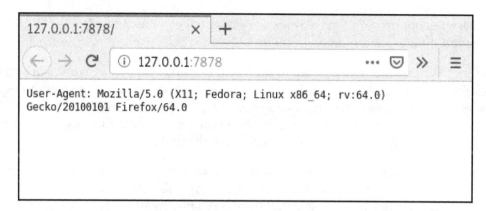

Gotham processed the request and returned a result to you. If you shut down the database, the server will return a response with a 500 error code and the *"connection closed"* string. The last thing we have to do is verify that the server added the records to the database, because we used an asynchronous approach to interact with the database and used the same Runtime to handle HTTP requests and perform SQL statements. Run the **psql** client for the postgres://postgres@localhost:5432 connection and enter a query:

```
postgres=# SELECT * FROM agents;
                                            agent
 | timestamp
-------------------------------------------------+--------------------------------
  Mozilla/5.0 Gecko/20100101 Firefox/64.0   | 2019-01-10 19:43:59.064265+00
  Chrome/71.0.3578.98 Safari/537.36         | 2019-01-10 19:44:08.264106+00
 (2 rows)
```

We made two requests from two different browsers and now we have two records in the agents table.

Summary

This chapter introduced you to comfortable frameworks that greatly simplify the writing of microservices: Rouille, Nickel, and Rocket.

The Rouille framework is built around the `router!` macro and helps you to declare all the paths and methods you need in a simple way. The routing declaration looks similar to how we did it with Hyper, but much, much simpler.

The Nickel framework is also pretty simple to use and is inspired by the Express framework of JavaScript.

The Rocket framework is pretty cool and helps you to write a handler in an intuitive, clear style, but it needs the nightly version of the compiler.

The Gotham framework is an asynchronous framework that's based on the `tokio` and `hyper` crates. It allows you to use all of the benefits of asynchronous applications: handling thousands of requests in parallel and utilizing all resources completely. We created an example that works with a database by sending queries to it using the asynchronous `tokio-postgres` crate.

But there are many more frameworks and we can't cover all of them. Most frameworks are synchronous and are simple to use. If you want to write an asynchronous microservice, I recommend you use, in most cases, the `actix-web` crate, which we will explore in the next chapter.

10
Background Tasks and Thread Pools in Microservices

In this chapter, you'll learn how to use background tasks in microservices. In `Chapter 5`, *Understanding Asynchronous Operations with the Futures Crate*, we created a microservice that provides a feature that enables the user to upload images. Now, we'll create another version of this service, which loads an image and returns a resized version of that image.

To utilize the available resources fully, microservices have to be implemented with asynchronous code, but not every part of a microservices can be asynchronous. For example, parts that require massive CPU load or parts that have to use shared resources should be implemented in a separate thread or use a pool of threads to avoid blocking the main threads that are used to process the event loops used by asynchronous code.

In this chapter, we'll cover the following topics:

- How to interact with spawned threads
- How to use the `futures-cpupool` and `tokio-threadpool` crates

Technical requirements

In this chapter, we'll improve the images microservice from `Chapter 5`, *Understanding Asynchronous Operations with the Futures Crate,* by adding an image-resizing feature. To compile the examples, you need the Rust compiler, version 1.31 or newer.

You can get the sources of the examples in this chapter from the project on GitHub: `https://github.com/PacktPublishing/Hands-On-Microservices-with-Rust/tree/master/Chapter10`.

Interacting with threads

We'll first implement this using a separate thread that will resize all incoming images. After that, we'll improve the microservice with multiple threads using thread pools. In this section, we'll start to use threads to perform tasks in the background.

Synchronous or asynchronous?

In this book, we prefer to create asynchronous microservices, because these can handle a lot of concurrent requests. Not every task, however, can be handled in an asynchronous way. Whether we can use an asynchronous microservice depends on the kind of task and the resources it needs. Let's explore the difference further.

IO-bound versus CPU-bound tasks

There are two types of tasks. If a task doesn't carry out many calculations, but it does do a lot of input/output operations, it's called an I/O-bound task. Since CPU is much faster than input/output buses, we have to wait a long time for a bus or device to be available for reading or writing. I/O-bound tasks can be handled well in an asynchronous way.

If a task does a lot operations using CPU, it's called a CPU-bound task. For example, image resizing is a kind of CPU-bound task, because it recalculates the pixels from an original image, but only saves the result when it's ready.

The difference between I/O-bound and CPU-bound tasks isn't obvious and not every task can be classified strictly to an I/O or CPU domain. To resize an image, you have to keep the whole image in the memory, but if your service transcodes video streams, it may take a lot of I/O and CPU resources simultaneously.

Synchronous tasks inside asynchronous contexts

Let's say you know which class the task belongs to, either I/O or CPU. IO tasks can be handled in a single thread, because they have to wait for a lot of I/O data. If your hardware has multicore CPUs and a lot of I/O devices, however, a single thread isn't enough. You may decide to use multiple threads with a single asynchronous context, but there's a problem—not every asynchronous task can be transferred between threads. For example, SQLite-embedded databases stores service data in thread-local storage, and you can't use the same database handle with multiple threads.

SQLite can't work with databases asynchronously; it has asynchronous methods that interact with instances that run in a separate thread, but you have to remember that not every task can be run in multithreaded contexts.

A good solution if we have a multicore hardware is to use a thread pool to handle connections. You can transfer connection contexts to any thread from the pool, which can handle connections asynchronously.

Rust and well-written crates prevent you from making mistakes; in my opinion, Rust is the best tool in existence for writing fast and secure software. However, it's important to be aware of a certain situation that's hard to detect with a compiler, which occurs when you call a blocking operation in an asynchronous context. Asynchronous applications use a reactor that calls the necessary code when a piece of data is ready to read or write, but if you've called the blocking method, the reactor can't be called and all connections that are handled by the blocked thread will be blocked as well. Even worse, the application might be completely blocked if you call a synchronous method related to the reactor. For example, if you try to send a message to a receiver handled by a reactor, but the channel is full, the program will be blocked, because the reactor must be called to drain the channel, but this can't be done because the thread is already blocked by the message being sent. Take a look at the following example: *deadlock*

```
fn do_send(tx: mpsc::Sender<Msg>) -> impl Future<Item = (), Error = ()> {
    future::lazy(|| {
        tx.send(Msg::Event).wait(); // The program will be blocked here
    })
}
```

The conclusion is simple—only use asynchronous operations in asynchronous contexts.

The limitations of using IO operations on files

As mentioned, some libraries, such as SQLite, use blocking operations to perform queries to a database and get the result back, but this depends on what kind of IO they use. A network stack is completely asynchronous in modern operating systems, but the input/output of files is harder to use asynchronously. Operating systems contain functions to carry out asynchronous reading or writing, but it's hard to implement this with cross-platform compatibility. It's simpler to use a separate thread to handle hard-drive IO interactions. The tokio crate uses a separate thread to handle the IO of files. Other platforms, such as Go or Erlang, do the same thing. You can use asynchronous IO for files for specific operating systems, but this isn't a very flexible approach.

Now that you know the difference between synchronous and asynchronous tasks, we're ready to create an asynchronous service that uses a separate thread for the CPU-bound task of resizing images.

Spawning a thread for image processing

In our first example, we'll create a microservice that expects a request with an image, loads it completely to the memory, sends it to a thread for resizing, and waits for the result. Let's start by creating a thread that expects image data and responses. To receive the request, we'll use the `mpsc::channel` module and `oneshot::channel` for responses, because multiple clients can't send requests and we only expect one response per image. For the requests, we'll use the following struct:

```
struct WorkerRequest {
    buffer: Vec<u8>,
    width: u16,
    height: u16,
    tx: oneshot::Sender<WorkerResponse>,
}
```

`WorkerRequest` contains the `buffer` field for binary image data, the desired `width` and `height` of the resized image, and a `tx` sender of the `oneshot::Sender` type for sending a `WorkerReponse` response.

The response is presented by a type alias to the `Result` type, which holds the successful result with the binary data of the resized image or an error:

```
type WorkerResponse = Result<Vec<u8>, Error>;
```

We can now create a thread that supports these messages and carries out resizing:

```
fn start_worker() -> mpsc::Sender<WorkerRequest> {
    let (tx, rx) = mpsc::channel::<WorkerRequest>(1);
    thread::spawn(move || {
        let requests = rx.wait();
        for req in requests {
            if let Ok(req) = req {
                let resp = convert(req.buffer, req.width,
req.height).map_err(other);
                req.tx.send(resp).ok();
            }
        }
    });
```

```
        tx
    }
```

Since we use a single thread for all resizing requests, we can use the `wait` method of the `Sender` and `Receiver` for interacting with clients. The preceding code creates a `channel` from the `mpsc` module that can keep one message in a buffer. We don't need more space in the buffer for the message, because resizing takes a long period of time and we just need to send the next message to a receiver while we're processing an image.

We use the `thread::spawn` method to spawn a new thread with a processing function. The `Receiver::wait` method converts a `Receiver` to a blocking iterator of the incoming messages. We use a simple loop to iterate over all the requests. The reactor isn't needed here. If the message is received successfully, we'll process the request. To convert the image, we use the `convert` method that's described in the following code snippet. We send the result to `oneshot::Sender`, which doesn't have a `wait` method; all we need to do is call the `send` method, which returns a `Result`. This operation won't block and doesn't need a reactor, because it uses `UnsafeCell` internally to provide a value for the `Receiver` that implements the `Future` trait.

To resize the image, we use an `image` crate. This contains a rich set of methods for image transformation and supports multiple image formats. Take a look at the implementation of the `convert` function:

```
fn convert(data: Vec<u8>, width: u16, height: u16) -> ImageResult<Vec<u8>>
{
    let format = image::guess_format(&data)?;
    let img = image::load_from_memory(&data)?;
    let scaled = img.resize(width as u32, height as u32,
FilterType::Lanczos3);
    let mut result = Vec::new();
    scaled.write_to(&mut result, format)?;
    Ok(result)
}
```

The function expects binary data of an image, related to its width and height. The `convert` function returns an `ImageResult`, which is a type alias for `Result` with `ImageError` as the error type. We use this error type, because some methods inside the `convert` function implementation can return errors of this type.

The first line of the implementation tries to guess the format of incoming data with the guess_format function. We can use this format value later on to use the same format for the output image. After that, we use the load_from_memory function to read an image from a data vector. This call reads the data and actually doubles the amount of consumed memory for the image – be aware of this if you want to process multiple images simultaneously. After resizing, we write the scaled image to a vector and return it as a Result. The scaled image also consumes some memory, meaning we're almost tripling the consumption. It's better to add limits for the size of the incoming message, the width, and the height to prevent memory overflow.

We can now implement the main function, which spawns a worker thread and starts a server instance:

```
fn main() {
    let addr = ([127, 0, 0, 1], 8080).into();
    let builder = Server::bind(&addr);
    let tx = start_worker();
    let server = builder.serve(move || {
        let tx = tx.clone();
        service_fn(move |req| microservice_handler(tx.clone(), req))
    });
    let server = server.map_err(drop);
    hyper::rt::run(server);
}
```

The only difference here from the main function of the previous chapter is that we call the start_worker function and use the returned Sender as a parameter for the handler function along with a request.

Let's look at an implementation of microservice_handler and learn how it interacts with a worker.

Interacting with a thread in an asynchronous way

The handler function of the image-resizing microservice contains two branches: one for the index page and one for the resize request. Take a look at the following code:

```
fn microservice_handler(tx: mpsc::Sender<WorkerRequest>, req:
Request<Body>)
    -> Box<Future<Item=Response<Body>, Error=Error> + Send>
{
    match (req.method(), req.uri().path().to_owned().as_ref()) {
        (&Method::GET, "/") => {
            Box::new(future::ok(Response::new(INDEX.into())))
```

```
        },
        (&Method::POST, "/resize") => {
            let (width, height) = {
                // Extracting parameters here
            };
            let body = ; // It's a Future for generating a body of the
Response
            Box::new(body)
        },
        _ => {
            response_with_code(StatusCode::NOT_FOUND)
        },
    }
}
```

In the `resize` branch part of the handler, we have to carry out various actions: extract parameters, collect a body from a stream, send a task to a worker, and generate a body. Since we use asynchronous code, we'll create a chain of method calls to construct the necessary `Future` object.

To extract the parameters, we use the following code:

```
let (width, height) = {
    let uri = req.uri().query().unwrap_or("");
    let query = queryst::parse(uri).unwrap_or(Value::Null);
    let w = to_number(&query["width"], 180);
    let h = to_number(&query["height"], 180);
    (w, h)
};
```

We use the `query` part of `uri` and the `parse` function of the `queryst` crate to parse the parameters to `Json::Value`. After that, we can extract the necessary values by index because the `Value` type implements the `std::ops::Index` trait. Taking a value by index returns a `Value`, which will be `Value::Null` if the value isn't set. The `to_number` function tries to represent a value as a string and parse it to the `u16` value. Alternatively, it returns a default value, which you set as a second parameter:

```
fn to_number(value: &Value, default: u16) -> u16 {
    value.as_str()
        .and_then(|x| x.parse::<u16>().ok())
        .unwrap_or(default)
}
```

By default, we'll use an image size of 180 × 180 pixels.

The next part of the handling branch creates the body of the response using the size parameters we extracted from the query string. The following code collects a stream of the request to a vector and uses a worker instance to resize an image:

```
let body = req.into_body()
    .map_err(other)
    .concat2()
    .map(|chunk| chunk.to_vec())
    .and_then(move |buffer| {
        let (resp_tx, resp_rx) = oneshot::channel();
        let resp_rx = resp_rx.map_err(other);
        let request = WorkerRequest { buffer, width, height, tx: resp_tx };
        tx.send(request)
            .map_err(other)
            .and_then(move |_| resp_rx)
            .and_then(|x| x)
    })
    .map(|resp|  Response::new(resp.into()));
```

To interact with a worker, we create a `oneshot::channel` instance and a `WorkerRequest` with the necessary parameters. After that, we `send` a request to a worker using the `tx` variable, which is a `Sender` instance connected to a worker and was provided with the `microservice_handler` function call. The `send` method creates a future that succeeds if a message is sent successfully. We add a step to this future with the `and_then` method, which reads a value from a `oneshot::Recevier` that implements the `Future` trait as well.

When the scaled message is ready, we take it as a result of `Future` and `map` it to a response.

Test the example by sending an image using `curl`:

```
curl --request POST \
    --data-binary "@../../media/image.jpg" \
    --output "files/resized.jpg" \
    "http://localhost:8080/resize?width=100&height=100"
```

We've sent `image.jpg` from the media folder and saved the result to the `files/resized.jpg` file.

The major drawback of this microservice is that it only uses a single thread, which will quickly become a bottleneck. To prevent this, we can use multiple threads to share CPU resources to handle more requests. Let's now look at how to use thread pools.

Using thread pools

To use thread pools, you don't need a special library. Instead, you can implement a scheduler that sends requests to a bunch of threads. You can even check the responses of workers to decide which thread to choose for processing, but there are ready-to-use crates that help to solve this issue more elegantly. In this section, we're going to look at the `futures-cpupool` and `tokio-threadpool` crates.

CpuPool

Here, we'll reuse an existing microservice and remove the `start_worker` function, and the `WorkerRequest` and `WorkerResult` types. Keep the `convert` function and add a new dependency to `Cargo.toml`:

```
futures-cpupool = "0.1"
```

Import the `CpuPool` type from that crate:

```
use futures_cpupool::CpuPool;
```

The pool is now ready to use in the request handler. We can pass it as a parameter, like we did with the `Sender` of the worker thread in the previous example:

```
fn main() {
    let addr = ([127, 0, 0, 1], 8080).into();
    let pool = CpuPool::new(4);
    let builder = Server::bind(&addr);
    let server = builder.serve(move || {
        let pool = pool.clone();
        service_fn(move |req| microservice_handler(pool.clone(), req))
    });
    let server = server.map_err(drop);
    hyper::rt::run(server);
}
```

In the preceding code, we created a thread pool with four threads and passed it to the `serve` function to `clone` it for the handler. The handler function takes a pool as the first argument:

```
fn microservice_handler(pool: CpuPool, req: Request<Body>)
    -> Box<Future<Item=Response<Body>, Error=Error> + Send>
```

We use the same branches and the code to extract the width and height parameters. We change how we convert the image, however:

```
let body = req.into_body()
    .map_err(other)
    .concat2()
    .map(|chunk| chunk.to_vec())
    .and_then(move |buffer| {
        let task = future::lazy(move || convert(&buffer, width, height));
        pool.spawn(task).map_err(other)
    })
    .map(|resp| Response::new(resp.into()));
```

The code of this implementation has become more compact and accurate. In this implementation, we also collect a body to a `Vec` binary, but to convert the image we use a lazy `Future` that spawned in a thread pool using the `spawn` method of `CpuPool`.

We use the `future::lazy` call to postpone the execution of the `convert` function. Without the `lazy` call, the `convert` function will be called immediately and will block all IO activities. You can also set specific parameters for `CpuPool` using `Bulder`. This helps to set the quantity of threads in a pool, the stack size, and the hooks that will be called after the start of a new thread and before it stops.

`CpuPool` is not the only way to use pools. Let's look at another example.

The blocking section

The `tokio-threadpool` crate contains a `blocking` function that's declared as follows:

```
pub fn blocking<F, T>(f: F) -> Poll<T, BlockingError> where F: FnOnce() ->
T
```

This function expects any function that performs blocking operations and runs it in a separate thread, providing a `Poll` result that can be used by a reactor. It is a slightly low-level approach but it's actively used by `tokio` and other crates (to perform IO operations on files).

The positive side of this approach is that we don't need to create a thread pool manually. We can use the simple `main` function, as we've done before:

```
fn main() {
    let addr = ([127, 0, 0, 1], 8080).into();
    let builder = Server::bind(&addr);
    let server = builder.serve(|| service_fn(|req|
```

```
    microservice_handler(req)));
        let server = server.map_err(drop);
        hyper::rt::run(server);
}
```

To spawn a task that calls the `convert` function, we can use the following code:

```
let body = req.into_body()
        .map_err(other)
        .concat2()
        .map(|chunk| chunk.to_vec())
            .and_then(move |buffer| {
                future::poll_fn(move || {
                    let buffer = &buffer;
                    blocking(move || {
                        convert(buffer, width, height).unwrap()
                    })
                })
                .map_err(other)
            })
            .map(|resp| Response::new(resp.into()));
```

The `blocking` function call delegates the task execution to another thread and returns a `Poll` for every call until the result of the execution is ready. To call a raw function that returns a `Poll` result, we can wrap that function with a `future::poll_fn` function call that converts any polling function to a Future instance. Looks simple, doesn't it? We didn't even create a thread pool manually.

For example, the `tokio-fs` crate uses this method to implement IO operations on files:

```
impl Write for File {
    fn write(&mut self, buf: &[u8]) -> io::Result<usize> {
        ::would_block(|| self.std().write(buf))
    }
    fn flush(&mut self) -> io::Result<()> {
        ::would_block(|| self.std().flush())
    }
}
```

`would_block` is a wrapper over the blocking function:

```
fn would_block<F, T>(f: F) -> io::Result<T>
where F: FnOnce() -> io::Result<T>,
{
    match tokio_threadpool::blocking(f) {
        Ok(Ready(Ok(v))) => Ok(v),
        Ok(Ready(Err(err))) => {
```

```
            debug_assert_ne!(err.kind(), WouldBlock);
            Err(err)
        }
        Ok(NotReady) => Err(WouldBlock.into()),
        Err(_) => Err(blocking_err()),
    }
}
```

You now know how any blocking operation can be joined with an asynchronous reactor. This approach is used not only to interact with filesystems, but also for databases and other crates that don't support the `futures` crate or that need massive calculations with CPU.

Actors

Threads and thread pools are good ways to utilize more resources of a server, but it's a tedious programming style. You have to think about a lot of details: sending and receiving messages, load distribution, and respawning failed threads.

There's another approach to run tasks concurrently: actors. The actors model is a computational model that uses computational primitives called **actors**. They work in parallel and interact with each other by passing messages. It's a more flexible approach than using threads or pools, because you delegate every complex task to a separate actor that receives messages and return results to any entity that sent a request to an actor. Your code becomes well structured and you can even reuse actors for different projects.

We already studied `futures` and `tokio` crates, which are tricky to use directly, but they're a good foundation to build asynchronous computational frameworks, and especially it's good to implement actors model. The `actix` crate already did that: it's based on both crates to bring an actors model to Rust. Let's study how we can use actors to perform background tasks.

We'll re-implement the resizing microservice, but add three actors: a resizing actor, a counting actor, which counts the amount of requests, and a logging actor, which will write the count values to `syslog`.

Basics of the actix framework

The actix crate provides a well-organized actors model that's simple to use. There are main concepts you should remember. At first, the actix crate has the System type, which is the main type to maintain actors system. You have to create the System instance before you create and spawn any actor. Actually, System is an Actor that controls the whole process and can be used to stop an application.

Actor is the most-used trait of the framework. Every type that implements the Actor trait can be spawned. We'll implement this trait for our types later in this chapter. Also, the actix crate contains the Arbiter type, which is an event loop controller that have to be one per thread. There's SyncArbiter to run CPU-boud tasks, and this arbiter uses pools of threads to perform actors.

Every Actor has to work in a Context, which is an environment to a runtime and can be used to spawn other tasks. Also, every Actor instance takes an Address and you can use it to send messages to actors and receive responses. We'll store in our example addresses of all necessary actors to a shared state to use them from different handlers in parallel.

Address provides a send method that expects a type that implements the Message trait. To implement message-handling for Actor, you have to implement the Handler trait for the actor's type.

Arbiter → Sync Arbiter
Actor → System

Let's create three actors for our resizing microservice.

Context
Address } send

Implementing actors

Message
Handler

First, we have to import all necessary dependencies. We'll use the same common dependencies from previous examples in this chapter, but you also have to add the following dependencies to Cargo.toml:

```
actix = "0.7"
failure = "0.1"
syslog = "4.0"
```

We added the actix crate. It's the main crate for the current example. Also, we imported the failure crate, because we'll use the Fail trait to get access to the compat method, which converts any error type that implements the Fail trait into a Compat type that implements the std::error::Error trait.

Also, we'll use `syslog` and we added the `syslog` crate to access the system API. `syslog` is a standard of system logging. We'll use it to demonstrate how actors can perform separate tasks of the whole process. Now we can add the `actors` module to our example and add three actors.

The count actor

The first actor we'll implement is a counter. It takes a message with a string and counts the number of the same strings. We will use it to count the amount of requests of specified paths.

Types

Create the `src/actors/count.rs` module and import the following types:

```
use actix::{Actor, Context, Handler, Message};
use std::collections::HashMap;

type Value = u64;
```

We'll use the `Actor` trait to implement an actor's behavior, which works in a `Context` and receive a `Message` and handle it by the `Handler` trait implementation. Also, we need `HashMap` to store all counts. We also add the `Value` types alias and use it as a type for counting.

Actor

Actor is a struct that implements the `Actor` trait. We'll use a struct with `HashMap` inside to count the number of incoming strings:

```
pub struct CountActor {
    counter: HashMap<String, Value>,
}

impl CountActor {
    pub fn new() -> Self {
        Self {
            counter: HashMap::new(),
        }
    }
}
```

We added a new method to create an empty `CountActor` instance.

Now we can implement the `Actor` trait for our struct. The implementation is simple:

```
impl Actor for CountActor {
    type Context = Context<Self>;
}
```

We specify a context and set it to the `Context` type. The actor trait contains the default implementation of different methods that help you to react on lifetime events of your actor:

- `started`: This is called when the `Actor` instance starts.
- `stopping`: This is called when the `Actor` instance switches to the Stopping state (if `Context::stop` is called, for example).
- `stopped`: This is called when the `Actor` instance stops.

Now, let's add a message type that will be handled by the actor.

Message

The counting actor expects a message with a string, and we'll add the following struct:

```
pub struct Count(pub String);

impl Message for Count {
    type Result = Value;
}
```

The `Count` struct has a single filed with the String type and implements the `Message` trait of the Actix framework. This implementation allows us to send `Count` instances using the address of the actor.

The Message trait needs type of associated type `Result`. This value will be returned after the message is processed. We'll return a counter value for the provided string.

Handler

To add support for incoming message types, we have to implement the `Handler` trait for our actor. Let's implement `Handler` of `Count` messages for our `CountActor`:

```
impl Handler<Count> for CountActor {
    type Result = Value;

    fn handle(&mut self, Count(path): Count, _: &mut Context<Self>) ->
Self::Result {
        let value = self.counter.entry(path).or_default();
        *value = *value + 1;
```

```
        *value
    }
}
```

We also have to set the associated type with the same type of a result.

Handling occurs in the body of the `handle` method of the `Handler` trait. We'll get entry for a provided String value with the `Count` message and extract the entry of `HashMap`. If no entry is found, we'll get a default value that equals 0 for `u64` type (`Value` alias) and add 1 to that `value`.

Now `ConnActor` is ready to use. We can instantiate it and use the address of the actor to count the paths of HTTP requests. Let's add two more actors.

The log actor

The logging actor will add records to `syslog`.

Types

We need basic types from the `actix` crate and import some types from the `syslog` crate:

```
use actix::{Actor, Context, Handler, Message};
use syslog::{Facility, Formatter3164, Logger, LoggerBackend};
```

We don't need to study the `syslog` crate in detail, but let's discuss basic some types.

You can also use `use actix::prelude::*;` to import all most-used types from the `actix` crate.

`Logger` is a main struct that allows writing methods to add records to `syslog`. It includes logging the methods order by level from highest to lowest: `emerg`, `alert`, `crit`, `err`, `warning`, `notice`, `info`, `debug`. The `LoggerBackend` enum specifies the type of a connection to a logger. It can be a socket or UNIX socket. The `Facility` enum specifies the type of application which writes logs. `Formatter3164` specifies the format of logging.

There are two `Syslog` protocols described in two RFCs: `3164` and `5424`. That's why formatters have such strange names.

Now we can implement the logging actor.

Actor

The main type is the LogActor struct, which contains a Logger instance in the writer field:

```
pub struct LogActor {
    writer: Logger<LoggerBackend, String, Formatter3164>,
}
```

We'll use this logger in the Handler trait implementation to write messages, but now we need a constructor for our struct, because we have to configure Logger on start:

```
impl LogActor {
    pub fn new() -> Self {
        let formatter = Formatter3164 {
            facility: Facility::LOG_USER,
            hostname: None,
            process: "rust-microservice".into(),
            pid: 0,
        };
        let writer = syslog::unix(formatter).unwrap();
        Self {
            writer,
        }
    }
}
```

We added new method that fills the Formatter3164 struct with the Facility value and process name. Other fields are set to blank values. We create a Logger instance by calling the syslog::unix method and providing a formatter to it. We store the Logger in the writer field and return an instance of the LogActor struct.

To add the actor's behavior, we'll implement the Actor trait for the LogActor struct:

```
impl Actor for LogActor {
    type Context = Context<Self>;
}
```

Since this actor will work in the same thread with a server instance and a counting actor, we'll use the basic Context type.

Message

We need a message to send messages for writing them to `syslog`. It's enough to have a simple struct with one public `String` filed:

```
pub struct Log(pub String);

impl Message for Log {
    type Result = ();
}
```

We added the `Log` struct and implemented the `Message` trait for it. We don't need the return value for this message since logging will be a one-way process and all errors will be ignored, since they aren't critical for a microservice application. But if your microservice has to work with a strict security environment, you'll also have to inform an administrator about logging issues.

Handler

`Handler` of the `Log` messages is quite simple. We call the info method of `Logger` with a provided message and ignore errors with by converting a `Result` into an `Option`:

```
impl Handler<Log> for LogActor {
    type Result = ();

    fn handle(&mut self, Log(mesg): Log, _: &mut Context<Self>) ->
Self::Result {
        self.writer.info(mesg).ok();
    }
  }
```

The last actor we have to implement is the resizing actor.

The resize actor

The resizing actor resizes incoming messages and return resized messages to a client.

Types

We don't need any special types and will use basic types of the `actix` crate and import types from the `image` crate that we've used before:

```
use actix::{Actor, Handler, Message, SyncContext};
use image::{ImageResult, FilterType};

type Buffer = Vec<u8>;
```

We'll convert the function body from previous examples in this chapter in handler implementation that's why we imported types from the `image` crate. We added the `Buffer` alias to the `Vec<u8>` type for convenience.

Actor

We need a struct without any fields, because we'll use it with `SyncArbiter`, which runs multiple actors in multiple threads. Add the `ResizeActor` struct:

```
pub struct ResizeActor;

impl Actor for ResizeActor {
    type Context = SyncContext<Self>;
}
```

We don't need a special constructor and we implemented the `Actor` trait with the `SyncContext` type for the associate `Context` type. We'll use this context type to make this actor suitable for the synchronous environment of `SyncArbiter`.

Message

We don't use the convert function in this example, but we need the same parameters and we'll take them from the `Resize` struct:

```
pub struct Resize {
    pub buffer: Buffer,
    pub width: u16,
    pub height: u16,
}

impl Message for Resize {
    type Result = ImageResult<Buffer>;
}
```

We provide a `buffer` with the image data, and the desired `width` and `height`. In the `Message` trait implementation of the `Resize` struct, we use the `ImageResult<Buffer>` type. The same result type that the `convert` function returns. We'll get this value from the actor in the HTTP handler implementation later.

Handler

We implement the `Handler` of the `Resize` message for `ResizeActor`, but use the body of the `convert` function with fields of the passed message:

```
impl Handler<Resize> for ResizeActor {
    type Result = ImageResult<Buffer>;

    fn handle(&mut self, data: Resize, _: &mut SyncContext<Self>) ->
Self::Result {
        let format = image::guess_format(&data.buffer)?;
        let img = image::load_from_memory(&data.buffer)?;
        let scaled = img.resize(data.width as u32, data.height as u32,
FilterType::Lanczos3);
        let mut result = Vec::new();
        scaled.write_to(&mut result, format)?;
        Ok(result)
    }
}
```

We also use `SyncContext` instead of `Context`, like we did for previous actors.

All actors are ready and you need to add all modules to the `src/actors/mod.rs` file:

```
pub mod count;
pub mod log;
pub mod resize;
```

Now we can implement a server with actors that perform resizing and other tasks for every request.

Using the server with actors

Import all necessary types for a server. It's worth noting only those with which you're unfamiliar:

```
use actix::{Actor, Addr};
use actix::sync::SyncArbiter;
```

Addr is an address of an actor. SyncArbiter is a synchronous event-loop controller that handles every message synchronously. We need it for resizing actors. Also, add the actors module and import all the types we declared in the submodules:

```
mod actors;

use self::actors::{
    count::{Count, CountActor},
    log::{Log, LogActor},
    resize::{Resize, ResizeActor},
};
```

We need a shared state to keep all the addresses of the actors that we'll use to handle requests:

```
#[derive(Clone)]
struct State {
    resize: Addr<ResizeActor>,
    count: Addr<CountActor>,
    log: Addr<LogActor>,
}
```

The Addr type is cloneable and we can derive the Clone trait for our State struct, because we have to clone for every service function of hyper. Let's implement the main function with a new shared State:

```
fn main() {
    actix::run(|| {
        let resize = SyncArbiter::start(2, || ResizeActor);
        let count = CountActor::new().start();
        let log = LogActor::new().start();

        let state = State { resize, count, log };

        let addr = ([127, 0, 0, 1], 8080).into();
        let builder = Server::bind(&addr);
        let server = builder.serve(move || {
            let state = state.clone();
            service_fn(move |req| microservice_handler(&state, req))
        });
        server.map_err(drop)
    });
}
```

First, we have to start the event loop. This makes with actix::run method call. We pass a closure that prepares all actors and return a Future to run. We'll use the Server type of hyper.

In closure, we start `SyncArbiter` with a function that produces a `ResizeActor` instance. With the first argument, we set the amount of thread that `SyncArbiter` will use to process requests. The `start` method returned an address of an arbiter that will route the message to both resizing actors.

To start other actors, we can use the start method of the `Actor` trait, because the `actix::run` method creates a `System` instance and a default `Arbiter` for us. We created `CountActor` and `LogActor` this way. The `start` method of the `Actor` trait also returns the addresses of actors. We put them all into a new `State` struct.

After, we create a `Server` instance, like we did in the previous example, but also pass a reference to the cloned `State`.

Requests handler

Before we implement a handler of HTTP requests, let's add a function that uses `State` to send a message to `CountActor` and use the returned value to print it with `LogActor`. Look at the following function:

```
fn count_up(state: &State, path: &str) -> impl Future<Item=(), Error=Error>
{
    let path = path.to_string();
    let log = state.log.clone();
    state.count.send(Count(path.clone()))
        .and_then(move |value| {
            let message = format!("total requests for '{}' is {}", path,
value);
            log.send(Log(message))
        })
        .map_err(|err| other(err.compat()))
}
```

We converted the path into a `String`, because we need this type for the `Count` message, and to move it to a `Future` that sends a `Log` message to `LogActor`. Also, we have to clone `Addr` to `LogActor`, because we'll need it later in the closure after the counter value become available. Now let's create a `Future` that sends the `Count` message and the `Log` message in turn.

The `Addr` struct has a `send` method that returns a `Request` instance that implements the `Future` trait. `Request` will return a counter value when it's available. We use the `and_then` method of `Future` to add extra `Future` to a chain. We need to prepare a message for `syslog` and send it to `LogActor` using the cloned `Addr`.

We also convert error to `io::Error`, but the send method returns `MaiboxError` as an error type that implements the `Fail` trait, but not implement `Error` trait from standard library and we have to use the `compat` method to convert an error to the `Compat` type of the `failure` crate that implements the standard `Error` trait.

We'll use the `count_up` method for both paths, / and /resize. Look at the `microservice_handler` implementation:

```
fn microservice_handler(state: &State, req: Request<Body>)
    -> Box<Future<Item=Response<Body>, Error=Error> + Send>
{
    match (req.method(), req.uri().path().to_owned().as_ref()) {
        (&Method::GET, "/") => {
            let fut = count_up(state, "/").map(|_|
Response::new(INDEX.into())));
            Box::new(fut)
        },
        (&Method::POST, "/resize") => {
            let (width, height) = {
                let uri = req.uri().query().unwrap_or("");
                let query = queryst::parse(uri).unwrap_or(Value::Null);
                let w = to_number(&query["width"], 180);
                let h = to_number(&query["height"], 180);
                (w, h)
            };
            // Add an implementation here
            Box::new(fut)
        },
        _ => {
            response_with_code(StatusCode::NOT_FOUND)
        },
    }
}
```

It remains the same in some parts, but now it takes a reference to `State` as a first argument. Since this handling function has to return a `Future` implementation, we can use the value returned by the `count_up` function call, but replace the value to `Response`. We already did it for the root path. Let's add a resizing functionality using `Addr` of `ResizeActor`.

To send an image buffer to an actor, we have to collect it from `Body` of `Request` using the `collect2` method, like we did before:

```
let resize = state.resize.clone();
let body = req.into_body()
    .map_err(other)
    .concat2()
```

```
        .map(|chunk| {
            chunk.to_vec()
        })
        .and_then(move |buffer| {
            let msg = Resize {
                buffer,
                width,
                height,
            };
            resize.send(msg)
                .map_err(|err| other(err.compat()))
                .and_then(|x| x.map_err(other))
        })
        .map(|resp| {
            Response::new(resp.into())
        });
    let fut = count_up(state, "/resize").and_then(move |_| body);
```

After that, we create the `Resize` message and send it to `ResizeActor` using the cloned `Addr` of that actor. We convert all errors to `io::Error`. But wait, we haven't added requests counting and logging. Add the `count_up` function call at the end and put it before the `Future` that resizes images by creating a chain using the `and_then` method.

That's all! Now every request send path to `CountActor` than send an informational message to `LogActor` and the resizing request also connect all data and send it for resizing to `ResizeActor`. It's time to test it.

Building and running

Build and run the code using the `cargo run` subcommand. When the server starts use the `curl` command to send `POST` request with an image. You can find example of parameters for this preceding command.

For example, I requested the root path five times with a browser and sent a resizing request once. It stored resized message to the `files` folder. Yeah, it works! Now we can check that the logging actor adds records to `syslog`. Use this command to print logs:

```
journalctl
```

You can find the following records:

```
Jan 11 19:48:53 localhost.localdomain rust-microservice[21466]: total
requests for '/' = 1
Jan 11 19:48:55 localhost.localdomain rust-microservice[21466]: total
```

```
requests for '/' = 2
Jan 11 19:48:55 localhost.localdomain rust-microservice[21466]: total
requests for '/' = 3
Jan 11 19:48:56 localhost.localdomain rust-microservice[21466]: total
requests for '/' = 4
Jan 11 19:48:56 localhost.localdomain rust-microservice[21466]: total
requests for '/' = 5
Jan 11 19:49:16 localhost.localdomain rust-microservice[21466]: total
requests for '/resize' = 1
```

As you can see, we have five requests to the root path and one to the /resize path.

If you don't have the jounrnalctl command, you can try to print logs with the less /var/log/syslog command.

This example used actors to run concurrent activities. Actually, only ResizeActor used a separate thread with SyncArbiter. CountActor and LogActor used the same thread with the hyper server. But it's OK, since neither actors don't load a lot of CPU.

Summary

In this chapter, we looked at how to use thread pools in microservices. We investigated three approaches: using plain threads, using the futures-cpupool crate, and using the tokio-threadpool crate. We used channels from the futures crate to interact with threads from asynchronous code. Special crates do all the interaction automatically; all you need to do is call a function that will be executed in a separate thread.

Also, we got acquainted with the actix crate and the actors model, which helps to split and run tasks as separate units that are managed by a smart runtime.

In the next chapter, we'll learn how to interact with different databases using Rust, including PostgreSQL, MySQL, Redis, MongoDB, and DynamoDB.

11
Involving Concurrency with Actors and the Actix Crate

This chapter will show an alternative approach to creating microservices based on the actors model (like Erlang or Akka). This approach allows you to write clear and effective code by splitting a microservice into small independent tasks that interact with each other by message passing.

By the end of this chapter, you will be able to do the following:

- Create a microservice using the Actix framework and the `actix-web` crate
- Create middleware for the Actix Web framework

Technical requirements

To implement and run all the examples of this chapter, you'll need the Rust compiler with version 1.31 as a minimum.

You can find the sources for the code examples in this chapter on GitHub: `https://github.com/PacktPublishing/Hands-On-Microservices-with-Rust/tree/master/Chapter11`

Actor concurrency in microservices

If you are familiar with Erlang or Akka, you may already know what actors are and how to use them. But in any case, we'll refresh our knowledge about the actors model in this section.

Understanding actors

We already became familiar with actors in `Chapter 10`, *Background Tasks and Thread Pools in Microservices*, but let's talk about using actors for microservices.

An actor is a model for doing concurrent computations. We should know the following models:

- **Threads**: In this model, every task works in a separate thread
- **Fibers or green threads**: In this model, every task has work scheduled by a special runtime
- **Asynchronous code**: In this model, every task is run by a reactor (actually, this is similar to fibers)

Actors combine all these approaches into an elegant one. To do any part of the work, you can implement actors that perform their own part of the work, and interact with other actors through messages to inform each other on the overall progress. Every actor has a mailbox for incoming messages and can send messages to other actors using this address.

Actors in microservices

To develop a microservice using actors, you should split your service into tasks that solves different kinds of work. For example, you can use a separate actor for every incoming connection or database interaction, and even as a supervisor to control other actors. Every actor is an asynchronous task that is executed in a reactor.

The benefits of this approach are as follows:

- It's simpler to write separate actors than a bulk of functions
- Actors can fail and respawn
- You can reuse actors

One important benefit of using actors is reliability, because every actor can be failed and respawned, so you don't need a long recovery code to handle failures. It doesn't mean your code can call the `panic!` macro everywhere, but this does mean that you can consider actors as short life cycle tasks that work concurrently on small tasks.

If you design actors well, you also gain great performance, because interaction with messages helps you to split work into short reactions, which won't block the reactor for a long time. Also, your source code becomes more structured.

The Actix framework

The Actix framework provides an actors model for Rust, based on the `futures` crate and some asynchronous code to allow actors to work concurrently with minimal resources needed.

I think this is one of the best tools for creating web applications and microservices with Rust. The framework includes two good crates—the `actix` crate that contains core structures, and the `actix-web` crate that implements the HTTP and WebSocket protocols. Let's create a microservice that routes requests to other microservices.

Creating a microservice with actix-web

In this section, we will create a microservice that looks similar to other microservices we created in Chapter 9, *Simple REST Definition and Requests Routing with Frameworks*, but use an actors model internally to achieve full resource utilization.

To create a microservice using `actix-web`, you need to add both the `actix` and `actix-web` crates. First, we need to start the `System` actor that manages the runtime of other actors. Let's create a `System` instance and start an `actix-web` server with the necessary routes.

Bootstrapping an actix-web server

Starting an `actix-web` server instance looks similar to other Rust web frameworks, but requires a `System` actor instance. We don't need to use `System` directly, but need to run it by calling the `run` method when everything is ready. This call starts the `System` actor and blocks the current thread. Internally, it uses the `block_on` method that we discussed in previous chapters.

Starting a server

Consider the following code:

```
fn main() {
    env_logger::init();
    let sys = actix::System::new("router");
    server::new(|| {
        // Insert `App` declaration here
    }).workers(1)
```

```
                .bind("127.0.0.1:8080")
                .unwrap()
                .start();
        let _ = sys.run();
    }
```

We create a new server with the `server::new` method call that expects a closure to return the `App` instance. Before we create the `App` instance, we have to finish our server and run it. The `workers` method sets the number of threads to run actors.

> You can choose not to set this value explicitly, and by default, it will be equal to the number of CPUs on the system. In many cases, it's the best possible value for performance.

The next call of the `bind` method binds the server's socket to an address. If it can't be bound to an address, the method returns `Err`, and we `unwrap` the result to halt a server if we can't start a server on a desired port. At the end, we call the `start` method to start the `Server` actor. It returns an `Addr` struct with an address that you can use to send messages to a `Server` actor instance.

Actually, the `Server` actor won't run until we call run the method of the `System` instance. Add this method call, and then we'll go on to look at creating an `App` instance in detail.

App creation

Insert the following code into a closure of the `server::new` function call:

```
let app = App::with_state(State::default())
    .middleware(middleware::Logger::default())
    .middleware(IdentityService::new(
            CookieIdentityPolicy::new(&[0; 32])
            .name("auth-example")
            .secure(false),
            ))
    .middleware(Counter);
```

The `App` struct contains information about the state, middleware, and the scopes of routes. To set shared state to our application, we use the `with_state` method to construct the `App` instance. We create a default instance of the `State` struct, which is declared as follows:

```
#[derive(Default)]
struct State(RefCell<i64>);
```

`State` contains a cell with an `i64` value to count all requests. By default, it is created with a 0 value.

After this, we use the middleware method of `App` to set the three following middlewares:

- `actix_web::middleware::Logger` is a logger that uses the `log` crate to log request and responses
- `actix_web::middleware::identity::IdentityService` helps to identity requests using an identity backend that implements the `IdentityPolicy` trait
- `Counter` is a piece of middleware that we will create in the following *Middleware* section, and uses `State` to count the total quantity of requests

For our `IdentityPolicy` backend, we use `CookieIdentityPolicy` from the same identity submodule where `IdentityService` lives. `CookieIdentityPolicy` expects a key with at least 32 bytes. When an instance of an identity policy for cookies has been created, we can use methods like `path`, `name`, and `domain` to set specific cookies parameters. We also allow the sending of cookies with insecure connections by using the `secure` method with a `false` value.

 There are two special parameters of cookies you should know about: `Secure` and `HttpOnly`. The first requires secure HTTPS connection to send cookies. If you run a service for testing and use plain HTTP to connect to it, then the `CookieIdentityPolicy` won't work. `HttpOnly` parameters don't allow the use of cookies from JavaScript. `CookieIdentityPolicy` sets this parameter to true and you can't override this behavior.

Scope and routes

The next thing we have to add to our `App` instance is routing. There is a `route` function that lets you set a handler for any route. But it's more thoughtful to use scopes to construct a structure of nested paths. Look at the following code:

```
app.scope("/api", |scope| {
    scope
        .route("/signup", http::Method::POST, signup)
        .route("/signin", http::Method::POST, signin)
        .route("/new_comment", http::Method::POST, new_comment)
        .route("/comments", http::Method::GET, comments)
})
```

The `scope` method of our `App` struct expects a prefix of a path and a closure with a `scope` as a single argument, and creates a scope that can contain subroutes. We create a `scope` for the `/api` path prefix and add four routes using the `route` method: `/signup`, `/signin`, `/new_comment`, and `/comments`. The `route` method expects a suffix including a path, a method, and a handler. For example, if a server now takes a request for `/api/singup` with the `POST` method, it will call the `signup` function. Let's add a default handler for other paths.

Our microservice also uses `Counter` middleware, which we will implement later, to count the total quantity of requests. We need to add a route to render statistics for the microservice, as follows:

```
.route("/counter", http::Method::GET, counter)
```

As you can see, we don't need `scope` here, since we have only one handler and can call the `route` method directly for the `App` instance (not `scope`).

Static files handler

For the other paths that were not listed in the previous `scope`, we will use a `handler` that will return a file's content from a folder to serve static assets. The `handler` method expects a prefix for a path, and a type that implements the `Handler` trait. In our case, we will use a ready-to-use static files handler, `actix_web::fs::StaticFiles`. It needs a path to a local folder and we can also set an index file by calling the `index_file` method:

```
app.handler(
    "/",
    fs::StaticFiles::new("./static/").unwrap().index_file("index.html")
)
```

Now, if a client send a `GET` request to a path such as `/index.html` or `/css/styles.css`, then the `StaticFiles` handler will send the contents of the corresponding files from the `./static/` local folder.

HTTP client

The handlers of this microservice work as proxies and resend incoming requests to other microservices, which will not be available to users directly. To send requests to other microservices, we need an HTTP client. The `actix_web` crate contains one. To use a client, we add two functions: one for proxfying `GET` requests, and the other to send `POST` requests.

GET requests

To send GET requests, we create a get_request function that expects a url parameter and returns a Future instance with binary data:

```
fn get_request(url: &str) -> impl Future<Item = Vec<u8>, Error = Error> {
    client::ClientRequest::get(url)
        .finish().into_future()
        .and_then(|req| {
            req.send()      → Send Request
                .map_err(Error::from)
                .and_then(|resp| resp.body().from_err())
                .map(|bytes| bytes.to_vec())
        })
}
```

We use ClientRequestBuilder to create the ClientRequest instance. The ClientRequest struct already has shortcuts that create builders with a preset HTTP method. We call the get method that only sets the Method::GET value to a request that is implemented as the calling method of the ClientRequestBuilder instance. You can also use a builder to set extra headers or cookies. When you are done with these values, you have to create a ClientRequest instance from a builder by calling one of the following methods:

- body sets a body value to binary data that can be converted Into<Body>
- json sets a body value to any type that can be serialized into JSON value
- form sets a body value to a type that can be serialized with serde_urlencoded: serializer
- streaming consumes a body value from a Stream instance
- finish creates a request without a body value

We use finish, because GET requests don't contain a body value. All these methods return a Result with a ClientRequest instance as a successful value. We don't unwrap the Result and will convert it into a Future value with the into_future method call to return an Error value to a client if the handler can't even build a request.

Since we have a Future value, we can use the and_then method to add the next processing step. We call the send method of a ClientRequest to create a SendRequest instance, which implements the Future trait and sends a request to a server. Since the send call can return the SendRequestError error type, we wrap it with failure::Error.

If a request has sent successfully we can take a `MessageBody` value with the `body` method call. This method is a part of the `HttpMessage` trait. `MessageBody` also implements a `Future` trait with a `Bytes` value and we use the `and_then` method to extend a chain of futures and transform a value from `SendRequest` to `Bytes`.

Finally, we use the `to_vec` method of `Bytes` to convert it into `Vec<u8>` and provide this value as a response to a client. We have finished our method that proxies GET requests to another microservice. Let's create a similar method for POST requests.

POST requests

For POST requests, we need input parameters that will be serialized to the request's body, and output parameters that will be deserialized from the request's response body. Look at the following function:

```
fn post_request<T, O>(url: &str, params: T) -> impl Future<Item = O, Error
= Error>
where
    T: Serialize,
    O: for <'de> Deserialize<'de> + 'static,
{
    client::ClientRequest::post(url)
        .form(params).into_future().and_then(|req| {
            req.send()
                .map_err(Error::from).and_then(|resp| {
                    if resp.status().is_success() {
                        let fut = resp.json::<O>().from_err();
                        boxed(fut)
                    } else {
                        error!("Microservice error: {}", resp.status());
                        let fut = Err(format_err!("microservice error"))
                            .into_future().from_err();
                        boxed(fut)
                    }
                })
        })
}
```

The `post_request` function creates `ClientRequestBuilder` with the `post` method of `ClientRequest` and fills a form with values from the `params` variable. We convert `Result` into `Future` and send a request to a server. Also, as in the GET version, we process a response, but do it another way. We get a status of a response with the `status` method call of `HttpResponse`, and check whether it's successful, with the `is_sucess` method call.

For successful responses, we use the `json` method of `HttpResponse` to get a `Future` that collects a body and deserializes it from JSON. If the response wasn't successful, we return an error to the client. Now, we have methods to send requests to other microservices, and can implement handlers for every route.

Handlers

We added methods to proxy incoming requests and resend them to other microservices. Now, we can implement handlers for every supported path of our microservice we will provide a holistic API to a client, but actually, we will use a set of microservices to provide all the necessary services to the client. Let's start with implementation of a handler for the /signup path.

Signup

The Router microservice uses the /signup route to resend a signup request to a users microservice bound to the `127.0.0.1:8001` address. This request creates a new users with filled from `UserForm`, passed with a parameter wrapped with the `Form` type. Look at the following code:

```
fn signup(params: Form<UserForm>) -> FutureResponse<HttpResponse> {
    let fut = post_request("http://127.0.0.1:8001/signup",
params.into_inner())
        .map(|_: ()| {
            HttpResponse::Found()
            .header(header::LOCATION, "/login.html")
            .finish()
        });
    Box::new(fut)
}
```

We call the `post_request` function that we declared before to send a `POST` request to a users microservice and if it returns a successful response, we return a response with a `302` status code. We create `HttpResponseBuilder` with the corresponding status code by the `HttpResponse::Found` function call. After this, we also set the `LOCATION` header to redirect the user to a login form with the `header` method call of `HttpResponseBuilder`. Lastly, we call `finish()` to create a `HttpResponse` from a builder and return it as a boxed `Future` object.

The function has a `FutureResponse` return type that is implemented as follows:

```
type FutureResponse<I, E = Error> = Box<dyn Future<Item = I, Error = E>>;
```

As you can see, it's a `Box` with a type that implements a `Future` trait.

Also, the function expects `Form<UserForm>` as a parameter. The `UserForm` structs are declared as follows:

```
#[derive(Deserialize, Serialize)]
pub struct UserForm {
    email: String,
    password: String,
}
```

As you can see, it expects two parameters: `email` and `password`. Both will be extracted from the query string of a request in the format of `email=user@example.com&password=<secret>`. The `Form` wrapper helps to extract data from the response's body.

> The `actix_web` crate limits requests and responses by size. If you want to send or receive huge payloads, you have to override defaults that often won't allow requests larger than 256 KB. For example, if you want to increase the limit, you can use the `FormConfig` struct provided with the `with_config` method call of `Route`, and call the `limit` method of a config with the desired quantity of bytes. The HTTP client is also limited by response size. For example, if you try to read a large JSON object from a `JsonBody` instance, you may need to limit it with the `limit` method call before you use it as a `Future` object.

Signin

Other methods allow users to sign in to a microservice with the provided credentials. Look at the following `signin` function that processes requests that are sent to the `/signin` path:

```
fn signin((req, params): (HttpRequest<State>, Form<UserForm>))
    -> FutureResponse<HttpResponse>
{
    let fut = post_request("http://127.0.0.1:8001/signin",
params.into_inner())
        .map(move |id: UserId| {
            req.remember(id.id);
            HttpResponse::build_from(&req)
            .status(StatusCode::FOUND)
```

```
                .header(header::LOCATION, "/comments.html")
                .finish()
        });
    Box::new(fut)
}
```

The function has two parameters: `HttpRequest` and `Form`. The first we need to get access to a shared `State` object. The second we need to extract the `UserForm` struct from the request body. We can also use the `post_request` function here, but expect it to return a `UserId` value in its response. The `UserId` struct is declared as follows:

```
#[derive(Deserialize)]
pub struct UserId {
    id: String,
}
```

Since `HttpRequest` implements the `RequestIdentity` trait and we plugged in `IdentityService` to App, we can call the `remember` method with a user's ID to associate the current session with a user.

After this, we create a response with the `302` status code, as we did in the previous handler, and redirect users to the `/comments.html` page. But we have to build an `HttpResponse` instance from `HttpRequest` to keep the changes of the `remember` function call.

New comment

The handler for creating new comments uses the identity of a user to check that there are credentials to add a new comment:

```
fn new_comment((req, params): (HttpRequest<State>, Form<AddComment>))
    -> FutureResponse<HttpResponse>
{
    let fut = req.identity()
        .ok_or(format_err!("not authorized").into())
        .into_future()
        .and_then(move |uid| {
            let params = NewComment {
                uid,
                text: params.into_inner().text,
            };
            post_request::<_, ()>("http://127.0.0.1:8003/new_comment",
params)
        })
        .then(move |_| {
            let res = HttpResponse::build_from(&req)
```

```
                          .status(StatusCode::FOUND)
                          .header(header::LOCATION, "/comments.html")
                          .finish();
                     Ok(res)
              });
          Box::new(fut)
      }
```

This handler allows every user who has signed it to leave a comment. Let's look at how this handler works.

First, it calls the `identity` method of the `RequestIdentity` trait that returns the user's ID. We convert it to `Result` to make it possible to convert it into `Future` and return an error if the user is not identified.

We use the returned user ID value to prepare a request for the comments microservice. We extract the `text` field from an `AddComment` form, and create a `NewComment` struct with the user's ID and a comment. Structs are declared as follows:

```
#[derive(Deserialize)]
pub struct AddComment {
    pub text: String,
}

#[derive(Serialize)]
pub struct NewComment {
    pub uid: String,
    pub text: String,
}
```

We can also use a single struct with an optional `uid`, but it's safer to use a separate struct for different needs, because if we use the same struct and resend it to another microservice without validation, we can create a vulnerability that allows any user to add a comment with another user's identity. Try to avoid these kind of mistakes by using exact, strict types, instead of universal, flexible ones.

Finally, we create a redirect a client as we did before, and send the user to the `/comments.html` page.

Comments

To view all comments that were created by the previous handler, we have to send a GET request to the comments microservice with the `get_request` function that we created before and resend the response data to a client:

```
fn comments(_req: HttpRequest<State>) -> FutureResponse<HttpResponse> {
    let fut = get_request("http://127.0.0.1:8003/list")
        .map(|data| {
            HttpResponse::Ok().body(data)
        });
    Box::new(fut)
}
```

Counter

The handler that prints the total quantity of requests also has quite simple implementation, but in this case, we get access to a shared state:

```
fn counter(req: HttpRequest<State>) -> String {
    format!("{}", req.state().0.borrow())
}
```

We use the `state` method of `HttpRequest` to get a reference to a `State` instance. Since the counter value is stored in `RefCell`, we use the `borrow` method to get the value from a cell. We implemented all handlers, and now we have to add some middleware that will count every request to the microservice.

Middleware

The `actix-web` crate supports middleware that can be attached to an `App` instance to process every request and response. Middleware helps to log requests, transform them, or even control access to a group of paths using regular expressions. Consider middleware as handlers for all incoming requests and outgoing responses. To create the middleware, we first have to implement the `Middleware` trait for it. Look at the following code:

```
pub struct Counter;

impl Middleware<State> for Counter {
    fn start(&self, req: &HttpRequest<State>) -> Result<Started> {
        let value = *req.state().0.borrow();
        *req.state().0.borrow_mut() = value + 1;
        Ok(Started::Done)
```

```
    }

    fn response(&self, _req: &HttpRequest<State>, resp: HttpResponse) ->
Result<Response> {
        Ok(Response::Done(resp))
    }

    fn finish(&self, _req: &HttpRequest<State>, _resp: &HttpResponse) ->
Finished {
        Finished::Done
    }
}
```

We declare an empty `Counter` struct and implement the `Middleware` trait for it.

> The `Middleware` trait has a type parameter with a state. Since we want to use the counter of our `State` struct, we set it as a type parameter, but if you want to create middleware that is compatible with different states, you need to add type parameters to your implementation and add an implementation of necessary traits that you can export to your module or crate.

The `Middleware` trait contains three methods. We implemented all of them:

- `start` is called when the request is ready and will be sent to a handler
- `response` is called after the handler returns a response
- `finish` is called when data has been sent to a client

We use the default implementation for the `response` and `finish` methods.

For the first method, we return a response without any changes in the `Response::Done` wrapper. `Response` also has a variant, `Future`, if you want to return a `Future` that generates an `HttpResponse`.

For the second method, we return a `Done` variant of the `Finished` enum. It also has a `Future` variant that can contain a boxed `Future` object, which will be run after the `finish` method ends. Let's explore how the `start` method works in our implementation.

In the `start` method implementation of the `Counter` middleware, we will count all incoming requests. To do this, we get the current counter value from `RefCell`, add 1, and replace the cell with a new value. At the end, the method returns a `Started::Done` value to notify you that the current request will be reused in the next handler/middleware of the processing chain. The `Started` enum also has variants:

- `Response` should be used if you want to return a response immediately
- `Future` should be used if you want to run a `Future` that will return a response

Now, the microservice is ready to build and run.

Building and running

To run a microservice, use the `cargo run` command. Since we don't have an other microservice for handlers, we can use the `counter` method to check that the server and `Counter` middleware works. Try to open `http://127.0.0.1:8080/stats/counter` in the browser. It will show a `1` value on a blank page. If you refresh the page, you will see a `3` value. That's because the browser also sends a request to get a `favicon.ico` file after the main request.

Using databases

Another good feature of `actix-web`, in combination with the `actix` crate, is the ability to use databases. Do you remember how we used `SyncArbyter` to perform background tasks? It's a good approach to implement database interaction since there are not enough asynchronous database connectors and we have to use synchronous ones. Let's add the caching of responses to a Redis database for our previous example.

The database interaction actor

We start by implementing an actor that interacts with a database. Copy the previous example and add the `redis` crate to the dependencies:

```
redis = "0.9"
```

We use Redis because it's great for caching, but we can also store cached values in memory.

Create a `src/cache.rs` module and add the following dependencies:

```
use actix::prelude::*;
use failure::Error;
use futures::Future;
use redis::{Commands, Client, RedisError};
```

It adds types from the `redis` crate that we already used in Chapter 7, *Reliable Integration with Databases*, to interact with Redis storage.

Actors

Our actor has to keep an instance of `Client`. We don't use a connection pool, because we will use multiple actors for handing parallel requests to a database. Look at the following struct:

```
pub struct CacheActor {
    client: Client,
    expiration: usize,
}
```

The struct also contains an `expiration` field that holds the **time-to-live** (**TTL**) period. This defines how long Redis will hold the value.

Add a `new` method to the implementation that uses a provided address string to create a `Client` instance, and adds both the `client` and `expiration` values to the `CacheActor` struct, as follows:

```
impl CacheActor {
    pub fn new(addr: &str, expiration: usize) -> Self {
        let client = Client::open(addr).unwrap();
        Self { client, expiration }
    }
}
```

Also, we have to implement an `Actor` trait for `SyncContext`, just as we did when resizing the worker in `Chapter 10`, *Background Tasks and Thread Pools in Microservices*:

```
impl Actor for CacheActor {
    type Context = SyncContext<Self>;
}
```

Now, we can add support for messages to set and get cached values.

Messages

To interact with `CacheActor`, we have to add two types of messages: to set a value and to get a value.

Setting a value message

The first message type we add is `SetValue`, which provides a pair of key and new value for caching. The struct has two fields—`path`, which is used as a key, and `content`, which holds a value:

```
struct SetValue {
    pub path: String,
    pub content: Vec<u8>,
}
```

Let's implement a `Message` trait for the `SetValue` struct with an empty unit type if the value is set, and return `RedisError` if there are issues with a database connection:

```
impl Message for SetValue {
    type Result = Result<(), RedisError>;
}
```

`CacheActor` has support for receiving `SetValue` messages. Let's implement this with the `Handler` trait:

```
impl Handler<SetValue> for CacheActor {
    type Result = Result<(), RedisError>;

    fn handle(&mut self, msg: SetValue, _: &mut Self::Context) ->
Self::Result {
        self.client.set_ex(msg.path, msg.content, self.expiration)
    }
}
```

We used a `Client` instance stored in `CacheActor` to execute the `SETEX` command from Redis with the `set_ex` method call. This command sets a value with an expiration period in seconds. As you can see, the implementation is close to the database interaction functions of `Chapter 7`, *Reliable Integration with Databases*, but implemented as a `Handler` of the specific message. This code structuring is simpler and more intuitive.

Get value message

The `GetValue` struct represents a message to extract a value from Redis by key (or path, in our case). It contains only one field with a `path` value:

```
struct GetValue {
    pub path: String,
}
```

We also have to implement the `Message` trait to it, but we want it to return an optional `Vec<u8>` value if Redis contains a value for the provided key:

```
impl Message for GetValue {
    type Result = Result<Option<Vec<u8>>, RedisError>;
}
```

CacheActor also implements a Handler trait for the GetValue message type, and uses the GET command of Redis storage by calling the get method of Client to extract a value from storage:

```
impl Handler<GetValue> for CacheActor {
    type Result = Result<Option<Vec<u8>>, RedisError>;

    fn handle(&mut self, msg: GetValue, _: &mut Self::Context) ->
Self::Result {
        self.client.get(&msg.path)
    }
}
```

As you can see, actors and messages are simple enough, but we have to use an Addr value to interact with them. It's not a concise approach. We will add a special type that allows methods to interact with the CacheActor instance.

Link to actor

The following struct wraps an address of CacheActor:

```
#[derive(Clone)]
pub struct CacheLink {
    addr: Addr<CacheActor>,
}
```

The constructor only fills this addr field with an Addr value:

```
impl CacheLink {
    pub fn new(addr: Addr<CacheActor>) -> Self {
        Self { addr }
    }
}
```

We need a CacheLink wrapping struct to add methods to get access to caching features, but need to hide the implementation details and message interchange. First, we need a method to get cached values:

```
pub fn get_value(&self, path: &str) -> Box<Future<Item = Option<Vec<u8>>,
Error = Error>> {
    let msg = GetValue {
        path: path.to_owned(),
    };
    let fut = self.addr.send(msg)
        .from_err::<Error>()
        .and_then(|x| x.map_err(Error::from));
```

```
        Box::new(fut)
    }
```

The preceding function creates a new GetValue message with a path inside, and sends this message to Addr, contained in CacheLink. After this, it waits for the result. The function returns this interaction sequence as a boxed Future.

The next method is implemented in a similar way—the set_value method sets a new value to a cache by sending a SetValue message to CacheActor:

```
pub fn set_value(&self, path: &str, value: &[u8]) -> Box<Future<Item = (),
Error = Error>> {
    let msg = SetValue {
        path: path.to_owned(),
        content: value.to_owned(),
    };
    let fut = self.addr.send(msg)
        .from_err::<Error>()
        .and_then(|x| x.map_err(Error::from));
    Box::new(fut)
}
```

To compose a message, we use a path and a bytes array reference converted into a Vec<u8> value. Now, we can use CacheActor and CacheLink in a server implementation.

Using database actors

In the previous example in this chapter, we used shared State to provide access to a counter stored as i64, wrapped with RefCell. We reuse this struct, but add a CacheLink field to use connections with a CacheActor to get or set cached values. Add this field:

```
struct State {
    counter: RefCell<i64>,
    cache: CacheLink,
}
```

We derived a Default trait for the State struct before, but now we need a new constructor, because we have to provide a CacheLink instance with the actual address of the caching actor:

```
impl State {
    fn new(cache: CacheLink) -> Self {
        Self {
            counter: RefCell::default(),
```

```
                cache,
        }
    }
}
```

In most cases, caching works this way—it tries to extract a value from a cache; if it exists and hasn't expired, then the value is returned to a client. If there is no valid value, we need to obtain a new one. After we have taken it, we have to store it in a cache for future use.

In the previous example, we often used a `Future` instance that receives a `Response` from another microservice. To simplify our use of caching, let's add the `cache` method to our `State` implementation. This method will wrap any provided `future` with a path and try to extract the cached value. If the value isn't available, it will obtain a new one, and afterwards, it receives the store-copied value to cache, and returns the value to the client. This method wraps the provided `Future` value with another `Future` trait implementation. Look at the following implementation:

```
fn cache<F>(&self, path: &str, fut: F)
    -> impl Future<Item = Vec<u8>, Error = Error>
where
    F: Future<Item = Vec<u8>, Error = Error> + 'static,
{
    let link = self.cache.clone();
    let path = path.to_owned();
    link.get_value(&path)
        .from_err::<Error>()
        .and_then(move |opt| {
            if let Some(cached) = opt {
                debug!("Cached value used");
                boxed(future::ok(cached))
            } else {
                let res = fut.and_then(move |data| {
                    link.set_value(&path, &data)
                        .then(move |_| {
                            debug!("Cache updated");
                            future::ok::<_, Error>(data)
                        })
                        .from_err::<Error>()
                });
                boxed(res)
            }
        })
}
```

The implementation uses the State instance to clone CacheLink. We have to use a cloned link because we have to move it to the closure that uses it to store a new value, should we need to obtain it.

First, we call the get_value method of CacheLink and get a Future that requests a value from the cache. Since the method returns Option, we will use the and_then method to check that the value exists in a cache, and return that value to the client. If the value is expired or not available, we will obtain it by executing the provided Future and use a link to call the set_value method if the new value is returned successfully.

Now, we can use the cache method to cache the list of comments that are returned for the comments handler of the previous example:

```
fn comments(req: HttpRequest<State>) -> FutureResponse<HttpResponse> {
    let fut = get_request("http://127.0.0.1:8003/list");
    let fut = req.state().cache("/list", fut)
        .map(|data| {
            HttpResponse::Ok().body(data)
        });
    Box::new(fut)
}
```

First, we create a Future to get a value from another microservice using the get_request method that we have implemented before. After that, we get a reference to State using the state method of the request, and call the cache method by passing the /list path, then create a Future instance to obtain a new value.

We have implemented all of the parts of our database actor. We still need to start a set of caching actors with SyncArbiter, and wrap the returned Addr value with CacheLink:

```
let addr = SyncArbiter::start(3, || {
    CacheActor::new("redis://127.0.0.1:6379/", 10)
});
let cache = CacheLink::new(addr);
server::new(move || {
    let state = State::new(cache.clone());
    App::with_state(state)
    // remains part App building
})
```

Now, you can build the server. It will return the cached value of the /api/list request every 10 seconds.

The other good benefit of using actors is WebSocket. With this, we can add stateful interaction to our microservices using a state-machine implemented as an actor. Let's look at this in the next section.

WebSocket

WebSocket is a full-duplex communication protocol worked over HTTP. WebSockets are often used as an extension of main HTTP interaction and can be used for live updates or notifications.

An actors model is well-suited for implementing WebSocket handlers, because you can combine and isolate code in a single place: in the implementation of the actor. `actix-web` supports the WebSocket protocol, and in this section, we will add notification functionality to our microservice. Maybe all the features we have implemented with `actix-web` make our example a bit complex, but it's important for demonstration purposes to keep all features to show how you can combine a server with multiple actors and tasks.

Repeater actor

We have to send notifications about new comments to all connected clients. To do this, we have to keep the list of all connected clients to send a notification to them. We could update the `State` instance on every connection to add every new client to it, but instead, we will create a more elegant solution with a router that resends messages to multiple subscribers. Subscribers or listeners, in this case, will be actors that handle incoming WebSocket connections.

Actors

We will add an actor to resend messages to other actors. We need some basic types from the `actix` crate, along with a `HashSet` to keep addresses of actors. Import the `NewComment` struct, which we will clone and resend:

```
use actix::{Actor, Context, Handler, Message, Recipient};
use std::collections::HashSet;
use super::NewComment;
```

Add a `RepeaterActor` struct with a `listeners` field of the `HashSet` type that contains `Recipient` instances:

```
pub struct RepeaterActor {
```

```
        listeners: HashSet<Recipient<RepeaterUpdate>>,
}
```

You are familiar with the `Addr` type, but we haven't used `Recipient` before. Actually, you can convert any `Addr` instance into a `Recipient` using the `recipient` method call. The `Recipient` type is an address that supports only one type of `Message`.

Add a constructor that creates an empty `HashSet`:

```
impl RepeaterActor {
    pub fn new() -> Self {
        Self {
            listeners: HashSet::new(),
        }
    }
}
```

Next, implement an `Actor` trait for this struct:

```
impl Actor for RepeaterActor {
    type Context = Context<Self>;
}
```

It's enough to have a standard `Context` type as an associated context type of `Actor`, because it can work asynchronously.

Now, we have to add messages to this actor type.

Messages

We will support two types of messages. The first is an update message that transfers a new comment from one actor to another. The second is a control message that adds or removes listeners to the actor.

Updating the message

We will start with updating the message. Add a `RepeaterUpdate` struct that wraps a `NewComment` type:

```
#[derive(Clone)]
pub struct RepeaterUpdate(pub NewComment);
```

As you can see, we also derived the `Clone` trait, because we need to clone this message to resend it to multiple subscribers. `NewComment` also has to be cloneable now.

Let's implement the `Message` trait for the `RepeaterUpdate` struct. We will use an empty type for the `Result` associated type, because we don't care about the delivery of these messages:

```
impl Message for RepeaterUpdate {
    type Result = ();
}
```

Now, we can implement a `Handler` for the `RepeaterUpdate` message type:

```
impl Handler<RepeaterUpdate> for RepeaterActor {
    type Result = ();

    fn handle(&mut self, msg: RepeaterUpdate, _: &mut Self::Context) ->
Self::Result {
        for listener in &self.listeners {
            listener.do_send(msg.clone()).ok();
        }
    }
}
```

The algorithm of the handler is simple: it iterates over all listeners (actually, addresses of listeners stored as `Recipient` instances) and sends a cloned message to them. In other words, this actor receives a message and immediately sends it to all known listeners.

Control message

The following message type is necessary to subscribe or unsubscribe from `RepeaterUpdate` messages. Add the following enumeration:

```
pub enum RepeaterControl {
    Subscribe(Recipient<RepeaterUpdate>),
    Unsubscribe(Recipient<RepeaterUpdate>),
}
```

It has two variants with the same `Recipient<RepeaterUpdate>` type inside. Actors will send their own `Recipient` addresses to start listening for updates or to stop any notifications about new comments.

Implement the `Message` trait for the `RepeaterControl` struct to turn it into the `message` type and use an empty `Result` associated type:

```
impl Message for RepeaterControl {
    type Result = ();
}
```

Now, we can implement a `Handler` trait for the `RepeaterControl` message:

```
impl Handler<RepeaterControl> for RepeaterActor {
    type Result = ();

    fn handle(&mut self, msg: RepeaterControl, _: &mut Self::Context) ->
Self::Result {
        match msg {
            RepeaterControl::Subscribe(listener) => {
                self.listeners.insert(listener);
            }
            RepeaterControl::Unsubscribe(listener) => {
                self.listeners.remove(&listener);
            }
        }
    }
}
```

The implementation of the preceding handler is also pretty simple: it adds a new `Recipient` to listeners set on the `Subscribe` message variant, and removes the `Recipient` upon `Unsubscribe` messages.

The actor that resends `NewComment` values to other actors is ready, and now we can start to implement an actor for handling WebSocket connections.

The notification actor

The notification actor is actually a handler of WebScoket connections, but it performs only one function—sending a `NewComment` value, serialized to JSON, to clients.

Since we need a JSON serializer, add the `serde_json` crate to dependencies:

```
serde_json = "1.0"
```

Then, add the `src/notify.rs` module and start implementing the actor.

Actor

The notification actor is more complex and we need more types to implement it. Let's look into them:

```
use actix::{Actor, ActorContext, AsyncContext, Handler, Recipient,
StreamHandler};
use actix_web::ws::{Message, ProtocolError, WebsocketContext};
use crate::repeater::{RepeaterControl, RepeaterUpdate};
use std::time::{Duration, Instant};
use super::State;
```

First, we started by using the `ws` module of the `actix_web` crate. It contains a necessary `WebsocketContext` that we will use as a context value in the `Actor` trait implementation. Also, we need `Message` and `ProtocolError` types to implement WebSocket stream handling. We also imported `ActorContext` to stop the method of the `Context` instance to break the connection with a client. We imported the `AsyncContext` trait to get an address of a context and to run a task that performs on time intervals. One new type that we have not used yet is `StreamHandler`. It is necessary to implement the handing of values that are sent from `Stream` to `Actor`.

> You can use either `Handler` or `StreamHandler` for handling messages of the same type. Which one is preferable? The rule is simple: if your actor will process a lot of messages, it's better to use `StreamHandler` and connect the messages flow as a `Stream` to an `Actor`. The `actix` runtime has check and if it calls the same `Handler`, you may receive warnings.

Add the constants that we will use for sending `ping` messages to our clients:

```
const PING_INTERVAL: Duration = Duration::from_secs(20);
const PING_TIMEOUT: Duration = Duration::from_secs(60);
```

The constants contain interval and timeout values.

> We will send pings to a client, because we have to keep a connection alive, since servers often have default timeouts for WebSocket connections. For example, `nginx` will close the connection after 60 seconds if there isn't any activity. And if you use `nginx` as a proxy with default configuration for WebSocket connections, then your connections can be broken. Browsers don't send pings and only send pongs for incoming pings. The server is responsible for sending pings to clients connected via browsers to prevent disconnecting through a timeout.

Add the following `NotifyActor` struct to the code:

```
pub struct NotifyActor {
    last_ping: Instant,
    repeater: Recipient<RepeaterControl>,
}
```

This actor has a `last_ping` of the `Instant` type to keep the timestamp of the latest ping. Also, the actor holds a `Recipient` address to send `RepeaterControl` messages. We will provide the address of `RepeaterActor` for this field with the constructor:

```
impl NotifyActor {
    pub fn new(repeater: Recipient<RepeaterControl>) -> Self {
        Self {
            last_ping: Instant::now(),
            repeater,
        }
    }
}
```

Now, we have to implement the `Actor` trait for the `NotifyActor` struct:

```
impl Actor for NotifyActor {
    type Context = WebsocketContext<Self, State>;

    fn started(&mut self, ctx: &mut Self::Context) {
        let msg = RepeaterControl::Subscribe(ctx.address().recipient());
        self.repeater.do_send(msg).ok();
        ctx.run_interval(PING_INTERVAL, |act, ctx| {
            if Instant::now().duration_since(act.last_ping) > PING_TIMEOUT
{
                ctx.stop();
                return;
            }
            ctx.ping("ping");
        });
    }

    fn stopped(&mut self, ctx: &mut Self::Context) {
        let msg = RepeaterControl::Unsubscribe(ctx.address().recipient());
        self.repeater.do_send(msg).ok();
    }
}
```

This is the first time where we need to override the empty `started` and `stopped` methods. In the `started` method implementation, we will create a `Subscribe` message and send it using `Repeater`. Also, we add a task that will be executed on `PING_INTERVAL` and will send a ping message using the `ping` method of `WebsocketContext`. If a client never responds to us, then the `last_ping` field won't be updated. If the interval is larger than our `PING_TIMEOUT` value, we will interrupt the connection using the `stop` method of the context.

The `stopped` method implementation is much simpler: it prepares an `Unsubscribe` event with the same address of the actor and sends it to `RepeaterActor`.

Our actor implementation is ready and now we have to add handlers for messages and a stream.

Handlers

First, we will implement a `StreamHandler` instance of the `ws::Message` messages:

```
impl StreamHandler<Message, ProtocolError> for NotifyActor {
    fn handle(&mut self, msg: Message, ctx: &mut Self::Context) {
        match msg {
            Message::Ping(msg) => {
                self.last_ping = Instant::now();
                ctx.pong(&msg);
            }
            Message::Pong(_) => {
                self.last_ping = Instant::now();
            }
            Message::Text(_) => { },
            Message::Binary(_) => { },
            Message::Close(_) => {
                ctx.stop();
            }
        }
    }
}
```

This is a basic approach for implementing the WebSocket protocol interaction with `actix-web`. We will use the `ws::start` method later to attach a `Stream` of WebSocket messages to this actor.

The `Message` type has multiple variants that reflects types of WebSocket messages from RFC 6455 (the official protocol specification). We use `Ping` and `Pong` to update the `last_ping` field of the actor's struct, and use `Close` to stop the connection by user's demand.

The last `Handler` we have to implement allows us to receive `RepeaterUpdate` messages and to send `NewComment` values to a client:

```
impl Handler<RepeaterUpdate> for NotifyActor {
    type Result = ();

    fn handle(&mut self, msg: RepeaterUpdate, ctx: &mut Self::Context) ->
Self::Result {
        let RepeaterUpdate(comment) = msg;
        if let Ok(data) = serde_json::to_string(&comment) {
            ctx.text(data);
        }
    }
}
```

The implementation destructs a `RepeaterUpdate` message to get a `NewComment` value, serializes it to JSON using the `serde_json` crate, and sends it to a client using the `text` method of `WebsocketContext`.

We have all necessary actors, so let's join them with a server.

Adding WebSocket support to a server

Since we will be extended the example from the previous section, we reuse the `State` struct, but add an `Addr` to the `Repeater` actor that we will create later in the `main` function:

```
pub struct State {
    counter: RefCell<i64>,
    cache: CacheLink,
    repeater: Addr<RepeaterActor>,
}
```

Update the constructor to fill the `repeater` field:

```
fn new(cache: CacheLink, repeater: Addr<RepeaterActor>) -> Self {
    Self {
        counter: RefCell::default(),
        cache,
        repeater,
    }
}
```

Now, we can spawn a `RepeaterActor`, set the address of the actor to `State`, and use it as the state for our `App`:

```
let repeater = RepeaterActor::new().start();

server::new(move || {
    let state = State::new(cache.clone(), repeater.clone());
    App::with_state(state)
        .resource("/ws", |r| r.method(http::Method::GET).f(ws_connect))
        // other
})
```

Also, we added a handler for HTTP requests with a resource method call of `App`, and passed the `ws_connect` function to it. Let's look at the implementation of this function:

```
fn ws_connect(req: &HttpRequest<State>) -> Result<HttpResponse, Error> {
    let repeater = req.state().repeater.clone().recipient();
    ws::start(req, NotifyActor::new(repeater))
}
```

This clones an address of `RepeaterActor`, converting it into a `Recipient` which is then used for creating a `NotifyActor` instance. To start that actor instance, you have to use the `ws::start` method that uses the current `Request` and bootstraps `WebsocketContext` for this actor.

The remaining thing is to send a `NewComment` to `RepeaterActor`, which will resend it to any `NotifyActor` instances of connected clients:

```
fn new_comment((req, params): (HttpRequest<State>, Form<AddComment>)) ->
FutureResponse<HttpResponse> {
    let repeater = req.state().repeater.clone();
    let fut = req.identity()
        .ok_or(format_err!("not authorized").into())
        .into_future()
        .and_then(move |uid| {
            let new_comment = NewComment {
                uid,
```

```
                    text: params.into_inner().text,
                };
                let update = RepeaterUpdate(new_comment.clone());
                repeater
                    .send(update)
                    .then(move |_| Ok(new_comment))
            })
            .and_then(move |params| {
                post_request::<_, ()>("http://127.0.0.1:8003/new_comment",
    params)
            })
            .then(move |_| {
                let res = HttpResponse::build_from(&req)
                    .status(StatusCode::FOUND)
                    .header(header::LOCATION, "/comments.html")
                    .finish();
                Ok(res)
            });
        Box::new(fut)
    }
```

We extended the `new_comment` handler that is called when a user adds a new comment, and add an extra step to send a `NewComment` value to a repeater. In any case, we ignore the result of delivery of this message to an actor, and we send a POST request to another microservice. It's worth noting that clients will be notified about the new comment, even it won't send to the other microservice, but you can improve it by changing the order of the corresponding `Future` in the chain.

Summary

In this chapter, we covered creating a microservice using the Actix framework. We discovered how to create and configure an `App` instance, which describes all routes and middleware to be used. After that, we implemented all handlers that return a `Future` instance. In all handlers, we also use `ClientRequest` to send a request to another microservice and return a response back to the client using an asynchronous approach with futures. Finally, we explored how to create our own `Middleware` for the `actix-web` crate.

In the next chapter, we'll examine the scalable microservices architecture, and look at how to achieve loose coupling of microservices. We'll also consider the use of message brokers to provide a flexible and manageable way to exchange messages between parts of a large application.

Scalable Microservices Architecture

This chapter describes the scalability of microservices. In this chapter, we will learn how to create microservices that use messages for passing interaction with other microservices. You will get acquainted with RabbitMQ message broker and how to use it in Rust with `lapin` crate.

We will cover the following concepts related to microservices scalability in this chapter:

- Scalable microservices design
- How to avoid bottlenecks in your app
- What are message brokers?
- How to use RabbitMQ with Rust

Technical requirements

To build scalable microservices you, need an infrastructure or resources to run multiple microservices in parallel. But for demonstration purposes, we will use Docker, which provides the ability to run multiple instances of our applications. We also need Docker to start a RabbitMQ instance.

To build all the examples, you will need version 1.31 of the Rust compiler.

You can get all the code for the examples in this chapter from the project on GitHub: https://github.com/PacktPublishing/Hands-On-Microservices-with-Rust/tree/master/Chapter12.

Scalable architecture

We avoid monoliths, and microservices can handle more requests per second if you develop them in the right way, but using microservices doesn't mean you have a scalable application effortlessly. It makes any part of an application flexible for scaling, and you have to write loosely coupled microservices that can run in many instances.

Basic ideas

To make an application scalable, you can choose one of two approaches.

In the first case, you can start more copies of the whole application. You may think it's impossible, but imagine a service that earns money from ads and provides a service to convert images into PDFs. This service can be scaled this way, and you can handle as many requests as the customers need, if you have enough hardware, of course.

The second approach is to split the application into separate services that handle the same types of task, and you can run as many instances of the services as you want. For example, your application is an online store and you have issues with load on servers with images or static assets. This problem is simple to solve, because you can use a **content delivery network** (**CDN**) or buy an extra server where you can put the necessary static files, run NGINX, and add this server to the DNS records of your domain. But for microservices, you can't always use this approach. This requires ingenuity. But the recipe is clear. You have to achieve loose coupling for your microservices when you add extra microservices to handle specific tasks or to speed up some processes by caching, or using other tricks.

To have a more abstract services interaction layer, you can use message brokers that know nothing about your application, but provide the ability to send messages from one microservice to another and return the result.

Message brokers and queues

Message brokers translate messages from one application to another. Clients of message brokers use APIs to send messages that are serialized to a specific format and subscribe to queues to be notified about all the new messages. There is the **AMQP** (short for **Advanced Message Queuing Protocol**) protocol, which provides a common API that's compatible with different products.

The main concept of message brokers is the queue. It is an abstraction that represents an entity used to collect messages until they will be consumed by clients.

Why is the concept of message brokers cool? Because it's the simplest way to achieve loose coupling for services and maintain the possibility of smooth updates. You can use a common message format and write microservices to read specific types of messages. It helps you to reroute all paths of messages. For examples, you can add a specific handler for the specific message type, or set a balancing rule to load more powerful services.

There are a lot of message brokers that can be used, depending on your needs. Some popular products are described in the following sections.

RabbitMQ

RabbitMQ is the most popular message broker. This message broker supports the AMQP protocol. It's fast and reliable. It also facilitates the creation of short-lifetime queues for implementing client-server interactions based on messages. We will use this message broker to create an example of a scalable application.

Kafka

Apache Kafka was originally created by LinkedIn and was donated to the Apache Software Foundation. It's implemented with Scala and works like a log that commits all information and provides access to it. It differs from traditional AMQP brokers, because it maintains a commit log that helps to achieve durable message storage.

Application bottlenecks

Any part of an application can be a bottleneck. At first, you may have issues with the infrastructure used by microservices, such as databases or message brokers. Scaling these parts is a complex concept, but here we will only touch upon the bottlenecks of microservices.

When you create a microservice, you may encounter problems with the quantity of requests it can handle. It depends on multiple factors. You can use a concept such as the actors model to spread a load across threads and event loops.

If you have issues with CPU performance, you can create a separate worker that handles CPU-intensive tasks and schedules tasks with message brokers to achieve loose coupling, because you can add more workers at any time to handle more requests.

It you have I/O-intensive tasks, you can use load balancers to direct load to a specific service, but your microservice should be replaceable and shouldn't keep a persistent state, but can load it from a database. It allows you to use products such as Kubernetes to scale your applications automatically.

You should also split large tasks into small and separate microservices by logical domain. For example, create a separate microservice for handling accounts and another to render and show shopping carts in the online store. You can also add another microservice that processes payments, and they interact with each other with messages transferred by a message broker.

Let's create an application that can be scaled by running extra instances of some of its components.

Scalable application with Rust and RabbitMQ

In this section, we will write an application that decodes QR codes from images to textual strings. We will create two services—one to handle incoming requests and for decoding tasks, and the second is a worker that will receive tasks and decode images to strings and return the result to a server. To implement interaction between services, we will use RabbitMQ. For the server and worker implementations, we will use the Actix framework. Before we start coding, let's start a RabbitMQ instance with Docker.

Bootstrap message broker for testing

To start RabbitMQ, we will use the official image for Docker from DockerHub, located here: `https://hub.docker.com/_/rabbitmq/`. We have already used Docker to start instances of databases. Starting RabbitMQ is similar:

```
docker run -it --rm --name test-rabbit -p 5672:5672 rabbitmq:3
```

We started a container called `test-rabbit` and forward port `5672` to the same port of the container. RabbitMQ images also exposes ports `4369`, `5671`, and `25672`. If you want to use the advanced features of the message broker, you need to open these ports too.

If you want to start an instance of RabbitMQ and have access to it from other containers, you can set the `--hostname` arguments for the `run` command and use the provided name from other containers to connect to the RabbitMQ instance.

When a message broker instance starts, you may need to get some statistics from it. The `rabbitmqctl` command can be executed inside the container using the `exec` command from Docker:

```
docker exec -it test-rabbit rabbitmqctl
```

It prints the available commands. Add any of them to the command, like this:

```
docker exec -it test-rabbit rabbitmqctl trace_on
```

The preceding command activates tracing all the messages pushed to queues, which you can see with the following command:

```
docker exec -it test-rabbit rabbitmqctl list_exchanges
```

It prints the following:

```
Listing exchanges for vhost / ...
amq.headers      headers
amq.direct       direct
amq.topic       topic
amq.rabbitmq.trace      topic
     direct
amq.fanout      fanout
amq.match      headers
```

Now, we can create a microservice that uses the message broker for interaction with the worker.

Dependencies

Create a new library crate (in which we will add two binaries later) called `rabbit-actix`:

```
[package]
name = "rabbit-actix"
version = "0.1.0"
edition = "2018"
```

As you can see, we are using the 2018 edition of Rust. We need a pretty big pile of crates:

```
[dependencies]
actix = "0.7"
actix-web = "0.7"
✓ askama = "0.7"        html render
chrono = "0.4"
env_logger = "0.6"
```

```
    image = "0.21"
✓   indexmap = "1.0"        ordered hmap?
    failure = "0.1"
    futures = "0.1"
    log = "0.4"
✓   queens-rock = "0.1"      QR
    rmp-serde = "0.13"
    serde = "1.0"
    serde_derive = "1.0"
    serde_json = "1.0"
    tokio = "0.1"
✓   uuid = "0.7"             uuid4
```

It's important to note that we use the actix framework with the actix-web crate. If you are not familiar with this crate, you can read more about it in Chapter 11, *Involving Concurrency with Actors and Actix Crate*. We also use the image crate to work with image formats, because this crate is used by queens-rock and implements a decoder for QR codes. We also use the askama crate to render HTML pages with posted tasks, and we use the indexmap crate to get an ordered hash map that keeps elements insertion order. To create unique names for the tasks, we will use the UUID4 format, which is implemented in the uuid crate.

To interact with RabbitMQ, we will use the lapin-futures crate, but we renamed it lapin because there are two implementations of this crate. The one that we use is based on the futures crate, and there is also the lapin-async crate version based on the mio crate. We will use the lapin-futures crate first, and name it lapin:

```
[dependencies.lapin]
version = "0.15"
package = "lapin-futures"    mq
```

Add the first binary with a server implementation pointing to the src/server.rs file:

```
[[bin]]
name = "rabbit-actix-server"
path = "src/server.rs"
test = false
```

Add the second binary for a worker that will be implemented in the src/worker.rs file:

```
[[bin]]
name = "rabbit-actix-worker"
path = "src/worker.rs"
test = false
```

We already use the askama crate as a dependency for the main code, but we also need it as a dependency for the build.rs script. Add this:

```
[build-dependencies]
askama = "0.7"
```

The preceding dependency needs to rebuild templates to embed them into code. Add the following code to a new build.rs script:

```
fn main() {
    askama::rerun_if_templates_changed();
}
```

All the dependencies are prepared, and we can create an abstract type to interact with queues in a message broker.

Abstract queue interaction actor

Add the src/queue_actor.rs actor, and let's create an actor that uses an abstract handler to process incoming messages and can send new messages to a queue. It also has to create all the necessary queues in RabbitMQ and subscribe to new events in the corresponding queue.

Dependencies

To create an actor, we need the following dependencies:

```
use super::{ensure_queue, spawn_client};
use actix::fut::wrap_future;
use actix::{Actor, Addr, AsyncContext, Context, Handler, Message,
StreamHandler, SystemRunner};
use failure::{format_err, Error};
use futures::Future;
use lapin::channel::{BasicConsumeOptions, BasicProperties,
BasicPublishOptions, Channel}; basic_consume, basic_publish
use lapin::error::Error as LapinError;
use lapin::message::Delivery;
use lapin::types::{FieldTable, ShortString};
use log::{debug, warn};
use serde::{Deserialize, Serialize};
use tokio::net::TcpStream;
use uuid::Uuid;

pub type TaskId = ShortString;
```

First, we use the `ensure_queue` function from the super module, which creates a new queue, but we will implement it later in this chapter. `spawn_client` lets us create a new `Client` connected to a message broker. We will use the `wrap_future` function, which converts any `Future` object into an `ActorFuture`, which can be spawned in the `Context` environment of the Actix framework.

Let's explore the types from the `lapin` crate. The `Channel` struct represents a connection channel with the RabbitMQ instance. `BasicConsumeOptions` represents options used for the `basic_consume` method of the `Channel` call to subscribe to new events in a queue. `BasicProperties` types are used as parameters for the `basic_publish` method call of the `Channel` type for add properties such as correlation IDs to distinct recipients of the message, or set the required quality level for delivery. `BasicPublishOptions` is used for the `basic_publish` call to set extra options for a message publishing activity.

We also need the `Error` type from the `lapin` crate, but we renamed it `LapinError` because we also use the generic `Error` from the `failure` crate. The `Delivery` struct represents an incoming message delivered from a queue. The `FieldTable` type is used as a parameter for the `basic_consume` method call of the `Channel` type. The `ShortString` type is a simple alias to a `String` that is used as a name of a queue in the `lapin` crate. The `Uuid` type is imported from the `uuid` crate to generate unique correlation IDs for messages to identify the origin of a message.

Now, we can declare the abstract handler for our messages.

Abstract messages handler

Create the `QueueHandler` struct in the `queue_actor.rs` file:

```
pub trait QueueHandler: 'static {
    type Incoming: for<'de> Deserialize<'de>;
    type Outgoing: Serialize;

    fn incoming(&self) -> &str;
    fn outgoing(&self) -> &str;
    fn handle(
        &self,
        id: &TaskId,
        incoming: Self::Incoming,
    ) -> Result<Option<Self::Outgoing>, Error>;
}
```

QueueHandler is a trait that has two associated types and three methods. It requires a static lifetime for types that will implement the QueueHandler trait, because instances of this trait will be used as fields of actors that have a static lifetime as well.

This trait has the Incoming associated type, which represents the incoming message type and requires the type to implement the Deserialize trait to be deserializable, because RabbitMQ transfers byte arrays only and you have to decide which format to use for serialization. The Outgoing associated type has to implement the Serialize trait to be serializable as a bytes array to be sent as an outgoing message.

The QueueHandler trait also has incoming and outgoing methods. The first returns the name of a queue to consume incoming messages. The second method returns the name of a queue in which an actor will write sending messages. There is also a handle method, which takes a reference to TaskId and incoming messages of the Self::Incoming associated type. The method returns a Result with an optional Self::Outgoing instance. If the implementation returns None then no messages will be sent to the outgoing channel. However, you can use a special SendMessage type to send a message later. We will declare this type later, after we add the actor's struct.

Actor

Add a new struct called QueueActor and add a type parameter that implements the QueueHandler trait:

```
pub struct QueueActor<T: QueueHandler> {
    channel: Channel<TcpStream>,
    handler: T,
}
```

The struct has a reference to a connection Channel to RabbitMQ. We build it over TcpStream. The struct also has a handler field that contains an instance of a handler that implements QueueHandler.

This struct also has to implement the Actor trait to become an actor. We also added a started method. It remains empty, but it's a good place to create all the queues. For example, you can create a message type that will attach a Stream of messages to this actor. With this approach, you can start consuming any queue at any time:

```
impl<T: QueueHandler> Actor for QueueActor<T> {
    type Context = Context<Self>;

    fn started(&mut self, _: &mut Self::Context) {}
}
```

We will initialize all the queues in the new method to interrupt actor creation if something goes wrong:

```
impl<T: QueueHandler> QueueActor<T> {
    pub fn new(handler: T, mut sys: &mut SystemRunner) ->
Result<Addr<Self>, Error> {
        let channel = spawn_client(&mut sys)?;     client → channel
        let chan = channel.clone();
        let fut = ensure_queue(&chan, handler.outgoing());  exist
        sys.block_on(fut)?;
        let fut = ensure_queue(&chan, handler.incoming()).and_then(move
|queue| {
            let opts = BasicConsumeOptions {
                ..Default::default()
            };
            let table = FieldTable::new();
            let name = format!("{}-consumer", queue.name());
            chan.basic_consume(&queue, &name, opts, table)  listen
        });
        let stream = sys.block_on(fut)?;
        let addr = QueueActor::create(move |ctx| {
            ctx.add_stream(stream);
            Self { channel, handler }
        });
        Ok(addr)
    }
}
```

We call the `spawn_client` function, which we will implement later, to create a `Client` that's connected to a message broker. The function returns a `Channel` instance, which is created by the connected `Client`. We use `Channel` to ensure the queue we need exists, or create it with `ensure_queue`. This method is implemented later in this chapter. We use the result of the `QueueHandler::outgoing` method to get the name of the queue to create.

This method expects `SystemRunner` to execute `Future` objects immediately by calling the `block_on` method. It lets us get a `Result` and interrupts other activities if the method call fails.

After that, we create a queue using the name we get with the `QueueHandler::incoming` method call. We will consume messages from this queue and use the `basic_consume` method of a `Channel` that starts listening for new messages. To call `basic_consume`, we also created default values of the `BasicConsumeOptions` and `FieldTable` types. `basic_consume` returns a `Future` that will be resolved to a `Stream` value. We use the `block_on` method call of the `SystemRunner` instance to execute this `Future` to get a `Stream` instance to attach it to `QueueActor`. We create the `QueueActor` instance using the `create` method call, which expects a closure, which in turn takes a reference to a `Context`.

Handling an incoming stream

We used the `basic_consume` method of a `Channel` to create a `Stream` that returns `Delivery` objects from a queue. Since we want to attach that `Stream` to the actor, we have to implement `StreamHandler` for the `QueueActor` type:

```
impl<T: QueueHandler> StreamHandler<Delivery, LapinError> for QueueActor<T>
{
    fn handle(&mut self, item: Delivery, ctx: &mut Context<Self>) {
        debug!("Message received!");
        let fut = self
            .channel
            .basic_ack(item.delivery_tag, false)    ack
            .map_err(drop);
        ctx.spawn(wrap_future(fut));
        match self.process_message(item, ctx) {     process
            Ok(pair) => {
                if let Some((corr_id, data)) = pair {
                    self.send_message(corr_id, data, ctx);   Outgoing
                }
            }
            Err(err) => {
                warn!("Message processing error: {}", err);
            }
        }
    }
}
```

Our `StreamHandler` implementation expects a `Delivery` instance. RabbitMQ expects that a client will send an acknowledgement when it consumes the delivered message. We do it with the `basic_ack` method call of a `Channel` instance stored as a field of `QueueActor`. This method call returns a `Future` instance that we will `spawn` in a `Context` to send an acknowledgement that the message was received.

RabbitMQ requires a consumer to notify with every message that is processed. If a consumer doesn't do this, then the message is left hanging in the queue. But you can set the `no_ack` field of the `BasicConsumeOptions` struct to `true` and the message will be marked as delivered as soon as the consumer reads it. But if your application fails before the message is processed, you will lose the message. It's only suitable for non-critical messages.

We use the `process_message` method that we will implement later to process a message using the `QueueHandler` instance. If this method returns a not `None` value, we will use it as a response message and send it to an outgoing queue using the `send_message` method, which we will also implement later in this chapter. But now we will add a message to initiate an outgoing message.

Sending a new message

`QueueActor` has to send a new message, because we will use this actor to send tasks to a worker. Add the corresponding struct:

```
pub struct SendMessage<T>(pub T);
```

Implement the `Message` trait for this type:

```
impl<T> Message for SendMessage<T> {
    type Result = TaskId;
}
```

We need to set the `Result` type to `TaskId`, because we will generate a new task ID for a new message to process the response with a handler later. If you are not familiar with the Actix framework and message, return to `Chapter 11`, *Involving Concurrency with Actors and Actix Crate.*

The `Handler` of this message type will generate a new UUID and convert it into a `String`. Then, the method will use the `send_message` method to send a message to an outgoing queue:

```
impl<T: QueueHandler> Handler<SendMessage<T::Outgoing>> for QueueActor<T> {
    type Result = TaskId;

    fn handle(&mut self, msg: SendMessage<T::Outgoing>, ctx: &mut
Self::Context) -> Self::Result {
        let corr_id = Uuid::new_v4().to_simple().to_string();
        self.send_message(corr_id.clone(), msg.0, ctx);
        corr_id
```

```
        }
    }
```

Now, we have to implement the `process_message` and `send_message` methods of `QueueActor`.

Utility methods

Let's add the `process_message` method, which processes incoming `Delivery` items:

```
impl<T: QueueHandler> QueueActor<T> {
    fn process_message(
        &self,
        item: Delivery,
        _: &mut Context<Self>,
    ) -> Result<Option<(ShortString, T::Outgoing)>, Error> {
        let corr_id = item
            .properties
            .correlation_id()
            .to_owned()
            .ok_or_else(|| format_err!("Message has no address for the
response"))?;
        let incoming = serde_json::from_slice(&item.data)?;
        let outgoing = self.handler.handle(&corr_id, incoming)?;
        if let Some(outgoing) = outgoing {
            Ok(Some((corr_id, outgoing)))
        } else {
            Ok(None)
        }
    }
}
```

First, we have to get a unique ID associated with a message. If you remember, we used the UUID in this case. We stored it in the correlation ID field of the message.

A correlation ID represents a value that is associated with a message as a tag for the response. This information is used to implement **Remote Procedure Calls** (**RPCs**) over RabbitMQ. If you skipped Chapter 6, *Reactive Microservices - Increasing Capacity and Performance*, you can return to it to read more about RPCs.

We use JSON format for our messages, and we parse using `serde_json` to create incoming data that is stored in the `data` field of the `Delivery` instance. If a deserialization was successful, we take the value of the `Self::Incoming` type. Now, we have all the information we need to call the `handle` method of the `QueueHandler` instance—the correlation ID and a deserialized incoming message. The handler returns a `Self::Outgoing` message instance, but we won't serialize it immediately for sending, because it will use the `send_message` method that we used to process incoming messages. Let's implement it.

The `send_message` method takes a correlation ID and an outgoing value to prepare and send a message:

```
impl<T: QueueHandler> QueueActor<T> {
    fn send_message(&self, corr_id: ShortString, outgoing: T::Outgoing,
ctx: &mut Context<Self>) {
        let data = serde_json::to_vec(&outgoing);
        match data {
            Ok(data) => {
                let opts = BasicPublishOptions::default();
                let props =
BasicProperties::default().with_correlation_id(corr_id);
                debug!("Sending to: {}", self.handler.outgoing());
                let fut = self
                    .channel
                    .basic_publish("", self.handler.outgoing(), data,
opts, props)
                    .map(drop)
                    .map_err(drop);
                ctx.spawn(wrap_future(fut));
            }
            Err(err) => {
                warn!("Can't encode an outgoing message: {}", err);
            }
        }
    }
}
```

First, the method serializes a value to binary data. If the value is serialized to JSON successfully, we prepare options and properties to call the `basic_publish` method of a `Channel` to send a message to an outgoing queue. It's worth noting that we associated the provided correlation ID to the `BasicProperties` struct that's used with the `basic_publish` call. Publishing a message returns a `Future` instance, which we have to spawn in the context of an `Actor`. If we can't serialize a value, we will log an error.

Now, we can finish implementing the library part of the crate by adding the `spawn_client` and `ensure_queue` functions.

Crate

Add the following imports to the `src/lib.rs` source file:

```
pub mod queue_actor;

use actix::{Message, SystemRunner};
use failure::Error;
use futures::Future;
use lapin::channel::{Channel, QueueDeclareOptions};
use lapin::client::{Client, ConnectionOptions};
use lapin::error::Error as LapinError;
use lapin::queue::Queue;
use lapin::types::FieldTable;
use serde_derive::{Deserialize, Serialize};
use tokio::net::TcpStream;
```

You are familiar with some types. Let's discuss some of the new ones. `Client` represents a client that connects to RabbitMQ. The `Channel` type will be created as a result of a connection and is returned by a `Client`. `QueueDeclareOptions` is used as a parameter for the `queue_declare` method call of a `Channel`. `ConnectionOptions` is necessary to establish a connection, but we will use default values. `Queue` represents a queue in RabbitMQ.

We need two queues: one for requests and one for responses. We will specify the destination of messages with the correlation ID. Add the following constants to be used as the names of queues:

```
pub const REQUESTS: &str = "requests";
pub const RESPONSES: &str = "responses";
```

To spawn a `Client` and create a `Channel`, we will add the `spawn_client` function, which creates a `Client` and produces a `Channel` from it:

```
pub fn spawn_client(sys: &mut SystemRunner) -> Result<Channel<TcpStream>,
Error> {
    let addr = "127.0.0.1:5672".parse().unwrap();
    let fut = TcpStream::connect(&addr)
        .map_err(Error::from)
        .and_then(|stream| {
            let options = ConnectionOptions::default();
            Client::connect(stream, options).from_err::<Error>()
```

```
        });
    let (client, heartbeat) = sys.block_on(fut)?;
    actix::spawn(heartbeat.map_err(drop));
    let channel = sys.block_on(client.create_channel())?;
    Ok(channel)
}
```

The implementation of the preceding function is simple enough. We create a `TcpStream` from a constant address with the `connect` method call. You can make the address parameter configurable if necessary. The `connect` method returns a `Future` that we use to create a combinator that maps to a new `Client` connected to RabbitMQ. We use `block_on` of `SystemRunner` to execute that `Future` immediately. It returns a `Client` and a `Heartbeat` instance. The `Client` instance is used to create an instance of `Channel`. The `Heartbeat` instance is a task that pings RabbitMQ with a connection that has to be spawned as a concurrent activity in the event loop. We use `actix::spawn` to run it, because we don't have the `Context` of an `Actor`.

Finally, we call the `create_channel` method of a `Client` to create a `Channel`. But the method returns a `Future`, which we also execute with the `block_on` method. Now, we can return the created `Channel` and implement the `ensure_queue` method, which expects that `Channel` instance as a parameter.

The `ensure_queue` method creates the option to call the `queue_declare` method, which creates a queue inside RabbitMQ:

```
pub fn ensure_queue(
    chan: &Channel<TcpStream>,
    name: &str,
) -> impl Future<Item = Queue, Error = LapinError> {
    let opts = QueueDeclareOptions {
        auto_delete: true,
        ..Default::default()
    };
    let table = FieldTable::new();
    chan.queue_declare(name, opts, table)
}
```

We fill `QueueDeclareOptions` with default parameters, but set the `auto_delete` field to `true`, because we want the created queues to be deleted when an application ends. It's suitable for testing purposes. In this method, we won't execute a `Future` that is returned by the `queue_declare` method immediately. We return it as is to enable the calling environment to make a combinator with the returned `Queue` value.

We have implemented all the necessary parts to create a server and a worker. Now, we need to declare request and response types to use them in a worker and in a server.

Request and response

The request type called QrRequest contains data about the QR image:

```
#[derive(Clone, Debug, Deserialize, Serialize)]
pub struct QrRequest {
    pub image: Vec<u8>,
}
```

It implements the Message trait from actix, which is to be set as an associated type of QueueHandler:

```
impl Message for QrRequest {
    type Result = ();
}
```

The response type is represented by the QrResponse enumeration:

```
#[derive(Clone, Debug, Deserialize, Serialize)]
pub enum QrResponse {
    Succeed(String),
    Failed(String),
}
```

It contains two variants: Succeed for successful results and Failed for errors. It is similar to the Result type of the standard library, but we decided to add our own type to have a chance to override the serialization behavior when we need it. But we can construct this response from a Result instance by implementing the From trait. It's useful because we can use a function to construct a value that returns the Result type. Look at the implementation here:

```
impl From<Result<String, Error>> for QrResponse {
    fn from(res: Result<String, Error>) -> Self {
        match res {
            Ok(data) => QrResponse::Succeed(data),
            Err(err) => QrResponse::Failed(err.to_string()),
        }
    }
}
```

QrResponse also has to implement the Message trait:

```
impl Message for QrResponse {
    type Result = ();
}
```

The library crate is ready to be used to create a worker and a server. Let's start by implementing a worker.

Worker

The worker will consume all the messages from the requests queue and try to decode them as QR images to strings.

Dependencies

We need the following types for the implementation of a worker:

```
use actix::System;
use failure::{format_err, Error};
use image::GenericImageView;
use log::debug;
use queens_rock::Scanner;
use rabbit_actix::queue_actor::{QueueActor, QueueHandler, TaskId};
use rabbit_actix::{QrRequest, QrResponse, REQUESTS, RESPONSES};
```

We imported all the necessary types earlier in this chapter. We also imported two types for decoding QR images. GenericImageView provides the to_luma method to convert an image into grayscale. The Scanner method is a decoder of QR codes provided as grayscale images.

Handler

We need to create an empty struct, because our worker doesn't have a state and will only transform incoming messages:

```
struct WokerHandler {}
```

We use the WorkerHandler struct as the handler for the queue and use it with QueueActor later. Implement the QueueHandler trait, which is required by QueueActor:

```
impl QueueHandler for WokerHandler {
    type Incoming = QrRequest;
```

```
        type Outgoing = QrResponse;

        fn incoming(&self) -> &str {
            REQUESTS
        }
        fn outgoing(&self) -> &str {
            RESPONSES
        }
        fn handle(
            &self,
            _: &TaskId,
            incoming: Self::Incoming,
        ) -> Result<Option<Self::Outgoing>, Error> {
            debug!("In: {:?}", incoming);
            let outgoing = self.scan(&incoming.image).into();
            debug!("Out: {:?}", outgoing);
            Ok(Some(outgoing))
        }
    }
```

Since this handler takes requests and prepares responses, we set QrRequest as
the Incoming type and QrResponse as the Outgoing type. The incoming method
returns the value of the REQUESTS constant that we will use as a name for incoming queues.
The outgoing method returns the RESPONSES constant, which is used as the name for the
queue of outgoing messages.

The handle method of QueueHandler takes a request and calls the scan method with
data. Then, it converts the Result into a QrResponse and returns it. Let's implement
the scan method, which decodes images:

```
impl WokerHandler {
    fn scan(&self, data: &[u8]) -> Result<String, Error> {
        let image = image::load_from_memory(data)?;
        let luma = image.to_luma().into_vec();
        let scanner = Scanner::new(
            luma.as_ref(),
            image.width() as usize,
            image.height() as usize,
        );
        scanner
            .scan()
            .extract(0)
            .ok_or_else(|| format_err!("can't extract"))
            .and_then(|code| code.decode().map_err(|_| format_err!("can't
decode")))
            .and_then(|data| {
                data.try_string()
```

```
                           .map_err(|_| format_err!("can't convert to a string"))
             })
      }
   }
```

The implementation of the function is not important from a microservices point of view, and I will describe it shortly—it loads an `Image` from the provided bytes, converts the `Image` to grayscale with the `to_luma` method, and provides the returned value as an argument for a `Scanner`. Then, it uses the `scan` method to decode the QR code and extracts the first `Code` converted to a `String`.

main function

Now, we can add a `main` function to spawn an actor with the decoding worker:

```
fn main() -> Result<(), Error> {
    env_logger::init();
    let mut sys = System::new("rabbit-actix-worker");
    let _ = QueueActor::new(WokerHandler {}, &mut sys)?;
    let _ = sys.run();
    Ok(())
}
```

P 314

This method starts a `System` and creates an instance of `QueueActor` with an instance of `WorkerHandler`. That's all. It's really simple—with `QueueActor`, it's enough to implement `QueueHandler` to make a processor to a queue. Let's create a server in a similar way.

Server

To implement a server, we don't just implement `QueueHandler`. We also have to implement handlers for HTTP requests. We will also use the `actix` and `actix-web` crates.

Dependencies

Add the following types to the `server.rs` file:

```
use actix::{Addr, System};
use actix_web::dev::Payload;
use actix_web::error::MultipartError;
use actix_web::http::{self, header, StatusCode};
use actix_web::multipart::MultipartItem;
use actix_web::{
```

```
    middleware, server, App, Error as WebError, HttpMessage, HttpRequest,
HttpResponse,
};
use askama::Template;
use chrono::{DateTime, Utc};
use failure::Error;
use futures::{future, Future, Stream};
use indexmap::IndexMap;
use log::debug;
use rabbit_actix::queue_actor::{QueueActor, QueueHandler, SendMessage,
TaskId};
use rabbit_actix::{QrRequest, QrResponse, REQUESTS, RESPONSES};
use std::fmt;
use std::sync::{Arc, Mutex};
```

You should be familiar with all the types, because we used most of them in the previous chapters, excluding `MultipartItem` and `MultipartError`. Both of these types are used to extract uploaded files from POST requests.

Shared state

We will also add the `SharedTasks` type alias, which represents an `IndexMap` wrapped with `Mutex` and `Arc`. We will use this type to store all the tasks and statuses for them:

```
type SharedTasks = Arc<Mutex<IndexMap<String, Record>>>;
```

`Record` is a struct that contains the unique identifier of the task, and is used as the correlation ID for the message. It also has a `timestamp` that denotes when the task was posted, and a `Status` that represents the status of the task:

```
#[derive(Clone)]
struct Record {
    task_id: TaskId,
    timestamp: DateTime<Utc>,
    status: Status,
}
```

`Status` is an enumeration that has two variants: `InProgress`, when a task is sent to a worker; and `Done`, when a worker returns a response as a `QrResponse` value:

```
#[derive(Clone)]
enum Status {
    InProgress,
    Done(QrResponse),
}
```

We need to implement the `Display` trait for `Status`, because we will use it to render the HTML template. Implement the trait:

```
impl fmt::Display for Status {
    fn fmt(&self, f: &mut fmt::Formatter) -> fmt::Result {
        match self {
            Status::InProgress => write!(f, "in progress"),
            Status::Done(resp) => match resp {
                QrResponse::Succeed(data) => write!(f, "done: {}", data),
                QrResponse::Failed(err) => write!(f, "failed: {}", err),
            },
        }
    }
}
```

We will show three statuses: in progress, succeed, and failed.

Our server needs a shared state. We will use the `State` struct with a map of tasks and an address of `QueueActor` and `ServerHandler`:

```
#[derive(Clone)]
struct State {
    tasks: SharedTasks,
    addr: Addr<QueueActor<ServerHandler>>,
}
```

Now, we can implement `ServerHandler` and spawn an actor with it.

Server handler

To consume responses from a worker, our server has to start `QueueActor` with a handler that will update the shared state of a server. Create a `ServerHandler` struct that keeps a copy of the `SharedTasks` reference:

```
struct ServerHandler {
    tasks: SharedTasks,
}
```

Implement the `QueueHandler` for this struct:

```
impl QueueHandler for ServerHandler {
    type Incoming = QrResponse;
    type Outgoing = QrRequest;

    fn incoming(&self) -> &str {
        RESPONSES
```

```
    }
    fn outgoing(&self) -> &str {
        REQUESTS
    }
    fn handle(
        &self,
        id: &TaskId,
        incoming: Self::Incoming,
    ) -> Result<Option<Self::Outgoing>, Error> {
        self.tasks.lock().unwrap().get_mut(id).map(move |rec| {
            rec.status = Status::Done(incoming);
        });
        Ok(None)
    }
}
```

The handler of the server has to use the RESPONSES queue to consume responses, and REQUESTS as the outgoing queue to send requests. Correspondingly, set QrResponse to the Incoming type and QrRequest to the Outgoing type.

The handle method locks a Mutex stored in the tasks field to get access to IndexMap and update the status field of Record if the record exists for a corresponding task ID. The ID of the task will be automatically extracted by QueueActor and is provided to this method by an immutable reference. It's time to implement all the necessary HTTP handlers.

Requests handlers

We need three handlers for requests: an index page to show the name of the microservice, a handler for rendering all tasks and their statuses, and an uploading handler for posing new tasks with QR codes.

Index handler

index_handler returns some text with the name of this microservice:

```
fn index_handler(_: &HttpRequest<State>) -> HttpResponse {
    HttpResponse::Ok().body("QR Parsing Microservice")
}
```

Tasks handler

`tasks_handler` locks a `Mutex` with `IndexMap` to iterate over all `Record` values to render them as a part of the `Tasks` struct:

```
fn tasks_handler(req: HttpRequest<State>) -> impl Future<Item =
HttpResponse, Error = WebError> {
    let tasks: Vec<_> = req
        .state()
        .tasks
        .lock()
        .unwrap()
        .values()
        .cloned()
        .collect();
    let tmpl = Tasks { tasks };
    future::ok(HttpResponse::Ok().body(tmpl.render().unwrap()))
}
```

If you remember, we added the `askama` crate to render templates. Create a `templates` folder in the root of project and add a `tasks.html` file with some HTML code that contains at least the following rendering table:

```
<table>
    <thead>
        <tr>
            <th>Task ID</th>
            <th>Timestamp</th>
            <th>Status</th>
        </tr>
    </thead>
    <tbody>
        {% for task in tasks %}
        <tr>
            <td>{{ task.task_id }}</td>
            <td>{{ task.timestamp }}</td>
            <td>{{ task.status }}</td>
        </tr>
        {% endfor %}
    </tbody>
</table>
```

This is a part of the full template that you can find in the examples folder for this book, but the preceding code contains code for rendering a table with all the tasks extracted from the `Tasks` struct, which is implemented as follows:

```
#[derive(Template)]
#[template(path = "tasks.html")]
```

```
struct Tasks {
    tasks: Vec<Record>,
}
```

Derive the `Template` type for this struct and attach the template with the `template` attribute. `askama` will embed the template into your code. That's very convenient.

Upload handler

`upload_handler` is a bit complex, because it takes POST requests with a form that contains the uploaded image:

```
fn upload_handler(req: HttpRequest<State>) -> impl Future<Item =
HttpResponse, Error = WebError> {
    req.multipart()
        .map(handle_multipart_item)
        .flatten()
        .into_future()
        .and_then(|(bytes, stream)| {
            if let Some(bytes) = bytes {
                Ok(bytes)
            } else {
                Err((MultipartError::Incomplete, stream))
            }
        })
        .map_err(|(err, _)| WebError::from(err))
        .and_then(move |image| {
            debug!("Image: {:?}", image);
            let request = QrRequest { image };
            req.state()
                .addr
                .send(SendMessage(request))
                .from_err()
                .map(move |task_id| {
                    let record = Record {
                        task_id: task_id.clone(),
                        timestamp: Utc::now(),
                        status: Status::InProgress,
                    };
                    req.state().tasks.lock().unwrap().insert(task_id,
record);
                    req
                })
        })
        .map(|req| {
            HttpResponse::build_from(&req)
                .status(StatusCode::FOUND)
```

P326   State

```
                    .header(header::LOCATION, "/tasks")
                    .finish()
            })
    }
```

The implementation gets a `Stream` of `MultipartItem`, the value of which could be either `Filed` or `Nested`. We use the following function to collect all items in a single uniform `Stream` of `Vec<u8>` objects:

```
pub fn handle_multipart_item(
    item: MultipartItem<Payload>,
) -> Box<Stream<Item = Vec<u8>, Error = MultipartError>> {
    match item {
        MultipartItem::Field(field) => {
            Box::new(field.concat2().map(|bytes|
bytes.to_vec()).into_stream())
        }
        MultipartItem::Nested(mp) =>
Box::new(mp.map(handle_multipart_item).flatten()),
    }
}
```

Then, we extract the first item with the `into_future` method. If the value exists, we map it to `QrRequest` and use the address of `QueueActor` to `send` a request to a worker.

 You may ask whether it is possible if a worker returns a result if the ID of task wasn't set. Potentially, it's possible. If you want to have a reliable changing of `State`, you should implement an actor that works with the `State` instance exclusively.

Finally, the handler constructs a `HttpResponse` value that redirects the client to the `/tasks` path.

Now, we can connect each part in a single function.

main function

We have already created functions that create app instances of `actix` in Chapter 11, *Involving Concurrency with Actors and Actix Crate*. Return to that chapter if you don't remember how to attach handlers and a state to an application, and look at the `main` function, as follows:

```
fn main() -> Result<(), Error> {
    env_logger::init();
    let mut sys = System::new("rabbit-actix-server");
```

```
let tasks = Arc::new(Mutex::new(IndexMap::new()));
let addr = QueueActor::new(
    ServerHandler {
        tasks: tasks.clone(),
    },
    &mut sys,
)?;

let state = State {
    tasks: tasks.clone(),
    addr,
};
server::new(move || {
    App::with_state(state.clone())
        .middleware(middleware::Logger::default())
        .resource("/", |r| r.f(index_handler))
        .resource("/task", |r| {
            r.method(http::Method::POST).with_async(upload_handler);
        })
        .resource("/tasks", |r|
r.method(http::Method::GET).with_async(tasks_handler))
    })
    .bind("127.0.0.1:8080")
    .unwrap()
    .start();

let _ = sys.run();
Ok(())
}
```

This function creates a System instance with a new method that returns a SystemRunner instance, which we will use to start QueueActor with ServerHandler inside. Then, it creates a State instance with the address of the spawned actor and fills the App object with all the necessary handlers.

When we start a SystemRunner, it creates an actor and connects to RabbitMQ to create all the necessary queues and starts consuming the responses.

 A good practice is to create the same queues from all the applications that use it, because you can't know which part will be started first—the server or the worker. That's why we implemented the creation of all the queues in the new method of QueueAction. All queues will be available before any piece of code uses them.

We are ready to test this example.

Testing

Let's build and run the server and worker of the application. You should start a container with a RabbitMQ instance, as we did in this chapter in the *Bootstrap message broker for testing* section. Then, use `cargo build` to build all the parts.

When compilation has finished, start a server instance:

```
RUST_LOG=rabbit_actix_server=debug ./target/debug/rabbit-actix-server
```

Also, start a worker instance with the following command:

```
RUST_LOG=rabbit_actix_worker=debug ./target/debug/rabbit-actix-worker
```

When both parts have started, you can explore RabbitMQ with the `rabbitmqctl` command and explore your queues:

```
docker exec -it test-rabbit rabbitmqctl list_queues
```

It prints both the queues that were created by the actors:

```
Timeout: 60.0 seconds ...
Listing queues for vhost / ...
responses    0
requests     0
```

If you want to see all connected consumers, you can do that with the following command:

```
docker exec -it test-rabbit rabbitmqctl list_consumers
```

It prints `responses-consumer`, which represents a server instance, and `requests-consumer`, which represents a worker instance:

```
Listing consumers on vhost / ...
responses    <rabbit@f137a225a709.3.697.0>   responses-consumer   true   0
[]
requests     <rabbit@f137a225a709.3.717.0>   requests-consumer    true   0
[]
```

Now that everything is connected to RabbitMQ, we can open `http://localhost:8080/tasks` in a browser. You will see an empty table and a form to upload a QR code. Choose a file and upload it using the form. It will refresh the page and you will see your task in progress:

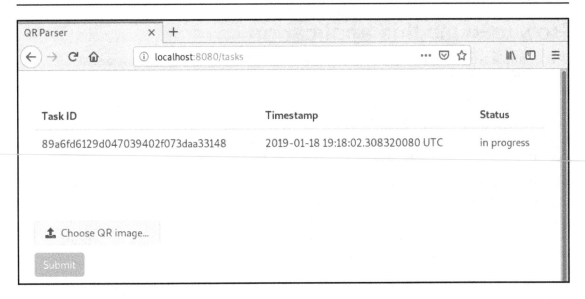

If the worker works properly and if you refresh the page after short period of time, you will see the decoded QR code:

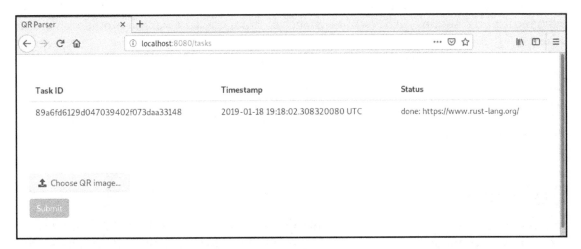

As you can see, the server and worker interact with a message that was delivered by RabbitMQ.

Let's discuss the benefits and drawbacks of this solution.

How to scale this application

The example we created in this chapter uses two parts that work separately and use RabbitMQ to exchange tasks and results.

Scaling this application is very easy—you just need to start as many workers as you want, and they don't have to work on the same server. You can run workers on a distributed cluster of servers. If your workers can't handle a load, you can start extra workers that will consume waiting tasks immediately and start the decoding process.

But this system has a potential bottleneck – the message broker. For this example, you can simply handle it if you start extra independent message brokers; for example, RabbitMQ support multiple instances with its clustering feature. Your server can have multiple connections with multiple message brokers, but you can't spawn as many servers as you want because they will have different sets of tasks.

Is it possible to share a list of tasks? Yes, you can use a traditional database or storage, such as Redis, but it becomes another bottleneck, because it's hard to use the same database instance for millions of clients.

How can we handle the bottleneck with a database? You can split the tasks list by client and keep the list for a specific client on one instance of storage. If you want to provide a feature where your clients share tasks with each other, you can create shared lists and store them in a database, which won't have a heavy load in this case.

As you can see, scaling is an undefined process, and you have to do some experimenting to achieve the desired result. But in any case, you should strive for separate tasks across microservices and use messages or RPCs to get loose coupling for your application, as well as good performance.

Summary

In this chapter, we discussed the important topic of scalable microservices. We started with the basics and continued with implementing two services that use RabbitMQ as a message broker to interact with each other. The example we created decodes QR codes to be processed by a separate worker. The benefit of the implemented application is that you can start as many workers as you want.

In the next chapter, we will learn how to test and debug microservices using unit tests, integration tests, and debuggers.

Testing and Debugging Rust Microservices

13

Microservices, like any other application, can have bugs. You can make a mistake when writing new code, or by adding extra features to an application. In this chapter, we will explore the available tools to test and debug your microservices.

We will start by creating unit and integration tests for an application. We will also examine the testing capabilities of the `actix` crate.

After this, we will study debugging with the LLDB Debugger, and also examine logging as a debugging technique, since not every bug can be caught with a traditional debugger. Furthermore, if you use a product in production, you can't attach a debugger to it.

We will cover the following topics in this chapter:

- Testing microservices

- Debugging microservices

Technical requirements

For the testing examples of this chapter, you need some extra software besides Rust compiler (which, of course, you'll need too). You will need to install Docker and Docker Compose to bootstrap the application from Chapter 15, *Packing Servers to Containers*. We will use this application to run integration tests.

You will also need to install the Postman tool, which we will use to test APIs manually, along with the LLDB debugger, which we'll learn how to use for debugging microservices. Also, Jaeger will need to be installed, but you can also use the all-in-one image running in Docker for this. Finally, we will use the OpenTracing API for distributed tracing.

The examples of this chapter are provided with sources on GitHub: `https://github.com/PacktPublishing/Hands-On-Microservices-with-Rust/tree/master/Chapter13`.

Testing microservices

Rust is an almost perfect tool for creating reliable applications. The compiler is so strict and never misses any potential memory access error or data race, but still there are many ways to make a mistake in the code. In other words, Rust helps you a lot, but it is not omnipotent.

Unit testing

Microservices can also have bugs, so you have to be armed to handle all possible bugs. The first line of defense is unit testing.

Unit testing involves using HTTP clients to send an isolated request to a server or a request handler. In a unit test, you should check only one function. It's necessary to cover the majority of the code that helps to keep the same behavior of a function that can be reimplemented or improved with tests.

Also, you can write a test before writing any piece of code. It's called **Test-Driven Development (TDD)**, but this approach is suitable for projects that have a good specification, because if you haven't decided on the solution, you will have to rewrite tests multiple times. In other words, TDD is not suitable for projects in which bugs are not critical, but where high-speed development is required.

Writing unit tests for traditional crates is simple, but for microservices, you have a lot of issues with emulating the environment in which a microservice will work in production. To emulate an environment, you can use mocking services that create HTTP servers with predefined responses for specified requests. Do you remember, in `Chapter 11`, *Involving Concurrency with Actors and Actix Crate*, when we created a routing microservice that we can't test, because we have to run a lot of microservices manually? In this section, we will create a unit test for that very routing microservice.

Mocking

Let's create a `mock` server that emulates responses for requests to three paths to a routing microservice: `/signin`, `/signup`, and `/comments`. There is the `mockito` crate that provides a server for emulating HTTP responses. We will use the example from `Chapter 11, Involving Concurrency with Actors and the Actix Crate`. Copy it and add these extra dependencies:

```
mockito = "0.15"
reqwest = "0.9"
```

We need the mockito crate to start a server with mocks, and the reqwest crate to make HTTP requests to our Actix server instance.

Create a `tests` module with the `#[cfg(test)]` attribute that will be compiled for testing only, and import the following types that we will use for testing:

```
use crate::{start, Comment, LinksMap, UserForm, UserId};
use lazy_static::lazy_static;
use mockito::{mock, Mock};
use reqwest::Client;
use serde::{Deserialize, Serialize};
use std::sync::Mutex;
use std::time::Duration;
use std::thread;
```

We use types of router microservices to prepare requests; namely, `Comment`, `UserForm`, and `UserId`. Also, we added the `LinksMap` struct to configure URLs to mocks:

```
#[derive(Clone)]
struct LinksMap {
    signup: String,
    signin: String,
    new_comment: String,
    comments: String,
}
```

Add this struct to `State` and use it with handlers to get the URLs of microservices:

```
#[derive(Clone)]
struct State {
    counter: RefCell<i64>,
    links: LinksMap,
}
```

Also, we imported the `lazy_static!` macro that we need to initialize a `Mutex`, which we will use to check that the Actix Server started once. Rust also has the `Once` type, which can also be used, but we need to wait a certain interval before letting the services perform requests, and the `is_completed` method of `Once` type is unstable. To create mocks, we will use the `mock` function of the `mockito` crate and a `Mock` type that represents a handler of a specific request.

Create a function to add mocks, as follows:

```
fn add_mock<T>(method: &str, path: &str, result: T) -> Mock
where
    T: Serialize,
{
    mock(method, path)
        .with_status(200)
        .with_header("Content-Type", "application/json")
        .with_body(serde_json::to_string(&result).unwrap())
        .create()
}
```

The `add_mock` function expects an HTTP method and path to emulated resource. Also, it takes a value returned as a response in JSON format.

We call the `mock` function to create a `Mock` instance and tune it with the following methods:

- `with_status` sets the status code of a response
- `with_header` sets a specific value for a header
- `with_body` sets the body of a response

Finally, we call the `create` method, which tries to start a `mock` server and attach our created `Mock` to it. Now, we can start a router microservice instance and prepare all the necessary mocks to emulate other microservices that the router expects.

Starting a server for testing

We will start a server instance in a separate thread, because Rust runs tests in multiple threads, and we won't create a server instance with a unique port for every test run to show how you can use a shared instance, because integration tests often need to reuse the same application instance. Create a shared flag that we will use to detect routers that have already started:

```
lazy_static! {
    static ref STARTED: Mutex<bool> = Mutex::new(false);
```

```
}
```

Now, we will use this `Mutex` to create a function to start a server. Look at the following `setup` function implementation:

```
fn setup() {
    let mut started = STARTED.lock().unwrap();
    if !*started {
        thread::spawn(|| {
            let url = mockito::server_url();
            let _signup = add_mock("POST", "/signup", ());
            let _signin = add_mock("POST", "/signin", UserId { id: "user-
id".into() });
            let _new_comment = add_mock("POST", "/new_comment", ());
            let comment = Comment {
                id: None,
                text: "comment".into(),
                uid: "user-id".into(),
            };
            let _comments = add_mock("GET", "/comments", vec![comment]);
            let links = LinksMap {
                signup: mock_url(&url, "/signup"),
                signin: mock_url(&url, "/signin"),
                new_comment: mock_url(&url, "/new_comment"),
                comments: mock_url(&url, "/comments"),
            };
            start(links);
        });
        thread::sleep(Duration::from_secs(5));
        *started = true;
    }
}
```

The preceding function locks a `Mutex` to get the value of the flag. If it equals `false`, we spawn a new thread with a server instance and mocks, and wait 5 seconds before we set the flag to `true` and release the `Mutex`.

In the spawned thread, we get a URL or `mock` server. It automatically starts that server if it wasn't started already. After this, we use the `add_mock` method to add all mocks to emulate other microservices.

 The `mockito` crate requires you to have added all the mocks in the same thread in which the `mock` server started.

Also, we keep all crated mocks in local variables. If any of them are dropped, then that mocking handler will be lost. You can also use the `std::mem::forget` method to ensure that the mock will be never dropped, but it's more accurate to leave the local variable.

We will employ `LinksMap` using the URL of the `mock` server and paths, both of which are concatenated with the following function:

```
fn mock_url(base: &str, path: &str) -> String {
    format!("{}{}", base, path)
}
```

Finally, we called the `start` function, which is actually a modified `main` function:

```
fn start(links: LinksMap) {
    let sys = actix::System::new("router");
    let state = State {
        counter: RefCell::default(),
        links,
    };
    server::new(move ||
        App::with_state(state.clone())
            // App resources attached here
    }).workers(1).bind("127.0.0.1:8080").unwrap().start();
    sys.run();
}
```

The difference between this and the `main` function of the router microservice of Chapter 11, *Involving Concurrency with Actors and Actix Crate*, is that it expects the `LinksMap` value to add it to `State`. Now, we can create methods to perform testing requests to a server that resends them to mocks.

Making requests

To make GET requests, we will use the `test_get` function, which creates a `Client` of the `reqwest` crate, sets a path, executes a `send` request, and deserializes the response from JSON:

```
fn test_get<T>(path: &str) -> T
where
    T: for <'de> Deserialize<'de>,
{
    let client = Client::new();
    let data = client.get(&test_url(path))
        .send()
        .unwrap()
```

```
        .text()
        .unwrap();
    serde_json::from_str(&data).unwrap()
}
```

If you are familiar with the reqwest crate, you may ask why we get text values, since Client has the json method that deserializes JSON? If we do that, we can't see the original value if we have deserialization issues, but using the original text of a response, we can log it for investigation.

To generate URLs, we use the following function:

```
fn test_url(path: &str) -> String {
    format!("http://127.0.0.1:8080/api{}", path)
}
```

This adds the address of a server to which we bind it, but for large projects, it's better to use dynamic addresses, especially if you want to use a fresh server instance in every test.

For POST requests, we will use similar method, but we won't deserialize the result because we don't need it and will check the status of a response only:

```
fn test_post<T>(path: &str, data: &T)
where
    T: Serialize,
{
    setup();
    let client =  Client::new();
    let resp = client.post(&test_url(path))
        .form(data)
        .send()
        .unwrap();
    let status = resp.status();
    assert!(status.is_success());
}
```

We have all the necessary functions to implement unit tests for every handler.

Implementing tests

With the utilities we've created so far in this chapter, the unit tests look pretty compact. To test the handler of the /signup path that expects UserForm, we will add a test_signup_with_client function with the #[test] attribute:

```
#[test]
fn test_signup_with_client() {
```

```
    let user = UserForm {
        email: "abc@example.com".into(),
        password: "abc".into(),
    };
    test_post("/signup", &user);
}
```

When we run the `cargo test` command, this function will be called and the `test_post` call, in turn, will bootstrap a server with a `mock` server as well.

To test a handler of the `/signin` path, we will use the following function:

```
#[test]
fn test_signin_with_client() {
    let user = UserForm {
        email: "abc@example.com".into(),
        password: "abc".into(),
    };
    test_post("/signin", &user);
}
```

This test uses the same input values with a `POST` request.

To fetch a list of comments, it's enough to call the `test_get` function with the `/comments` path:

```
#[test]
fn test_list_with_client() {
    let _: Vec<Comment> = test_get("/comments");
}
```

Now, we can start these tests to check the router microservice that forwards requests to a `mock` server.

Running our tests

To run the unit test, run Cargo's `test` command in the folder of this project. It will start three tests and you will see, in the Terminal, the output of the command:

```
running 3 tests
test tests::test_list_with_client ... ok
test tests::test_signup_with_client ... ok
test tests::test_signin_with_client ... ok

test result: ok. 3 passed; 0 failed; 0 ignored; 0 measured; 0 filtered out
```

All of the tests have passed, but let's check what happens if we change something in the implementation. Let's remove a `Mock` for the `/signin` path. The test will print that one test has failed:

```
running 3 tests
test tests::test_list_with_client ... ok
test tests::test_signin_with_client ... FAILED
test tests::test_signup_with_client ... ok

failures:
---- tests::test_signin_with_client stdout ----
thread 'tests::test_signin_with_client' panicked at 'assertion failed:
status.is_success()', src/lib.rs:291:9
note: Run with `RUST_BACKTRACE=1` environment variable to display a
backtrace.

failures:
    tests::test_signin_with_client

test result: FAILED. 2 passed; 1 failed; 0 ignored; 0 measured; 0 filtered
out
```

As expected, the `tests::test_signin_with_client` test failed, because it can't get a response from the `/signin` request. Unit testing will help you ensure the behavior of a handler won't be changed, even if you rewrite the implementation from scratch.

We covered a microservice with a unit test using predefined methods to simplify bootstrapping a server and to send HTTP requests to it. If you want to test complex interaction with an application, you should implement integration tests, which we will cover now.

Integration testing

Unit testing can't guarantee that the whole application works, because it tests only a small piece of implementation. By contrast, integration tests are more complex and they help to ensure your whole application works properly. We combined some microservices that we created for this book into one application. Let's create integration tests to check the application.

Starting an application instance

Before we write the first line of a testing code, we have to start an application with Docker. It's complex and you will learn how to make it in Chapter 15, *Packing Servers to Containers*, but for now, open the code samples folder of that chapter and start a project from the Docker Compose script. However, you will also have to prepare an image for building microservices. Enter these two commands into a Terminal:

```
docker build -t rust:nightly nightly
docker-compose -f docker-compose.test.yml up
```

The project already contains a special Compose file, `docker-compose.test.yml`, that opens the ports of the containers to make it possible to connect to them from our local Rust application.

It takes time to start, but when the application has started, you will see the log in a Terminal window. Then, we can write some integration tests.

Dependencies

You might be surprised, but for integration testing, we don't need a lot of dependencies, because we will use an HTTP client and the `serde` family of crates to serialize requests and deserialize responses:

```
cookie = "0.11"
rand = "0.6"
reqwest = "0.9"
serde = "1.0"
serde_derive = "1.0"
serde_json = "1.0"
uuid = { version = "0.5", features = ["serde", "v4"] }
```

Also, we need the `uuid` crate to generate unique values, and the cookie crate to support cookies in our HTTP requests, because integration tests have to keep the session to make a sequence of meaningful requests.

Utils

Like we did for unit tests, we'll add some utility function to avoid creating HTTP clients for every test. We will use predefined methods to health-check and to send POST and GET requests to microservices included in the application. Create a utils.rs file and import the necessary types:

```
use cookie::{Cookie, CookieJar};
use rand::{Rng, thread_rng};
use rand::distributions::Alphanumeric;
pub use reqwest::{self, Client, Method, RedirectPolicy, StatusCode};
use reqwest::header::{COOKIE, SET_COOKIE};
use serde::Deserialize;
use std::collections::HashMap;
use std::iter;
use std::time::Duration;
use std::thread;
```

We will use a Client instance from the reqwest crate, just as we did for the unit test, but we'll need to import extra types: Method to set different HTTP methods exactly; RedirectPolicy to control redirects, since the router microservice will redirect us to other pages; and Client, which will perform those redirects, but we want to turn off this behavior. StatusCode is used to check returned HTTP status codes.

We imported the COOKIE and SET_COOKIE headers to set the values of those headers for requests, and get their values from the responses. But the values of those headers are formal and we need to parse them. To simplify this, we will use the Cookie and CookieJar types of the cookie crate, since the reqwest crate doesn't support cookies now.

Also, we use the rand crate and the imported Alphanumeric distribution from it to generate unique logins for testing, because we will interact with a working application and simply can't restart it now.

Our application contains four microservices with the following addresses, all of which are available from the Docker containers of our application:

```
const USERS: &str = "http://localhost:8001";
const MAILER: &str = "http://localhost:8002";
const CONTENT: &str = "http://localhost:8003";
const ROUTER: &str = "http://localhost:8000";
```

We declared addresses as constant, so that we have a single place to update them if necessary:

```
pub fn url(url: &str, path: &str) -> String {
    url.to_owned() + path
}
```

Also, we need a function to generate random strings that consist of alphanumeric characters:

```
pub fn rand_str() -> String {
    let mut rng = thread_rng();
    iter::repeat(())
            .map(|()| rng.sample(Alphanumeric))
            .take(7)
            .collect()
}
```

The preceding code uses a random number generator that's initialized for the current thread, and an iterator that generates random values, to take 7 characters and join them into `String` values.

Since integration tests work with live systems, we need a function to sleep the current thread:

```
pub fn wait(s: u64) {
    thread::sleep(Duration::from_secs(s));
}
```

This function is a short alias for the `thread::sleep` call.

But it's not all about utilities—we also need a universal client to send requests to all working microservices.

The integration testing client

Add the following struct to your `utils.rs` source file:

```
pub struct WebApi {
    client: Client,
    url: String,
    jar: CookieJar,
}
```

It has three fields—an HTTP `Client`; a base `url`, which is used to construct full URLs with added paths; and a `CookieJar` instance to keep cookie values between requests.

The constructor of this struct takes a URL and builds a `Client` instance with redirects disabled:

```
impl WebApi {
    fn new(url: &str) -> Self {
        let client = Client::builder()
            .redirect(RedirectPolicy::none())
            .build()
            .unwrap();
        Self {
            client,
            url: url.into(),
            jar: CookieJar::new(),
        }
    }
}
```

We can add shortcuts to create instances of `WebApi` for the specific microservice of our application:

```
pub fn users()   -> Self { WebApi::new(USERS)   }
pub fn mailer()  -> Self { WebApi::new(MAILER)  }
pub fn content() -> Self { WebApi::new(CONTENT) }
pub fn router()  -> Self { WebApi::new(ROUTER)  }
```

We will check that every microservice is alive. To do this, we need a method for `WebApi` that sends GET requests to a specified path and checks the response:

```
pub fn healthcheck(&mut self, path: &str, content: &str) {
    let url = url(&self.url, path);
    let mut resp = reqwest::get(&url).unwrap();
    assert_eq!(resp.status(), StatusCode::OK);
    let text = resp.text().unwrap();
    assert_eq!(text, content);
}
```

Every microservice of our application has a special path to get the name of microservice, which we will use for health-checking.

To send requests to microservices, we will use the following function:

```
pub fn request<'a, I, J>(&mut self, method: Method, path: &'a str, values:
I) -> J
where
```

```
        I: IntoIterator<Item = (&'a str, &'a str)>,
        J: for <'de> Deserialize<'de>,
{
    let url = url(&self.url, path);
    let params = values.into_iter().collect::<HashMap<_, _>>();
    let mut resp = self.client.request(method, &url)
        .form(&params)
        .send()
        .unwrap();

    let status = resp.status().to_owned();

    let text = resp
        .text()
        .unwrap();

    if status != StatusCode::OK {
        panic!("Bad response [{}] of '{}': {}", resp.status(), path, text);
    }

    let value = serde_json::from_str(&text);
    match value {
        Ok(value) => value,
        Err(err) => {
            panic!("Can't convert '{}': {}", text, err);
        },
    }
}
```

It's a useful function that sends a request in JSON format and receives a response in JSON format, which it deserializes into the necessary native struct. The implementation of this method is not crazy. It expects a HTTP method, path, and values that will be used as form parameters in a request.

We use a textual response to print values if the microservice returns an HTTP status other than OK. If a response is successful, we will deserialize the body from JSON format to the necessary output type.

Since the whole application won't return internal service information to us, we need a method that creates a request and checks the status code of a response, but also stores cookies to have a chance to sign up and sign in to our application. Create the check_status method for the WebApi struct implementation:

```
pub fn check_status<'a, I>(&mut self, method: Method, path: &'a str,
values: I, status: StatusCode)
where
    I: IntoIterator<Item = (&'a str, &'a str)>,
```

```
{
    let url = url(&self.url, path);
    let params = values.into_iter().collect::<HashMap<_, _>>();
    let cookies = self.jar.iter()
        .map(|kv| format!("{}={}", kv.name(), kv.value()))
        .collect::<Vec<_>>()
        .join(";");
    let resp = self.client.request(method, &url)
        .header(COOKIE, cookies)
        .form(&params)
        .send()
        .unwrap();
    if let Some(value) = resp.headers().get(SET_COOKIE) {
        let raw_cookie = value.to_str().unwrap().to_owned();
        let cookie = Cookie::parse(raw_cookie).unwrap();
        self.jar.add(cookie);
    }
    assert_eq!(status, resp.status());
}
```

The preceding implementation also uses values to make a request with a form, but it also prepares cookies and sends them with the Cookie header after the function expects a response from a server. If a response contains a SetCookie header, we use it to update our CookieJar. With such simple manipulations, we take a method that can keep the connection session.

Types

Before we start implementing tests, we need to add some types that we need to interact with microservices. Create a types.rs source file with types:

```
use serde_derive::Deserialize;
use uuid::Uuid;
```

Now, add a UserId struct that will be used to parse raw responses from the users microservices (yes, we will also test it directly):

```
#[derive(Deserialize)]
pub struct UserId {
    id: Uuid,
}
```

Also, add a Comment struct that we will use to post new comments to our content microservice:

```
#[derive(Deserialize)]
```

```
pub struct Comment {
    pub id: i32,
    pub uid: String,
    pub text: String,
}
```

Now, we can write tests for every microservice separately, and after that, create a test for complex interaction.

Users

We will start the `users` microservice test coverage. Create a `users.rs` file and import the created modules into it with the necessary types:

```
mod types;
mod utils;

use self::types::UserId;
use self::utils::{Method, WebApi};
```

At first, we have to check that the microservice is alive. Add the `users_healthcheck` method:

```
#[test]
fn users_healthcheck() {
    let mut api = WebApi::users();
    api.healthcheck("/", "Users Microservice");
}
```

It creates an instance of the `WebApi` struct using the `users` method that already configures it for interaction with the users microservice. We use the `healthcheck` method to check the root path of a service that has to return the `"Users Microservice"` string.

The main purpose of the `users` microservice is a new users' registration, and the authorization of registered users. Create a `check_signup_and_signin` function that will generate a new user, register it by sending a request to the `/signup` path, and then try to log in using the `/signin` path:

```
#[test]
fn check_signup_and_signin() {
    let mut api = WebApi::users();
    let username = utils::rand_str() + "@example.com";
    let password = utils::rand_str();
    let params = vec![
        ("email", username.as_ref()),
```

```
            ("password", password.as_ref()),
    ];
    let _: () = api.request(Method::POST, "/signup", params);

    let params = vec![
        ("email", username.as_ref()),
        ("password", password.as_ref()),
    ];
    let _: UserId = api.request(Method::POST, "/signin", params);
}
```

We created a new `WebApi` instance that has targeted to our `users` microservice. The values
of the `username` and `password` are generated by the `rand_str` function call of the `utils`
module that we created earlier. After this, we prepare parameters to emulate sending an
HTML form to a server with a `POST` request. The first request registers a new user; the
second request tries to authorize it with the same form parameters.

Since the users microservice is used internally by the router microservice, it returns a raw
`UserId` struct. We will parse it, but won't use it, because we have already checked that the
microservice works, as it won't return users' IDs for bad credentials.

Content

The next microservice we need to test is a content microservice that allows users to post
comments. Create a `content.rs` file and import the `types` and `utils` modules with the
necessary types:

```
mod types;
mod utils;

use self::utils::{Method, WebApi};
use self::types::Comment;
```

We also will check that the service is available in the `content_healthcheck` test:

```
#[test]
fn content_healthcheck() {
    let mut api = WebApi::content();
    api.healthcheck("/", "Content Microservice");
}
```

This service is necessary for users to be able to add a new comment, and is loose-coupled (it doesn't need to check that the user exists, because it is protected from non-existent users by router microservices). We will generate a new ID of the user and send a request to post a new comment:

```
#[test]
fn add_comment() {
    let mut api = WebApi::content();
    let uuid = uuid::Uuid::new_v4().to_string();
    let comment = utils::rand_str();
    let params = vec![
        ("uid", uuid.as_ref()),
        ("text", comment.as_ref()),
    ];
    let _: () = api.request(Method::POST, "/new_comment", params);

    let comments: Vec<Comment> = api.request(Method::GET, "/list", vec![]);
    assert!(comments.into_iter().any(|Comment { text, ..}| { text ==
comment }))
}
```

We prepared a form to create a new comment and sent a POST request to the /new_comment path. After that, we take a list of comments and check that there is a comment with generated text in a list. This means that the comment was added and that the content microservice works properly.

Mailer

Our application also has a mailer microservice that sends notifications to users. It needs the utils module for testing only:

```
mod utils;

use self::utils::{Method, WebApi};
```

Put the preceding code into a new mailer.rs file and add a healthcheck to test that a microservice instance is alive:

```
#[test]
fn mails_healthcheck() {
    let mut api = WebApi::mailer();
    api.healthcheck("/", "Mailer Microservice");
}
```

The Mailer microservice also doesn't need to know users to notify them. It only requires an email address and some content. This microservice will send confirmation codes to a user, so let's simulate this behavior in our `send_mail` test:

```
#[test]
fn send_mail() {
    let mut api = WebApi::mailer();
    let email = utils::rand_str() + "@example.com";
    let code = utils::rand_str();
    let params = vec![
        ("to", email.as_ref()),
        ("code", code.as_ref()),
    ];
    let sent: bool = api.request(Method::POST, "/send", params);
    assert!(sent);
}
```

We created a `WebApi` instance with the `mailer` function call to target a client to the Mailer microservice. After that, we generated a new email and code, and put them into a form. The microservice returns a Boolean value, indicating that the email was sent. We use it with the `asser!` macro to check that it worked correctly.

We have covered all of the microservices of the application with tests, and now we can add a full integration test that checks a complex interaction with the application.

Router

Create a `router.rs` file and add the following modules and types:

```
mod types;
mod utils;

use self::utils::{Method, StatusCode, WebApi};
use self::types::Comment;
```

Since the router microservice also serves static files by the root path that we used for the other microservice, to check that they are alive, we will use a special /healthcheck path that returns the name of that microservice:

```
#[test]
fn router_healthcheck() {
    let mut api = WebApi::router();
    api.healthcheck("/healthcheck", "Router Microservice");
}
```

The complete test is implemented in the `check_router_full` test. Look at the following code:

```
#[test]
fn check_router_full() {
    let mut api = WebApi::router();
    let username = utils::rand_str() + "@example.com";
    let password = utils::rand_str();
    let params = vec![
        ("email", username.as_ref()),
        ("password", password.as_ref()),
    ];
    api.check_status(Method::POST, "/api/signup", params,
StatusCode::FOUND);

    let params = vec![
        ("email", username.as_ref()),
        ("password", password.as_ref()),
    ];
    api.check_status(Method::POST, "/api/signin", params,
StatusCode::FOUND);

    let comment = utils::rand_str();
    let params = vec![
        ("text", comment.as_ref()),
    ];
    api.check_status(Method::POST, "/api/new_comment", params,
StatusCode::FOUND);

    let comments: Vec<Comment> = api.request(Method::GET, "/api/comments",
vec![]);
    assert!(comments.into_iter().any(|Comment { text, ..}| { text ==
comment }))
}
```

It creates a new `WebApi` instance that's targeted at the router microservice. After this, it creates random credentials for a user and calls the router's method in `/api` scope. But in this case, we use the `check_status` method, because the router microservice creates and keeps session IDs internally and returns cookies to identify us.

We sent requests to `/api/signup` and `/api/signin` to register a user account and to authorize it. After this, we called the `/api/new_comment` method of the application API to post a new comment by user of the current session. Finally, we check in the open `/api/comments` endpoint that our comment exits.

We covered the basic functionality of applications with this integration test, but for large applications, you can also check records in databases, cached values, and uploaded files to ensure that the application works as you expected. If your microservice works incorrectly and you can't find a reason, you can try to debug it with the instruments that we will learn about in the next section.

Debugging microservices

If your program does go wrong, you need debugging tools to fix that, which we will explore in this section. Debugging not only means interactive debugging using a debugger—a special tool that helps you to execute program step by step—you can also use logging to trace all activities of the code. To understand the cause of the error, you can use the following tools:

- **curl**: a command-line tool that we already used to send HTTP requests
- **Postman:** a GUI tool for testing REST APIs
- **mitmproxy:** a proxy to trace all requests passing through it
- **LLDB:** a traditional command-line debugger
- **VS Code:** an editor with good LLDB integration

Let's explore all of them.

curl

The most commonly used tool to perform HTTP requests is `curl`. It's a command-line tool with a boatload of parameters. Some of the most useful ones are as follows:

- `--request <METHOD>` (or `-X`) sets the HTTP method to use
- `--header "Header: Value"` (or `-H`) sets an extra header to the request
- `--data <data>` (of `-d`) sets a body to a request, and uses `@filename` as a data value to attach the contents of a file
- `--form "field=value"` (or `-F`) sets a field of a form
- `--cookie <file>` (or `-b`) sets a file with cookies to send
- `--cookie-jar <file>` (or `-c`) sets a file with cookies to store

For example, if you want to send a request with a JSON file, use the following command:

```
curl -X POST -H "Content-Type: application/json" -d @file.json
http://localhost:8080/upload
```

Or, to send a form, use the following command:

```
curl -X POST -F login=user -F password=secret
http://localhost:8080/register
```

If you want to keep cookies between calls, use the same file to read and write cookie values with the following code: `-b session.file -c session.file`.

If you prefer to use GUI tools, you can consider using Postman.

Postman

Postman is a popular extension for browsers that is also available as a desktop application. You can get it from here: `https://www.getpostman.com/`. The coolest features of Postman include that you can group requests and use configurable variables in requests.

For example, let's send a sign-in request to our application that we started with Docker Compose. Install Postman and create a new workspace called **Rust Microservices**. Enter the URL of an application, set the method to `POST`, and add the body as `x-www-form-unlencoded`, with two parameters, `email` and `password` (the user has to have been created with /*signup* before). Click the **Send** button:

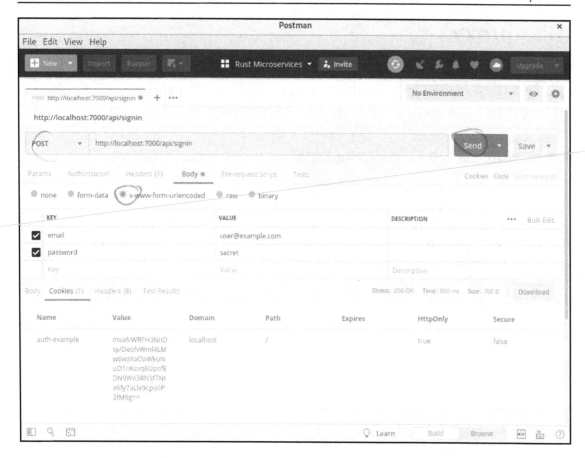

As you can see, the microservices returned a response with cookies, which contain an `auth-example` named value.

But what about if we want to use a browser to perform all activities, but explore sent request and responses later? We can start a tracing proxy. Let's do it.

mitmproxy

mitmproxy is a good proxy that logs all request and responses, and can work as a transparent proxy, as a SOCKS5 proxy, or as a reverse proxy. This tool is useful when you want to interact with the running application with a browser, but want to record all request and responses of the interaction session. You can get this tool from here: `https://mitmproxy.org/`.

Install a proxy and start it by forwarding it to the server's ports:

```
mitmweb --mode reverse:http://localhost:7000 --web-port 7777 --listen-port 7780
```

As you may already know by talking parameters, we used reverse-proxy mode. It used the `7777` port to provide access to the mitmproxy UI and port `7780` to connect to our application through proxy. In other words, the proxy redirects all requests from port `7780` to port `7000` of our application.

Open `127.0.0.1:7777` in a browser, and `127.0.0.1:7780` in a separate tab, and try to interact with the application. The mitmproxy web app will show you a flow of request and the responses the browser made:

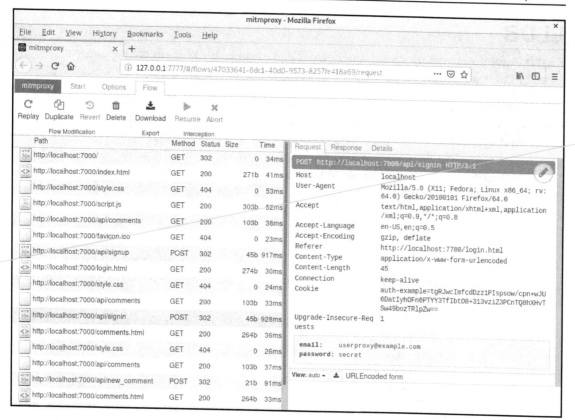

Like with Postman, we also can explore the headers of the /signin response, and see the cookie header with the auth-example value set.

Sometimes, you might see incorrect behavior in your application, but can't find a bug in the code. For these cases, you may consider trying debuggers.

LLDB

Rust has good support for two debuggers—GDB and LLDB. We will try the second here. LLDB is a modern command-line debugger. It's a part of the LLVM project.

Let's try to look inside our working router microservice. Move to the directory with the microservice and compile it with the `cargo build` command. However, you have to be sure you don't set the `--release` flag, because it removes all debugging information. If you don't use cargo and want to add debugging information directly using `rustc`, add the `-g -C debuginfo=2` arguments to keep debugging symbols in the output file. After the building is finished, use a command to start a debugger with scripts to support the Rust programming language:

```
rust-lldb ./target/debug/router-microservice
```

This command is already installed if you used the `rustup` installation tool to install Rust. You will have also installed LLDB debugger on your machine. When the debugger starts, it will print something like this:

```
(lldb) command script import "/home/user/.rustup/toolchains/nightly-x86_64-
unknown-linux-gnu/lib/rustlib/etc/lldb_rust_formatters.py"
(lldb) type summary add --no-value --python-function
lldb_rust_formatters.print_val -x ".*" --category Rust
(lldb) type category enable Rust
(lldb) target create "./target/debug/router-microservice"
Current executable set to './target/debug/router-microservice' (x86_64).
(lldb)
```

It will prompt for your input.

Let's set a breakpoint to the `comments` handler. You can do that with the following command:

```
breakpoint set --name comments
```

It will print that your breakpoint was set:

```
Breakpoint 1: where = router-
microservice`router_microservice::comments::h50a827d1180e4955 + 7 at
main.rs:152, address = 0x00000000001d3c77
```

Now, we can start the microservice with this command:

```
run
```

It will inform you that the process has launched:

```
Process 10143 launched:
'/home/user/sources/Chapter15/deploy/microservices/router/target/debug/rout
er-microservice'
```

Now, if you try to open the `http://localhost:8080/comments` URL in a browser, then the debugger will interrupt the execution of the handler in the breakpoint you set, and the debugger will show you the position of the line of code where it has interrupted:

```
    151         fn comments(req: HttpRequest<State>) ->
FutureResponse<HttpResponse> {
->  152             debug!("/api/comments called");
    153             let url = format!("{}/list", req.state().content());
    154             let fut = get_req(&url)
    155                 .map(|data| {
```

At this point, you can explore the running microservices. For example, you can get to know which alive threads exists with the following command:

```
thread list
```

It will show you the main thread and arbiter threads of actix:

```
    thread #3: tid = 10147, 0x00007ffff7e939d7
libc.so.6`.annobin_epoll_wait.c + 87, name = 'actix-web accep'
    thread #4: tid = 10148, 0x00007ffff7f88b4d
libpthread.so.0`__lll_lock_wait + 29, name = 'arbiter:77596ed'
    thread #5: tid = 10149, 0x00007ffff7f8573c
libpthread.so.0`__pthread_cond_wait + 508, name = 'arbiter:77596ed'
```

To see the variables that are available for the current context, you can use the `frame variable` command. To move execution to the next line of code, use the `next` command. To continue execution, use the `continue` command.

Using this tool, you can go through buggy handlers step by step and find the reason for the problem. Many developers prefer GUI debuggers and we'll also try one.

Visual Studio Code

Visual Studio Code is a convenient editor for developers with a lot of extensions, including for the Rust language and the LLDB debugger support. Let's try to use it.

First, you have to download and install Visual Studio Code from here: `https://code.visualstudio.com/`. After this, you need to install two extensions—`rust-lang.rust` and `vadimcn.vscode-lldb`. The first adds Rust support while the second integrates VS Code with LLDB.

The integration with Rust is based on the **Rust Language Server** (**RLS**) project that, which provides information about Rust code for IDEs.

Open the router microservice project with *File > Add Folder To A Workspace...* and choose the folder with a project. When it's open, set a breakpoint—set a cursor to the desired line and choose *Debug > Toggle Breakpoint* command. Now, we can start debugging with the *Debug | Start Debugging* command. On the first run, it takes some time to prepare LLDB, but when debugger starts, it prints some information to the *Output* tab.

Open a browser and try to open the `http://localhost:8080/comments` URL that activates the breakpoint of our `comments` handler:

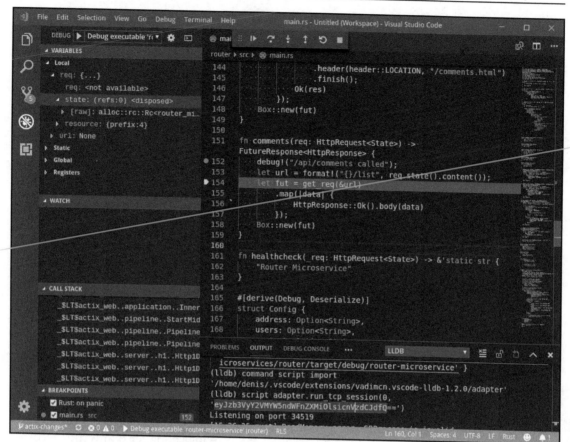

Use the bar at the top to move the execution pointer to the next line. With a GUI debugger, you can explore variables and the call stack. It's simple and useful. But not every case can be fixed with debugger, because there's types of bugs (called **Heisenbugs**) that disappear at the moment of debugging or studying them. The only thing that can help with that is logging.

Structural logging

I believe the logging is the silver bullet of debugging, because it works everywhere—on tests, on production servers, in cloud infrastructure. Also, you don't have to reproduce the activity that produces bugs – you can take the logs of a working application and read them to detect problems. Sometimes, you will have bugs that you can't reproduce, and logs can help to fix them.

We already studied the basics of logging in Chapter 3, *Logging and Configuring Microservices*. We used the simple env_logger and log crates, but for large applications, it may not be enough, because you will need to collect all logs for analyzing, and it's simpler to parse logs from a formal format like JSON. There are structural logging crates for this case. Let's explore a tiny example of using structural logging with the slog crate.

Example

We will crate a tiny application that writes logs to a file and to a console. Create a new crate and add the following dependencies:

```
slog = "2.4"
slog-async = "2.3"
slog-json = "2.3"
slog-term = "2.4"
```

We need slog as the main logging crate for the application. The slog-async crate helps to move log processing to a separate thread. slog-json provides a logger that writes records in JSON format. slog-term provides formats to write messages to a Terminal.

We will import the following types:

```
use slog::{crit, debug, error, Drain, Duplicate, Level, LevelFilter};
use slog_async::Async;
use slog_term::{CompactFormat, PlainDecorator};
use slog_json::Json;
use std::fs::OpenOptions;
use std::sync::Mutex;
```

From the main slog crate, we will use the crit, debug, and error macros, which are an alternative to the logging macro of the log crate. Drain is the main trait that provides logging functionality. Ultimately, we must create a Drain instance to log something. Duplicate is a kind of Drain that duplicates records to two Drain instances. Level and LevelFilter allow us to filter records by desired level.

From the `slog-async` crate, we will use the `Async` type, which is a `Drain` that moves records processing to a separate thread. `PlainDecorator`, which is imported from the `slog-term` crate, prints logs without any coloring. Also, we imported the `CompactFormat` type, which is a `Drain` that writes records in a short format. From the `slog-json` crate, we imported the `Json` form of `Drain` that writes logs in JSON format.

Please note that the `Drain` trait has a default implementation for `Mutex` values that contains a value that has already implemented the `Drain` trait. It allows us to wrap any `Drain` with a `Mutex` to make it safe for use in multiple threads. The `OpenOptions` type is imported to open a file for writing and truncate the contents of it.

Now, we can add the `main` function with sample logging:

```
fn main() {
    let log_path = "app.log";
    let file = OpenOptions::new()
        .create(true)
        .write(true)
        .truncate(true)
        .open(log_path)
        .unwrap();

    let drain = Mutex::new(Json::default(file)).fuse();
    let file_drain = LevelFilter::new(drain, Level::Error);

    let decorator = PlainDecorator::new(std::io::stderr());
    let err_drain = CompactFormat::new(decorator).build().fuse();

    let drain_pair = Duplicate::new(file_drain, err_drain).fuse();
    let drain = Async::new(drain_pair).build().fuse();

    let log = slog::Logger::root(drain, slog::o!(
        "version" => env!("CARGO_PKG_VERSION"),
        "host" => "localhost",
        "port" => 8080,
    ));
    debug!(log, "started");
    debug!(log, "{} workers", 2;);
    debug!(log, "request"; "from" => "example.com");
    error!(log, "worker failed"; "worker_id" => 1);
    crit!(log, "server can't continue to work");
}
```

This function opens a file and creates two `Drain` instances. The first is a `Json` wrapped with a `Mutex`, because `Json` is not a thread-safe type. We also wrap it with `LevelFilter` to filter messages at a level lower than `Error`.

After this, we used `PlainDecorator` to write logs to the `stderr` stream. It implements the `Decorator` trait, which can be used as a stream for creating `Drain` instances. We wrap it with `CompactFormat` and now we have two `Drain` instances that we will combine.

We use `Duplicate` to duplicate records to the two created `Drain` instances, but we also wrap it with `Async` to move logs that are processing to a separate thread. Now, we can create a `Logger` instance and fill it with basic information about the application.

We use the `root` method to create the root logger. This method can also get a map of values, which will be added to records. We used the `o!` macro to create a map. After this, we added calls of different macros to show you how to use a structural logger.

Any logging macro expects some arguments—a reference to a `Logger` instance, a message, optional parameters to fill a message, or a key-value map with extra parameters that can be extracted later from logs for analysis.

The demo application is ready and we can start to test it.

Building and testing

Build this application with `cargo build`, or with the following command, if you want to play with the code:

```
cargo watch --ignore *.log -x run
```

We use the `cargo-watch` tool, but ignore log files, because these will be created when the application is run. After the application has started, you will the following records in the Terminal:

```
version: 0.1.0
 host: localhost
  port: 8080
    Jan 20 18:13:53.061 DEBG started
    Jan 20 18:13:53.062 DEBG 2 workers
    Jan 20 18:13:53.062 DEBG request, from: example.com
    Jan 20 18:13:53.062 ERRO worker failed, worker_id: 1
    Jan 20 18:13:53.063 CRIT server can't continue to work
```

As you can see, no records with the Debug level were filtered in the Terminal output. As you may remember, we duplicated logging into two Drain instances. The first writes errors to the app.log file, and if you open this file, you can see the filtered records that don't contain records with a Debug level:

```
{"msg":"worker
failed","level":"ERRO","ts":"2019-01-20T18:13:53.061797633+03:00","port":80
80,"host":"localhost","version":"0.1.0","worker_id":1}
{"msg":"server can't continue to
work","level":"CRIT","ts":"2019-01-20T18:13:53.062762204+03:00","port":8080
,"host":"localhost","version":"0.1.0"}
```

There are only records with the level above or equal to Error.

In Chapter 3, *Logging and Configuring Microservice,* in the example with the env_logger crate, we used environment variables to configure a logger. slog also provides this feature with the slog_envlogger crate.

Logging is an awesome tool that's used to trace every action of a single microservice, but if your application consists of multiple microservices, it can be hard to understand why some error happened, because it is affected by multiple factors. To find and repair this hardest type of bug, there is distributed tracing.

Distributed tracing

Distributed tracing helps to collect information about related parts of an application as a **distributed acyclic graph (DAG)**. You can use collected information to analyze a path of any activity in a distributed application.

There is an open standard—OpenTracing, which is supported by multiple products, including Jaeger. The most minimal unit of tracing is called a **span**. Spans can have relationships with other spans to construct a report with tracing paths. In this section, we'll write a tiny application that will send some spans to a Jaeger instance.

Starting Jaeger

First, we need a working Jaeger instance that you can start as a Docker container from the official Docker image that contains all of the parts of the application in one. It's even called **jaegertracing/all-in-one**:

```
$ docker run --rm --name jaeger \
    -e COLLECTOR_ZIPKIN_HTTP_PORT=9411 \
    -p 5775:5775/udp \
    -p 6831:6831/udp \
    -p 6832:6832/udp \
    -p 5778:5778 \
    -p 16686:16686 \
    -p 14268:14268 \
    -p 9411:9411 \
    jaegertracing/all-in-one:1.8
```

Open all the necessary ports, and access the web UI of Jaeger at `http://localhost:16686`.

Now, we can write an application to interact with this instance.

Generating spans

We will use two crates to make a test example—`rustracing` and `rustracing_jaeger`. Create a new crate and add it to the `[dependencies]` section of `Cargo.toml`:

```
rustracing = "0.1"
rustracing_jaeger = "0.1"
```

Add the following dependencies to the `main.rs` source file:

```
use rustracing::sampler::AllSampler;
use rustracing::tag::Tag;
use rustracing_jaeger::Tracer;
use rustracing_jaeger::reporter::JaegerCompactReporter;
use std::time::Duration;
use std::thread;
```

`AppSampler` implements the `Sampler` trait that is used to decide whether every new trace will be sampled or not. Consider samplers as filters of loggers, but smart ones that can limit the amount of traces per second or use other conditions. `Tag` is used to set extra data for spans. `Tracer` is the main object that's used for creating spans.
The `JaegerCompactReporter` type is used to group spans and send them to the Jaeger instance.

Also, we need a function to sleep the current thread for milliseconds:

```
fn wait(ms: u64) {
    thread::sleep(Duration::from_millis(ms));
}
```

Now, you can add the main function, and add the first part of the example to it:

```
let (tracer1, span_rx1) = Tracer::new(AllSampler);
let (tracer2, span_rx2) = Tracer::new(AllSampler);
thread::spawn(move || {
    loop {
        {
            let req_span = tracer1
                .span("incoming request")
                .start();
            wait(50);
            {
                let db_span = tracer2
                    .span("database query")
                    .child_of(&req_span)
                    .tag(Tag::new("query", "SELECT column FROM table;"))
                    .start();
                wait(100);
                let _resp_span = tracer2
                    .span("generating response")
                    .follows_from(&db_span)
                    .tag(Tag::new("user_id", "1234"))
                    .start();
                wait(10);
            }
        }
        wait(150);
    }
});
```

In this code, we did a major part of the tracing routine. First, we created two `Tracer` instances that will pass all values by `AllSampler`. After this, we used `spawn` to create a new thread and created a loop that generated spans. You have to remember that the `rustracing` crate uses a `Drop` trait implementation to send a span value to a `Reciever` that was also created with the `Tracer::new` method call, and we have to drop values (we used the scoping rules of Rust to do dropping automatically).

We used the `Tracer` instance stored in the `tracer1` variable to create a span with the `span` method call. It expects a name for the span and created a `StartSpanOptions` struct that can be used to configure a future `Span` value. For configuring, we can use the `child_of` method to set a parent, or the `follows_from` method to set a reference to the previous `Span`. Also, we can set extra information with the `tag` method call and provide a key-value pair called `Tag`, just as we did in structural logging before. After configuring, we have to call the `start` method of the `StartSpanOptions` instance to create a `Span` instance with a set span starting time. Using scopes and tracer, we emulated two parts of an application: the first that processes a request, and the second that performs a database query and generates a response, where the first is a parent of the latter.

Now, we have to use `SpanReciever` instances to collect all dropped `Span` values. (They've actually been sent to `Reciever`.) Also, we create two `JaegerCompactReporter` instances with names and add spans to reports using the `report` method call in the loop:

```
let reporter1 = JaegerCompactReporter::new("router").unwrap();
let reporter2 = JaegerCompactReporter::new("dbaccess").unwrap();
loop {
    if let Ok(span) = span_rx1.try_recv() {
        reporter1.report(&[span]).unwrap();
    }
    if let Ok(span) = span_rx2.try_recv() {
        reporter2.report(&[span]).unwrap();
    }
    thread::yield_now();
}
```

Now, we can compile and run this tracing example.

Compile and run

To start this example, you can use the `cargo run` command. When the example starts, it will continuously produce spans and send them to the running Jaeger instance. You will need to wait for a short interval and interrupt the application, otherwise it will generate too many spans.

Open the web UI of Jaeger in a browser. Choose `router` in the **Service** field, and click the **Find Traces** button to find the corresponding spans. You will see recent traces, and if you click on one of them, you will see the details of the tracing:

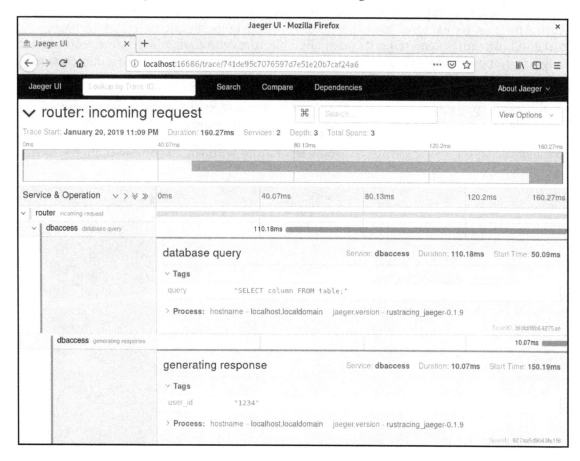

As you can see, distributed tracing registered activities of our application, and we can use it as a tool for logging the distributed activities of microservices that are included in our application.

Summary

In this chapter, we discussed a lot of topics on testing and debugging microservices. First, we considered unit and integration tests, and also saw some examples of using these in Rust. After this, we explored tools that help us with debugging microservices, including curl and Postman, to send requests manually; mitmproxy to trace all incoming requests and outgoing responses of a microservice; LLDB to explore the running code of a microservice; and Visual Studio Code as a GUI frontend for the LLDB Debugger.

Lastly, we discussed two techniques that used for the largest applications, where you can't simply debug: structural logging and distributed tracing using OpenTracing API.

In the next chapter, you'll learn about some techniques with which you can optimize Rust microservices.

Optimization of Microservices

14

Optimization is an important part of the microservice development process. With optimization, you can increase the performance of a microservice and reduce costs for infrastructure and hardware. In this chapter, we will shed light on benchmarking, along with some optimization techniques, such as caching, reusing shared data with structs without taking ownership, and how you can use a compiler's options to optimize a microservice. This chapter will help you to improve the performance of your microservices using optimization techniques.

In this chapter, we will cover the following topics:

- Performance-measuring tools
- Techniques of optimizations

Technical requirements

To run the examples in this chapter, you need a Rust compiler (version 1.31 and above) to build the examples for testing and to build the tools you need to measure performance.

There are sources of the examples of this chapter on GitHub: https://github.com/PacktPublishing/Hands-On-Microservices-with-Rust/tree/master/Chapter14.

Performance-measuring tools

Before you decide to optimize something in a microservice, you have to measure its performance. You shouldn't write optimal and fast microservices from the start, because not every microservice needs good performance, and if your microservice has bottlenecks inside, it will stumble on heavy loads.

Let's explore a pair of benchmarking tools. We will explore tools that are written in Rust, because they can be simply used to construct your own measuring tool if you need to test a special case with extremely high load.

Welle

Welle is an alternative to the popular **Apache Benchmarking tool** (**ab**) that is used to benchmark HTTP servers. It can produce a batch of requests to a specified URL and measure the time to response for every request. At the end, it collects statistics about the average response time and quantity of failed requests.

To install this tool, use the following command:

```
cargo install welle
```

Using this tool is simple: set a URL to test with a number of requests you want to send to a server:

```
welle --num-requests 10000 http://localhost:8080
```

By default, the tool uses a single thread to send a request and wait for the response to send the next request. But you can split requests across more threads by setting a `--concurrent-requests` command-line parameter with the number of necessary threads.

When a measurement is finished, it will print a report similar to this:

```
Total Requests: 10000
Concurrency Count: 1
Total Completed Requests: 10000
Total Errored Requests: 0
Total 5XX Requests: 0

Total Time Taken: 6.170019816s
Avg Time Taken: 617.001µs
Total Time In Flight: 5.47647967s
Avg Time In Flight: 547.647µs
```

```
Percentage of the requests served within a certain time:
50%:  786.541µs
66%:  891.163µs
75%:  947.87µs
80%:  982.323µs
90%:  1.052751ms
95%:  1.107814ms
99%:  1.210104ms
100%: 2.676919ms
```

If you want to use a HTTP method other than GET, you can set it using the --method command-line parameter.

Drill

Drill is more complex and lets you perform load tests on microservices. It not only sends batches of requests, it also uses a testing script to produce a sequence of activities. It helps you to perform a load test that you can use to measure performance of the entire application.

To install drill, use the following command:

```
cargo install drill
```

After it's installed, you have to configure the load testing you will perform. Create a benchmark.yml file and add the following load test script:

```
---

threads: 4
base: 'http://localhost:8080'
iterations: 5
rampup: 2

plan:
  - name: Index Page
    request:
      url: /
```

To start testing using this script, run the following command:

```
drill --benchmark benchmark.yml --stats
```

It will perform a load test of your microservice by sending HTTP request constructed with rules from the script and print a report like the following:

```
Threads 4
Iterations 5
Rampup 2
Base URL http://localhost:8080

Index Page                    http://localhost:8080/ 200 OK 7ms
Index Page                    http://localhost:8080/ 200 OK 8ms
...
Index Page                    http://localhost:8080/ 200 OK 1ms

Concurrency Level 4
Time taken for tests 0.2 seconds
Total requests 20
Successful requests 20
Failed requests 0
Requests per second 126.01 [#/sec]
Median time per request 1ms
Average time per request 3ms
Sample standard deviation 3ms
```

Both tools are suitable for testing the performance of your microservices. Welle is good for measuring the performance of a single request type if you want to optimize the specified handler. Drill is good to produce a complex load to measure how much users can be served by an application.

Let's look at an example in which we add some optimizations and test the difference using Welle.

Measuring and optimizing performance

In this section, we will measure the performance of an example microservice compiled with two options: without optimizations, and with optimizations made by a compiler. The microservice will send rendered index page to clients. And we will use the Welle tool to measure the performance of this microservice to see if we can improve it.

Basic example

Let's create a microservice in a new crate based on the `actix-web` crate.

Add the following dependencies to `Cargo.toml`:

```
[dependencies]
actix = "0.7"
actix-web = "0.7"
askama = "0.6"
chrono = "0.4"
env_logger = "0.5"
futures = "0.1"

[build-dependencies]
askama = "0.6"
```

We will construct a tiny server that will render an index page asynchronously with the current time, with one-minute precision. As a matter of fact, there is a shortcut function that does this:

```
fn now() -> String {
    Utc::now().to_string()
}
```

We use the `askama` crate to render the template of the index page and insert the current time taken from a shared state it it. For the time value, we use a `String` instead of types directly from the `chrono` crate, in order to get a value that uses a memory heap:

```
#[derive(Template)]
#[template(path = "index.html")]
struct IndexTemplate {
    time: String,
}
```

For a shared state, we will use a struct with a `last_minute` value, represented as a `String` wrapped with a `Mutex`:

```
#[derive(Clone)]
struct State {
    last_minute: Arc<Mutex<String>>,
}
```

As you may remember, `Mutex` provides concurrent access to any type for multiple threads. It's locked for both reading and writing the value.

For the index page, we will use the following handler:

```
fn index(req: &HttpRequest<State>) -> HttpResponse {
    let last_minute = req.state().last_minute.lock().unwrap();
    let template = IndexTemplate { time: last_minute.to_owned() };
```

```
        let body = template.render().unwrap();
        HttpResponse::Ok().body(body)
}
```

The handler shown in the preceding code block locks the `last_minute` field of a `State` instance available in `HttpRequest`. Then we use this value to fill the `IndexTemplate` struct and call the `render` method to render the template and use the generated value as a body for a new `HttpResponse`.

We start the application with the `main` function that prepares the `Server` instance and spawns a separate thread that updates a shared `State`:

```
fn main() {
    let sys = actix::System::new("fast-service");

    let value = now();
    let last_minute = Arc::new(Mutex::new(value));

    let last_minute_ref = last_minute.clone();
    thread::spawn(move || {
        loop {
            {
                let mut last_minute = last_minute_ref.lock().unwrap();
                *last_minute = now();
            }
            thread::sleep(Duration::from_secs(3));
        }
    });

    let state = State {
        last_minute,
    };
    server::new(move || {
        App::with_state(state.clone())
            .middleware(middleware::Logger::default())
            .resource("/", |r| r.f(index))
    })
    .bind("127.0.0.1:8080")
    .unwrap()
    .start();
    let _ = sys.run();
}
```

We used the Actix Web framework for this example. You can read more about this framework in Chapter 11, *Involving Concurrency with Actors and the Actix Crate*. This simple example is ready to compile and start. We will also check the performance of this code using the Welle tool.

Performance

First, we will build and run the code using a standard command without any flags:

```
cargo run
```

We build a binary with a lot of debugging information, which can be used with LLDB as we did in Chapter 13, *Testing and Debugging Rust Microservices*. A debugging symbol reduces performance, but we will check it to compare it with a version without these symbols later.

Let's load the running server with 100000 requests from 10 concurrent activities. Since our server was bound to port 8080 of localhost, we can use the welle command with the following arguments to measure the performance:

```
welle --concurrent-requests 10 --num-requests 100000 http://localhost:8080
```

It takes about 30 seconds (depending on your system) and the tool will print the report:

```
Total Requests: 100000
Concurrency Count: 10
Total Completed Requests: 100000
Total Errored Requests: 0
Total 5XX Requests: 0

Total Time Taken: 29.883248121s
Avg Time Taken: 298.832µs
Total Time In Flight: 287.14008722s
Avg Time In Flight: 2.8714ms

Percentage of the requests served within a certain time:
50%: 3.347297ms
66%: 4.487828ms
75%: 5.456439ms
80%: 6.15643ms
90%: 8.40495ms
95%: 10.27307ms
99%: 14.99426ms
100%: 144.630208ms
```

In the report, you can see that there is an average response time of 300 milliseconds. It was a service that was burdened with debugging. Let's recompile this example with optimizations. Set the --release flag on the cargo run command:

```
cargo run --release
```

This command passed the -C opt-level=3 optimization flag to the rustc compiler. If you use cargo without a --release flag, it sets opt-level to 2.

After the server has recompiled and started, we use the Welle tool again with the same parameters. It reports the other values:

```
Total Requests: 100000
Concurrency Count: 10
Total Completed Requests: 100000
Total Errored Requests: 0
Total 5XX Requests: 0

Total Time Taken: 8.010280915s
Avg Time Taken: 80.102µs
Total Time In Flight: 63.961189338s
Avg Time In Flight: 639.611µs

Percentage of the requests served within a certain time:
50%: 806.717µs
66%: 983.35µs
75%: 1.118933ms
80%: 1.215726ms
90%: 1.557405ms
95%: 1.972497ms
99%: 3.500056ms
100%: 37.844721ms
```

As we can see, the average time taken for a request has been reduced to more than 70%. The result is already pretty good. But could we reduce it a little more? Let's try to do it with some optimizations.

Optimizations

We will try to apply three optimizations to the code we created in the previous section:

- We will try to reduce the blocking of a shared state.
- We will reuse a value in a state by reference.
- We will add caching of responses.

After we implement them, we will check the performance after the first two improvements, and later check it again with caching.

In the code of this section, we will implement all optimizations gradually, step by step, but if you downloaded the example from the GitHub repository of this book, you will find the following features in the `Cargo.toml` file of the project of this chapter:

```
[features]
default = []
```

```
cache = []
rwlock = []
borrow = []
fast = ["cache", "rwlock", "borrow"]
```

The code here uses features to provide you a capability to activate or deactivate any optimization separately. We see the following:

- cache: activates the caching of requests
- rwlock: uses RwLock instead of Mutex for State
- borrow: reuses a value by reference

Let's implement all of these optimizations and apply all of them to measure differences in the performance.

State sharing without blocking

In the first optimization, we will replace Mutex with RwLock, because Mutex is locked for both reading and writing, but RwLock allows us to have a single writer or multiple readers. It allows you to avoid blocking for reading the value if no one updates the value. This applies to our example, as we rarely update a shared value, but have to read it from multiple instances of handlers.

RwLock is an alternative to Mutex that separates readers and writers, but the usage of RwLock is as simple as Mutex. Replace Mutex to RwLock in the State struct:

```
#[derive(Clone)]
struct State {
    // last_minute: Arc<Mutex<String>>,
    last_minute: Arc<RwLock<String>>,
}
```

Also, we have to replace a creation of the last_minute reference counter to the corresponding type:

```
// let last_minute = Arc::new(Mutex::new(value));
let last_minute = Arc::new(RwLock::new(value));
```

In the code of the worker, we will use the write method of RwLock to lock the value for writing to set a new time value. Its exclusive lock will block all potential readers and writers with a single writer that can change the value:

```
// let mut last_minute = last_minute_ref.lock().unwrap();
let mut last_minute = last_minute_ref.write().unwrap();
```

Since the worker will take an exclusive lock once per three seconds, it's a small price to pay to increase the amount of simultaneous readers.

In the handler, we will use the `read` method to lock `RwLock` for reading:

```
// let last_minute = req.state().last_minute.lock().unwrap();
let last_minute = req.state().last_minute.read().unwrap();
```

This code won't be blocked by other handlers, excluding the case when a worker updates a value. It allows all handlers to work simultaneously.

Now we can implement the second improvement—avoid cloning of values and using them by references.

Reusing values by references

To render a template of an index page, we use a struct with a `String` field and we have to fill the `IndexTemplate` struct to call the `render` method on it. But the template needs an ownership for the value and we have to clone it. Cloning in turn takes time. To avoid this CPU cost, we can use a reference to a value, because if we clone a value that uses a memory heap, we have to allocate a new memory space and copy bytes of the value to a new place.

This is how we can add a reference to a value:

```
struct IndexTemplate<'a> {
    // time: String,
    time: &'a str,
}
```

We have added the `'a` lifetime to a struct, because we use a reference inside and the struct that can't live longer than the string value we referred to.

Using references is not always possible for combinations of `Future` instances, because we have to construct a `Future` that generates an `HttpResponse`, but lives longer than calling a handler. In this case, you can reuse a value if you take ownership of it and use methods such as fold to pass the value through all the steps of the combinator's chain. It is valuable for large values, which can consume a lot of CPU time, to be cloned.

Now we can use a reference to the borrowed `last_minute` value:

```
// let template = IndexTemplate { time: last_minute.to_owned() };
let template = IndexTemplate { time: &last_minute };
```

The `to_owned` method, which we used before, cloned the value that we put to `IndexTemplate`, but we can now use a reference and avoid cloning at all.

All we need to do now is implement caching, which can help to avoid template rendering.

Caching

We will use a cache to store rendered template and returns it as a response for future requests. Ideally, the cache should have a lifetime, because if the cache is not updated, then clients won't see any updates on the page. But for our demo application, we won't reset the cache to make sure it works, because our small microservice renders a time and we can see if it's frozen. Now we will add a new field to the `State` struct to keep a rendered template for future responses:

```
cached: Arc<RwLock<Option<String>>>
```

We will use `RwLock` because we have to update this value at least once, but for values that won't be updated and can be initialized, we can use the `String` type without any wrapper for protection from concurrent access, such as `RwLock` or `Mutex`. In other words, you can use the `String` type directly if you only read it.

We also have to initialize the value with `None`, because we need to render a template once to get the value for caching.

Add an empty value to a `State` instance:

```
let cached = Arc::new(RwLock::new(None));
let state = State {
    last_minute,
    cached,
};
```

Now we can use a `cached` value to construct a fast response to the user's request. But you have to take into account that not all the information can be shown to every user. The cache can separate values by some information about users, for example, it can use location information to get the same cached value for users from the same country. The following code improves the `index` handler and takes a `cached` value, and if the cached value exists, it is used to produce a new `HttpResponse`:

```
let cached = req.state().cached.read().unwrap();
if let Some(ref body) = *cached {
    return HttpResponse::Ok().body(body.to_owned());
}
```

We immediately return a cached value because there is a rendered template stored and we don't have to spend time on rendering. But if no value exists, we can produce it with the following code and set the cached value at the same time:

```
let mut cached = req.state().cached.write().unwrap();
*cached = Some(body.clone());
```

After this, we keep the original code that returns HttpResponse to a client.

Now we have implemented and compiled the code with all the optimizations and can measure performance of the new version with optimizations.

Compilation with optimizations

The code included three optimizations. We can use some of them to check the difference in performance. First, we will compile the code with RwLock and borrow the state's value features. If you use the code from the book's GitHub repository, you can run the necessary optimizations using the --features argument with the corresponding feature names:

```
cargo run --release --features rwlock,borrow
```

Once the server is ready, we can start running the same test we used to measure performance of this microservice before, with Welle, to measure how many incoming requests the optimized version of the server can handle.

After testing, the tool will print a report like this:

```
Total Requests: 100000
Concurrency Count: 10
Total Completed Requests: 100000
Total Errored Requests: 0
Total 5XX Requests: 0

Total Time Taken: 7.94342667s
Avg Time Taken: 79.434µs
Total Time In Flight: 64.120106299s
Avg Time In Flight: 641.201µs

Percentage of the requests served within a certain time:
50%: 791.554µs
66%: 976.074µs
75%: 1.120545ms
80%: 1.225029ms
90%: 1.585564ms
95%: 2.049917ms
```

```
99%:  3.749288ms
100%: 13.867011ms
```

As you can see, the application is faster—it takes `79.434` microseconds instead of `80.10`. The difference is less than 1%, but it's good for a handler that already worked faster.

Let's try to activate all the optimizations we implemented, including caching. To do this with examples from GitHub, use the following arguments:

`cargo run --release --features fast`

Let's start testing again once the server is ready. With the same testing parameters, we get a better report:

```
Total Requests: 100000
Concurrency Count: 10
Total Completed Requests: 100000
Total Errored Requests: 0
Total 5XX Requests: 0

Total Time Taken: 7.820692644s
Avg Time Taken: 78.206µs
Total Time In Flight: 62.359549787s
Avg Time In Flight: 623.595µs

Percentage of the requests served within a certain time:
50%:  787.329µs
66%:  963.956µs
75%:  1.099572ms
80%:  1.199914ms
90%:  1.530326ms
95%:  1.939557ms
99%:  3.410659ms
100%: 10.272402ms
```

It takes `78.206` microseconds to get a response for a request from the server. It's more than 2% faster than the original version without optimization, which takes 80.10 microseconds per request on average.

You may think the difference is not very big, but in reality, it is. This is a tiny example, but try to imagine the difference of optimizing a handler that makes three requests to databases, and renders a 200 KB template with arrays of values to insert. For heavy handlers, you can improve performance by 20%, or even more. But remember, you should remember the over-optimization is an extreme measure, because it makes code harder to develop and add more features without affecting achieved performance.

It's better not to consider any optimization as a daily task, because you may spend a lot of time on optimization of short pieces of code to get a 2% performance for features your customers don't need.

Optimization techniques

In the previous section, we optimized the source code, but there are also alternative techniques of optimization by using special compilation flags and third-party tools. In this section, we will cover some of these optimization techniques. We will talk a little about reducing sizes, benchmarks, and profiling Rust code.

Optimization is a creative topic. There is no special recipe for optimization, but in this section, we will create a small microservice that generates an index page with the current time, and then we will try to optimize it. With this example, I hope to show you some optimization ideas for your projects.

Link-time optimizations

The compiler does a lot of optimizations automatically during the compilation process, but we can also activate some optimizations after the sources compiled. This technique called **Link Time Optimizations** (**LTO**) and applied after code linked and the whole program available. You can activate this optimization for Rust program by adding an extra section to the `Cargo.toml` file in your project:

```
[profile.release]
lto = true
```

If you have already compiled the project with this optimization, force a complete rebuild of your project. But this option also takes much more time for compilation. This optimization does not necessarily improve the performance, but can help to reduce the size of a binary.

 If you activate all optimization options, it doesn't mean you have made the fastest version of an application. Too many optimizations can reduce the performance of a program and you should compare the results with an original version. Most often, just using the standard `--release` helps the compiler to produces a binary with an optimal balance of compilation speed and performance.

Normal Rust programs use panic macros for unhandled errors and print backtraces. For optimization, you can consider turning this off. Let's look at this technique in the next section.

Abort instead of panicking

Error-handling code also requires space and can affect performance. If you try to write microservices that won't panic, and will try to solve problems, and fail only when there's an unsolvable problem, you can consider using aborts (immediate termination of the program without unwinding the stack), instead of Rust's `panic`.

To activate it, add the following to your `Cargo.toml` file:

```
[profile.release]
panic = "abort"
```

Now, if your program fails, it won't make a `panic` and will be stopped immediately without printing backtraces.

> Aborting is dangerous. If your program will be aborted, it has less chance to write logs corectly or deliver spans to distributed tracing. For microservices, you can create a separate thread for tracing, and even if the main thread failed, wait till all available tracing records will be stored.

Sometimes, you not only need to improve the performance, but also have to reduce the size of the binary. Let's see how to do it.

Reducing the size of binaries

You may want to reduce the size of binaries. Often it's not necessary, but it may be useful if you have a distributed application that uses some hardware with limited space that requires tiny binaries. To reduce the size of your compiled application, you can use the `strip` command, which is part of the **binutils** package:

```
strip <path_to_your_binary>
```

For example, I tried to strip a compiled binary of the microservice we created in the *Basic example* section of this chapter. The binary with debugging symbols compiled with the `cargo build` command reduced from 79 MB to 12 MB. The version compiled with the `--release` flag reduced from 8.5 MB to 4.7 MB.

> But remember that you can't debug a stripped binary, because the tool will remove all necessary information for debugging.

Sometimes, you may want to compare some ideas of optimizations and want to measure which one is better. You can use benchmarks for that. Let's look at the benchmark feature supplied with `cargo`.

Isolated benchmarks

Rust supports benchmark testing out of the box. You can use it to compare the performance of different solutions of the same problem or to get to know the time of execution of some parts of your application.

To use benchmarks, you have to add a function with the `#[bench]` attribute. The function expects a mutable reference to the `Bencher` instance. For example, let's compare cloning a `String` with taking a reference to it:

```
#![feature(test)]
extern crate test;
use test::Bencher;

#[bench]
fn bench_clone(b: &mut Bencher) {
    let data = "data".to_string();
    b.iter(move || {
        let _data = data.clone();
    });
}

#[bench]
fn bench_ref(b: &mut Bencher) {
    let data = "data".to_string();
    b.iter(move || {
        let _data = &data;
    });
}
```

To benchmark, you have to provide a closure with a code you want to measure to the `iter` method of the `Bencher` instance. You also need to add a `test` feature with `#![feature(test)]` to testing module and use `extern crate test` to import `test` crate to import the `Bencher` type from this module.

The `bench_clone` function has a `String` value and clones it on every measurement by `Bencher`. In `bench_ref`, we take a reference to a `String` value.

Now you can start a benchmark test with `cargo`:

```
cargo bench
```

It compiles the code for testing (the code items with the `#[cfg(test)]` attribute will be activated) and then runs the benchmarks. For our examples, we have the following results:

```
running 2 tests
test bench_clone ... bench:          32 ns/iter (+/- 9)
test bench_ref   ... bench:           0 ns/iter (+/- 0)

test result: ok. 0 passed; 0 failed; 0 ignored; 2 measured; 0 filtered out
```

As we expected, taking the reference to a `String` takes no time, but the cloning of a `String` takes 32 nanoseconds per call of the `clone` method.

> Remember, you can do good benchmark testing for CPU-bound tasks, but not I/O-bound tasks, because I/O tasks are more dependent on the quality of hardware and operating system performance.

If you want to benchmark the operation of some functions in the running application, then you have to use a profiler. Let's try to analyze some code with a profiler.

Profiling

Benchmark tests are useful for checking a portion of code, but they are not suitable for checking the performance of a working application. If you need to explore the performance of some of the functions of the code, you have to use a profiler.

Profilers dump information about code and function executions and record the time spans during which the code works. There is a profiler in the Rust ecosystem called **flame**. Let's explore how to use it.

Profiling takes time and you should use it as a feature to avoid affecting performance in production installations. Add the `flame` crate to your project and use it as an optional. Add a feature (such as the official examples from the `flamer` crate repository; I named the feature `flame_it`) and add the flame dependency to it:

```
[dependencies]
flame = { version = "0.2", optional = true }

[features]
default = []
```

```
flame_it = ["flame"]
```

Now, if you want to activate profiling, you have to compile the project with the `flame_it` feature.

Using the `flame` crate is pretty simple and includes three scenarios:

- Use the `start` and `end` methods directly.
- Use the `start_guard` method, which creates a `Span` that is used to measure execution time. A `Span` instance ends measurement automatically when it's dropped.
- Use `span_of` to measure code isolated in a closure.

We will use spans like we did in the `OpenTracing` example in `Chapter 13`, *Testing and Debugging Rust Microservices*:

```rust
use std::fs::File;

pub fn main() {
    {
        let _req_span = flame::start_guard("incoming request");
        {
            let _db_span = flame::start_guard("database query");
            let _resp_span = flame::start_guard("generating response");
        }
    }

    flame::dump_html(&mut File::create("out.html").unwrap()).unwrap();
    flame::dump_json(&mut File::create("out.json").unwrap()).unwrap();
    flame::dump_stdout();
}
```

You don't need to collect spans or send them to `Receiver`, as we did for Jaeger, but profiling with `flame` looks like tracing.

At the end of the execution, you have to dump a report in the appropriate format, such as HTML or JSON, print it to a console, or write it to a `Writer` instance. We used the first three of them. We have implemented the main function and used the `start_quard` method to create `Span` instances to measure the execution time of some pieces of the code. After this, we will write reports.

Compile and run this example with the activated profiling feature:

```
cargo run --features flame_it
```

The preceding command compiles and prints the report to the console:

```
THREAD: 140431102022912
| incoming request: 0.033606ms
  | database query: 0.016583ms
    | generating response: 0.008326ms
    + 0.008257ms
  + 0.017023ms
```

As you can see, we have created three spans. You can also find two reports in files, out.json and out.html. If you open the HTML report in a browser, it renders like so:

In the preceding screenshot, you can see the relative duration of execution of every activity of our program. A longer colored block means longer execution time. As you can see, profiling is useful for finding a slow section of code that you can optimize with other techniques.

Summary

In this chapter, we discussed optimizations. First, we explored tools for measuring performance—Welle, which is an alternative to the classic **Apache Benchmarking tool**, and Drill, which uses scripts to perform load tests.

Then we created a tiny microservice and measured its performance. Focusing on results, we applied some optimizations to that microservice—we avoided blocking a shared state for reading, we reused a value by a reference instead of cloning it, and we added the caching of rendered templates. Then we measured the performance of the optimized microservice and compared it with the original version.

In the last section of this chapter, we got acquainted with alternative techniques of optimization—using LTO, aborting execution without backtracing instead of panicking, reducing the size of a compiled binary, benchmarking small pieces of code, and using profiling for your projects.

In the next chapter, we will look at creating images with Rust microservices using Docker to run microservices in containers with preconfigured environments to speed up delivery of your product to customers.

15
Packing Servers to Containers

Microservices created with Rust are pretty simple to deploy: it's sufficient to build a binary for your server, upload that binary to your server, and start it. But that's not a flexible approach for real applications. Firstly, your microservice may need files, templates, and configuration. On the other hand, you may want to use servers with different operating systems. In that case, you would have to build a binary for every system. To reduce the amount of issues with deployment, modern microservices are packed to containers and use virtualization to launch. Virtualization helps to simplify the deployment of a set of microservices. Also, it can help to scale a microservice, because to run an extra instance of a microservice you should only start another copy of the container.

This chapter will immerse you in building Docker images with Rust microservices. We will look at the following:

- Compiling microservices with Docker.
- Preparing a necessary Rust version in a container.
- Reducing time spent building images with a Rust microservice. After we have prepared an image, we will create images for multiple microservices.
- Creating a compose file for the Docker Compose utility to bootstrap a set of microservices to show how to run a complex project consisting of multiple microservices that interact with each other.
- Configuring a set of microservices and adding a database instance to let those microservices store persistent state to a database.

Technical requirements

This chapter requires a full Docker installation with the Docker Compose utility. It doesn't require the Rust compiler, since we will build microservices with Docker containers, but it's good to have the nightly Rust compiler if you want to build and test any microservices locally or play with configuration parameters without patching the `docker-cocmpose.yml` file.

To install Docker, follow the instructions for your operating system here: `https://docs.docker.com/compose/install/`.

To install the Docker Compose utility, look at these docs: `https://docs.docker.com/compose/install/`.

You can find the examples for this chapter in the `Chapter15` folder of the GitHub project: `https://github.com/PacktPublishing/Hands-On-Microservices-with-Rust-2018/`.

Building a Docker image with a microservice

In the first part of this chapter, we will build a Docker image with the necessary version of the Rust compiler and build an image with a compiled microservice. We will use a set of microservices from other chapters to show how to join microservices created with different frameworks. We will use the *users*, *emails*, and *content* microservices from `Chapter 9`, *Simple REST Definition and Request Routing with Frameworks* and the *router* microservice from `Chapter 11`, *Involving Concurrency with Actors and Actix Crate*, and we'll also tune them to be configurable. Also, we will add a `dbsync` microservice, which will do all of the necessary migrations to a database, because we will use two microservices that use the database with the `diesel` crate and there will be a conflict if both microservices try to apply migrations for their own schema. That's because we'll use a single database, but if you use separate databases (not necessarily different database management applications, but only database files) for every microservice, you can use an individual migration set for every database. It's time to prepare an image with the nightly Rust compiler.

Creating an image with the Rust compiler

There are many ready-to-use images on Docker Hub. You can also find an official image here: `https://hub.docker.com/_/rust/`. But we will create our own image since official images contain a stable compiler version only. If it's enough for you, it's better to use official images, but if you use crates such as `diesel`, which need the nightly version of the Rust compiler, you will have to build your own image to build microservices.

Create a new `Dockerfile` and add the following content to it:

```
FROM buildpack-deps:stretch

ENV RUSTUP_HOME=/usr/local/rustup \
    CARGO_HOME=/usr/local/cargo \
```

```
      PATH=/usr/local/cargo/bin:$PATH

RUN set -eux; \
url="https://static.rust-lang.org/rustup/dist/x86_64-unknown-linux-gnu/rust
up-init"; \
    wget "$url"; \
    chmod +x rustup-init; \
    ./rustup-init -y --no-modify-path --default-toolchain nightly; \
    rm rustup-init; \
    chmod -R a+w $RUSTUP_HOME $CARGO_HOME; \
    rustup --version; \
    cargo --version; \
    rustc --version;
```

I've borrowed this `Dockerfile` from the official Rust Docker image located here: `https://github.com/rust-lang-nursery/docker-rust-nightly/blob/master/nightly/Dockerfile`. This file is a good starting point for good practices when creating images with the Rust compiler.

Our Rust image is based on the `buildpack-deps` image, which contains all of the necessary dependencies commonly used by developers. This dependency is indicated in the first line with the FROM command.

 `buildpack-deps` is an official Docker image based on Ubuntu (a free open-source Linux distribution based on Debian). The image includes a lot of headers for libraries such as OpenSSL and curl, and packages with all of the necessary certificates, and so on. It's very useful as a build environment for your Docker images.

The next line, which contains the ENV command, sets three environment variables in the image:

- RUSTUP_HOME: Sets the root folder of the `rustup` utility, which contains a configuration and installs toolchains
- CARGO_HOME: Contains cached files used by the `cargo` utility
- PATH: The system environment variable that contains paths to executable binaries

We target all utilities to the `/usr/local` folder by setting these environment variables.

 We use the `rustup` utility here to bootstrap the Rust environment. It's an official Rust installation tool that helps you to maintain and keep multiple Rust installations up-to-date. In my opinion, using `rustup` is the best way to install Rust locally or in a container.

The last `Dockerfile` command, `RUN`, is complex and we will analyze this set of commands line by line. The first shell command is the following:

```
set -eux
```

Since the default shell in Ubuntu is the Bash shell, we can set three useful flags:

- `-e`: This flag tells the shell to run the next line (command) only if the previous one finished successfully
- `-u`: With this flag, the shell will print an error to `stderr` if the command tries to expand a variable that is not set
- `-x`: With this flag, the shell will print every command to `stderr` before running it

The next three lines download the `rustup-init` binary and set the executable flag to the downloaded file:

```
url="https://static.rust-lang.org/rustup/dist/x86_64-unknown-linux-gnu/rust
up-init"; \
wget "$url"; \
chmod +x rustup-init; \
```

The next pair runs the `rustup-init` command with parameters and removes the binary after running:

```
./rustup-init -y --no-modify-path --default-toolchain nightly; \
rm rustup-init; \
```

The following flags were used:

- `-y`: Suppresses any confirmation prompts
- `--no-modify-path`: Won't modify the `PATH` environment variable (we set it manually before, for the image)
- `--default-toolchain`: The type of the default toolchain (we will use `nightly`)

The remaining lines set write permissions to the `RUSTUP_HOME` and `CARGO_HOME` folders and print the version for all the installed tools:

```
chmod -R a+w $RUSTUP_HOME $CARGO_HOME; \
rustup --version; \
cargo --version; \
rustc --version;
```

Now you can build the `Dockerfile` to get an image that contains the preconfigured Rust compiler:

```
docker build -t rust:nightly .
```

This command takes some time to complete, but after it has finished, you will have an image that you can use as a base for building images for microservices. If you type the docker images command, you will see something like this:

```
REPOSITORY   TAG       IMAGE ID     CREATED            SIZE
rust         nightly   91e52fb2cea5 About an hour ago  1.67GB
```

Now we will use the image tagged as rust:nightly and create images for microservices from it. Let's start by creating an image for the users microservice.

Users microservice image

The users microservice provides users with registration capabilities. This chapter contains a modified version of the users microservice from Chapter 9, *Simple REST Definition and Request Routing with Frameworks*. Since this service requires a database and uses the diesel crate to interact with it, we need to use the diesel.toml config in the process of building the image.

.dockerignore

Since Docker copies all files from the building folder, we have to add the .dockerignore file that contains the patterns of paths to avoid copying these files. It's useful, for example, to skip the target building folder, because it may contain gigabytes of data for large projects, but in any case, we don't need all of them since we'll build a microservice using the image with the Rust compiler. Add the .dockerignore file:

```
target
Cargo.lock
**/*.rs.bk
files
*.db
```

We will ignore all Rust's build artifacts (such as the target, Cargo.lock, and *.bk files that are produced by the rustfmt tool that we will use later) in the next chapter, where we will explore continuous integration tools. We also included two patterns: files—this folder will be created by this microservice to store files if you try to run it locally, and *.db—not a necessary pattern for SQLite Database, because this version uses PostgreSQL instead of SQLite, but useful if you want to support both databases for testing reasons later.

Dockerfile

Now everything is ready to build and pack the microservice to an image. To do this, add the `Dockerfile` file to the folder with the microservice and add the following lines to it:

```
FROM rust:nightly

RUN USER=root cargo new --bin users-microservice
WORKDIR /users-microservice
COPY ./Cargo.toml ./Cargo.toml
RUN cargo build

RUN rm src/*.rs
COPY ./src ./src
COPY ./diesel.toml ./diesel.toml
RUN rm ./target/debug/deps/users_microservice*
RUN cargo build

CMD ["./target/debug/users-microservice"]

EXPOSE 8000
```

We created the image based on the `rust:nightly` images that we created earlier in this chapter. We set it using the `FROM` command. The next line creates a new crate:

```
RUN USER=root cargo new --bin users-microservice
```

You might ask why we did that and didn't use an existing crate. That's because we will reproduce the creation of the crate inside the container to build dependencies first, to avoid the lengthy process of rebuilding them, when you would add any tiny change to the source code of the microservice. This approach will save you a lot of time. Copy `Cargo.toml` to the image and build all of the dependencies without the sources of the microservice (since we have not copied them yet):

```
WORKDIR /users-microservice
COPY ./Cargo.toml ./Cargo.toml
RUN cargo build                     bring in dep.
```

The next set of commands adds sources and the `diesel.toml` file to the image, removes previous build results, and builds the crate again with the new sources:

```
RUN rm src/*.rs
COPY ./src ./src
COPY ./diesel.toml ./diesel.toml
RUN rm ./target/debug/deps/users_microservice*
RUN cargo build
```

At this moment, the image contains a binary of a microservice that we can use as a starting command for containers:

```
CMD ["./target/debug/users-microservice"]
```

By default, a container doesn't open a port and you can't connect to it with another container or forward the port of a container to a local port. Since our microservice starts at port 8000, we have to expose it using the following command:

```
EXPOSE 8000
```

The image is ready to build and run a container. Let's do it.

Building an image

We have prepared the Dockerfile to build an image that first builds all the dependencies for our microservice and then builds all the source code. To start this process, you have to use the Docker `build` command:

```
docker build -t users-microservice:latest
```

When you run this command, you will see how Docker prepares files to build an image and builds all the dependencies, but only for the empty crate without the sources of a microservice:

```
Sending build context to Docker daemon  13.82kB
Step 1/12 : FROM rust:nightly
 ---> 91e52fb2cea5
Step 2/12 : RUN USER=root cargo new --bin users-microservice
 ---> Running in 3ff6b18a9c72
    Created binary (application) `users-microservice` package
Removing intermediate container 3ff6b18a9c72
 ---> 85f700c4a567
Step 3/12 : WORKDIR /users-microservice
 ---> Running in eff894de0a40
Removing intermediate container eff894de0a40
 ---> 66366486b1e2
Step 4/12 : COPY ./Cargo.toml ./Cargo.toml
 ---> 8864ae055d16
Step 5/12 : RUN cargo build
 ---> Running in 1f1150ae4661
    Updating crates.io index
 Downloading crates ...
 Compiling crates ...
    Compiling users-microservice v0.1.0 (/users-microservice)
```

```
    Finished dev [unoptimized + debuginfo] target(s) in 2m 37s
Removing intermediate container 1f1150ae4661
 ---> 7868ea6bf9b3
```

Our image needs 12 steps in total to build the microservice. As you can see, the building of dependencies takes two and a half minutes. It's not fast. But we don't need to repeat this step till `Cargo.toml` has changed. The next steps copy the source code of the microservices into a container and build them with prebuilt dependencies:

```
Step 6/12 : RUN rm src/*.rs
 ---> Running in 5b7d9a1f96cf
Removing intermediate container 5b7d9a1f96cf
 ---> b03e7d0b23cc
Step 7/12 : COPY ./src ./src
 ---> 2212e3db5223
Step 8/12 : COPY ./diesel.toml ./diesel.toml
 ---> 5d4c59d31614
Step 9/12 : RUN rm ./target/debug/deps/users_microservice*
 ---> Running in 6bc9df93ebc1
Removing intermediate container 6bc9df93ebc1
 ---> c2e3d67d3bf8
Step 10/12 : RUN cargo build
 ---> Running in b985b6c793d1
   Compiling users-microservice v0.1.0 (/users-microservice)
    Finished dev [unoptimized + debuginfo] target(s) in 4.98s
Removing intermediate container b985b6c793d1
 ---> 553156f97943
Step 11/12 : CMD ["./target/debug/users-microservice"]
 ---> Running in c36ff8e44db3
Removing intermediate container c36ff8e44db3
 ---> 56e7eb1144aa
Step 12/12 : EXPOSE 8000
 ---> Running in 5e76a47a0ded
Removing intermediate container 5e76a47a0ded
 ---> 4b6fc8aa6f1b
Successfully built 4b6fc8aa6f1b
Successfully tagged users-microservice:latest
```

As you can see in the output, building the microservice takes just 5 seconds. It's fast enough and you can rebuild it as many times as you want. Since the image has been built, we can start a container with our microservice.

Starting a container

The image we built has been stored in Docker and we can see it using the `docker images` command:

```
REPOSITORY            TAG       IMAGE ID        CREATED         SIZE
users-microservice    latest    4b6fc8aa6f1b    7 minutes ago   2.3GB
rust                  nightly   91e52fb2cea5    3 hours ago     1.67GB
```

To start the microservice from an image, use the following command:

```
docker run -it --rm -p 8080:8000 users-microservice
```

The container with the microservice instance will start but it won't work since we haven't run a container with a database instance. We won't connect containers manually, since it's part of the subtleties of Docker usage, and you can read about that in Docker's documentation; however, we will learn how to connect containers with the Docker Compose tool later in this chapter, in the *Composing a microservice set* section.

You might also ask: Why is our microservice so big? We will try to reduce it later in this chapter. But now we should pack other microservices to images.

Content microservice image

The second microservice we will use is the content microservice that we created in `Chapter 9`, *Simple REST Definition and Request Routing with Frameworks*. We also prepared this service for use with the PostgreSQL database. We borrowed the `dockerignore` file from the previous example and adapted the `Dockerfile` file for this microservice. Look at the following code:

```
FROM rust:nightly

RUN USER=root cargo new --bin content-microservice
WORKDIR /content-microservice
COPY ./Cargo.toml ./Cargo.toml
RUN cargo build

RUN rm src/*.rs
COPY ./src ./src
RUN rm ./target/debug/deps/content_microservice*
RUN cargo build

CMD ["./target/debug/content-microservice"]
EXPOSE 8000
```

As you can see, this `Dockerfile` is the same as the `Dockerfile` of the previous image, but it has one difference: it doesn't copy any configuration files. We'll are using the Rocket framework, but we will set all the parameters using the environment variables in the Docker Compose file.

You can build this image with the following command to check how it works:

```
docker build -t content-microservice:latest .
```

But it's not necessary to build this image, because we won't start containers manually—we will use Docker Compose. Let's pack an email microservice to an image too.

Email microservice image

The email microservice doesn't use the `diesel` crate and we can use the official Rust image to build a microservice. Also, the email microservice has templates that are used to prepare the contents of emails. We will use the same `.dockerignore` file, but will copy `Dockerfile` from the previous example and add some changes related to the email microservice:

```
FROM rust:1.30.1

RUN USER=root cargo new --bin mails-microservice
WORKDIR /mails-microservice
COPY ./Cargo.toml ./Cargo.toml
RUN cargo build

RUN rm src/*.rs
COPY ./src ./src
COPY ./templates ./templates
RUN rm ./target/debug/deps/mails_microservice*
RUN cargo build

CMD ["./target/debug/mails-microservice"]
```

We created this image from the `rust:1.30.1` image. The stable version of the compiler is suitable to compile this simple microservice. We also added a command to copy all the templates into the image:

```
COPY ./templates ./templates
```

Now we can prepare the image with the router microservice.

Router microservice image

If you remember, we created the router microservice in Chapter 11, *Involving Concurrency with Actors and the Actix Crate,* where we explored features of the Actix framework. We adapted the router microservice to work with other microservices—we added a Config and a State that share configuration values with handlers. Also, the improved router microservice serves assets that are in the static folder. We also have to copy this folder to an image. Look at the Dockerfile of the router microservice:

```
FROM rust:1.30.1

RUN USER=root cargo new --bin router-microservice
WORKDIR /router-microservice
COPY ./Cargo.toml ./Cargo.toml
RUN cargo build

RUN rm src/*.rs
COPY ./src ./src
COPY ./static ./static
RUN rm ./target/debug/deps/router_microservice*
RUN cargo build

CMD ["./target/debug/router-microservice"]

EXPOSE 8000
```

We also used the official Rust image with the stable compiler. The one difference you will notice in comparison with the previous example is copying the static folder into an image. We use the same .dockerignore file as we used for the previous examples.

We have built images for all of the microservices, but the last element we need to add is a worker that will apply migrations to a database. We will use it with Docker Compose later to apply all migrations automatically. Let's create this Docker image.

DBSync worker image

The DBSync worker has only one function—waiting for a connection with the database and applying all migrations. We'll also pack this worker to a Docker image to use it in a compose file that we will create in the next section of this chapter.

Dependencies

The worker needs the following dependencies:

```
clap = "2.32"
config = "0.9"
diesel = { version = "^1.1.0", features = ["postgres", "r2d2"] }
diesel_migrations = "1.3"
env_logger = "0.6"
failure = "0.1"
log = "0.4"
postgres = "0.15"
r2d2 = "0.8"
serde = "1.0"
serde_derive = "1.0"
```

We need the `diesel` crate with `diesel_migrations` to embed all the migrations into the code. It's not necessary, but useful. We need the `config` and `serde` crates to configure the worker. The other crates are more common and you can see how we used them in the previous chapters.

Add those dependencies to `Cargo.toml` and import the types that we will use in the `main` function:

```
use diesel::prelude::*;
use diesel::connection::Connection;
use failure::{format_err, Error};
use log::debug;
use serde_derive::Deserialize;
```

Now let's create code that will wait for a connection to the database and apply all embedded migrations.

The main function

Before we create the main function, we have to embed migrations using the `embed_migrations!` macro call:

```
embed_migrations!();
```

This call creates an `embedded_migrations` module, which contains the `run` function, which applies all migrations to a database. But before we use it, let's add the `Config` struct to read the database connection link from a configuration file or an environment variable using the `config` crate:

```
#[derive(Deserialize)]
struct Config {
    database: Option<String>,
}
```

This struct contains only a single parameter—the optional `String` with a connection link to the database. We will set this parameter later with Docker Compose using the `DBSYNC_DATABASE` environment variable. We have added the `DBSYNC` prefix in the `main` function. Look at the full code of the `main` function:

```
fn main() -> Result<(), Error> {
    env_logger::init();
    let mut config = config::Config::default();
    config.merge(config::Environment::with_prefix("DBSYNC"))?;
    let config: Config = config.try_into()?;
    let db_address =
config.database.unwrap_or("postgres://localhost/".into());
    debug!("Waiting for database...");
    loop {
        let conn: Result<PgConnection, _> =
Connection::establish(&db_address);
        if let Ok(conn) = conn {
            debug!("Database connected");
            embedded_migrations::run(&conn)?;
            break;
        }
    }
    debug!("Database migrated");
    Ok(())
}
```

In the preceding code, we initialized `env_logger` to print information to strerr. After, we created a generic `Config` instance from the `config` module and merged environment variables with the `DBSYNC` prefix. If the config merged successfully, we try to convert it to a value of our own `Config` type that we declared before. We'll use a config to extract a link of a connection to the database. If the value is not provided, we will use the `postgres://localhost/` link.

When a connection link is ready, we use a loop to try to connect to the database. We will try to connect to it until it succeeds, because we will use this worker with Docker Compose, and despite the fact we will start a container with the database, it can be unavailable when a database instance is starting. We use a loop to wait for the connection to be ready.

When the connection is ready, we use it to apply embedded migrations with the `run` method of the `embedded_migrations` module. After the migrations have been applied, we break the loop and stop the worker.

We have all the microservices ready to launch, but their disadvantage is that their source code also remains in the image. This is not good if we want to hide the implementation details of our microservices. Let's explore a technique that hides the sources of microservices using the image building cache.

Hiding microservice source code

The main drawback of building microservices inside an image is that all of the sources and build artifacts will be available for anyone who has access to a Docker image. If you want to remove sources and other building artifacts, you can use one of two approaches.

1. The first approach is to build all sources using a Docker image with the Rust compiler, providing access to sources through a linked virtual volume. In Docker, you can map any local folder to a volume inside a container using the `-v` argument of the `docker run` command. The disadvantage of this approach is that Docker uses another ID inside the container that you have in your local session. It can create files you can't delete without changing the user ID. Also, this approach is harder to maintain. But it's useful if you need the result of compilation only. If you plan to run a microservice inside a container, it's better to build everything inside an image.

2. The second approach involves building everything with Docker, but using a building cache to get the compilation result and putting it into a newly created container. Let's explore the `Dockerfile` that implements this approach:

```
FROM rust:nightly as builder

RUN USER=root cargo new --bin dbsync-worker
WORKDIR /dbsync-worker
COPY ./Cargo.toml ./Cargo.toml
RUN cargo build

RUN rm src/*.rs
COPY ./src ./src
COPY ./migrations ./migrations
COPY ./diesel.toml ./diesel.toml
RUN rm ./target/debug/deps/dbsync_worker*
RUN cargo build

FROM buildpack-deps:stretch
```

```
COPY --from=builder /dbsync-worker/target/debug/dbsync-worker
/app/
ENV RUST_LOG=debug
EXPOSE 8000
ENTRYPOINT ["/app/dbsync-worker"]
```

We used the `Dockerfile` of the dbsync microservice and the first part of the file was the same as the original with one small improvement—we set that name as an image we built in the first line:

```
FROM rust:nightly as builder
```

Now we can use the cached data of the image using the `builder` name.

After this section, we start a new empty image from the `buildpack-deps` image that was originally used to build the preceding `rust:nightly` image. We copy a binary executable file from the builder image using the `COPY` command with the `--from` parameter where we set the name of the image:

```
COPY --from=builder /dbsync-worker/target/debug/dbsync-worker  /app/
```

This command copies the binary to the `/app` folder inside the image and we can use it as the entry point of the container:

```
ENTRYPOINT ["/app/dbsync-worker"]
```

We also set the `RUST_LOG` environment variable and expose the port. Build this image by passing the name of this `Dockerfile` with the `-f` argument of the Docker build command and you will get an image with a single binary of the microservice inside. In other words, this approach allows us to build a microservice and reuse the compiled binary for a new image. You now know enough to pack your microservices to an image and now we can explore Docker Compose's ability to start a set of microservices and connect all launched containers to each other.

Composing a microservice set

Docker Compose is an awesome tool for deploying and running a set of microservices that can be connected each other. It helps you to define a multi-container application with configuration parameters in a human-readable YAML file. You are not limited to local deployment only and you can deploy it on a remote server on which the Docker daemon is also running.

In this section of the chapter, we will pack all our microservices with a database into a single application. You will learn how to set variables for Rust frameworks and loggers, how to connect microservices, how to define the order to start containers, how to read the logs of a running application, and how to use different configurations for testing and production.

Application definition

Docker Compose is a tool that works with the YAML definition of an application. A YAML file can contain a declaration of containers, networks, and volumes. We will use version 3.6. Create a `docker-compose.test.yml` file and add the following sections:

```
version: "3.6"
services:
    # the place for containers definition
```

In the `services` section, we will add all our microservices. Let's look at each container configuration.

Database container

Our application needs a database instance. Both user and content microservices use the PostgreSQL database, and the dbsync worker applies all migrations if necessary. Look at these settings:

```
db:
    image: postgres:latest
    restart: always
    environment:
        - POSTGRES_USER=postgres
        - POSTGRES_PASSWORD=password
    ports:
        - 5432:5432
```

We use the official PostgreSQL image. If the database fails, it will have to be restarted. We set the `restart` policy to `always`, which means the container will be restarted if it fails. We also set the user and password with environment variables.

Since we created a compose file for testing purposes, we forward a port of the container outside to connect to the database using the local client.

A container with an email server

We need the SMTP server for our mailer service. We use the `juanluisbaptiste/postfix` image with the Postfix mail server. The server also has to be restarted if it fails and we set the `restart` policy to `always`. Look at the following code:

```
smtp:
  image: juanluisbaptiste/postfix
  restart: always
  environment:
    - SMTP_SERVER=smtp.example.com
    - SMTP_USERNAME=admin@example.com
    - SMTP_PASSWORD=password
    - SERVER_HOSTNAME=smtp.example.com
  ports:
    - "2525:25"
```
      local   docker

We also configure the server using the environment variables and set the server name, username, password, and a hostname. To test the mail server, we forward port 25 of the mail server to a local 2525 port.

DBSync worker container

Now we can add the dbsync worker that applies migrations to a database instance. We use a local image that will be built with `Dockerfile` from the `./microservices/dbsync` folder that we used as a value for the `build` parameter. This worker depends on a database container (called db) and we set this dependency with the `depends_on` parameter.

> Dependencies don't mean the dependant container will be started when the necessary application is ready to work. It only refers to the order in which containers are started; the application that your microservice needs might not be ready. You have to control the readiness of the application, as we did for dbsync, with a loop that tries to connect to a database till it is available.

Also, we set the `RUST_LOG` variable with the filtering of messages with one level less than `debug` and printed messages related to the `dbsync_worker` module only:

```
dbsync:
  build: ./microservices/dbsync
  depends_on:
    - db
  environment:
```

```
    - RUST_LOG=dbsync_worker=debug
    - RUST_BACKTRACE=1
    - DBSYNC_DATABASE=postgresql://postgres:password@db:5432
```

We also activated backtrace printing by setting the `RUST_BACKTRACE` variable.

The last variable sets a connection link to a database. As you can see, we use the db name of the host since Docker configures containers to resolve names and match the names of other containers, so you don't need to set or remember the IP address of the container. You can use the names of containers as host names.

Mails microservice container

The microservice that sends emails to users builds on the image from the `Dockerfile` stored in the `./microservices/mails` folder. This microservice depends on the `smtp` container, but this microservice doesn't check that the mail service is ready for work. If you want to check that the mail server is ready, add a piece of code that will try to connect to the SMTP server before starting any activity. Look at the following settings:

```
mails:
  build: ./microservices/mails
  depends_on:
    - smtp
  environment:
    - RUST_LOG=mails_microservice=debug
    - RUST_BACKTRACE=1
    - MAILS_ADDRESS=0.0.0.0:8000
    - MAILS_SMTP_ADDRESS=smtp:2525
    - MAILS_SMTP_LOGIN=admin@example.com
    - MAILS_SMTP_PASSWORD=password
  ports:
    - 8002:8000
```

We also configure a microservice with environment variables and forward port 8002 to port 8000 of the container. You can use port 8002 to check that the microservice started and works.

Users microservice container

The users microservice is built from the `Dockerfile` we created before. This microservice depends on two other containers—dbsync and mails. First, we need to have a table of users in the database to keep user records in; secondly, we need to have the ability to send email notifications to a user. We also set the address of the socket in the `USERS_ADDRESS` variable and the link for the connection in the `USERS_DATABASE` variable:

```
users:
  build: ./microservices/users
  environment:
    - RUST_LOG=users_microservice=debug
    - RUST_BACKTRACE=1
    - USERS_ADDRESS=0.0.0.0:8000
    - USERS_DATABASE=postgresql://postgres:password@db:5432
  depends_on:
    - dbsync
    - mails
  ports:
    - 8001:8000
```

Also, there is a setting to forward port 8000 of the container to the local port, 8001, which you can use to access the microservice for testing.

Content microservice container

The content microservice is built with the `Dockerfile` file in the `./microservices/content` folder. We also created this file earlier in this chapter. Since the content microservice is based on the Rocket framework, we can use the environment variables with the `ROCKET` prefix to configure the microservice:

```
content:
  build: ./microservices/content
  depends_on:
    - dbsync
  ports:
    - 8888:8000
  environment:
    - RUST_LOG=content_microservice=debug
    - RUST_BACKTRACE=1
    - ROCKET_ADDRESS=0.0.0.0
    - ROCKET_PORT=8000
    -
ROCKET_DATABASES={postgres_database={url="postgresql://postgres:password@db
```

```
:5432"}}
    ports:
        - 8003:8000
```

This microservice uses the database and depends on the `dbsync` container, which in turn depends on the `db` container with a database instance. We open port `8003` to access this microservice outside Docker.

Router microservice container

The last service we'll configure before we start the whole application is the router microservice. This service depends on the users and content microservices, because router proxies request these microservices:

```
router:
    build: ./microservices/router
    depends_on:
        - users
        - content
    environment:
        - RUST_LOG=router_microservice=debug
        - RUST_BACKTRACE=1
        - ROUTER_ADDRESS=0.0.0.0:8000
        - ROUTER_USERS=http://users:8000
        - ROUTER_CONTENT=http://content:8000
    ports:
        - 8000:8000
```

We also configured logging with the `debug` level for the `router_microservice` namespace, turned on backtrace printing, set the socket address to bind this microservice to, and set paths to the users and content microservices with environment variables supported by the configuration. We used container names as host names, since Docker Compose configures containers to reach each other by name. We also forwarded port `8000` to the same system port. Now we can start the application with all of the containers.

Running the application

To run the application, we will use the Docker Compose tool, which has to be installed (you can find useful links in the Technical Requirements section of this chapter). If the utility installed successfully, you'll have the `docker-compose` command. Change the directory to a directory called `docker-compose.test.yml` and run the `up` subcommand:

```
docker-compose -f docker-compose.test.yml up
```

Thus, it will build all the images if necessary and start the application:

```
Creating network "deploy_default" with the default driver
Creating deploy_smtp_1 ... done
Creating deploy_db_1     ... done
Creating deploy_mails_1  ... done
Creating deploy_dbsync_1 ... done
Creating deploy_users_1   ... done
Creating deploy_content_1 ... done
Creating deploy_router_1 ... done
Attaching to deploy_smtp_1, deploy_db_1, deploy_mails_1, deploy_dbsync_1,
deploy_content_1, deploy_users_1, deploy_router_1
```

When all the containers are started, you will see the logs of all the containers in the terminal, prefixed by the name of the container:

```
smtp_1     | Setting configuration option smtp_sasl_password_maps with
value: hash:\/etc\/postfix\/sasl_passwd
mails_1    | [2018-12-24T19:08:20Z DEBUG mails_microservice] Waiting for
SMTP server
smtp_1     | Setting configuration option smtp_sasl_security_options with
value: noanonymous
dbsync_1   | [2018-12-24T19:08:20Z DEBUG dbsync_worker] Waiting for
database...
db_1       |
db_1       | fixing permissions on existing directory
/var/lib/postgresql/data ... ok
mails_1    | [2018-12-24T19:08:20Z DEBUG mails_microservice] SMTP connected
smtp_1     | Adding SASL authentication configuration
mails_1    | Listening on http://0.0.0.0:8000
mails_1    | Ctrl-C to shutdown server
content_1  | Configured for development.
router_1   | DEBUG 2018-12-24T19:08:22Z: router_microservice: Started http
server: 0.0.0.0:8000
content_1  | Rocket has launched from http://0.0.0.0:8000
users_1    | [2018-12-24T19:08:24Z DEBUG users_microservice] Starting
microservice...
```

Now the application is started and you can connect to it with the browser using this link: http://localhost:8000.

To stop the application, use the *Ctrl+C* key combination. That will start the termination process and you will see it reflected in the Terminal:

```
Gracefully stopping... (press Ctrl+C again to force)
Stopping deploy_router_1  ... done
Stopping deploy_users_1   ... done
Stopping deploy_content_1 ... done
```

```
Stopping deploy_mails_1    ... done
Stopping deploy_db_1       ... done
Stopping deploy_smtp_1     ... do
```

If you restart the application, the database will be empty. Why? Because we stored the database on a temporary filesystem of the container. If you need persistence, you can attach a local folder to the container as a virtual volume. Let's explore this feature.

Adding persistent state to the application

We created an application that consists of microservices, and that doesn't have a persistent state – the application is empty on every restart. Fixing this is simple: map the persistent volume to a folder of the container. Since no one microservice of our application keeps the data in files, but the PostgreSQL database does, we only need to attach a folder to a database container. Copy docker-compose.test.yml to docker-compose.prod.yml and add the following changes:

```
services:
  db:
    image: postgres:latest
    restart: always
    environment:
      - POSTGRES_USER=postgres
      - POSTGRES_PASSWORD=password
    volumes:
      - database_data:/var/lib/postgresql/data
  # other containers definition
volumes:
  database_data:
    driver: local
```

We attached a volume with the name database_data to the /var/lib/postgresql/data path of the database container. PostgreSQL uses this path by default to store database files. To declare a persistent volume, we use the volume section with the name of the volume. We set the driver parameter to local to keep the data on the local hard drive. Now the data is saved between restarts.

We also removed port forwarding for all of the microservices, excluding the router microservice, since all of the microservices are available via the inner virtual network of Docker and only the router has to be available outside the container.

Running the application in the background

We started the application by attaching the terminal to the output of the containers, but that's inconvenient if you want to deploy an application to a remote server. To detach the terminal, use the –d parameter when you start:

```
docker-compose -f docker-compose.prod.yml up -d
```

This will start the application with a persistent state, and print something like the following:

```
Starting deploy_db_1     ... done
Starting deploy_smtp_1    ... done
Starting deploy_dbsync_1 ... done
Starting deploy_mails_1   ... done
Starting deploy_content_1 ... done
Starting deploy_users_1   ... done
Starting deploy_router_1  ... done
```

It also detaches from the Terminal. You might ask: How can I read the logs that microservices print using env_logger and the log crate? Use the following command with the name of the service at the end:

```
docker-compose -f docker-compose.prod.yml logs users
```

This command will print the logs of the users_1 container, which represents the users service of the application. You can use the grep command to filter unnecessary records in logs.

Since the application detached from the terminal, you should use the down command to stop the application:

```
docker-compose -f docker-compose.test.yml stop
```

This will stop all containers and finish with the output:

```
Stopping deploy_router_1   ... done
Stopping deploy_users_1    ... done
Stopping deploy_content_1 ... done
Stopping deploy_mails_1    ... done
Stopping deploy_db_1       ... done
Stopping deploy_smtp_1     ... done
```

The application has stopped and now you know how to use the Docker Compose tool to run a multi-container application. If you want to learn more about using Docker Compose on local and remote machines, read this book.

Summary

This chapter introduced you to how to build images and run containers with your own microservices using Docker. We packed all of the microservices we created in Chapter 9, *Simple REST Definition and Request Routing with Frameworks*, and Chapter 11, *Involving Concurrency with Actors and the Actix Crate*, and learned how to build images manually and start a container. We also added the dbsync worker, which applied all necessary migrations and prepared a database for use with the users and content microservices.

Also, we considered approaches to hiding the source code of a microservice and used the cache of a container to copy a compiled binary to an empty image without building artifacts.

In the second half of the chapter, we learned how to run multiple microservices with necessary dependencies (such as databases and mail servers) at once. We used the Docker Compose tool to describe the configuration of a microservice set with a running order and port forwarding. We also learned how to attach volumes to services (containers), to store persistent data, and to allow you to restart an application without any risk of losing data.

In the next chapter, we will learn how to automate building microservices using continuous integration tools, helping you deliver the latest release of your product faster.

16
DevOps of Rust Microservices - Continuous Integration and Delivery

This chapter covers the widely used practices of **continuous integration** (**CI**) and **continuous delivery** (**CD**). When a microservice is being developed, you have to be sure that every feature is tested and works and think about how to deliver an application to your servers or deploy it to the cloud.

In this chapter, we'll study how to do the following:

- How to use tools to check the code
- How to build the code automatically using CI tools
- How to deploy the compiled code to servers

Technical requirements

This chapter requires the Rust compiler, and you have to install at least version 1.31. Also, you need the `rustup` tool to add extra components, such as `rustfmt` and `clippy`. If you don't have it, you can find it here: `https://rustup.rs/`

Also in this chapter, we will try to bootstrap a CI system that will build and test a microservice. Since manual installation of these kinds of tools is long and complex, we will use Docker with Docker Compose to start and prepare the building environment faster. But in any case, you need a browser to be able to connect to the management console UI of the TeamCity tool to configure it.

The examples for this chapter can be found on GitHub: `https://github.com/ PacktPublishing/Hands-On-Microservices-with-Rust/tree/master/Chapter16.`

Continuous integration and continuous delivery

In the modern world, speed is a decisive factor of success for applications and products. The competition has become fierce and every company has to release new features as fast as possible.

For microservice developers, this means we need a continuous process for building and delivering new versions of our products to be timely and competitive. In terms of software, this means you need to automate this process—maybe a special product or a set of scripts. Fortunately, this class of products already exists; called CI tools.

Continuous integration

CI is the process of merging all incoming features and patches into a single, well-tested application. It is important to note that this should happen several times a day—you will get a freshly *baked* version, like from a conveyor belt.

Nowadays, many products are offered to provide you a tool to test, build, and deploy your product unclear. In most cases, CI products work as a server that uses remote build agents to build code pulled from a repository. This process is approximately depicted in the following diagram:

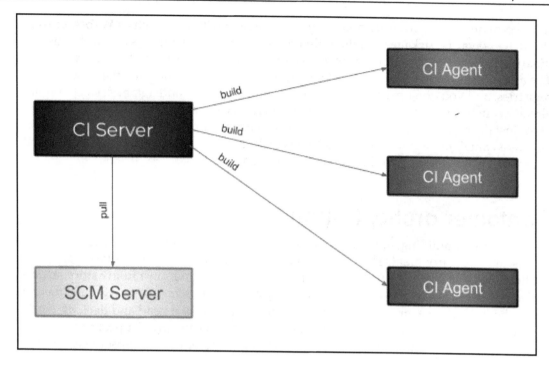

The CI server is responsible for getting updates from a source code management server (such as Git) to pull a fresh version of the code and start building on using agents that are already connected and registered on the server. Some software can use Docker as a runtime for the necessary build agents. In this case, you don't even need to run agents manually. But this is not suitable for every part of an application, because some parts need to be built in an environment that can't be started as a Docker container.

Microservices that have been compiled and tested successfully can be moved to a deployment process that also can be automated using CD.

Continuous delivery

When an application is built and is ready for deployment, the process of deployment automation is called CD. Often, this functionality is provided by CI products by using special plugins called configuration management and deployment tools, such as Ansible, Chef, Puppet, and Salt.

In the past, microservices were delivered as an archive with files such as **Web ARchives (WAR)**, in Java, as packages installed directly on a server's operating system, and as binaries. Nowadays, companies prefer to deliver containers, instead of these other formats. The advantages of containers are undeniable: they're compact and safe, they use shared registries, and you don't need to prepare environments again and again. A Docker image already contains what you need, and if your microservices can work without collisions with other instances of the same microservice, you can consider delivering your product not only as a container deployed to a remote server, but also using an orchestration tool that automatically scales your application depending on your customers' needs.

Container orchestration

With automated building and delivery processes, you can still deploy a microservice into an unscalable environment. This means you lose the important benefit of fast-scaling your application. Developers of one huge internet hiring service told me a funny story about the peak load they experience—the greatest activity on their servers falls on Monday morning. That's the time when every worker visits the office after the weekend and decides, *that's finished*. The reality of application maintenance is that you can't predict peaks of activity for your services, so you should be able to run more instances of your microservices quickly.

There are some products that can orchestrate containers, and one of the most popular is Kubernetes. The only thing you have to do is to upload containers to a registry. Kubernetes can route requests and run extra instances of microservices that can't process all incoming requests. However, you still need to provide hardware resources to it and write loosely coupled microservices so that you can run as many as you want.

In any case, to automate the delivery process of your application, you have to start with a CI system and improve it. Let's look at the tools that we can use to write CI scripts for Rust projects.

Rust tools

The first line of quality control of microservices is checking that the code does not contain explicit blunders. The compiler checks the cases with mutability, references, ownership, and lifetimes, and also prints warnings if you have unused code, but there are more complex cases that require a special tool to detect.

In this section, we cover the following tools commonly used in CI agents to prepare a code for merging. Let's explore all of them, starting with code formatting styles.

Rustfmt

Rustfmt is a tool that helps you to fit your code to style guidelines. It doesn't mean you have to use one common style: the tool provides multiple configuration parameters that you can use to set a preferred style.

This tool is mature, but it wasn't included in the Rust distribution until version 1.31. Since edition 2018 was released, the rustfmt tool has been available and is recommended for use in your projects; however, Rust doesn't force your code to have a standard format. Let's install it and try to use it.

Installation

If you use the `rustup` tool, then to install `rustfmt`, you need to add the corresponding component using the following command:

```
rustup component add rustfmt
```

If you want to install the latest version, you can do it directly from the repository:

```
cargo install --git https://github.com/rust-lang/rustfmt
```

The installation from source code requires compilation time and can be unstable, but you will have the latest features.

Usage

Since `rustfmt` was added as a command, using it is as simple as calling a special command:

```
cargo fmt
```

This command fixes all sources to default style guidelines. But it works quietly and we have to look at the differences between files to see the changes.

The tool patches files from your project, and you have to commit all the changes before you attempt to fix the code styles.

But we will use this tool to check the code styles with CI, and stop building if the code was formatted incorrectly. To check the code and also to see potential changes, you have to pass the --check argument to rustfmt:

```
cargo fmt -- --check
```

As you can see, we used an extra -- parameter, because without it, we pass arguments to a tool that calls rustfmt, but to send arguments directly to rustfmt we have to add this extra pair of dashes. The checking has a 0 code if sources don't contain issues, and a non-zero code if errors are present, printing a potential diff:

```
Diff in ./microservice/src/main.rs at line 1:
-use actix_web::{App, middleware, server, App};
+use actix_web::{middleware, server, App, App};

 fn index(_req: &HttpRequest) -> &'static str {
     "Microservice"
Diff in ./microservice/src/main.rs at line 8:
     env_logger::init();
     let sys = actix::System::new("microservice");
     server::new(|| {
-          App::new().middleware(middleware::Logger::default()).resource("/",
|r|  r.f(index))
+          App::new()
+              .middleware(middleware::Logger::default())
+              .resource("/", |r| r.f(index))
     })
     .bind("127.0.0.1:8080")
     .unwrap()
```

This is exactly what we need to use in CI to interrupt the building, and to see the reason for the interruption in order to fix it.

Configuration

You can change the behavior of rustfmt with a configuration to set your preferred styles. Add the rustfmt.toml configuration file to your project. The defaults of the current version can be described with the following configuration file contents:

```
max_width = 100
hard_tabs = false
tab_spaces = 4
newline_style = "Auto"
use_small_heuristics = "Default"
reorder_imports = true
```

```
reorder_modules = true
remove_nested_parens = true
edition = "2015"
merge_derives = true
use_try_shorthand = false
use_field_init_shorthand = false
force_explicit_abi = true
```

Most parameters have descriptive names, but if you want to read a description of the parameters, you can pass the --help=config argument to rustfmt to see the details. You can create a rustfmt.toml file and set parameters that are different from the default values.

Often, code style checking is the first step of a CI script, because it's the fastest check and is best done before a long compilation process. There is also another code check that we should do before compilation—lint checking.

Clippy

In addition to the problems with the format of your code, you may also face more serious problems that can be fixed with another kind of tool—linters. A linter is a program that finds bad practices of writing code that can affect the future performance if the problem can be solved more simply. Rust has a good linter called clippy, included as a component since version 1.31, when it became a part of edition 2018. It's a good tool to use when building scripts to prevent a flood of bad coding practices. Let's install it and try to use it.

Installation

You can install clippy in two ways, as we did with the rustfmt tool: by adding the component using the rustup command or by installing the latest version from the GitHub repository of the project. To add it as a prebuilt component, use the following command:

```
rustup component add clippy
```

You also can install the latest version directly from the repository of the project using this command:

```
cargo install --git https://github.com/rust-lang/rust-clippy
```

But remember, this version is potentially unstable, and the lints it contains might be changed in the future.

Usage

To use `clippy`, it's enough to start it as the subcommand of `cargo`:

```
cargo clippy
```

This sub-command starts checking the code and will inform you about possible improvements. For example, imagine that you have a struct like this in your code:

```
struct State {
    vec: Box<Vec<u8>>,
}
```

Then, `clippy` will inform you that `Box` is unnecessary, since `Vec` is already placed in a memory heap:

```
warning: you seem to be trying to use `Box<Vec<T>>`. Consider using just
`Vec<T>`
 --> src/main.rs:4:10
  |
4 |     vec: Box<Vec<u8>>,
  |          ^^^^^^^^^^^^
  |
  = note: #[warn(clippy::box_vec)] on by default
  = help: `Vec<T>` is already on the heap, `Box<Vec<T>>` makes an extra
allocation.
  = help: for further information visit
https://rust-lang.github.io/rust-clippy/master/index.html#box_vec
```

But if you really want to box a vector, you can disable this warning for this line of code by adding the `#[allow(clippy::box_vec)]` attribute to the field or the struct, and the warning for this field will be suppressed.

The preceding example is a warning that means the code will be compiled successfully and the building won't be interrupted by `clippy`. In CI scripts, `clippy` has to interrupt execution if it gets a warning from the code, because we should merge code that doesn't contain any warnings, as well as ambiguous code. To let `clippy` fail when there's warning, we can set the extra argument:

```
cargo clippy -- -D warnings
```

Now, `clippy` denies all warnings. But there is still a loophole if your crate contains non-default features: `clippy` won't check all of them. To do a full check, you can use the following arguments:

```
cargo clippy --all-targets --all-features -- -D warnings
```

Of course, it will take more time, but all potential problems known to `clippy` will be checked.

Configuration

The `clippy` tool can be very annoying. To tighten or loosen checks, you can configure the tool using the `clippy.toml` configuration file.

For example, if we activate all lints with the `-W clippy::pedantic` argument, we can get a warning like this:

```
warning: you should put `MyCompany` between ticks in the documentation
  --> src/main.rs:8:29
   |
8  | /// This method connects to MyCompany API.
   |                              ^^^^^^^^^^
   |
   = note: `-W clippy::doc-markdown` implied by `-W clippy::pedantic`
   = help: for further information visit
   https://rust-lang.github.io/rust-clippy/master/index.html#doc_markdown
```

This happened because `clippy` thinks there is the name of a variable that we forget to include in ticks. To avoid this behavior, we can add an extra word to the `clippy.toml` configuration to ignore markdown comments:

```
doc-valid-idents = ["MyCompany"]
```

Now the tool won't interpret `MyCompany` as the name of a variable.

Recommended code attributes

As you saw, it's possible to allow or deny some warnings for lints, but there are some attributes that can be used to make your code cleaner:

```
#![deny(
    bare_trait_objects,
    dead_code,
)]
#![warn(
    missing_debug_implementations,
    missing_docs,
    while_true,
    unreachable_pub,
)]
```

```
#![cfg_attr(
    feature = "cargo-clippy",
    deny(
        clippy::doc_markdown,
    ),
)]
```

This is an example of stricter requirements for a code. The compiler deny unused code of missing docs, will require `loop` instead of `while true` and check all published types have to be reachable. Also, we completely deny using variable names in markdown docs without ticks. You can add whatever requirements you need to your project.

Also, the preceding requirements force us to use `dyn Trait` for trait objects, instead of a bare `Trait` name. This may come in handy if you use the 2015 edition but want to prepare the project for Edition 2018, but it's better to use the latest edition where possible, and there is a tool that can help you to move to the freshest edition of Rust—`rustfix`.

Rustfix

You may have thought, if Rust can find a problem in a code and suggest a solution, why hasn't it applied the changes immediately? This is a reasonable idea, and it may be possible in the future, but now this feature in active development with the `rustfix` tool.

This project aims to provide a tool that can fix all compiler warnings, and today you can try to use it to move your project from Edition 2015 to Edition 2018. We don't need this tool in CI processes directly, but it can help to satisfy CI checks more quickly.

Installation

To install `rustfix`, use the following command:

```
cargo install cargo-fix
```

After installation, you can use the `cargo fix` subcommand with the necessary parameters.

Usage

Let's consider moving the project from Edition 2015 to Edition 2018. Which arguments do you have to set to do this transformation of your code? First, you can prepare your code for transformation with this command:

```
cargo fix --edition
```

This command will make your code compatible with both editions, but if you want to use idioms of an edition, you have to set the edition version to be used in the `edition` field of the `[package]` section of the `Cargo.toml` file, and run the following command:

```
cargo fix --edition-idioms
```

After running this, your code will potentially be compatible with the selected edition. You can also do more with `rustfix`, but some issues can be fixed if you use an IDE, but this topic is out of the scope of this book; and let's explore other cargo commands.

Cargo test

To be perfectly honest, the most important tool for checking in CI is the testing tool. We already learned about writing tests in `Chapter 13`, *Testing and Debugging Rust Microservices*, but in this section we explore some useful arguments for the `cargo test` command.

There are some useful arguments for CI:

- `--no-run`: Compiles, but doesn't run tests, which is useful for checking the compilation of tests for different targets, without wasting time for extra running
- `--all-targets`: Runs tests for all targets
- `--all-features`: Runs tests with all features
- `--examples`: Tests all examples
- `--jobs <N>`: Runs tests in multiple jobs, which is useful if the test uses one database instance only and you want to run tests sequentially to avoid a situation where one test affects the results of another

Now we are ready to bootstrap a CI tool and configure it for building a microservice.

CI and CD tools

In this section, we will discuss systems for CI, and bootstrap a CI server instance with a build agent using Docker Compose. But first, let's look at some popular CI products and their delivery capabilities.

TravisCI

TravisCI is the most popular CI service for open source projects, because it provides a free plan for such projects and is integrated well with GitHub. To use it, all you have to do is add the .travis.yml file to the root of repository of your project. It supports Rust out of the box.

With TravisCI, you can build your projects in either Linux or macOS environments. Let's write a simple example of a .travis.yml file. The first part of this file is a building matrix declaration:

```
language: rust
cache: cargo
matrix:
  include:
    - os: linux
      rust: stable
      env: TARGET=x86_64-unknown-linux-gnu
    - os: linux
      rust: nightly
      env: TARGET=x86_64-unknown-linux-gnu
    - os: osx
      rust: stable
      env: TARGET=x86_64-apple-darwin
    - os: osx
      rust: nightly
      env: TARGET=x86_64-apple-darwin
```

We chose the Rust language with caching for cargo to speed up building updates. Also, we declared a matrix of environments. TravisCI automatically prepared the Rust environment for us with four variants: linux with a stable compiler, linux with a nightly compiler, and a pair of stable and nightly compiler versions for osx. For microservices, you often need linux builds only. Also, we specified targets, but you can use musl instead of gnu, for example.

The following code installs extra packages:

```
addons:
  apt:
    packages:
      - build-essential
      - libcurl4-openssl-dev
      - libssl-dev
```

Also, you can add environment variables that you can use in building and test running:

```
env:
  global:
    - APPNAME="myapp"
```

Finally, you have to add a script that will be used as the CI script. You can put the `script` section with a command directly into `.travis.yml` as items to that section, or add a `jobs` section that can contain concurrent jobs to run:

```
jobs:
  include:
    - name: rustfmt
      install:
        - rustup component add rustfmt
      script:
        - cargo fmt -- --check
    - name: clippy
      install:
        - rustup component add clippy
      script:
        - cargo clippy
    - name: test
      script:
        - cargo build --target $TARGET --verbose
        - cargo test --target $TARGET --verbose
```

The `jobs` section can also contain an install subsection to provide a list of commands to install extra dependencies for a job.

Now you can put this `.travis.yml` file into the root of the repository of your project to allow Travis CI to check the pull requests of your project. But remember that you have to pay for private repositories with the TravisCI service, while GitHub allows you to have private repositories for free. You can test your Rust application for Linux and macOS, but there is another service that provides another set of operating systems.

AppVeyor

AppVeyor is a CI service for Linux and Windows. It's also free for open source projects and provides good integration with GitHub. To start using this service, you have to add an `appveyor.yml` file to your project. Let's look at the example configuration:

```
os: Visual Studio 2015
environment:
  matrix:
```

```
    - channel: stable
      target: x86_64-pc-windows-msvc
    - channel: nightly
      target: i686-pc-windows-msvc
    - channel: stable
      target: x86_64-pc-windows-gnu
    - channel: nightly
      target: i686-pc-windows-gnu
```

The configuration looks similar to the configuration for TravisCI. We also created a matrix of builds and will use MSVC and GNU toolchains for stable and nightly compiler versions. After this, we use these values to install the required tools using `rustup`:

```
install:
    - appveyor DownloadFile https://win.rustup.rs/ -FileName rustup-init.exe
    - rustup-init -yv --default-toolchain %channel% --default-host %target%
    - set PATH=%PATH%;%USERPROFILE%\.cargo\bin
    - rustup component add rustfmt
    - rustup component add clippy
    - rustc -vV
    - cargo -vV
```

We also installed the `rustfmt` and `clippy` tools after the `PATH` environment variable was updated. Finally, we can build the projects as follows:

```
build: false
test_script:
    - cargo fmt -- --check
    - cargo clippy
    - cargo build
    - cargo test
```

We set the `build` field to `false` to prevent the building agent from starting the MSBuild tool, which is not necessary for Rust crates.

Jenkins

This is a popular CI system created originally for and with Java. Jenkins is an open source product and has no limits on usage. These are both reasons why some growing companies choose this product, and you might too, if you want to customize the build process and want to control costs for CI.

Jenkins offers you two approaches for building applications.The first is running a plain script and the second is using pipeline, the feature that allows you to include a CI script in the root of the repository, like we did with TravisCI and AppVeyor.

Here is an example of the `pipeline` configuration that has to be stored in a `Jenkinsfile` configuration file in the root of your project if you want to pull this script with a repository automatically and update it using SCM:

```
pipeline {
    agent { dockerfile true }
    stages {
        stage('Rustfmt') {
            steps {
                sh "cargo fmt -- --check"
            }
        }
        stage('Clippy') {
            steps {
                sh "cargo clippy"
            }
        }
        stage('Build') {
            steps {
                sh "cargo build"
            }
        }
        stage('Test') {
            steps {
                sh "cargo test"
            }
        }
    }
}
```

The preceding `pipeline` configuration means that Jenkins requires Docker to build the attached `Dockerfile` and to run all commands for all stages. This feature utilizes Docker containers instead of agents, but you can also connect traditional building agents to a CI server.

Demonstration of continuous integration

To create a demonstration, we will use TeamCity CI, developed by JetBrains. This product is similar to Jenkins in some features, but it's simpler to bootstrap and deploy for our demonstration. We will bootstrap our own CI environment and configure our own building tasks for it. TeamCity has a free plan that's enough for building small and medium projects. We will also use a Gogs Git server to have a private SCM server for our building needs. Let's start.

Docker Compose

Create an empty `docker-compose.yml` file and add a `services` section to it:

```
version: '3.1'
services:
```

The SCM server

To the `services` section, add the SCM server Gogs first:

```
git-server:
    image: gogs/gogs
    ports:
        - '10022:22'
        - '10080:3000'
    volumes:
        - ./gogs:/data
```

We'll use an official Docker image. We set a persistent volume to keep all created repositories between starts. Also, we forwarded two ports—SSH (from local port `10022` to port `22` in the container) and HTTP (from local port `10080` to port `3000` in the container). To upload data with the Git client, we will use the local port, but to use the server from TeamCity, we have to use the port of the container.

The CI server

The next service we need is a CI server. We will use the official image of TeamCity:

```
teamcity:
    image: jetbrains/teamcity-server
    ports:
        - '8111:8111'
    volumes:
        - ./teamcity/datadir:/data/teamcity_server/datadir
        - ./teamcity/logs:/opt/teamcity/logs
```

The container requires two persistent volumes for data and logs. We also forward port `8111` of the container to the same local port to connect to the UI with a browser.

The CI agent

To use the TeamCity server for builds, we need at least one agent. It works as a sibling container in Docker, and we also declare it as a service, but provide the SERVER_URL environment variable targeted to the CI server we created before:

```
agent:
    build: ./images/rust-slave
    environment:
        - SERVER_URL=http://teamcity:8111
    volumes:
        - ./teamcity/agent:/data/teamcity_agent/conf
```

There is the official image for an agent, but we don't use it directly here, because we need to add the Rust compiler and extra tools, which is why we build our own image for this service. Also, we need to provide a persistent volume to it to keep the configuration of the running agent that will be connected to the server.

Agents don't need to open ports, because they are non-interactive and don't have any UI. Often, agents are also called slaves.

The image

The image for the agent service created from the official image of minimal agent for TeamCity is as follows:

```
FROM jetbrains/teamcity-minimal-agent:latest

RUN apt-get update
RUN apt-get install -y build-essential

ENV RUST_VERSION=1.32.0

RUN curl https://sh.rustup.rs -sSf \
  | sh -s -- -y --no-modify-path --default-toolchain $RUST_VERSION

ENV PATH=/root/.cargo/bin:$PATH

RUN rustup --version; \
  cargo --version; \
  rustc --version;

RUN rustup component add rustfmt
RUN rustup component add clippy
```

As you can see, we installed the Rust compiler and added `rustfmt` and `clippy` as components with `rustup`.

Configuring Gogs

Let's configure the SCM server and push a tiny microservice to it:

1. Start up Docker Compose from our CI services bundle with this command:

```
docker-compose up
```

2. When all services are started, open `http://localhost:10080` in a browser to configure the Gogs server. You will see the following configuration form:

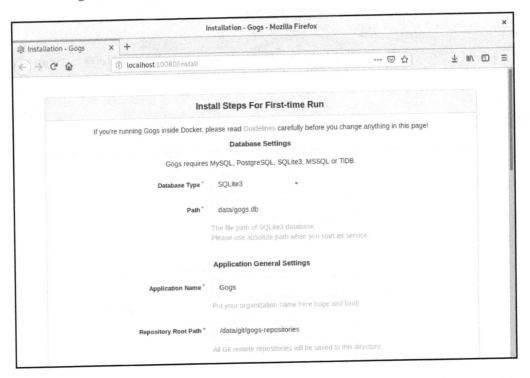

3. Set **SQLite3** in the **Database Type** field (because we won't spend time configuring an external database), leave the default values in the other fields, and hit the **Install Gogs** button. It will redirect you to port `3000`, but recall that, it's available inside Docker only and you have to open the previous URL again.

4. Click the **Register** link and register a new account:

I set `developer` as the username and `secret` as the password. We need these credentials to both upload our code to a created repository and to pull it with CI.

5. Create a new private repository with the + sing button and call it `microservice`. Now you can upload the code to this repository using `http://localhost:3000/developer/microservice.git`. If you use the code of this chapter from the repository of the book, you can use the microservice crate in that folder, but you have to initialize it and add the remote server with these commands:

```
git init
git add -A
git commit
git remote add origin
```

```
http://localhost:10080/developer/microservice.git
git push origin master
```

It's a trivial command, but one to remember if you forget something.

6. Enter the username and password we set before, and you have got an empty repository in SCM:

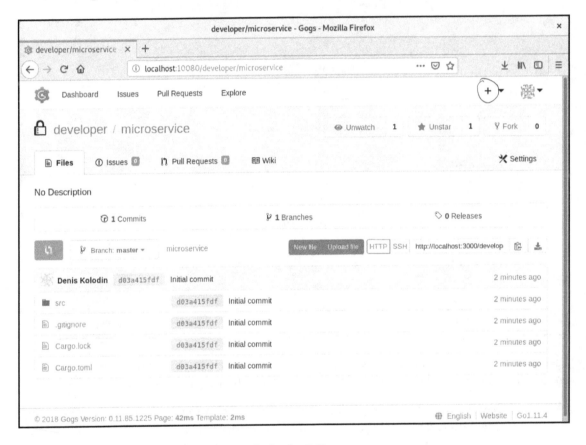

Now we can configure CI to get this code for building.

Configuring TeamCity

1. First, open the `http://localhost:8111` URL, where we bind the CI server in a browser and pass the first steps of configuring the TeamCity instance. Set a **DataDirectory** the same as we attached as a persistent volume (default value):

TeamCity First Start

Please review the settings below before proceeding with the first TeamCity start.

TeamCity server stores server configuration settings, project definitions, build results and caches on disk in a **Data Directory**.⊘

Location of the Data Directory: **/data/teamcity_server/datadir**

If you already worked with TeamCity and want to use existing directory or you want to use another location for creating fresh setup, check the documentation to change the directory location.

Proceed

TeamCity 2018.2.1 (build 61078)

2. Click the **Proceed** button, and in the next step, create a database of the **HSQLDB** type. There are options for other external databases, and it's better to use them for production, but for testing it's enough to keep all data in the data directory of TeamCity:

Database connection setup

TeamCity server stores builds history and users-related data in an SQL database.

Select the database type*: [Internal (HSQLDB) ∨]

The internal database suits evaluation purposes only and is not intended for production. We strongly recommend using an external database in a production environment.

You can start with the internal database and then migrate the data to an external one after successful evaluation.

[Proceed]

TeamCity 2018.2.1 (build 61078)

3. Create an administrator account that you will use to access the TeamCity UI:

I used the admin value for username and the secret value for the password fields. Now it takes time to initialize and start, but after the initialization process is finished, we can add external agents.

Authorizing agents

Since we have an agent in a sibling container, it already tried to connect to a server, but we have to authorize it because if an agent is authorized it can steal the source code of the microservices. Click the **Authorize** button in the **Unauthorized** tab of the **Agents** page:

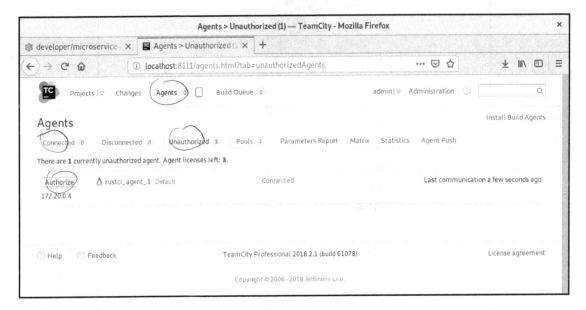

When the agent is authorized, you can see it in the **Connected** tab and can control it. You can also add more sibling workers to the Docker Compose configuration.

Creating a project

Now we have connected agents and can create a project that will build our microservice. Click the **Create Project** button on the **Projects** page and fill in the form with the parameters of the repository that we want to build:

We set the repository URL
to `http://git-server:3000/developer/microservice.git`, because the CI server instance works inside a virtual network and can connect to other services by the names and original ports exposed by Docker images.

When you click the **Proceed** button, you can specify the name of the project:

Click **Proceed** again, and you have an empty project that we can configure with steps.

Building steps for Rust

On the project's page, click the link to **configure build steps manually** and add a new build step to our project:

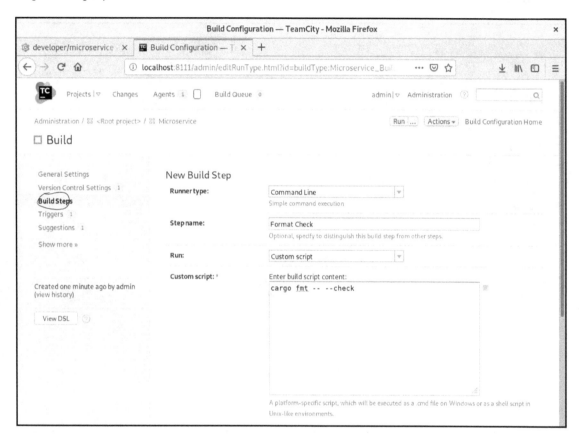

The first step, called `Format Check`, is a **Command Line** that runs **Custom script** with a single command: `cargo fmt -- --check`. This command will check the style of the code with the `rustfmt` tool. Add the next build step, called Build (you can use your own name), with the `cargo build` command:

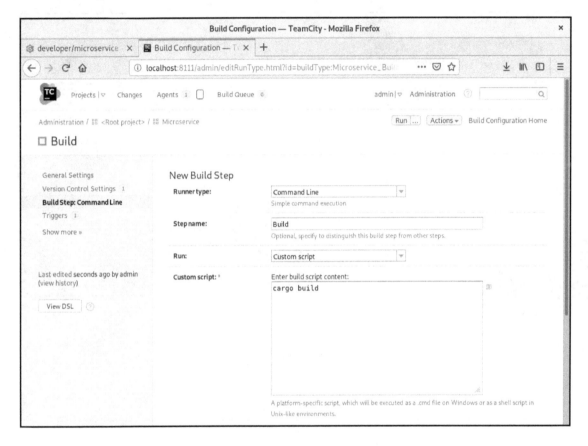

Now, if you click the **Build Steps** menu item, you will see the steps we created:

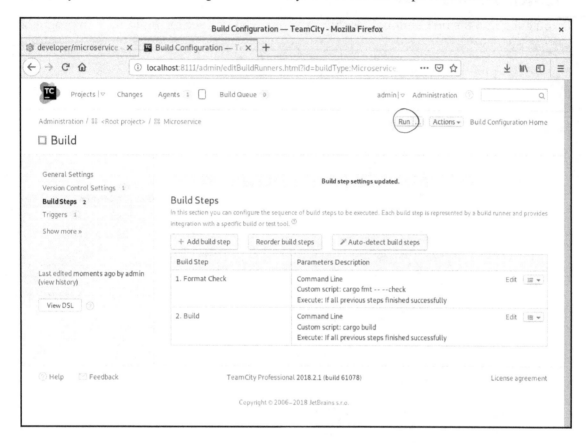

Now you can start this building process by clicking the **Run** button, as shown in the preceding screenshot. It will immediately start building with the agent container.

Building with CI

If you enter into the first building task that appears, you will see the building is in progress:

As you can see, the first step is finished successfully and the `cargo build` command is in progress. When it is complete, the status of this building task will be changed to success. It works!

Also, projects by default create a trigger to run the build process when you push new changes to the repository:

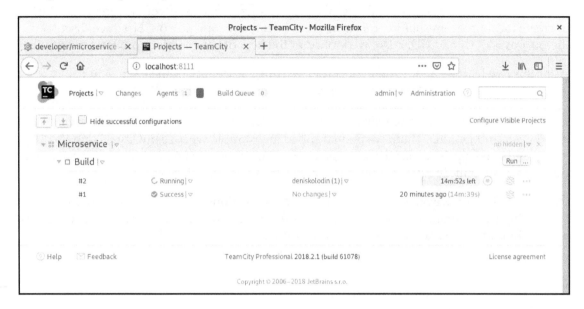

I pushed one extra commit to a repository and the building process started. As you can see in the preceding screenshot, an estimated time for building has appeared. According to the previous build, it's estimated at 15 minutes, but actually it takes only 40 seconds, because agents keep a building cache.

As an experiment, you can add more steps that test and check the code with `clippy`, and also add steps to upload the binary to servers.

You can also configure Jenkins to work in a similar way, but it takes a little more time to configure.

Summary

In this chapter, we got acquainted with CI of Rust microservices. If you haven't used Rust to create local programs before, this may seem like a new topic to you. First, we discussed the purposes of CI and CD. Also, we looked at the benefits of container orchestration tools.

After this, we learned about some tools for checking the quality of the code—`rustfmt`, `clippy`, and `rustfix`. Then we figured out how to configure them.

Next, we studied examples of using some popular CI services and servers—TravisCI, AppVeyor, and Jenkins. Then, we bootstrapped an example with TeamCity CI and its agent, and used a private Git server to push our Rust project to be built with CI. Lastly, we configured the building process of a microservice and checked it with UI.

In the next chapter, we have a look at serverless applications: what is it, and how to write them using Rust. Amazon Web Services offers AWS Lambda product for hosting serverless applications and had started to support Rust officially.

17
Bounded Microservices with AWS Lambda

In the Last chapter we learned how to create serverless applications using AWS Lambda and the official `lambda-runtime` crate. It is useful for developers who use **Amazon Web Services** (**AWS**) and who especially want to use AWS Lambda. It differs from the approach where we created a standalone web server, because AWS Lambda stores, scales, and runs automatically, and the only thing we should provide is the compiled code of a microservice.

The following topics will be covered in this chapter:

- Dealing with the AWS Lambda Rust runtime
- Deploying a microservice to AWS using the Serverless Framework

Technical requirements

To use the techniques from this chapter, you need a configured Docker instance, because AWS uses Amazon Linux AMI distribution to run lambdas, and we need the special environment to compile Rust code for that environment. You also need an account in AWS. Create one if you don't have one. AWS provides a free trial period called Free Tier, which includes 1 million requests to AWS Lambda per month over the course of one year. You can read more about this trial period here: `https://aws.amazon.com/free/`.

You should also know how to use AWS Console. There will be some examples of using it in this chapter, but for production you have to know all its features, including using access controls to prevent malicious penetration to your microservice. You can read about AWS in a book called *Learning AWS*: `https://www.packtpub.com/virtualization-and-cloud/learning-aws-second-edition`.

In this chapter, we will create two examples of a serverless application. The first requires the Rust compiler 1.31 version or above and the musl library, and the second needs npm and Docker.

You can find sources of all examples of this chapter on GitHub: `https://github.com/PacktPublishing/Hands-On-Microservices-with-Rust/tree/master/Chapter17/`

Serverless architecture

For the most part, in this book we have created microservices as standalone server applications. To deploy them you have to upload binaries to remote servers using continuous delivery tools. If you don't want to worry about making the binaries compatible with operating systems, you can use containers to deliver and deploy applications packed to images. It gives you the opportunity to use container orchestration services, such as Kubernetes. Container orchestration software simplifies scaling and configuring large applications that use containers to run microservices. If you try to think about this simplification further, you can find it helpful to use a predefined and preinstalled pool of containers with generic environment that will run small binaries with request-handling functions and without any HTTP middleware. In other words, you could write handlers for events and no more HTTP code. This approach is called serverless.

In the next section we list the platforms that provide serverless infrastructure and that can be used to deploy serverless applications.

AWS Lambda

AWS Lambda is an Amazon product that you can find here: `https://aws.amazon.com/lambda/`.

There is official support for the Rust programming language with the `lambda-runtime` crate: `https://github.com/awslabs/aws-lambda-rust-runtime`. We will use this crate in this chapter to demonstrate the serverless approach.

Azure Functions

Azure Functions is the serverless product of Microsoft, and is part of the Azure platform: https://azure.microsoft.com/en-us/services/functions/.

There is no official Rust support at the moment, but you can use the azure-functions crate, which uses the internal worker protocol of Azure Functions based on GRPC to interact between the host and the language worker.

Cloudflare Workers

Cloudflare offers its own serverless product called Cloudflare Workers: https://www.cloudflare.com/products/cloudflare-workers/.

This service is compatible with Rust because Cloudflare Workers implemented an awesome idea: **workers compiled to WebAssebly (WASM)**. Since Rust has good support for WASM, you can easily use it to produce serverless workers for Cloudflare.

IBM Cloud Functions

IBM provides its own serverless product based on Apache OpenWhisk: https://console.bluemix.net/openwhisk/.

You can write serverless functions using Rust, because the platform supports functions provided as Docker images and you can create a Docker image with your Rust functions.

Google Cloud Functions

Google Cloud Functions is a product of Google provided as a part of Google Cloud: `https://cloud.google.com/functions/`.

There is no support for Rust. Potentially, you can write native modules for Python environments using Rust and try to start them using Python code, but I can't find confirmation that this approach will work. In any case, I'm sure there will be an opportunity in the future to run Rust code.

Minimal Rust microservices for AWS Lambda

In this section, we will create a microservice that works in a serverless environment using AWS Lambda. We will reimplement the random number generator from Chapter 4, *Data Serialization and Deserialization with Serde Crate*, in the *Data format for interaction with microservices* section.

Dependencies

First, we need to create a new `minimal-lambda` crate and add the following dependencies to it:

```
[dependencies]
lambda_runtime = { git =
"https://github.com/awslabs/aws-lambda-rust-runtime" }
log = "0.4"
rand = "0.5"
serde = "1.0"
serde_derive = "1.0"
simple_logger = "1.0"
```

The main dependency we need is `lambda_runtime`, which is an official crate for writing `lambda` functions for AWS Lambda platform using Rust. We used a version from GitHub because, at the time of writing, this crate was in active development.

AWS prints the output of all the `lambda` functions as logs, and we will use the `simple_logger` crate, which prints all logs to *stdout*.

We also need to override the name of a binary with lambda, because an environment that run, AWS Lambda expects to find a binary called `bootstrap` that implements the `lambda` function. Let's rename the binary produced by our example:

```
[[bin]]
name = "bootstrap"
path = "src/main.rs"
```

That's enough to start writing a minimal microservice for a serverless environment.

Developing a microservice

We need the following types in our code:

```
use serde_derive::{Serialize, Deserialize};
use lambda_runtime::{lambda, Context, error::HandlerError};
use rand::Rng;
use rand::distributions::{Bernoulli, Normal, Uniform};
use std::error::Error;
use std::ops::Range;
```

It make sense to look at imports from the `lambda_runtime` crate. The `lambda` macro is used to export a handler from a binary, which will be used by the AWS Lambda runtime. Context is a required parameter of a handler, and we also have imported HandlerError to use in the returning `Result` value of a handler.

Then we can write a main function that initializes `simple_logger` and wraps `rng_handler`, which we will implement in the following code, to export the handler of a lambda function:

```
fn main() -> Result<(), Box<dyn Error>> {
    simple_logger::init_with_level(log::Level::Debug).unwrap();
    lambda!(rng_handler);
    Ok(())
}
```

`rng_handler` is a function that expects a request and returns a response:

```
fn rng_handler(event: RngRequest, _ctx: Context) -> Result<RngResponse,
HandlerError> {
    let mut rng = rand::thread_rng();
    let value = {
        match event {
            RngRequest::Uniform { range } => {
                rng.sample(Uniform::from(range)) as f64
```

```
            },
            RngRequest::Normal { mean, std_dev } => {
                rng.sample(Normal::new(mean, std_dev)) as f64
            },
            RngRequest::Bernoulli { p } => {
                rng.sample(Bernoulli::new(p)) as i8 as f64
            },
        }
    };
    Ok(RngResponse { value })
}
```

In the implementation, we used a generator from the example in Chapter 4, *Data Serialization and Deserialization with the Serde Crate,* in the *Data format for interaction with microservices* section, and also borrowed a request type that has to be deserializable:

```
#[derive(Deserialize)]
#[serde(tag = "distribution", content = "parameters", rename_all =
"lowercase")]
enum RngRequest {
    Uniform {
        #[serde(flatten)]
        range: Range<i32>,
    },
    Normal {
        mean: f64,
        std_dev: f64,
    },
    Bernoulli {
        p: f64,
    },
}
```

The preceding request type is an enumeration that has three variants that let a client choose one of three probability distributions to generate a random value. We also need a type to return responses with random values. We will also borrow it from the preceding code. Look at the struct we will use for responses:

```
#[derive(Serialize)]
struct RngResponse {
    value: f64,
}
```

Now, this lambda function expects an `RngRequest` value in JSON format as a request that will be deserialized automatically, and a `RngResponse` result that will be serialized to JSON and returned to a client. Let's build this code and check how it works.

Building

To build a lambda function, we need to produce a binary that is compatible with Amazon Linux. You can use three methods to build a corresponding binary:

- Build it with a Linux distribution (compatible with x86_64).
- Build it in a Docker container of Amazon Linux.
- Build it with the `musl` standard C library.

We will use the latter method, because it minimizes the external dependencies of the produced binary. First, you have to install the `musl` library, which you can get here: `https://www.musl-libc.org/`.

I did this with the following commands:

```
git clone git://git.musl-libc.org/musl
  cd musl
  ./configure
  make
  sudo make install
```

But if there is a package for your operating system, you should to install that instead.

To build the code with the `musl` library we have to use `x86_64-unknown-linux-musl` as the target value. But we can set this target as the default for this project with a configuration file for cargo. Add a `.cargo/config` file to the project's folder and add the following configuration to it:

```
[build]
target = "x86_64-unknown-linux-musl"
```

Make sure the compiler supports `musl` or add it using `rustup`:

```
rustup target add x86_64-unknown-linux-musl
```

Now you can simply build the lambda using the `cargo build` command. That produces a binary that's compiled with the `musl` library that we can upload to AWS.

Deployment

We can deploy lambda to AWS using two tools:

- AWS CLI tool
- Web AWS Console

The first is a little tedious, and in the next section of this chapter, you will see how to use the Serverless Framework to deploy an application consists of `lambda` functions. For this example, enter the AWS Console and go to the AWS Lambda product page. Click the **Create Function** button and, in the form that appears, enter the following values:

- **Name**: `minimal-lambda`
- **Runtime**: Choose **Use custom runtime in function code or layer**
- **Role**: Choose **Create a new role from one or more templates**
- **Role name**: `minimal-lambda-role`

This is what the form should look like when you've finished:

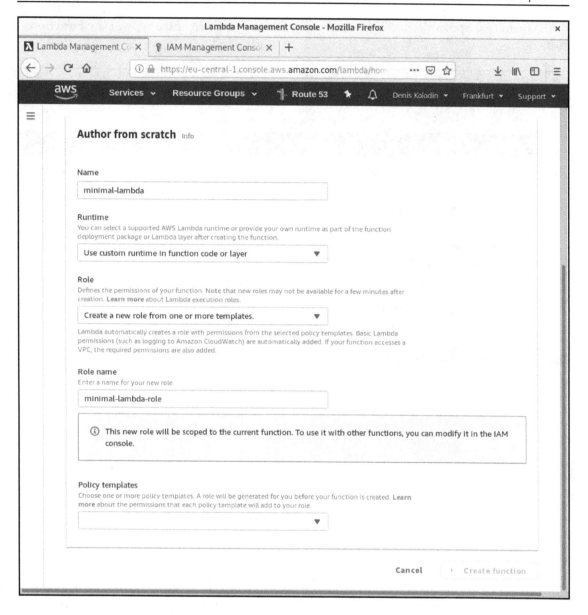

Click the **Create function** button, and while the function is being created, pack the binary to the zip file using the following command:

```
zip -j minimal-lambda.zip target/x86_64-unknown-linux-musl/debug/bootstrap
```

In the form that appears, choose **Upload a .zip file** in the **Code entry type** of the **Function code** section:

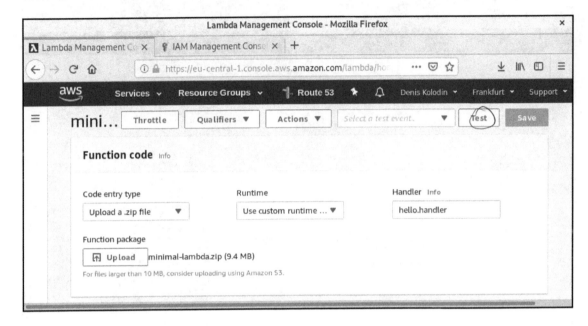

Choose the file and upload it using the form. When the archive with the Rust function is uploaded, the function is ready to be called. Click on the **Test** button, and you will see a form in which you can enter the testing request in JSON format:

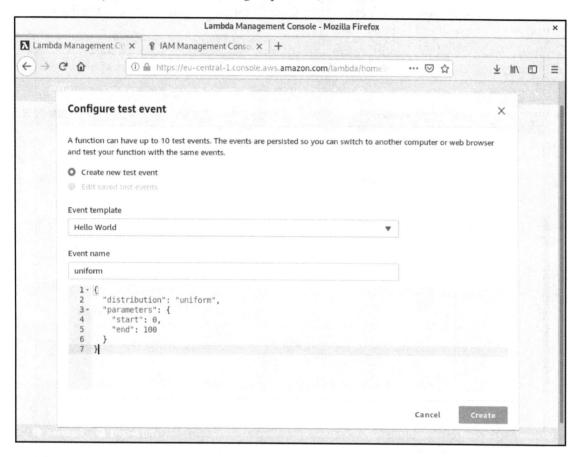

Enter the following JSON in it:

```
{
  "distribution": "uniform",
  "parameters": {
    "start": 0,
    "end": 100
  }
}
```

This is a serialized `RngRequest` value that generates random a value in the range 0-100 using uniform distribution. Enter `uniform` in the **Event name** field and click the **Create** button, and the testing prerequisites will be stored. Now you can choose this request in the drop-down list to the left of the **Test** button. Choose **uniform** value and click the **Test** button to see the result of the response:

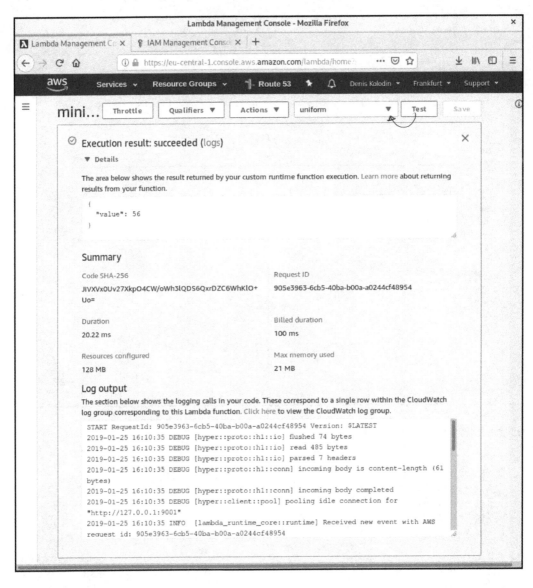

Our microservice generated a value. If you click the **Test** button again, it will generate the next value. As you can see, there are log records printed by the `simple_logger` crate in the **Log output** section. And the execution of this function takes about 20 milliseconds.

The main benefit of AWS Lambda is access to all other AWS services. Let's create a more complex example that utilizes more services in order to show how to integrate `lambda` functions with other AWS infrastructure.

Serverless Framework

In this section, we will port a serverless application from the Wild Rydes Serverless Workshops to Rust: `https://github.com/aws-samples/aws-serverless-workshops`. The idea of this example to provide a service that emulates ordering a ride on a unicorn.

We will use the Serverless Framework, which provides a useful tool that simplifies the deployment of applications using a declaration of the resources and their relations. This section was inspired by an example of Serverless Framework usage created by Andrei Maksimov, which is located here:`https://github.com/andreivmaksimov/serverless-framework-aws-lambda-amazon-api-gateway-s3-dynamodb-and-cognito`. Let's prepare the environment to write and build an application using the Serverless Framework.

Preparation

First, you need to install the Serverless Framework using npm, which is supplied with Node.js:

```
sudo npm install -g serverless
```

I installed it globally because I want to use it to create a new project from a Rust template of an application with multiple lambdas:

```
sls install --url https://github.com/softprops/serverless-aws-rust-multi --name rust-sls
```

This command downloads the template automatically and will use the name provided to construct a blank application. It prints the following to the console:

```
Serverless: Downloading and installing "serverless-aws-rust-multi"...
Serverless: Successfully installed "rust-sls"
```

When the project is initialized, enter a folder of this project and add the `serverless-finch` plugin, which we will use to upload the assets of our application:

```
npm install --save serverless-finch
```

The `serverless-aws-rust-multi` template is a workspace and contains two crates: `hello` and `world`. Let's rename them `lambda_1` and `lambda_2`. I have used this template to show you how an application can include more than one crate. After renaming the folders, we also have to replace the `members` of a `workspace` in the `Cargo.toml` configuration of the project:

```
[workspace]
 members = [
     "lambda_1",
     "lambda_2",
 ]
```

Now we can leave `lambda_2` without changes and implement the functionality of the Wild Rydes example in the `lambda_1` crate.

Implementation

The original sources of the templates contain some code similar to the previous example, but we will write the code from scratch, and you have to remove the original `main.rs` file.

Dependencies

In the `lambda_1` crate's folder, add the following dependencies to `Cargo.toml`:

```
[dependencies]
chrono = "0.4"
lambda_runtime = { git =
"https://github.com/awslabs/aws-lambda-rust-runtime" }
log = "0.4"
rand = "0.6"
rusoto_core = {version = "0.35.0", default_features = false,
features=["rustls"]}
rusoto_dynamodb = {version = "0.35.0", default_features = false,
features=["rustls"]}
serde = "1.0"
serde_derive = "1.0"
serde_json = "1.0"
simple_logger = "1.0"
uuid = { version = "0.7", features = ["v4"] }
```

If you read the previous chapters, you will be familiar with all crates from the list, including `lambda_runtime`, which we used in the previous section of this chapter. Let's look at the types in `src/main.rs` that we will use from this crate:

```
use chrono::Utc;
use lambda_runtime::{error::HandlerError, lambda, Context};
use log::debug;
use rand::thread_rng;
use rand::seq::IteratorRandom;
use rusoto_core::Region;
use rusoto_dynamodb::{AttributeValue, DynamoDb, DynamoDbClient,
PutItemError, PutItemInput, PutItemOutput};
use serde_derive::{Serialize, Deserialize};
use std::collections::HashMap;
use std::error::Error;
use uuid::Uuid;
```

We used the preceding types to implement the following sequence of actions:

- Parsing the request
- Finding (generating) a `Unicorn` instance that will be declared later
- Adding a record to the `DynamoDb` table

Our `main` function only calls a handler function that performs these steps:

```
fn main() -> Result<(), Box<dyn Error>> {
    simple_logger::init_with_level(log::Level::Debug)?;
    debug!("Starting lambda with Rust...");
    lambda!(handler);
    Ok(())
}
```

We also initialized the logger to have to read them with CloudWatch services.

Handler

The handler performs the same logic as the original example, but it is completely rewritten with Rust and the `lambda_runtime` crate. Look at the implementation of the `handler` function:

```
fn handler(event: Request, _: Context) -> Result<Response, HandlerError> {
    let region = Region::default();
    let client = DynamoDbClient::new(region);
    let username = event
        .request_context
```

```
            .authorizer
            .claims
            .get("cognito:username")
            .unwrap()
            .to_owned();
    debug!("USERNAME: {}", username);
    let ride_id = Uuid::new_v4().to_string();
    let request: RequestBody = serde_json::from_str(&event.body).unwrap();
    let unicorn = find_unicorn(&request.pickup_location);
    record_ride(&client, &ride_id, &username, &unicorn).unwrap();
    let body = ResponseBody {
        ride_id: ride_id.clone(),
        unicorn_name: unicorn.name.clone(),
        unicorn,
        eta: "30 seconds".into(),
        rider: username.clone(),
    };
    let mut headers = HashMap::new();
    headers.insert("Access-Control-Allow-Origin".into(), "*".into());
    let body = serde_json::to_string(&body).unwrap();
    let resp = Response {
        status_code: 201,
        body,
        headers,
    };
    Ok(resp)
}
```

Initially, this function creates a connection to DynamoDB using the default Region value, which initially reads environment variables to get an actual value, and if it doesn't find a region, it uses the us-east-1 region. Then, the handler extracts a username provided by Cognito that we will use to authorize users and won't implement user registration manually.

Then we generate the unique ID of a ride and extract the body of a request that is provided by a JSON string. You can't declare a complete Request struct, you have to parse it with two steps. The first uses the lambda! macro, and the second uses the serde_json::from_str function call. Then, we call the find_unicorn function, which we will implement later, and add a record to a database using the record_ride function call, which we will implement later in this section.

When the record is added, we construct a response in two steps. First, we create the body of a response, and then we wrap it with extra values. We have to do this wrapping because we will use API Gateway to call the lambda with an external application shared by s3.

Now we can have a look at structs that we need.

Request and response types

The main struct is Unicorn, which contains the creature we will ride:

```
#[derive(Clone, Serialize)]
#[serde(rename_all = "PascalCase")]
struct Unicorn {
    name: String,
    color: String,
    gender: String,
}
```

Every Unicorn has a name, color, and gender. We will store these values as items in a DynamoDB record. To simplify the creation of the instance in the code, we will add the following constructor:

```
impl Unicorn {
    fn new(name: &str, color: &str, gender: &str) -> Self {
        Unicorn {
            name: name.to_owned(),
            color: color.to_owned(),
            gender: gender.to_owned(),
        }
    }
}
```

You may ask why we don't represent color and gender with enumerations. It's possible, but you have to be sure that the serialized values are exactly what you want.

The Location struct represents a point on a map that will be set by the UI of the application:

```
#[derive(Deserialize)]
#[serde(rename_all = "PascalCase")]
struct Location {
    latitude: f64,
    longitude: f64,
}
```

Now we can declare a `Request` struct that contains `body` and `request_context` fields, which we will use to get a username provided by `Cognito`. You may have noticed that the `Location` structs have different renaming rules than other structs. That's because the `Request` struct was parsed by API Gateway, but `Location` and `RequestBody` will be created by the frontend application, which uses other identifiers. `Request` represents the body as a `String`:

```
#[derive(Deserialize)]
#[serde(rename_all = "camelCase")]
struct Request {
    body: String,
    request_context: RequestContext,
}
```

`RequestContext` is a map that is filled by the runtime, and we will parse it to a struct:

```
#[derive(Deserialize)]
#[serde(rename_all = "camelCase")]
struct RequestContext {
    authorizer: Authorizer,
}
```

We need an `Authorizer` field that only contains `claims` values:

```
#[derive(Deserialize)]
#[serde(rename_all = "camelCase")]
struct Authorizer {
    claims: HashMap<String, String>,
}
```

We used `claims` to get the `cognito:username` value in the `handler`.

```
#[derive(Deserialize)]
#[serde(rename_all = "PascalCase")]
struct RequestBody {
    pickup_location: Location,
}
```

Now we can declare a `Response`. It is also used by API Gateway and has to contain `status_code` and `headers`:

```
#[derive(Serialize)]
 #[serde(rename_all = "camelCase")]
 struct Response {
     body: String,
     status_code: u16,
     headers: HashMap<String, String>,
 }
```

The `body` field is represented by a `String` type that we will deserialize separately to the `ResponseBody` struct:

```
#[derive(Serialize)]
 #[serde(rename_all = "PascalCase")]
 struct ResponseBody {
     ride_id: String,
     unicorn: Unicorn,
     unicorn_name: String,
     eta: String,
     rider: String,
 }
```

The preceding fields are necessary for frontend applications from the workshop.

Now we can add functions to generate the `Unicorn` instance and to add a record to a database.

Functions

The `find_unicorn` function picks one of the three predefined values of `Unicorn`:

```
fn find_unicorn(location: &Location) -> Unicorn {
    debug!("Finding unicorn for {}, {}", location.latitude,
location.longitude);
    let unicorns = [
        Unicorn::new("Bucephalus", "Golden", "Male"),
        Unicorn::new("Shadowfax", "White", "Male"),
        Unicorn::new("Rocinante", "Yellow", "Female"),
    ];
    let mut rng = thread_rng();
    unicorns.iter().choose(&mut rng).cloned().unwrap()
}
```

The `record_ride` function constructs put requests from DynamoDB. To make this kind of request, we need to fill a `HashMap` with attributes only. If you want to learn more about how to interact with DynamoDB, you can return to Chapter 7, *Reliable Integration with Databases*, in which we explored interaction with databases in detail.

```
fn record_ride(
    conn: &DynamoDbClient,
    ride_id: &str,
    username: &str,
    unicorn: &Unicorn,
) -> Result<PutItemOutput, PutItemError> {
    let mut item: HashMap<String, AttributeValue> = HashMap::new();
    item.insert("RideId".into(), s_attr(ride_id));
    item.insert("User".into(), s_attr(username));
    item.insert("UnicornName".into(), s_attr(&unicorn.name));
    let timestamp = Utc::now().to_string();
    item.insert("RequestTime".into(), s_attr(&timestamp));
    item.insert("Unicorn".into(), unicorn_map(unicorn));
    let put = PutItemInput {
        table_name: "Rides".into(),
        item,
        ..Default::default()
    };
    conn.put_item(put).sync()
}
```

We also need a function to prepare `AttributeValues` used by the `rusoto_dynamodb` crate from the types that can be represented as references to a string value:

```
fn s_attr<T: AsRef<str>>(s: T) -> AttributeValue {
    AttributeValue {
        s: Some(s.as_ref().to_owned()),
        ..Default::default()
    }
}
```

The last function we need is to convert the fields of Unicorn into a map:

```
fn unicorn_map(unicorn: &Unicorn) -> AttributeValue {
    let mut item = HashMap::new();
    item.insert("Name".into(), s_attr(&unicorn.name));
    item.insert("Color".into(), s_attr(&unicorn.color));
    item.insert("Gender".into(), s_attr(&unicorn.gender));
    AttributeValue {
        m: Some(item),
        ..Default::default()
    }
}
```

You will see a stored value that uses this layout with AWS Console later in this chapter.

Configuration

The Serverless Framework uses a serverless.yml configuration file to deploy lambdas to AWS. Since we installed the serverless-rust plugin (which comes with the Rust template), we can use it to set a runtime. Fill in the parameters of the service described:

```
service: rust-sls
 provider:
   name: aws
   runtime: rust
   memorySize: 128
```

The following parameter takes more control for configuring functions:

```
package:
   individually: true
```

We also have to activate two plugins: one for building Rust lambdas and another for uploading assets to S3:

```
plugins:
   - serverless-rust
   - serverless-finch
```

Now we can declare our functions:

```
functions:
   lambda_1:
     handler: lambda_1
     role: RustSlsLambdaRole
     events:
```

```
        - http:
            path: ride
            method: post
            cors: true
            authorizer:
              type: COGNITO_USER_POOLS
              authorizerId:
                Ref: RustSlsApiGatewayAuthorizer
  lambda_2:
    handler: lambda_2
    events:
      - http:
          path: check
          method: get
```

The first function has the associated `RustSlsLambdaRole` role that we will declare later. We need it to get access to some resources. The lambda takes a post and supports CORS to be called from the frontend, which works in a browser. We have also associated an authorizer, and use `RustSlsApiGatewayAuthorizer`, which we will declare later.

Resources

Add a resources section that contains `Resources` and `Outputs` maps to declare the necessary resources and output variables. Let's add `Resources`:

```
resources:
  Resources:
```

Add an `S3` bucket declaration, where we place all the assets and set `WebsiteConfiguration` to set the default index file:

```
RustSlsBucket:
    Type: AWS::S3::Bucket
    Properties:
      BucketName: rust-sls-aws
      WebsiteConfiguration:
        IndexDocument: index.html
```

We also have to add a policy to allow these files to be read by an external client, such as a browser:

```
RustSlsBucketPolicy:
    Type: AWS::S3::BucketPolicy
    Properties:
      Bucket:
        Ref: "RustSlsBucket"
```

```
PolicyDocument:
  Statement:
    -
      Effect: "Allow"
      Principal: "*"
      Action:
        - "s3:GetObject"
      Resource:
        Fn::Join:
          - ""
          -
            - "arn:aws:s3:::"
            -
              Ref: "RustSlsBucket"
            - "/*"
```

The Wild Rydes application is configured to use `Cognito` with a client to authorize users with their accounts. Let's configure it with the following declaration and activate email confirmations:

```
RustSlsCognitoUserPool:
  Type: AWS::Cognito::UserPool
  Properties:
    UserPoolName: RustSls
    UsernameAttributes:
      - email
    AutoVerifiedAttributes:
      - email
RustSlsCognitoUserPoolClient:
  Type: AWS::Cognito::UserPoolClient
  Properties:
    ClientName: RustSlsWebApp
    GenerateSecret: false
    UserPoolId:
      Ref: "RustSlsCognitoUserPool"
```

In `Chapter 7`, *Reliable Integration with Databases,* we used a JSON declaration of a table. You can configure a `DynamoDB` table using the Serverless Framework as well:

```
RustSlsDynamoDBTable:
  Type: AWS::DynamoDB::Table
  Properties:
    TableName: Rides
    AttributeDefinitions:
      - AttributeName: RideId
        AttributeType: S
    KeySchema:
      - AttributeName: RideId
```

```
       KeyType: HASH
    ProvisionedThroughput:
      ReadCapacityUnits: 1
      WriteCapacityUnits: 1
```

Add a role for our `lambda_1` crate:

```
RustSlsLambdaRole:
    Type: AWS::IAM::Role
    Properties:
      RoleName: RustSlsLambda
      AssumeRolePolicyDocument:
        Version: '2012-10-17'
        Statement:
          - Effect: Allow
            Principal:
              Service:
                - lambda.amazonaws.com
            Action: sts:AssumeRole
```

And add these policies to this role:

```
Policies:
    - PolicyName: DynamoDBWriteAccess
      PolicyDocument:
        Version: '2012-10-17'
        Statement:
          - Effect: Allow
            Action:
              - logs:CreateLogGroup
              - logs:CreateLogStream
              - logs:PutLogEvents
            Resource:
              - 'Fn::Join':
                - ':'
                -
                  - 'arn:aws:logs'
                  - Ref: 'AWS::Region'
                  - Ref: 'AWS::AccountId'
                  - 'log-group:/aws/lambda/*:*:*'
          - Effect: Allow
            Action:
              - dynamodb:PutItem
            Resource:
              'Fn::GetAtt': [ RustSlsDynamoDBTable, Arn ]
```

We have to provide write access to the `DynamoDB` table for this role.

Create an `authorizer`:

```
RustSlsApiGatewayAuthorizer:
  Type: AWS::ApiGateway::Authorizer
  Properties:
    Name: RustSls
    RestApiId:
      Ref: ApiGatewayRestApi
    Type: COGNITO_USER_POOLS
    ProviderARNs:
      - Fn::GetAtt: [ RustSlsCognitoUserPool, Arn ]
    IdentitySource: method.request.header.Authorization
```

Declare the output variables:

```
Outputs:
  RustSlsBucketURL:
    Description: "RustSls Bucket Website URL"
    Value:
      "Fn::GetAtt": [ RustSlsBucket, WebsiteURL ]
  RustSlsCognitoUserPoolId:
    Description: "RustSls Cognito User Pool ID"
    Value:
      Ref: "RustSlsCognitoUserPool"
  RustSlsCognitoUserPoolClientId:
    Description: "RustSls Cognito User Pool Client ID"
    Value:
      Ref: "RustSlsCognitoUserPoolClient"
  RustSlsDynamoDbARN:
    Description: "RustSls DynamoDB ARN"
    Value:
      "Fn::GetAtt": [ RustSlsDynamoDBTable, Arn ]
```

The last section of this long config declares the folder that the `serverless-finch` plugin will use to upload:

```
custom:
  client:
    bucketName: rust-sls-aws
    distributionFolder: assets
```

As you can see, I used `rust-sls-aws` as the bucket name, but every S3 bucket needs a unique global name, and you have to replace the bucket name in all the configs to deploy it.

Deployment

Everything is ready for deployment. You need a working AWS account to run this application. But let's start by creating a user with the necessary permissions to deploy the application using AWS CLI.

Permissions

To deploy this application, you need to have configured the AWS CLI tool and a user with the following permissions:

- AWSLambdaFullAccess
- IAMFullAccess
- AmazonDynamoDBFullAccess
- AmazonAPIGatewayAdministrator
- AmazonCognitoPowerUser
- CloudFormationAdministrator

It is worth noting that the latter was created manually and can be added when configuring the user by adding a JSON definition to the policy:

```
{
    "Version": "2012-10-17",
    "Statement": [
        {
            "Sid": "Stmt1449904348000",
            "Effect": "Allow",
            "Action": [
                "cloudformation:CreateStack",
                "cloudformation:CreateChangeSet",
                "cloudformation:ListStacks",
                "cloudformation:UpdateStack",
                "cloudformation:DeleteStack",
                "cloudformation:DescribeStacks",
                "cloudformation:DescribeStackResource",
                "cloudformation:DescribeStackEvents",
                "cloudformation:ValidateTemplate",
                "cloudformation:DescribeChangeSet",
                "cloudformation:ExecuteChangeSet"
            ],
            "Resource": [
                "*"
            ]
        }
```

```
        ]
    }
```

When you have created a user with the necessary credentials, you can build and deploy the application using the Serverless Framework, which builds all the lambdas automatically.

Script

We need some values that are not known before deployment. We will use the `sls info -v` command to get the actual values that we need to configure the frontend. Create a bash script to add the necessary deployment functions. First, we need an `extract` function to get the second column (aster) space delimited of `sls info` output:

```
extract() {
    echo "$DATA" | grep $1 | cut -d " " -f2
}
```

To deploy an application with the Serverless Framework, you have to call the `sls deploy` command, but our application is more complex and we have to use a sequence of commands:

```
deploy() {
    echo "ASSETS DOWNLOADING"
    curl -L
https://api.github.com/repos/aws-samples/aws-serverless-workshops/tarball \
    | tar xz --directory assets --wildcards
"*/WebApplication/1_StaticWebHosting/website" --strip-components=4
    echo "LAMBDAS BUILDING"
    sls deploy
    echo "ASSETS UPLOADING"
    sls client deploy
    echo "CONFIGURATION UPLOADING"
    DATA=`sls info -v`
    POOL_ID=`extract PoolId`
    POOL_CLIENT_ID=`extract PoolClientId`
    REGION=`extract region`
    ENDPOINT=`extract ServiceEndpoint`
    CONFIG="
    window._config = {
        cognito: {
            userPoolId: '$POOL_ID',
            userPoolClientId: '$POOL_CLIENT_ID',
            region: '$REGION'
        },
        api: {
            invokeUrl: '$ENDPOINT'
```

```
            }
        };
        "
        echo "$CONFIG" | aws s3 cp - s3://rust-sls-aws/js/config.js
        INDEX=`extract BucketURL`
        echo "INDEX: $INDEX"
    }
```

In the `deploy` function we download the frontend part of the Wild Rydes application from GitHub and only extract the folder we need to the `assets` folder of our project. Then we call `sls deploy` to deploy a stack of the application. Then we call `sls client deploy` to publish all assets to S3. When all parts are deployed we use the `extract` function to get all the necessary values to fill the `config.js` file, which is necessary to connect the deployed frontend with our lambda implemented with Rust. We construct a `config.js` file from the embedded template and upload it with the `aws s3 cp` command.

Let's run this command.

Running

If you have downloaded the sources of the project for this chapter from GitHub, you can use the `deploy.sh` script to call the function we implemented previously. Provide the name of the `deploy` function to call it:

`./deploy.sh deploy`

It will start the building and deployment process with the Serverless Framework and will print something like this:

```
ASSETS DOWNLOADING
    % Total    % Received % Xferd  Average Speed   Time    Time     Time
Current
                                   Dload  Upload   Total   Spent    Left
Speed
    0     0    0     0     0      0       0         0 --:--:-- --:--:-- --:--:--
0
  100 65.7M    0 65.7M     0      0    7647k         0 --:--:--  0:00:08 --:--:--
9968k
LAMBDAS BUILDING
 Serverless: Building native Rust lambda_1 func...
    Finished release [optimized] target(s) in 0.56s
   adding: bootstrap (deflated 60%)
 Serverless: Building native Rust lambda_2 func...
    Finished release [optimized] target(s) in 0.32s
   adding: bootstrap (deflated 61%)
```

```
Serverless: Packaging service...
Serverless: Creating Stack...
Serverless: Checking Stack create progress...
.....
Serverless: Stack create finished...
Serverless: Uploading CloudFormation file to S3...
Serverless: Uploading artifacts...
Serverless: Uploading service .zip file to S3 (2.75 MB)...
Serverless: Uploading service .zip file to S3 (1.12 MB)...
Serverless: Validating template...
Serverless: Updating Stack...
Serverless: Checking Stack update progress...
.........................................................................
Serverless: Stack update finished...
Service Information
service: rust-sls
stage: dev
region: us-east-1
stack: rust-sls-dev
api keys:
  None
endpoints:
  POST - https://48eggoi698.execute-api.us-east-1.amazonaws.com/dev/ride
  GET - https://48eggoi698.execute-api.us-east-1.amazonaws.com/dev/check
functions:
  lambda_1: rust-sls-dev-lambda_1
  lambda_2: rust-sls-dev-lambda_2
layers:
  None
```

The deployment takes time, and when it is finished the second command, `sls client deploy`, will be called to upload the assets folder with the `serverless-finch` plugin, and it prints the following:

```
ASSETS UPLOADING
Serverless: This deployment will:
Serverless: - Upload all files from 'assets' to bucket 'rust-sls-aws'
Serverless: - Set (and overwrite) bucket 'rust-sls-aws' configuration
Serverless: - Set (and overwrite) bucket 'rust-sls-aws' bucket policy
Serverless: - Set (and overwrite) bucket 'rust-sls-aws' CORS policy
? Do you want to proceed? true
Serverless: Looking for bucket...
Serverless: Bucket found...
Serverless: Deleting all objects from bucket...
Serverless: Configuring bucket...
Serverless: Configuring policy for bucket...
Serverless: Configuring CORS for bucket...
Serverless: Uploading client files to bucket...
```

```
Serverless: Success! Your site should be available at
http://rust-sls-aws.s3-website-us-east-1.amazonaws.com/
CONFIGURATION UPLOADING
INDEX: http://rust-sls-aws.s3-website-us-east-1.amazonaws.com
```

The script printed the link that we can use to connect to and test the application.

Testing

Open the provided URL in a browser, and you will see the frontend Wild Rydes app.

Users have to click the **GIDDY UP!** button and register an account using `Cognito`, which is actually used in the background, and users don't need to interact directly with that service.

You will see the cute UI. Click on the map and click the **Set Pickup** button, and you will see how the head of a unicorn moves to the point you set:

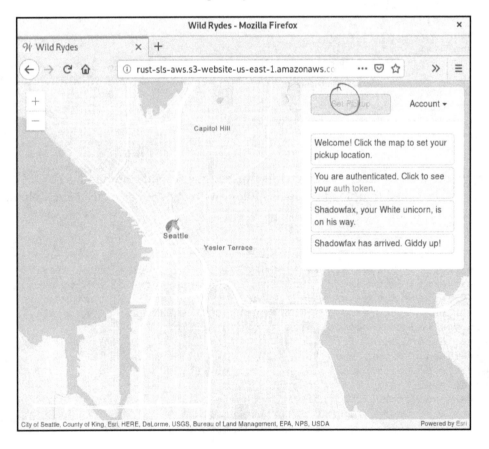

The name and the color of unicorn is generated by our `lambda` function that was created with Rust. If you open some pages of AWS Console you can see that there is a registered user on the **Users and groups** page of the **User Pools** section:

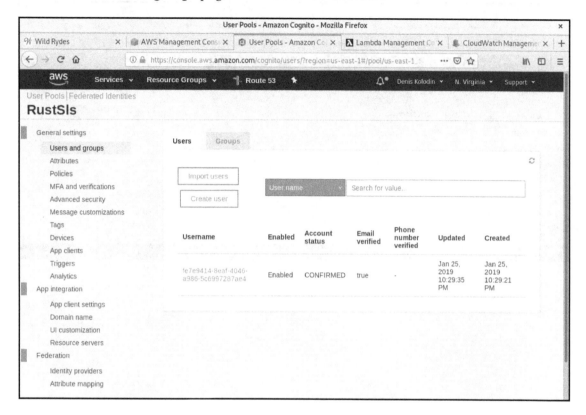

We have two deployed lambdas, but actually the application only uses the first, which is called `rust-sls-dev-lambda_1`:

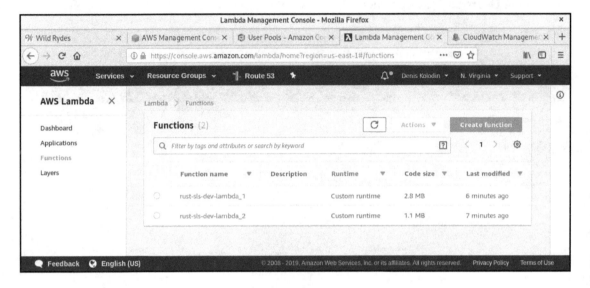

If you enter the lambda's page, click on the **Monitoring** tab, and open `CloudWatch` logs of the lambda, you can see the lambda generated a username and, is stored in the location we set:

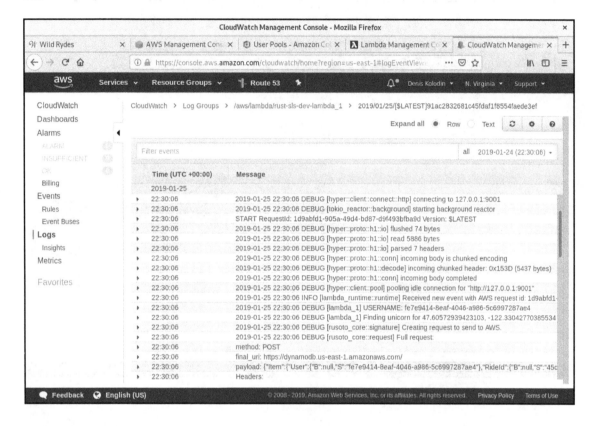

The lambda also stored a record in DynamoDB, and you can also find it on the **Tables** page of the **DynamoDB** section:

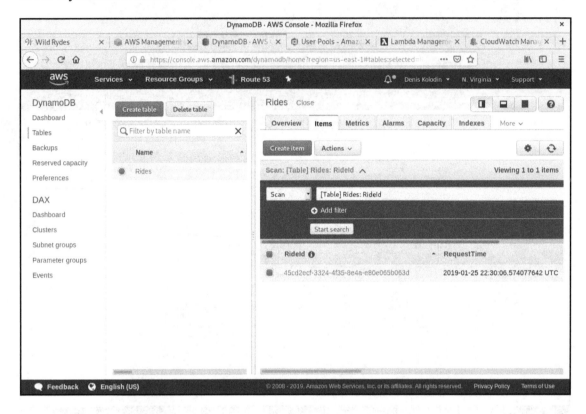

You can see the record that the lambda added. And if you click on the record, you will see the all the fields we populated with the `record_ride` function earlier:

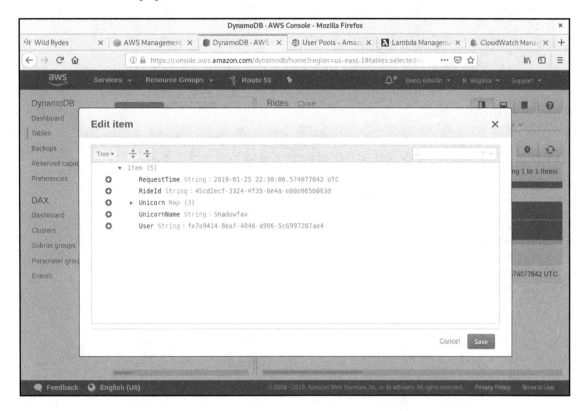

The application has been successfully ported to Rust, and it works as expected. Let's look at how we can clean up the resources we've used.

Updating and removing

The Serverless Framework also provides the ability to update resources automatically if you call `sls deploy` again. We can add this as a function to the deployment bash script:

```
update() {
    sls deploy
}
```

This command is useful if you want to update the code of some of the lambdas, but don't want to leave the session maintained by `Cognito`.

To remove everything we deployed, we can use the following function:

```
remove() {
    echo "ASSETS REMOVING"
    sls client remove
    echo "LAMBDAS REMOVING"
    sls remove
    echo "ASSETS CLEANUP"
    rm -rf assets
    mkdir assets
    touch assets/.gitkeep
}
```

It works because the Serverless Framework supports removing declared resources. I recommend you clean up everything after experimenting, because AWS will produce bills for services even if you don't use this demo.

Summary

In this chapter, we studied an alternative approach to microservice implementation—serverless architecture. This approach involves direct usage of functions that handle incoming requests. There are many providers of serverless infrastructure, and we used the popular AWS platform to port a serverless application to Rust.

Other Books You May Enjoy

If you enjoyed this book, you may be interested in these other books by Packt:

Hands-On Concurrency with Rust

Brian L. Troutwine

ISBN: 9781788399975

- Probe your programs for performance and accuracy issues
- Create your own threading and multi-processing environment in Rust
- Use coarse locks from Rust's Standard library
- Solve common synchronization problems or avoid synchronization using atomic programming
- Build lock-free/wait-free structures in Rust and understand their implementations in the crates ecosystem
- Leverage Rust's memory model and type system to build safety properties into your parallel programs
- Understand the new features of the Rust programming language to ease the writing of parallel programs

Rust Quick Start Guide
Daniel Arbuckle

ISBN: 9781789616705

- Install Rust and write your first program with it
- Understand ownership in Rust
- Handle different data types
- Make decisions by pattern matching
- Use smart pointers
- Use generic types and type specialization
- Write code that works with many data types
- Tap into the standard library

Leave a review - let other readers know what you think

Please share your thoughts on this book with others by leaving a review on the site that you bought it from. If you purchased the book from Amazon, please leave us an honest review on this book's Amazon page. This is vital so that other potential readers can see and use your unbiased opinion to make purchasing decisions, we can understand what our customers think about our products, and our authors can see your feedback on the title that they have worked with Packt to create. It will only take a few minutes of your time, but is valuable to other potential customers, our authors, and Packt. Thank you!

Index

M

CPSIA information can be obtained
at www.ICGtesting.com
Printed in the USA
LVHW100429060820
662527LV00012B/1439